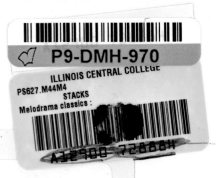

# Melodrama Classics ⚹

## Six Plays and How to Stage Them

### Dorothy Mackin

STERLING PUBLISHING CO., INC.   NEW YORK

**Other Books of Interest**

Actors on Acting
Clown for Circus and Stage
Exploring Mime
Make-Up, Costumes & Masks for the Stage

**Library of Congress Cataloging in Publication Data**

Main entry under title:

Melodrama classics.

Includes index.
1. American drama—19th century.   2. Melodrama
3. English drama—19th century.   I. Mackin, Dorothy.
PS627.M44M4        812'.0527'08        81-8856
ISBN 0-8069-7036-7                     AACR2
ISBN 0-8069-7037-5 (lib. bdg.)

Song "Don't Go in the Lions' Cage Tonight"
Copyright © Larry Spier, Inc., New York, N.Y.
Copyright © renewed.
Reprinted with permission of the Copyright Owner.

Copyright © 1982 by Sterling Publishing Co., Inc.
Two Park Avenue, New York, N.Y. 10016
Distributed in Australia by Oak Tree Press Co., Ltd.
P.O. Box J34, Brickfield Hill, Sydney 2000, N.S.W.
Distributed in the United Kingdom by Blandford Press
Link House, West Street, Poole, Dorset BH15 1LL, England
Distributed in Canada by Oak Tree Press Ltd.
℅ Canadian Manda Group, 215 Lakeshore Boulevard East
Toronto, Ontario M5A 3W9
*Manufactured in the United States of America*

# Contents

To all the young actors and actresses who have brought these plays to vibrant life on the Imperial stage, and with whom it has been my pleasure and privilege to work.

It is my sincere hope that this book may be instrumental in helping to move melodrama out of the theatrical trash heap into which it has been tossed, and back into the realm of "legitimate theatre" from whence it came.

## Credits

Musical references and
  research ................ Danny Griffith
Scene plot sketches ........ John Masterman
Music scores .............. Robert Goodnow
Lyrics ................... Danny Griffith,
.................... Max Morath
.................... Dorothy Mackin
Scene design washes ....... Walter Wilson
Costume designs ......... William Damron, Jr.
Photograph on cover ....... PhotoGraphics,
                                 Colorado Springs

# 1 The Many Faces of Melodrama

Although it has never been explicitly documented in theatrical history, melodrama must first have taken root in the same areas around the Mediterranean that nurtured the Commedia dell'Arte. That motley assortment of gypsy players, comprised of writers, actors, mimes, jugglers, singers and musicians, must have provided the common background that eventually branched into opera and operetta on the musical side and into the prose and poetry of drama. In opera and operetta, the spoken word was used only for transitions from one musical rendition to another, whereas in melodrama, music and musical numbers were used only to accent and punctuate the spoken word.

In recent times, the word "melodrama" has most often been used in a derogatory context. Any review of theatre history, however, reveals that in one form or another, melodrama dominated the stage for most of the 19th Century in France, England and America, and during periods of their colonization and settlement, Canada and Australia, as well. It entertained the perfumed and bejeweled upper-class audiences in such theatres as the Porte St. Martin and the Ambigu in Paris, Covent Garden and the Drury Lane in London, the Abbey Theatre in Dublin, the Theatre Royal in Sydney, the Park and Union Square in New York.

It is illuminating to observe the change in definition that transpires from an 1899 edition of Peter Fenelon Collier's *Universal Dictionary of the English Language* through a 1977 *Morris Dictionary* to *The American Heritage Dictionary* of 1980.

*Collier's*, 1899: (Fr. *melodrame* — acting with songs) 1. Orig. A dramatic piece in which the interest is heightened by the character of the vocal or instrumental music accompanying certain situations. The melodrama is of French invention and was introduced into England at the end of the last century; the subjects are generally of a romantic character, illustrated with picturesque costumes and scenery, and having serious and sensational incidents. Although sometimes confounded with the opera, it differs from that form of work insomuch that the action is carried on in speaking and not in recitative and aria.

2. A play of strong situations, resembling both the domestic and sensational drama, and characterized more by bold colouring than artistic finish. The more thrilling passages are accentuated by musical accompaniments, known as the "hurries," the only relic of the original musical character of the melodrama, which has now come to designate a romantic play, depending mainly on sensational incidents, thrilling situations, and an effective denouement, and often paying little attention to the probability or naturalness of incident in the effort to produce strong effects. Such pieces are often staged at great expense for scenery, costume, and mechanical arrangements, moving machinery, locomotives that cross the stage, falling bridges, burning houses, and a great variety of such mechanism being introduced.

*Morris Dictionary*, 1977: (from the French, *melodrame*) The first melodramas were more like opera than the melodrama of yesteryear, complete with song and orchestral music. They were sensational, extravagant and romantic, but not as violent as later ones. Although the "melo" part of the word comes from the Greek *melos* (song), the entire name melodrama was retained long after songs and music were deleted.

*American Heritage Dictionary*, 1980: A sentimental dramatic presentation characterized by heavy use of suspense and sensational episodes. (F. *melodrame*, "musical drama").

Note that over the years, definitions became less detailed and placed greater emphasis upon the sensation elements and less upon the musical.

Whatever the definitions, the term has been used to describe such widely diverse pieces as Shakespeare's *Othello*,

D'Ennery & Corman's *The Two Orphans, The Drunkard* —
allegedly authored by a gentleman actor of Boston who chose
to remain anonymous — and Harriet Beecher Stowe's *Uncle
Tom's Cabin.*

In the final analysis, the word "melodrama" has been used
to mean whatever the writer wants. As Humpty Dumpty said,
"It means just what I choose it to mean — neither more nor
less."

In recent decades, as a longer view is taken of developments
in the theatre in the past 100 years, an increasing amount of
scholarly attention has been directed toward melodrama. It
has pointed out important trends and changes, such as playwright Steele MacKaye, a Parisian disciple of the Delsarte
school, moving into realistic drama with such plays as *Hazel
Kirke*. The introduction of gas lights, as early as 1816 when
they were introduced at the Chestnut Theatre in Philadelphia,
altered the approach to scene design and stage lighting.

The French playwright Rene Pixérecourt is often mentioned as the first of the melodrama writers; however,
Alexandre Dumas preceded him in the dramatic treatment of
many of his characters and situations. Adolphe D'Ennery and
Eugene Corman wrote melodrama for the French stage; Edward Bulwer-Lytton, Tom Taylor and Dion Boucicault for
England; Bartley Campbell, Steele MacKaye, Augustin Daly
and David Belasco for the United States. Boucicault, an Irish
playwright who was one of the most prolific of the period,
later joined his talents to those of Augustin Daly and David
Belasco for a long and brilliant career in the American
theatre. It is ironic that Boucicault, who so liberally adapted
from the French and German playwrights and productions,
should have been instrumental in securing the enactment of
the first American copyright law on plays.

Melodrama nurtured and refined the talents of important
playwrights, actors and actresses, and stage and theatrical
managers of the time. The great Edmund Kean of the British
stage gained considerable fame in melodrama as well as in
his unforgettable Shakespearean roles. During his career, it
was written of him, "To see Kean play is like reading Shakespeare by flashes of lightning."

In the United States, Blanche Bates, Lotta Crabtree, Henry
Miller, Charles Couldock, Lola Montez and Bijou Heron
created memorable characterizations in British, French, and
later, American melodramas.

Another form of theatre, known as the "ten-twent-thirt"

sensation melodrama, simultaneously flourished in tent shows and country fairs, providing welcome diversion for people of simpler tastes and lesser purse who could afford the ten to thirty cents, pence or sous that gave the shows their name. This "sensation drama," still presented as melodrama, originated in the streets of Paris and London when playwrights picked sensational crimes from the police files and put them into dramatic form. One of these plays, recently revived in a New York musical, *Sweeney Todd, the Demon Barber of Fleet Street*, brought to the stage the gruesome tale of a barber who entices well-to-do customers into his chair, only to rob them of their valuables. He then pitches them backward through a trap door into the basement, where a crone of an accomplice makes them into succulent meat pies to be purveyed in her bake shop!

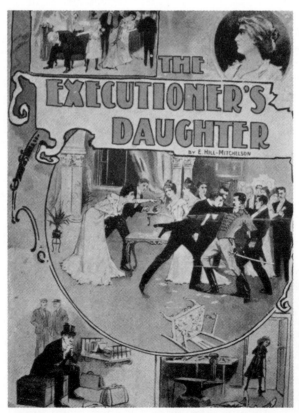

*Posters for sensation melodrama depicted scenes of real or threatened violence and featured elaborately constructed theatrical effects.*

Another type of play misnamed melodrama is the temperance drama, doubtless an offspring of the earlier ecclesiastical "morality" plays. As Allardyce Nicoll states in his *World Drama*:

> The morality tradition laid stress upon the eternal conflict of good and evil, while in practice it set forth, crudely but not ineffectively, the inner struggle within man of these two forces. Good was always triumphant in the end, but that end might come, and generally did come, only at the very conclusion of each drama, so that essentially the morality play was concerned with an exhibition of evil rampant against a field of eternity.

Surely this description fits such plays as *Ten Nights in a Barroom, Fifty Years of a Gambler's Fate*, or *The Drunkard*. These

*A performance of* Ten Nights in a Barroom, *one of the most popular of the temperance plays. The cartoonist has drawn a look of terror on the face of the youth in the front row, possibly to indicate that he was beginning to understand the pitfalls of alcohol. These plays, performed often just prior to World War I, may well have been influential in the passing of the U.S. Eighteenth Amendment (Prohibition) in 1920.*

A PERFORMANCE OF "TEN NIGHTS IN A BARROOM."—"Frank Slade, you have killed your own father!"

*Blind Louise (Mary Stevens) and crippled Pierre (Allen Fearon) shiver in despair in front of Notre Dame Cathedral in Paris. The city is painted on the backdrop. The scene takes place at night, adding to the feeling of cold and misery that permeates this emotional scene.*

dramas were enthusiastically performed in London and the United States in a vain effort to stem the flow of alcohol or the curse of gambling in the lives of the poor.

As a matter of practice, melodrama can currently mean anything from the quiet poignancy of the tender love scene between Pierre Frochard and blind orphan Louise in *The Two Orphans* to the overdrawn suspense of the heroine tied to the railroad track in *Under the Gaslight*, to the unmitigated vulgarity of deliberate double entendre in the worst of the modern rewrites.

*About ten years after Dion Boucicault portrayed the London underground railway in* After Dark, *Augustin Daly elaborated on the railroad scene in his New York presentation of* Under the Gaslight.

Wherever British and French colonists settled, they soon found ways and places in which to present their favorite plays, adapting to local and public tastes, but always preserving their own cultures in any corner of the world. In America, proscribed by much of the Puritan population of the northern territories with their Cromwellian heritage, theatre naturally flourished in the liberal areas of the south, settled by French and Spanish colonists and British gentry. The first building in America designed solely for use as a theatre was the Dock Street Theatre at 135 Church Street in Charleston, South Carolina. This theatre opened on February 12, 1736. An old theatre program of the time preserves the record that "A Tragedy, called *The Orphan* or *The Unhappy Marriage*" was to be enacted "on Monday next, February 21, 1736." The Dock Street Theatre has been twice burned and twice rebuilt and now serves as a museum and active theatre in historic Charleston.

As cities expanded along the eastern seaboard, theatres were established in Boston, Philadelphia, Baltimore and New York, presenting plays, concerts and operas imported from abroad. From the early 1800's, melodrama comprised a major and important portion of all the plays presented on the American stage.

In Charleston in the year 1820, out of 100 plays presented, 38 were melodramas, with the balance distributed among Shakespeare, 17th and 18th Century Restoration dramas, 19th Century comedies and tragedies, and a total of only two performances of opera and ballet. That same year, Philadelphia saw 10 Shakespearean plays, 11 Restoration dramas, 24 comedies and tragedies of the 19th Century and 30 melodramas on its stages.

Melodrama went west with the California gold seekers. The first performances in California under American rule were given by an amateur Thespian Club organized by Col. J.D. Steven's Seventh Regiment of the New York Volunteers. The play, presented in Sonoma, California in late 1847, was an English melodrama by Benjamin Webster, *The Golden Farmer*. On October 4, 1851, the new Jenny Lind Theatre in San Francisco opened with *All That Glitters Is Not Gold*. A newspaper account reported, "The opening night presented a brilliant display of beauty and fashion, and every part of the immense building was crowded to excess."

A logical extension of any New York or Boston stage success was the proliferation of touring companies sent on the road by such ambitious entrepreneurs as Augustin Daly, actor-playwright Dion Boucicault, Daniel Frohman and David Belasco. Historians record that 100 companies were touring in the winter of 1876-77. This accelerated to 300 in 1880 and increased to 500 by the year 1900. The Chautauqua and Orpheum circuits spread the fame of players and playwrights across the land, to the mid-west, to Mississippi river towns and the glittering gold coast of California. In the winter of 1893-94, with the silver panic having a serious effect on American road companies, Boucicault and Frohman organized the first successful Canadian touring company.

Melodrama flourished in remote mining camps around the world. In Alaska, Circle City was dubbed "The Paris of Alaska," when, in 1896, the Grand Opera House opened, featuring popular melodramas alternating with Shakespearean plays and vaudeville. In Dawson, 1898 playbills advertised *East Lynne, Camille* and a production of *Uncle Tom's Cabin*, in which Eliza is chased across the ice by a malamute puppy, whose movement across the stage was guided by invisible wires. *Uncle Tom*, about the same time, was presented in New South Wales, Australia, where sheep dogs pursued the heroine.

The first ships carrying convicts from England to Australia had docked in Sydney Cove in 1788. Less than 17 months later, with convicts providing most of the talent, George Farquhar's *The Recruiting Officer* was presented in a makeshift theatre and seats were paid for in rum, tobacco, corn and chickens. It was not until 50 years later that The Theatre Royal, the first professional playhouse, opened in Sydney, offering almost entirely English and American plays.

And preserved in the Lakes District Centennial Museum in Arrowtown, New Zealand, is a program for Saturday, the 17th of November, 1900, for *The Ticket-of-Leave Man* at the Atheneum Hall, presented by the Arrow Dramatic Society, with a Mr. J. T. McBride playing Robert Brierly, and Miss Low as May Edwards.

# Melodrama in Cripple Creek

In Nevada, Goldfield and Virginia City lured prospectors and travellers alike. In Colorado, gold was discovered in Gregory Gulch, near Denver in 1859, and there was a silver bonanza in Leadville. The latest of the gold discoveries was in Cripple Creek on the west slope of famed Pikes Peak, where commercial quantities were confirmed in 1891. As in every other location, soon after the discovery, the rush of gold seekers arrived, bringing the familiar tent and shack city into existence, as they feverishly dug for the yellow metal.

Saloons, gambling houses and prostitutes followed close behind the prospectors. It was not until after two disastrous fires destroyed the central part of town that more permanent structures of brick were erected. Two opera houses were built, and to them came the popular entertainments of the day: travelling troupes with plays, opera, vaudeville, variety and minstrel shows.

During just one week in the spring of 1900, for example, the Grand Opera House in Cripple Creek presented Miss Leonora Jackson in a violin concert, a hit play, two performances by the Lombardi Grand Opera Company and a production of *Uncle Tom's Cabin*. The *Cripple Creek Times* announced, "This Sunday evening, the Dobbins Brothers' big production of *Uncle Tom's Cabin* will hold the boards at the Grand. Be sure to see the big parade at noon on Sunday with two bands, ten Shetland ponies, bloodhounds, floats and gorgeous banners." Cripple Creek also had a vaudeville theatre called The Crystal. On the top circuits, three shows were presented every night and two matinees each week.

The lights went down on melodrama, vaudeville and much of the live stage, as talent and interest shifted to a new entertainment medium. Silent film darkened opera houses and theatres across the country, but much of melodrama remained on the flickering screen. Many of the plays were adapted to film, among the most famous, D.W. Griffith's *Orphans of the Storm*, starring Lillian and Dorothy Gish, which was an adaptation of *Les Deux Orphelines*, or *The Two Orphans*. And sitting in the darkened house, watching avidly in order not to miss a mood or gesture, sat the house pianist, adding that all-important "melo" to the thrilling drama on the screen.

*Dorothy and Lillian Gish in D.W. Griffith's* Orphans of the Storm, *the film version of* The Two Orphans. *This photo courtesy of Lillian Gish, from her own collection.*

*This cartoon of* After Dark *from the late 1920's depicts the characters in burlesqued melodrama style, with emphasis on the sensation themes, rather than the quieter moments of the drama.*

# 2 The Revival of Melodrama

No significant attempts were made to revive live melodrama until the late Christopher Morley opened Dion Boucicault's *After Dark* in a warehouse in Hoboken, New Jersey, in 1928. It proved most popular, playing for one-and-one-half years, and it was followed by a less successful run of *The Blue and the Gray*.

In October of 1947 Wayne Mackin and I inaugurated what is now the longest running melodrama theatre in the United States in the historic Imperial Hotel in Cripple Creek, Colorado. We began with an inauspicious performance of a simple modern melodrama presented by a travelling troupe of young actors and actresses who had spent the summer in Colorado. From that modest beginning has grown an internationally known summer melodrama theatre. The cabaret-style basement theatre that seated fewer than 100 for the first season in 1948 has been remodelled and expanded several times until it now seats 285. Since the 1953 presentation of Bartley Campbell's *My Partner*, only plays of the 1850-1900 period have been presented. The one exception to this is the 1901 *The Spoilers*, presented on the Imperial stage in 1959 and repeated in 1970.

The number of melodramas written and produced between 1800 and 1900 stagger the imagination. The ones that have been published or preserved in manuscript form are scattered from the well-organized collections of Paris and London, across the United States in various public and private collections and in the dusty drawers and attics of aging actors or their heirs.

In the process of researching, selecting, revising and producing the plays that have been staged at the Imperial, my husband and I have read and evaluated several hundred manuscripts. Some of them are excellent plays, well written, and, in their time, popular. The vast majority, however, as in any period of theatrical endeavor, are simply poor plays—or hopelessly outdated. A great many of them depended for their success on the unusual and outstanding talents of a single actor or actress who created a role and used it as a personal tour de force. Others reflected the political events of a time or place. During the period when new wealth was being created on the frontiers of mining, railroads and commerce, and the *nouveau riche* sent their daughters abroad to be educated in the social graces (often to return wed to a minor French or British nobleman), characters and plots leaned heavily on social status and caste. Each in its own time, the noble savage and the buckskin-clad frontiersman were favorite new characters introduced on the British and American stage.

"WOLVES! What can save us?" | "The strong arm of a Backwoodsman."

*Europeans were especially enchanted with plays portraying the American fron-tier. (English) J.T. Haines adapted (American) Robert Montgomery Bird's novel,* Nick of the Woods. Metamora, *the most popular of the plays portraying the American Indian as the noble savage, played to enthusiastic British and Ameri-can audiences for many years.*

For the Gold Bar Room stage at the Imperial Hotel, quite a few considerations are important in selecting a script suitable for a 12-week, 150-performance run. The plot and language of the play must be understandable to a wide range of audiences of different levels of education and interest, to children as well as to more mature and elderly patrons. It must be excit-ing and entertaining enough to hold an audience and keep them enjoying the experience for approximately two-and-one-half hours.

To attract and hold the many gifted young actors and ac-tresses who portray their roles 12 times each week, parts should be of sufficient significance and scope to engage their talents throughout the season.

In selecting which play to do each season, we give a great deal of consideration to period and location of each of the scripts. As a general rule, a play with a British setting and a prison theme might be followed with a play set in France and a travel theme, with an American frontier play chosen for the third season. This has been necessary since the Imperial is fortunate enough to count well over 60 percent repeat business from season to season, and by judicious change of time and place, there is little similarity in each year's choices.

The plays in this volume are representative of the selection offered to Imperial Players' audiences over the past 13 years. All of them have had long, successful modern-day runs. Several of them have played a second full season after an interval of 10 to 15 years.

In every instance, cuts and changes have been made to enhance their appeal to audiences of widely divergent backgrounds and tastes. Archaic language has been revised to be comprehensible without disturbing the flavor of characterization and setting so crucial to the presentation of melodrama.

When these plays were written, production costs and performers' salaries were much lower than today and could be more easily absorbed. Consequently, many of the plays of the period called for 20 or 30 characters. Crowd scenes have been deleted or altered in all of the plays included here, and some of the scenes have been rewritten, in the interest of clarity of plot and practicability of production.

All the plays depend for their success on the wonderful delicate balance everyone in theatre thrives upon—that great coming together of script, players, direction, music, scene design, costuming and choreography. With luck, all of these combine with good box office, theatre management, advertising and press to create that greatest of all magic: audience aglow and players eating up every moment of performance.

Whatever else it may be, at whatever time or place, melodrama is good entertainment, fun for audiences who take its messages seriously as well as for those who ridicule the virtues and vices it portrays. It still brings into the theatre people who would otherwise never become acquainted with flesh-and-blood live stage performance, and it introduces young actors and actresses to a wide variety of audience responses at close range.

# 3 The Plays

The Ticket-of-Leave Man

Under Two Flags

The Two Orphans

After Dark

Hazel Kirke

The Spoilers

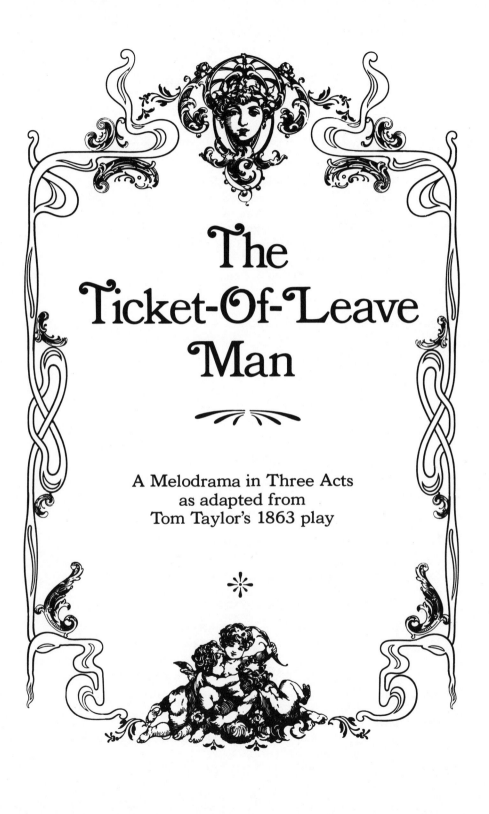

# The Ticket-Of-Leave Man

A Melodrama in Three Acts
as adapted from
Tom Taylor's 1863 play

# CAST OF CHARACTERS

ROBERT BRIERLY, a Lancashire lad
JAMES DALTON, alias Downey, alias the Tiger
MELTER MOSS, the Tiger's henchman
HAWKSHAW, the Detective
GREEN JONES, married to "St. Evremond"
MR. GIBSON, a bill broker
MRS. WILLOUGHBY, proprietor of Mrs. Willoughby's rooming house
SAM WILLOUGHBY, her grandson, growing up in London
MALTBY, proprietor of the Bellevue Tea Garden
MAY EDWARDS, loyal friend and wife
EMILY ST. EVREMOND, nightclub nightingale
WAITER
DETECTIVE
GUESTS at the Bellevue Tea Gardens

# SYNOPSIS OF SCENES

Time: 1864-1868                                    Place: London

### PROLOGUE

Bellevue Tea Gardens, in the southwest suburbs of London on a
summer evening.
"Kind words are hard to bear."

### ACT ONE

May Edwards' room at Mrs. Willoughby's, three years later.
"Honesty has brought us a blessing already."

### ACT TWO

Mr. Gibson's bill-broking office, six months later.
"We were wrong to hide the truth."

### ACT THREE

**Scene One:**   The Bridgewater Arms, four months later.
"Now's the time."
**Scene Two:**   St. Nicholas' Churchyard.
"There may be some good left in a ticket-of-leave man,
after all."

## About the Play

The Ticket-of-Leave Man *was the play in which Hawkshaw the Detective first spoke. As a contemporary writer put it, "Who can forget Bob Brierly, framed by dastardly villains and sent to Portland Prison, then exonerated by Hawkshaw, who perceived his noble qualities, donned a wig, and lent his aid!"*

Probably no Victorian melodrama has been so long remembered and so widely presented as playwright Tom Taylor's *The Ticket-of-Leave Man*. The most popular of his more than one hundred plays, it introduces the character of "Hawkshaw, the Detective." This character was doubtless the model for Conan Doyle's later Sherlock Holmes, who first appeared in *A Study in Scarlet* in 1887. Since that time there have been 54 plays, 116 silent films, 81 talkies, a ballet and a Broadway musical based on the master detective character, and the name "Hawkshaw" has become synonymous with "detective."

The play, probably a rewrite of Edouard Louis Alexandere Brisebarre and Eugene Nus' *Leonard ou la retour de Brest*, presents a remarkably British picture of the life of a paroled—or "ticket-of-leave"—prisoner, hounded from place to place for his past record. In its initial London run at the Guard's Opera House in 1863, the melodrama achieved the then remarkable record of 407 continuous performances. The following year it opened in New York at the Winter Garden Theatre with W.J. Florence playing Bob Brierly, the "ticket-of-leave man," for a series of 102 performances. Florence eventually acted the role more than 1,500 times.

The play enjoyed wide popularity. Lotta Crabtree carried it in her repertoire at the California Opera House in San Francisco. Performances were recorded at the Denver Theatre and the Guard's Opera

House in Denver in the late 1860's. A *London Times* article of September 21, 1946 states, "Its main personalities, Bob Brierly and Hawkshaw, have made *The Ticket-of-Leave Man* immortal. . . . By any standard other than that of the 'reformers' it is the outstanding play of the Victorian drama."

When first presented by the Imperial players in 1964, the play was 101 years old. Many archaic passages of speech made it incomprehensible to a modern audience. In the adaptation here, words such as "darbies" for handcuffs, "flimsies" for counterfeit bills, or the phrase, "spoil my squeeze"—for ruining a chance for a crack at a safe—have been retained, since the actions explain them. Only where absolutely necessary has the language been altered to clarify meaning, thus keeping the play's original flavor.

Tom Taylor also wrote the very popular *Our American Cousin*, the play that Abraham Lincoln and his party were watching on the night of his assassination.

See page 382 for definitions of the Victorian slang in this play.

*Hawkshaw (with newspaper, center) explains to James Dalton (left) and Bob Brierly that newspapers can be most valuable to anyone becoming acquainted in a new city, in this case, London. Left to right: Dennis MacRae, Michael Brody and Manzy Mooney in the 1964 Imperial production.*

# PROLOGUE

SCENE: *The Bellevue Tea Gardens, in the southwest suburbs of London on a summer evening. The front of the tavern U.L. is an ornamental verandah; there are tables and seats, trees, shrubs, statues. As the curtain rises,* MALTBY, *the steady and philosophical proprietor of the Bellevue Tea Gardens, is moving about with an eye to the guests. He is a portly man, about forty, neatly dressed, hair carefully arranged. He prides himself on running a first-rate establishment.* DETECTIVE *is seated at the table U.L.* MALTBY *moves to the* DETECTIVE'*s table with his order and places it before him.*

MALT. There you are, sir, dry sherry, one shilling. *(Takes money, moves about.)* Now three teas to table six, three toddies inside *(to table six.)* Uncommon thirsty weather, sir, uncommon. *(To front table.)* If I might recommend champagne for the lady, sir, delicious refreshment for July. *(Calls to bartender off.)* James, look after them brandies in three. *(Moves off.)*

    *(Enter* HAWKSHAW, *R., detective of Scotland Yard, master of many disguises, defender of the law and relentless pursuer of all wrong-doers. He is tall, thin, in his mid-thirties, and he combines an air of mystery and authority. His customary garb is tweed knee breeches, plaid Norfolk jacket, plaid deerstalker's cap with front and rear bills, and jaunty bow on top. For outdoor wear, he adds a colorful Inverness cape. He strolls carelessly to the* DETECTIVE'*s table; then in an undertone and without looking at him:)*

HAWK. Report.

DETECTIVE *(in the same tone and without looking at Hawkshaw).* All right.

HAWK *(same tone).* Here's old Moss. Keep an eye on him. *(Strolls off L.)*

    *(Enter* MELTER MOSS, *sits at table R. He is a petty crook, down-at-the-heels. Enter* MALTBY.*)*

MOSS *(to* MALTBY*).* Good evening, Maltby, four pennyworth of brandy, if you please *(Sits.),* and a little peppermint. *(Coughs, looks around.)* Tiger not here yet.

    *(Bell rings.)*

MALT. The curtain bell, ladies and gentlemen—in the gardens *(Pointing off).* The first talent—selections from the best classical music—this way. *(Exit.)*

    *(Enter* DALTON.*)*

MOSS *(stirring and sipping his brandy and peppermint).* Warm and comfortable. Tiger ought to be here before this. *(As he stirs, his eye falls upon the spoon; he takes it up, weighs it in his fingers.)* Uncommon neat article—might take in a good many people—plated, though, plated.

    *(While* MOSS *is looking at the spoon,* DALTON *takes a seat at Moss' table, unobserved by him.* JAMES DALTON, *alias "Downey," alias*

*"The Tiger," is good-looking, in his early forties, well-groomed and somewhat flashily dressed. He wears conspicuous jewelry, highly polished shoes, and a dark, soft felt hat.)*

DAL. Not worth flimping, eh?

MOSS *(starting, but not recognizing him).* Eh, did you speak to me, sir?

DAL. What? Don't know me? Then it is a good get up. *(He lifts his hat and gives* MOSS *a peculiar look.)* Eh, Melter?

MOSS *(recognizing him).* What, Tiger!

DAL. Stow that. There's no tigers here. My name's Downey; now mind that. John Downey, from Rotherham, jobber and general dealer.

MALT *(coming down to* DALTON*).* Now, sir, what can I have the pleasure of ordering you?

DAL. My good friend, Mr. Moss, here insists on standing a bottle of sherry.

MOSS *(in alarm).* No, no!

DAL. What, will you make it champagne? Very well. *(To* MALTBY.*)* I like it dry, mind you, and none of your home-brewed.

*(Exit* MALTBY.*)*

MOSS. Come, Tiger. *(*DALTON *gives him a look which stops him.)* A joke's a joke. But a bottle of real champagne at ten and six—

DAL. That's serious, eh? Well, I've taken a serious turn, always do when it's low tide here. *(Patting his pocket.)*

MOSS. Down on your luck, eh?

DAL *(shrugs his shoulders).* The bobbies are getting to know too much; then there's the Nailer's been after me.

MOSS. What, Hawkshaw, the best detective on the force after you?

DAL. He's taken his oath at Bow Street Office to be square with me for that Peckham job—

MOSS. Ah!

DAL. When I spoiled his friend.

MOSS *(shaking his head).* Ah, I always said that blackjack would be doing somebody a mischief.

*(Re-enter* MALTBY *with champagne and glasses.)*

DAL. Hush, here's the tipple.

MALT *(at back of table uncorking and pouring out).* And though I say it myself, there ain't a better bottle opened at Buckingham Palace. Ten and six, Mr. Moss—there's a color—there's a bouquet!

MOSS *(grumbling as he pays).* There ought to be at that price.

*(Exit* MALTBY.*)*

DAL *(drinking).* Ah, tidy swizzle!

MOSS. And so you're keeping dark, eh?

DAL. Yes, getting about a bit on the sneak, picking up a little when I get the chance; but the Nailer's too hard on me. There's no making a gentlemanly livelihood. Hang me, if I haven't often thought of turning respectable.

MOSS. No, no; it's not that bad yet. *(Looking about and speaking cautiously.*) Now, I have the beautifullest lot of Bank of England flimsies that ever came out of Birmingham. It's the safest paper to work, and you shall have it cheap, dirt cheap, and credit till you've planted it.

DAL. None of that for me! If I'm caught it's a lifer.

MOSS. Bless you, I wouldn't have you chance it; but in the high society you keep, you could surely pick up some innocent to pass on the paper.

DAL *(hits table with fist)*. I've the very man. I gave him an appointment here, for this evening.

MOSS. Did you though! How pat things come about! Who is he?

DAL. A Lancashire lad—an only son—he tells me. The old folks spoiled him as long as they lived, left him a few hundreds, and now he's kicking 'em down, seeing life. *(Laughs.)* And life in London ain't to be seen, without paying at the doors, eh Melter? *(Slaps him on back.)*

MOSS. Ha, ha, ha! and you're selling him the bill of the play?

DAL. I'm putting him up to a thing or two—cards, races, billiards, sporting houses, night life and casinos—every short cut to the devil and the bottom of a man's purse. He's green as a leek, and soft as new cheese. *(Rises.)*

MOSS *(rising)*. Oh, beautiful, beautiful! *(Rubs his hands.)* It would be a sin to drop such a live one! Suppose we take him in partnership?

DAL. Thank you, I know *your* partnerships—me all the kicks and you all the money. But if I can work him to pass these flimsies of yours, I don't mind; remember, though. I won't go higher than fifteen bob for a fiver.

MOSS. What! Only fifteen bob! And such beauties too, they'd take in the bank chairman—fifteen! I'd rather chance it myself! Only fifteen—it's robbery!

DAL. Take it or leave it. *(Takes up newspaper and sits at table.)*

MOSS. I must take a turn and think it over. *(Going, returns.)* I'll bring the notes to you. Come, you'll allow me a pound?

DAL. Bid me down again, and I'll stand on ten shillings—like it or lump it. *(He returns to his paper.)*

MOSS *(holding up his hands)*. Oh dear, oh dear! What it is to deal with people that have no consciences! *(Exit.)*

BRIERLY *(heard off L.)*. A bottle of champagne, lad, and half a dozen Cabanas—and look sharp!

DAL *(looking up from paper)*. Here's my pigeon!

*(Enter* ROBERT BRIERLY, *looking feverish and dishevelled. A young lad from Lancashire in his early twenties, he is seeing the city for the first time. He is innocent, but trying to appear sophisticated. He is dressed in exaggerated sporting style.)*

DAL *(setting the paper down)*. Ah, Bob, up to time as usual! *(They shake hands.)*

BRI. Aye! Nobody shall say Bob Brierly quit while he could yet keep going.

*(WAITER brings another glass. BRIERLY pours out wine.)*

BRI. It puts heart into a chap! *(Drinks eagerly.)* I've nearly lived on it this fortnight past. *(Drinks.)*

DAL *(reaches out to stop his hand).* Take care, Bob, or we shall have you in the doctor's hands.

BRI. Doctor? Nay, I'm as game as a pebble and strong as a tree! *(Fills DALTON's glass with shaking hand.)* Curse the glass! Here—drink, man, drink. I can't bear drinking single-handed. I like company—I always did. *(Looking around uneasily.)* And now, I don't know how it is—*(Nervously looking down near the table.)* No, no, it's nothing! Here, have a weed. *(Offers cigar.)*

DAL. I'll take a light from you. *(As DALTON lights his cigar at BRIER-LY's, the shaking of BRIERLY's hand becomes more apparent.)* Come, come, Master Bob *(Puffs.)*, you're getting shaky. *(Takes match.)* This wont' do.

BRI. It's the waking—waking—if I could only sleep. *(Earnestly.)* I don't know, how it is—I get no rest—and when I do, it's worse than none—there's great black crawling things about me. *(Gulps down a glass of wine.)* I say, Downey, do you know how a chap feels when he's going mad?

DAL. I know the symptoms of delirium tremens well enough—sit down, sit down. First and foremost *(Puts him in a chair.)* I prescribe a devilled biscuit—I'll doctor one for you. *(Calling.)* Here—a plate of biscuit, toasted hot, butter and cayenne. *(BRIERLY hides his head in his hands. Aside, looking at him contemptuously.)* The horrors! Ah, he's seen too much of life lately—Bob, are you in cash?

BRI. Cleaned out—I've written to the lawyer chap down at Glossop—him that's got all my property to manage, you know—for more brass.

DAL *(aside).* Now, if I'd a few of Moss' fivers—here's a chance—*(To BRIERLY.)* You must bank with me until your money comes. Delighted to lend you a sovereign—five, ten, anything you want.

*(Enter MOSS.)*

BRI. Will you though? That's friendly of you. Here's luck and sink the expense! *(He pours out wine, standing in front of table.)*

MOSS *(aside to Dalton).* I've got the flimsies—I'll do it at seven-ten.

DAL *(aside).* Fork over.

MOSS *(aside, giving him a roll of notes).* There's fifty to begin with—twenty, a tenner, and four fives. Plant the big one first.

*(Enter HAWKSHAW C. He meets MOSS at back of chair and approaches the table where DETECTIVE is. He nods towards MOSS and DALTON.)*

MOSS. Good evening, gentlemen. *(Crosses behind DALTON.)* You'll find my friend, Mr. Downey, excellent company, sir. Very improving for a young man from the country. *(Aside.)* That's an honestly earned seven-ten!

*(Exit MOSS. MALTBY brings biscuits and cayenne, exits.)*

DAL. Now for your devil, Master Bob.

*(As* DALTON *prepares the biscuit,* HAWKSHAW *approaches table and takes up the paper which* DALTON *has put down.* DALTON *pushes the biscuit across to* BRIERLY.)*

Try that?

HAWK *(speaks with cultivated British speech).* Beg pardon, sir, but if the paper's not in hand.

DAL *(rudely and pocketing the note hastily).* Eh, sir?

HAWK *(sitting down coolly at the table and unfolding the paper).* Paper's very dull lately, don't you think so, sir?

DAL *(assuming a country dialect).* I never trouble 'em much myself, sir, except for the livestock lists, in the way of business.

HAWK. Ah, much my own case. They put a fellow up to the dodges of the town, though; for instance, these cases of forged notes offered at the Bank lately. *(Watching him closely.)*

DAL. I never took a bad note in my life.

HAWK. You've been very lucky—in the livestock line, too, I think you said. In the jobbing way, may I ask, sir, or in the breeding?

DAL. Sometimes one, and sometimes t'other—always ready to turn the nimble shilling.

HAWK. My own rule.

DAL. May I ask your business?

HAWK. The fancy iron trade. My principle is to get as much of my stock on other people's hands as I can. From the country, I think.

DAL. Yes, Yorkshire.

HAWK. Ah! Durham, myself; and this young gent?

BRI. What's that to you? *(Pushing away biscuit.)* It's no use—I can't swallow a morsel.

HAWK. From Lancashire, I see. Why, we are quite neighbors when we are at home—and neighbors ought to be neighborly in this overgrown city, so I hope you'll allow me to stand treat—give it a name, gentlemen.

DAL *(roughly).* Thank you, I never drink with strangers.

BRI. They've a saying down in Glossop, where I came from: if you want a welcome, wait to be asked.

HAWK. Ah, quite right to be cautious about the company you keep, young man. Perhaps I could give you a bit of good advice.

BRI. Thank you! I'm not in the way of taking good advice.

HAWK. Well, don't take bad; and you won't easy find a worse advisor than your thieving companion here.

DAL *(starting).* Eh? What do you mean by that?

HAWK. Not you, sir. *(Tapping the champagne bottle.)* This gentleman here. He robs people of their brains—their digestion—and their conscience—to say nothing of their money. But since you won't allow me to stand anything—

DAL. And wish to keep ourselves to ourselves.

BRI. And think your room a deal better than your company. *(To*

HAWKSHAW.*)* Meanin' no offence, you know.

HAWK *(rises and crosses)*. Not in the least. If gentlemen can't please themselves in a public establishment! I'll wish you a very good evening. *(Aside.)* A plant! I'll keep an eye on 'em! *(Exit.)*

DAL *(aside)*. I don't half like the look of that fellow. There's something about his eye—I must make out if Moss knows him—Bob, will you excuse me for five minutes?

BRI *(to DALTON)*. Don't be long—I can't bear my own company.

DAL. I've only a word to say to a customer. *(Exit.)*

*(HAWKSHAW re-appears, watches DALTON off and follows him after a moment's interval).*

BRI *(goes to chair)*. And I'll try to sleep till he comes back. If I could only sleep without dreaming! I never close my eyes but I'm back at Glossop with the folks at home—with mother stroking my head, and calling me her bonny boy—no, no, I mustn't think of it—or I shall go mad. *(Sinking his head in his hands.)*

*(Music. Enter MAY EDWARDS with guitar. She is a very pretty girl, about 20, a street singer with a lovely voice.)*

MAY. If only they'll let me sing tonight. *(Tuning guitar.)*

*(MALTBY enters.)*

MALT. Hello—hello! What's this? Oh, it's you, is it, Edwards? Come, I'm glad to see you're about again, but I can't have you begging here.

MAY. Oh, Mr. Maltby, please only allow me to try one song, and go round after it—I promise I'll stop right after one song.

MALT. Well, well, you was always a well-behaved girl, so for once, in a way—

MAY. Oh, thank you, thank you, and if you should have an opening for me, sir, when I'm quite strong again—

MALT. No chance of it, we're chuck full of talent; but if I *should* be able to find room for you in the chorus, and to double Miss Plantagenet when she's in the tantrums, ten shillings a week and find your own wardrobe, you know *(To audience.)*—I'm not the man to shrink from a generous action. *(Exit.)*

MAY. (SONG: *"Keep on the Sunny Side"* *)

> Keep on the sunny side
> And let dull care pass you by.
> Just figure out you're a long time dead,
> Don't start to worry or sigh.
> Weep, and you weep alone,
> Don't give up hope till you've tried,
> Don't join the crowds that walk under dark clouds,
> But keep on the sunny side.

*Music on page 370.

(MAY *goes to the tables. All repulse her.*)

1ST PARTY. The concert's bad enough without caterwauling between the acts.

2ND PARTY. We've no small change, miss.

3RD PARTY. Be off!

MAY (*to* BRIERLY). Please, sir—

BRI. Be off, lass, I'm in no mood for music.

MAY (*suppressing her tears*). Not a penny!

BRI. Stop, lass. (*Feels in his pocket.*) Not a farthing. Where's Downey? Here, now, what'st crying for?

MAY. I've had no food all day and I've not been well lately. (*She turns faint and grasps a seat to support herself.*)

BRI (*rising*). Poor thing, here—(*Places chair.*) Come, sit down. How pale you look! (*Offers her a biscuit.*) Here—try and eat a bit.

MAY. Thank you, sir, you're very kind. (*She tries to swallow but cannot. To* BOB.) If I had a drink of water . . .

BRI. Water? (*At back of table.*) Nay, a sip of this will hearten you. (*Gives her wine from his bottle.*) There, lass, sip that.

MAY (*drinks*). It's wine.

BRI. So it is; drink it up.

MAY. It makes me so warm.

BRI. It'll put some heart in you. Here, again, this will tune up your pipes. Now try and eat a bit.

MAY. Oh, sir, you're too good.

BRI. Good? Me? Nay—

(*Enter* MALTBY.)

MALT (*presenting check*). Your check, sir—

BRI. Here (*Feels in his pockets.*) Eh? Empty—well, score it down.

MALT. We ain't in the habit of scoring, sir, not to strangers.

BRI. Then, you'd better begin. My name's Bob Brierly.

MALT. Your name may be Bob Brierly, sir, or Bob Anybody, sir, but when people take wine in this establishment, sir, they pay for it.

(DALTON *re-appears from L.*)

BRI. I tell you—I'll pay as soon as my friend comes back.

MALT. Oh, your friend! A regular case of bilking—

BRI. Now you take care! (*Threatening him.*)

MAY (*frightened*). Oh, please, sir, please, Mr. Maltby.

DAL (*coming forward*). Hello! What's all this?

BRI (*seizing him*). Here, Downey, lend me a sovereign to pay this chap.

DAL. Sorry, I haven't change, but we'll manage it directly. (*To* MALTBY.) It's all right. I'll stand good for my friend here.

MALT. Your word's quite enough, sir. Any friend of Mr. Moss—

DAL. Come, Bob, don't be a fool, take a turn and cool yourself. (*Drawing him off, aside.*) Now to plant the big one.

(*They exit U.L.*)

MALT (*to guests*). Sorry for this disturbance, gents, quite out of keeping with the character of my establishment. (*Fiercely to* MAY.)

This is all along of your cadging, Edwards, sitting down to drink with a promiscuous party.

MAY. Oh, I'm so sorry—he never thought—it was all his kindness.

MALT (sneeringly). Kindness! Much kindness he'd have shown you, if you'd been old and ugly. You ought to be ashamed of yourself.

MAY (indignantly). You ought to be ashamed of yourself! It is cruel in you to insult a helpless and friendless girl.

MALT. Insult! Ho, ho, ha, here's a lark! A half-starved street-singer cheeking me in my own establishment! You'd better apply for an engagement, you had, on the first vacancy. (Looking off.) Hello, what's this? Carriage company! Heavy swells out on the lark, white ties and pink bonnets! I've business to attend to, girl, now, be off! (Exit.)

MAY (sinks down at one of tables). I'm foolish to be angry; my bread depends on such as he. Oh, if I could only get away from this weary work! I'm quick at my needle, but who'd take me, a vagabond, without a friend to speak for me? It's strange how people's lives are made for them. I see so many girls, nicely dressed, well off, with parents to love and care for them. I can't bear it sometimes. When I think what I am, and what's before me—(Puts her hand to her face.) I'm a silly girl; it's all because of the fever. There's nothing like keeping a good heart. How good he was—it was all through looking after me he got into trouble—but I mustn't think of him. Come along old friend (She pats guitar.), you've got to earn my supper yet. (Takes her guitar and exits.)

(Enter GREEN JONES, a London man about town, and EMILY ST. EVREMOND. He is well-to-do, and somewhat snobbish about it. EMILY is a dance hall girl, trying to rise in the world. She is very pretty, vivacious and eager to please. She is well—but somewhat fussily—dressed.)

GREEN (speaking as he enters). Excuse me, Emily. Anything but that concert. If your mama likes music, let her enjoy it.

EMILY. The music's very nice, Mr. Jones.

GREEN. Mr. Jones! Miss St. Evremond! What have I done that you keep me at arm's length? Was it to be called Mr. Jones that I thawed the thick-ribbed ice of Mrs. Traddles?

EMILY. Thick-ribbed ain't a proper word to use to any lady, and I tell you my ma's name ain't Traddles; it's the same as mine— St. Evremond. She's changed it at my wish.

GREEN. I beg pardon of your stern parent (Sits.), Mrs. St. Evremond, late Traddles; but I repeat, was it to be called Mister Jones that I treated Mrs. St. Evremond and child to the Star and Garter; and her child—without Mrs. St. Evremond—to the Trafalgar, where from the moonlit balcony that overhung the fragrant river, we watched the sunset together.

EMILY. And very wrong it was of me to go to the Trafalgar without ma; and preciously she blew up about it, though I told her you couldn't have treated me with more respect if I'd been a countess instead of a chorus girl.

GREEN. Emily, you only did me justice. My intentions are honorable. If you are in the ballet, that's no reason you shouldn't be a dear, good girl. You've been a trump of a daughter, I don't see why you shouldn't turn out a trump of a wife. Emily, accept my hand.

EMILY. Nonsense, Green, you don't mean it.

GREEN. I'm perfectly serious. My hand and my heart, my fortune and my future. Don't stare, Emily. It's as true as that my name is Green. I'm quite in earnest—I am indeed.

EMILY. Oh! Green, dear, I'm in such agitation!

GREEN. We will spend a rosy existence. You like life, and I flatter myself I understand how to enjoy it.

EMILY. And don't I? I call this life—the music and the company, and the singing and the trapeze. Oh, Green, I thought that man must surely break his neck. It's all so beautiful!

GREEN. Yes, I like to associate with all classes. "Survey mankind", you know, Emily—"from China"—to earthenware.

*(Re-enter* MAY. *She begins to sing.)*

Oh, anything but that! Now do oblige me by shutting up—there's a good girl.

EMILY. No, no, poor thing. Let her sing; she has a sweet voice.

GREEN. Flat, decidedly.

EMILY *(contemptuously).* You're another. Give me a half crown for her.

GREEN *(gives one, she asks by gesture for another).* Two? Such a bore—I shall have to change a note at the bar.

EMILY. You'll have to change a good many notes when we're married.

*(Exit* GREEN JONES *and* EMILY, MAY *following. Enter* BRIERLY.*)*

BRI. Downey not here? He said I was to bring the money to our table.

MAY *(Recognizing him).* 'Tis he. Oh, sir, I'm so sorry—

BRI. Why, it's the singing lass. *(Crosses to her.)* I say, have you seen my friend?

MAY. No, sir.

BRI. And where's the landlord? Here's that will make him civil enough. *(Shows a number of sovereigns in his hand.)*

MAY. Oh, what a lot of money!

BRI. Brass for a twenty pound note. I got it changed at the cigar shop down the road. He's a good one, Downey is, lends me whatever I want—here, landlord.

MALT *(entering).* Coming! Coming! *(Recognizing him.)* Oh, it's you.

BRI *(flinging a half sovereign to Maltby).* There; seven and six is for the wine and the other half crown is for the thrashing I owe you. *(Approaches him threateningly.)*

MALT *(pocketing the money and retreating).* Take care—I'll teach you to insult a respectable licensed saloon keeper. *(To* MAY, *who tries to calm* BRIERLY.*)* And you too, you tramp, I'll have you locked up for annoying my customers. How do I know my spoons are safe?

BRI. You cur! *(He breaks away.* MALTBY *exits crying "Police.")*

MAY. I cannot bear you should trouble for me, indeed, sir. *(Concealing her tears.)*

BRI. Nay, never heed that muck-worm. Come, dry your tears. You're too soft a creature for this kind of life.

MAY *(apologetically).* It's the fever, I think, sir—I didn't used to mind unkind looks and words.

BRI. Here, take this *(Puts money into her hand.)* and stay quiet at home till you're back in health.

MAY. Two sovereigns! Oh, sir, I couldn't.

BRI. Take them—you'll make better use of them than I—What crying again? Come, never heed that old brute. Hard words break no bones, you know.

MAY. It's not the hard words I'm crying for now, sir.

BRI. What then?

MAY. Your kind ones, they're harder to bear—they sound so strange to me.

BRI. Poor thing! Heaven help you. You remind me of a sister I lost. She had eyes like yours, and hair, and much the same voice. It would be good to have a sweet lass like you to talk to.

MAY. But where I live, sir, it's a very poor place, and I'm by myself, and—

BRI *(hesitates).* Of course, you're right—I couldn't come there, but I'm loath to lose sight of you.

*(Enter* DALTON *hastily.)*

DAL. Brierly!

BRI. Here's the change—I've borrowed five of the twenty.

DAL. All right, now let's be off—I've a cab outside.

BRI *(to* MAY*).* Mind, if you want a friend, write to Bob Brierly, at the Lancashire Arms, Air Street. You'll not forget?

MAY. Never—I'll set it down *(Aside.)* in my heart.

DAL. Come!

BRI. And you—tell me your name—will you?

MAY. May Edwards.

DAL. Confound your billing and cooing—come on! *(As* BRIERLY *follows* DALTON, HAWKSHAW *and* DETECTIVE *re-appear.)*

HAWKSHAW. You're wanted for passing a forged note!

DAL *(aside).* The crushers! Run, Bob!

*(Music.* DALTON *attempts to escape.* DETECTIVE *detains* BRIERLY. HAWKSHAW *seizes* DALTON. *In the scuffle,* DALTON's *hat and wig are knocked off.)*

HAWK. I know you, James Dalton!

DAL *(starting).* Ah!

HAWK. Remember the Peckham job!

DAL. The Nailer! Hit out, Bob!

(BRIERLY *has been wrestling with the* DETECTIVE. *As* DALTON *speaks, he knocks him down.*)

BRI. I have.

MAY *(cries).* Help! Help! *(Wringing her hands.)*

(A *fierce struggle,* DALTON *escapes from* HAWKSHAW *and throws him. He draws a pistol.* DALTON *strikes him down with a black-jack and makes his escape.* BRIERLY *is overpowered and hand-cuffed by* DETECTIVE.)

**CURTAIN**

*The garrulous and goodhearted Mrs. Willoughby explains the hardships of a landlady's life to one of her tenants, May Edwards. Shown here are Kathleen McCreery as May, Jane Ellen Drake as Mrs. Willoughby.*

# ACT ONE

SCENE: *The room occupied by* MAY EDWARDS *in* MRS. WILLOUGHBY's *house, humbly but neatly furnished, flowers in the window, a worktable with needlework on it, stool; a door communicating with her bedroom; door leading to the staircase; guitar hanging against wall.* MAY *is discovered with a birdcage on the table, arranging a piece of sugar and groundsel between the bars.*

MAY. There, Goldie, I must give *you* your breakfast, though I don't care a bit for my own. I'm sure I shall have a letter from Robert this morning. I've kept all his letters here. *(She takes a packet from her work-box.)* How he has improved his handwriting. *(Opening letter.)* That's more than three years now. Goldie, if you'll be quiet, I'll read you Robert's last letter. *(Reads.)* "Portland, February 25th, 1860. My own dearest May *(Kisses letter.)*, as the last year keeps slipping away, I think more and more of our happy meeting. But for your love and comfort, I think I should have broken down." *(To bird.)* Goldie, do you hear that? *(Bird chirps.)* "But now we both see how things are guided for the best. But for my being sent to prison, I should have died before this, a broken-down drunkard, if not worse; and you might still have been earning hard bread as a street singer, or carried from a hospital ward to a pauper's grave." Yes, yes *(Shuddering.)*, that's true. "I count the days till we meet. Goodbye and heaven bless you, prays your ever affectionate Robert Brierly." *(Kisses letter.)* And don't I count the days, too? They seem so slow—when one looks forward—and yet they pass so quickly!

*(Picks up birdcage. A knock at the door. Enter EMILY.)*

EMILY *(entering)*. May I come in?

MAY. Oh, yes, Mrs. Jones.

EMILY. St. Evremond, please, Miss Edwards. Jones has changed his name. When people have come down in circumstances, the best they can do is to keep up their names. I like St. Evremond: It looks well on the bill and sounds foreign. That's always attractive—and I dress my hair à la Francaise, to keep up the effect. I've brought back the shawl you were kind enough to lend me.

MAY. I hope you got the engagement, dear?

EMILY *(sighs)*. No, the proprietor said my appearance was quite the thing—good stage face and figure, and all that; you know how those creatures always flatter one; but they hadn't an opening just now in the comic duet and character-dance business.

MAY. I'm so sorry. Your husband will be so disappointed.

EMILY. Oh! Bless you, he doesn't know what I've been after. I couldn't bear to worry him, poor fellow! He's had so many troubles. I've been used to roughing it—before we came into our fortune.

*(Noise heard overhead. MAY starts.)*

MAY. What noise is that? It's in your room.

EMILY. Don't be alarmed—it's only Green. I left him to practice the clog-dance while I went out. He's so clumsy, but he gets on very nicely in comic duets.

MAY. It's very fortunate he's willing to turn his hand to anything.

EMILY. Yes, he's willing enough to turn his hand, only he is so slow in turning his feet. Ah, my dear, you're so lucky only having yourself to keep.

MAY. I find it hard enough sometimes. But after the life I had before I came here, it seems paradise.

EMILY. Oh! I couldn't bear it; such a want of excitement and you that was brought up to the public life, too. *(Rises.)* Every night about six, when they begin to light up the gas, I feel so fidgety, I can't think—of course, it was very different the three years we had our fortune. *(Sighs with an air of martyrdom.)*

MAY. I'm afraid Mr. Jones ran through a great deal in a very short time.

EMILY. Well, we were both fast, dear, and to do Jones justice, I don't think he was the fastest. You see, he was used to spending and I wasn't. It seemed so jolly at first to have everything one liked.

*(A knock.)*

MAY. Come in!

*(Enter* GREEN JONES, *much dilapidated; he wears a decayed dressing gown and a stocking cap, and carries a pair of clogs in his hands. He throws himself into a chair.)*

MAY. Your wife is here, Mr. Jones.

EMILY. St. Evremond, please, dear.

GREEN. Yes, Montague St. Evremond. I thought you would be here, Milly. I saw you come in the street door.

*(*MAY *takes up her work.)*

EMILY. Oh, you were watching for me out the window, I suppose, instead of practicing your *pas*.

GREEN. I was allowing my shins an interval of refreshment. I hope, Miss Edwards, you may never be reduced to earn a subsistence by the clog hornpipe, or if you are, that you will be allowed to practice in your stockings. The way I've barked my poor shins! *(He lifts trouser leg.)*

EMILY. Poor dear fellow! There, there! He's a good boy, and shall have a piece of sugar, he shall. *(Kissing him.)*

GREEN. Sugar is all very well, Emily, but I'm satisfied I shall never electrify the British public in this kind of pump. *(Showing clog.)* The truth is, Miss Edwards, I'm not meant for a star of the ballet. As Emily says, I'm too fleshy.

EMILY. Stout was the word.

GREEN. Oh, was it? Anyway, you meant short-winded. My vocation is in the more private walks of existence. If I'd a nice light porter's place, now—

EMILY. Oh! Montague, how can you be so mean-spirited?

GREEN. Or if there's nothing else open to us but the music hall, I always said I should do better with performing dogs.

EMILY. Performing dogs!

GREEN. Yes, I've a turn for puppies. I'm at home with them. But we're interrupting Miss Edwards. Come along, Emily, if you're at liberty to give your Montague a lesson in the poetry of motion under difficulties—*(Showing the clog.)* But, oh, remember your Montague has shins. *(Rises, leaving clogs.)*

EMILY. You poor dear soft-headed, soft-hearted, soft-shinned creature! What *would* you do without me? *(Comes back.)* Oh, what a man he is! He has forgotten his dancing pumps!

*(Exit EMILY and GREEN JONES.)*

MAY *(folding up her shawl).* How times are changed since she made him give me a half-a-crown that dreadful night, when Robert—I can't bear to think of it—

*(Enter MRS. WILLOUGHBY, proprietor of MRS. WILLOUGHBY's rooming house. She is in her 50's, good-hearted, a "salt-of-the-earth" kind of woman, but a busybody.)*

Ah, Mrs. Willoughby, I was expecting a visit from you. I've the week's rent all ready. *(Gives her a folded parcel from small box on table.)*

MRS. W. *(takes deep breath).* Which ready you always was, to the minute, that I will say, my dear. You'll excuse me if I take a chair. *(Sits.)* These stairs is trying to an elderly woman, and that's the truth.

MAY. At all events, Mrs. Willoughby, you're looking very, very well this morning.

MRS. W. Ah, my dear, you are very good to say so *(Breath.)*, which if it wasn't for the rheumatics and the rates, one on top of another, and that boy Sam, though which is the worse, I'm sure is hard to say, only a grandmother's feelings is not to be told *(Breath.)*, which sweet oil can't be rubbed into the heart, as I said to Mrs. Molloy—her that has my first floor front—which she says to me, "Mrs. Willoughby," says she, "nine oils is the thing," she says *(Breath.)*, "rubbed in warm," she says. "Which is all very well, Mrs. Molloy," says I, "but how is a lone woman to rub it in the back of her neck," and Sam, that giddy and distressing me to that degree. "No, Mrs. Molloy *(Breath.)*," I says, "What's sent us we must bear it, and parties that's reduced to let lodgings can't afford easy chairs." *(Sigh.)*

MAY. I'm sure you ought to have one, so hard as you've worked all your life, and when Sam gets a situation—

MRS. W. Sam, ah, that boy— I came here about him. Hasn't he been here this morning?

MAY. No, not yet. I was expecting him—he promised to carry some things home for me.

MRS. W. Ah, Miss Edwards, if you would only talk to him; he don't mind anything that I say, no more than if I was a flat-iron, and his poor mother. Which was the only one I brought up and had five *(Breath.)*, she says to me, "Mother," she says, "he's a big child," she says, "and he's a beautiful child, but he have a temper of his own," which, "Mary," I says *(Breath.)* —she was called Mary after her aunt, from which we had expectations, but which was left to the Blind Asylum, and the Fishmongers' Alms Houses, and very like you she was, only she had light hair and blue eyes. *(Breath.).* "Mary, my dear," I says, "I hope you'll never live to see it," and took she was, at twenty-three, sudden, and that boy I've had to mend and wash and do for ever since, and hard lines it is.

MAY. I'm sure he loves you very dearly, and has an excellent heart.

MRS. W. Heart, my dear—which I wish it had been his heart I found in his right-'and pocket, as I was a-mending his best trousers last night, which it was a short pipe, and smoked as if it had been black-leaded. Many's the time when he've come in, I've said, "Sam," I've said, "I smell tobacco," I've said. "Grandmother," he'd say to me, quite grave and innocent, "p'raps it's the chimbley"—and him a child of fifteen, and a short pipe in his pocket! I'm sure I could have broke my heart over it, I could, let alone the pipe—which I flung it into the fire—but a happy moment since is a thing I have not known. *(Pauses for breath.)*

MAY. Oh! He'll get rid of his bad habits in time. I've taught him to carry my parcels already.

MRS. W. Yes, indeed! And how you can trust him to carry parcels; but oh, Miss Edwards, if you'd talk to him, and tell him pipes is the thief of time, and tobacco's the root of all evil—*(Rummaging in her pocket.)*

*(Knock at door.)*

That's at your door—which, if you're expecting a caller *(Rises.)* —

MAY. No, I expect no one—unless it's Sam.

*(Knock repeated.)*

Come in. *(Lays down her work.)*

*(BRIERLY opens the door timidly. He is dressed in rough clothing and is pale.)*

BRI *(doubtfully).* Miss Edwards, please?

MAY *(rushing into his arms).* Robert! You here!

BRI. My own dear May!

MAY *(confused).* I'm so glad! *(Steps back.)* But, how is it that you're *(Moves in.)* —how well you look!

MRS. W. Well, I'm sure!

MAY. Oh, you mustn't mind, Mrs. Willoughby, it's Robert.

MRS. W. Oh—Robert! I suppose by the way he's goin' on Robert's your brother—leastways, if he ain't your brother—

BRI. Her brother? Yes, ma'am, I'm her brother. *(Kisses her.)*

MRS. W. Indeed! And if I might make bold to ask where you come from—

BRI. I'm just discharged.

*(He pauses. MAY gives him a look.)*

MRS. W. Discharged! *(Moves toward him.)* Well, not from your situation, I hope.

BRI. From Her Majesty's Service, if you must know.

MAY. I've not seen him for three years, and more. I didn't expect him so soon, Mrs. Willoughby, so it's quite natural the sight of him should startle me.

MRS. W. Which well I know it—not 'avin' had brothers myself, but an uncle that ran away for a soldier and came back on the parish with a wooden leg, and a shillin' a day pension, and always in arrears for liquor, *(Sits.)*—which the way that man could drink beer!

BRI. I should have written to prepare you, but I thought I might be here as soon as my letter, so I jumped into the train at Dorchester, and here I am.

MAY. That was very thoughtless of you—no, it was very thoughtful and kind, but, I don't understand—

BRI. How come I to be here before the time I told you in my letter? You see, I had full marks and nothing against me, and the regulations—

*(MAY gives him a look which interrupts him.)*

MAY *(crosses to MRS. W.).* If Sam comes, shall I tell him to go downstairs to you, Mrs. Willoughby?

MRS. W. I shall be much obliged to you, my dear—which I know when brothers and sisters meet they'll have a great deal to talk over, and I never was one to stand listening' when other folks is talkin'— and one thing I may say, as I told Mrs. Molloy, only last week when the first floor had a little tiff, "Mrs. Molloy," says I, "Nobody ever heard me put in my oar when I wasn't asked," I says, "and idle chatterin' and gossip," I says, "is a thing that I was never given to, and I ain't a-goin' to begin now," I says, which good morning to you, young man, and a better girl and a nicer girl and a harder-working girl than your sister, I hope and trust, may never darken my doors again,

*(BRIERLY throws open the door.)*

which her rent was ever ready to the day. No, my dear, it's the truth.

*(During this, BRIERLY urges her toward the door.)*

Thank you, I can find the way myself, young man *(Turns to him.)* and a very nice-looking head you have on your shoulders, though you have had your hair cut uncommon short, which, I must say, good mornin', my dear, and anything I can do for you. *(Exit still talking.)*

BRI. Phew! One would think she'd been on the silent system for a twelvemonth! Now, we're alone at last. Let me have a good look at you. *(He takes her by the hand.)*

MAY. Well—

BRI. Prettier than ever—

MAY. Now, come sit down and don't talk nonsense.

BRI. Sit down! Not till I've had a good look at you; now I must have a good look at the place. How snug it is, neat as the cell I've just left. But it wasn't hard to keep that in order—a stool, a basin and a hammock. But here you have no end of things—a sofa and carpet— and chairs *(Going round as he speaks.)* —

MAY. And look at the chiffonier—I picked that up at a bargain and all out of my own earnings.

BRI. It's the coziest little nest for my bird—*(Sees the guitar.)* And there's the old bread winner—I'm glad you've not parted with that.

MAY. I should be most ungrateful if I did. Many a dinner it's earned for me, and many a week's rent it's paid. But tell me, how are you out so long before your time?

BRI. Here's my ticket of leave. They've given me every week of my nine months—they hadn't a mark against me. But when I was sent for to the Governor's room yesterday, and told I was a free man, everything swam round and round. They had to give me water, or I think I should have fainted like a girl.

MAY. Ah, as I felt that night when you gave me the wine.

BRI. Poor dear, I remember it as if it were yesterday. But when I passed out at the gate a free man—free to go where I liked, do what I liked, speak to whom I liked—I thought I should go crazy. But there was the convict's taint about me. You can't fling that off with the convict's jacket.

MAY. But here, no one knows you. You can make a fresh start now.

BRI. I hope so, but it's awfully uphill work. May—I've heard enough down yonder of all that stands between a poor fellow who's been in trouble—and an honest life. But just let me get a chance.

MAY. Oh—if only Mr. Gibson would give you one.

BRI. Who's he?

MAY. The husband of the lady who was my first and best friend. *(BRIERLY looks uneasy.)* After you, of course, you jealous thing. It was she gave me work—recommended me to her friends—and now I've quite a nice little business. If only Mr. Gibson would give you employment. He has some kind of office in the city.

BRI. No chance of that, May. I must begin lower down, and when I've got a character, then I may reach a step higher, and so creep back little by little to the level of honest men. *(Gloomily.)* There's no other way.

MAY *(putting her hands on his shoulders)*. At all events, you can wait and look about a little—you've money coming in, you know.

BRI. Money?

MAY. Yes. You forgot those two sovereigns you lent me. I've put away a shilling a week out of my savings, and then there's the interest, you know, ever so much. It's all here *(Goes to table and puts savings-box in his hand.)* You needn't count it. There'd have been more if you hadn't come so soon.

BRI. My good, kind May, do you think I'd touch a farthing of your savings?

MAY. Oh, do take it, Robert, or I shall be so unhappy! I've had more pleasure out of that money that any I ever earned, because I thought it would go to help you.

BRI. Bless your kind heart! To think of those little fingers working for me—why, May, lass, I've some twenty pounds of my own earnings at Pentonville and Portland, overtime and allowances. The Governor paid it over to me before I started yesterday—aye—and shook hands with me. God bless him for that.

MAY. Twenty pounds! Oh, I was so proud of my little earnings.

BRI. Well, keep them, May. Keep them to buy your wedding-gown. *(Takes her in his arms and kisses her. Enter* SAM, *grandson of* MRS. WILLOUGHBY, *a smart aleck 15-year-old. He gives a significant cough.)*

MAY. Oh! Sam!

BRI *(hastily)*. Sam, is it! Confound him! I'll teach him. *(Crosses, sees it is a boy and pauses.)*

SAM. You will, though? Granny would be uncommon obliged to you. *(To* MAY.*)* She says I want teaching, don't she?

MAY. How dare you come in like that, Sam, without so much as knocking?

SAM. How was I to know you had company? Of course, I'd knocked if I'd known you had your young man.

BRI. I tell you what, young'un. If you don't make yourself scarce—

SAM. Well, what? *(Retreating.)* If I don't make myself scarce, you'll pitch into me. Just you try it! *(Squaring.)* Yah! Hit one your own size, why don't you?

BRI. Go it, Master Sam! Ha, ha, ha!

SAM. My name's not Sam. It's Samuel Willoughby, Esquire, most respectable references given and required *(Pulls up collar.)*, as Granny says when she advertises the first floor.

BRI. Now be off, like a good little chap.

SAM. Come, cheeky! Don't you use bad language. I'm rising fifteen, stand five-feet-five in my stockings, and I'm sprouting—why, by summer—

MAY *(crosses to* SAM*)*. Hold your tongue! You're a naughty, impudent little boy.

SAM. Come, I'm bigger than you are, I'll bet a bob!

*(Stands on his toes. Enter* MRS. WILLOUGHBY.*)*

MRS. W. Oh, here's that boy at last! Which upstairs and downstairs and all along the street have I been a-seekin' of him. Which, if you don't believe me, Miss Edwards, I left a fourpenny bit in the china dog on the mantel piece only yesterday morning as ever was, and the trouble I've had to keep that boy's 'ands off it—where's that fourpenny piece *(Seizes him.)*, you young villain, which you know you took it.

SAM. Well, then, I did—to buy 'bacca with.

MRS. W. Bacca! And him not fifteen—and the only one left of three! *(Falls in chair.)*

SAM. If you will nobble a fellow's 'bacca, you must take the consequences, and just you mind—it ain't no use trying it on breaking my pipes, Granny. I've given up Brosley's and started a briar root. *(Pulls pipe out.)* It's a stunner.

MRS. W. Oh dear! Oh dear! If it ain't enough to melt a 'eart of stone. Oh, the grey hairs that boy have determined to bring me with sorrow to my grave.

SAM. What? 'Cause I smoke? Why, there's Jim Keggles smokes, and he's a year younger'n me. His father is going to take him to see the badger fights one of these days, and *his* mother don't go into hysterics.

MAY. Sam, I'm surprised you should take pleasure in making your grandmother unhappy!

SAM. I don't take no pleasure—she won't let me. She's always a-naggin' and aggravatin' me. Here, dry your eyes, Granny *(Goes to her.)*, and I'll be a good boy, and I won't go after the rats and I won't aggravate old Miggles' bullfinches.

MRS. W. And you'll give up that nasty tobacco, and not go slidin' down ladders in your Sunday trousers—

SAM. Best put me in charity leathers at once—wouldn't I look stunnin'?

MRS. W. There he goes with that impertinent chaff—I know he gets it from that young Miggles. Enough to stop his Granny's mouth with.

SAM. No. *(Kisses her.)* That's the only way to stop it. Come, I'm a-goin' to take myself up short and be a real swell, Granny—only I'm waitin' till I come into my fortune—you know, that twenty pounds you was robbed of, three years ago.

MRS. W. Which robbery is too good a word for it. It was forgery! Aye, and most as good as murder, which it might-a been my death. Yes, my dears, as nice-lookin' civil spoken a young man as you would want to see, and a broad way of speaking, and "Would you change me a twenty-pound note, ma'am?" he says. "And it ain't very often," I says, "you could have come into this shop"—which I was in the cigar and periodical line at the time.

BRI. Where was your shop?

MRS. W. In Fulham Road, three doors outside the Bellevue Gardens—"And a note is all the same to me," I says, "if all correct," I says, and when I looked in that young man's face, I had no more suspicion than I should of either of yours, my dears; so he gave me the note, and he took the sovereigns. And the next thing I saw was a gent, which his name he told me was Hawkshaw, and he were in the police, only in plain clothes, and asked to look at the note, and told me it was a bad 'un. And if that man left me on the sofa, in the back shop, or behind the counter with my head among the ginger beer bottles, is more than I can tell—for fits it was for days and days, and when I worked out of 'em, then I was short of my rent, and the stock sold up, and me ruined—

*(BRIERLY shows signs of agitation while she is speaking.)*

BRI. And you never recovered your money?

MRS. W. Not a penny, my dear, and if it hadn't been for a kind friend that set me up in my own furniture, it's Fulham Workhouse where I might have been at this moment—and that blessed boy—*(She cries.)*

SAM (*gaily*). In a suit of grey dittos, a-stepping out to church of a Sunday, to such a jolly long sermon! (*Mimes the stepping.*) Shouldn't I like that! (*Consolingly, and changing his tone, touching her.*) I say, don't cry. Granny, we ain't come to the poorhouse yet.

MRS. W. Which if that young man knew the mischief he'd done—

MAY. Perhaps he does, and is sorry for it.

MRS. W. (*crosses with* SAM). Not he, the wretch! What do the like o' them care for the poor creatures they robs—hanging's too good for 'em, the villains.

BRI (*crosses, takes his hat to go*). Will you excuse me?

MAY. You're not going?

BRI. No, I'll be back directly. (*Aside.*) Thank heaven, I can make it up to her! (*Exit.*)

MAY (*aside*). Poor fellow! He can't bear it—she little thinks—

MRS. W. You'll excuse me, it's not often I talk about it, Miss Edwards, which it's no use a-cryin' over spilt milk, and there's HIM as tempers the wind to the shorn lamb—and if it wasn't for this boy—

SAM. There, she's at me again.

MRS. W. Which if I'd only the means to put him to school and out of the streets, and clear of the Jim Miggles and them rats—

SAM (*half crying*). Bother the rats!

MAY (*crosses to* SAM). You see, Sam, how unhappy you make your grandmother.

SAM (*to* MAY). And don't you see how unhappy she makes me, talkin' of sendin' me to school.

MAY (*pushing him to* MRS. W.). Ah, Sam, you don't understand the blessing of having one who loves you as she does.

SAM. Then what does she break my pipes for?

MRS. W. Oh, them pipes!

(*A knock.*)

MAY. More visitors! What a busy morning! Come in.

(*Enter* MR. GIBSON, *a substantial, conservative London businessman, middle-aged, of careful but kindly disposition.*)

MR. G. Miss Edwards?

MAY. Yes, sir.

MR. G. Glad I'm right. My name is Gibson.

MAY. Oh, sir, I've never been able to say what I felt to your good kind lady, but I hope you will tell her how grateful I am.

MR. G. She knows it by the return you have made. You've showed you deserved her kindness.

MRS. W. Which you can tell your good lady, sir, from me, Miss Edwards' rent were always ready to the days and minutes—as I was telling her brother just now.

MR. G. Brother? My wife said you were alone in the world.

MAY. And so I was, sir, when she found me. He was (*She hesitates.*) away.

MR. G. (*pointing to* SAM, *who has put down a chair and is balancing himself acrobatically*). Is this the young gentleman? (SAM *pitches over with chair, and* MRS. W. *lugs him up.*)

MRS. W. Oh dear, no, sir, begging your pardon, which that is my grandson, Samuel Willoughby—which—take your cap out of your mouth, Samuel, and stand straight, and let the gentleman see you.

SAM *(sulkily)*. The old gent can see well enough—it don't want a telescope *(Slinks across at back.)* I ain't going to be inspected. I'll mizzle! *(Takes flying leap over chair and exits.)*

MRS. W. Which Miss Edwards' brother is grown up, and only come back this blessed mornin' as ever was, discharged from Her Majesty's Service, and by the name of Robert—

MR. G. With a good character, I hope.

MAY *(eagerly)*. Oh, yes, the very best, sir.

*(Re-enter BRIERLY.)*

BRI *(aside)*. I've done it. I can face her now.

MR. G. *(rises)*. I suppose this is Robert, a likely young fellow.

MAY. This is Mr. Gibson, Robert, the husband of the lady who was so good to me.

BRI. Heaven bless her, and you too, sir, for your kindness to this poor girl, while I was unable to help her.

MR. G. But now you've got your discharge, she'll have a protector.

BRI. I hope so, sir, as long as I live, and can earn a crust, I suppose I shall be able to do that.

MR. G. What do you mean to do?

BRI. Ah, there it is. I wish I knew what I could get to do, sir. There are not many things in the way of work that would frighten me, I think.

MR. G. That's the spirit I like! Your sister speaks well of you, and you've come out of Her Majesty's Service with a good character.

*(BRIERLY sighs relief.)*

You write a good hand?

*(MAY goes to table, gets letters from box.)*

BRI. Tolerably good, sir.

MAY. Beautiful, sir. Here are some of his letters. Look, sir *(Going to show him, but pauses.)*—Portland! Not this, sir. *(Turns page.)* This side is better written.

MR. G. A capital hand. Can you keep accounts?

BRI. Yes, sir. I helped to keep the books—yonder.

*(Re-enter SAM, comes over rapidly at back, to MRS. WILLOUGHBY.)*

SAM. Hello, Granny, here's a parcel I found for you in the letter-box. Ain't it heavy?

MRS. W. For me! *(Takes it.)* Whatever is it? Eh, money? Oh, Sam, you've gone and done something wrong?

SAM. Bother! Do you think if I had I'd come to you with the swag?

*(MRS. WILLOUGHBY, who has opened the packet, screams, and lets paper fall from the packet.)*

MAY. What's the matter, Mrs. Willoughby?

MRS. W. Sovereigns! Real gold sovereigns!

MAY & MR. G. Sovereigns!

SAM. Oh, crikey! *(Goes up and down in exultation.)*

MAY (*picks up paper* MRS. WILLOUGHBY *has let fall*). Here's a note—
"For Mrs. Willoughby—20 pounds in payment of an old debt."

MR. G. (*who has seated himself and begun to write, rises and comes down*). Yes, and no signature. Come, don't faint. Here, give her a glass of water. (*To* MAY.)

MRS. W. (*recovering*). Sovereigns! For me? Oh, sir, let me look at 'em, the beauties, eight, nine, ten, twelve, fifteen, eighteen, twenty! Just the money I lost.

SAM. There, Granny—I always said we was comin' into our fortune.

MRS. W. (*with sudden flash of doubt*). I shouldn't wonder if it was some nasty trick.

BRI. Perhaps it's somebody that wronged you and wants to clear his conscience.

MR. G. Ah! Eccentric people will do that sort of thing—even with income tax. Take my advice, lady, and keep the cash.

MRS. W. Which in course a gentleman like you knows best.

BRI. Amen!

MRS. W. Which, first and foremost, there's my silver teapot, I'll have out of pawn this blessed day, and I'll ask Mrs. Molloy to a cup of tea in my best blue china, and then this blessed boy shall have a year of finishin' school.

SAM. I wish the party had kept his money. I do!

(MRS. WILLOUGHBY *is counting the money over and over.*)
I say, Granny, you couldn't spare a young chap a couple of them, could you?

MRS. W. Drat the boy's impertinence! Him askin' for sovereigns as natural—Ah! They'll all be for you, Sam, one of these days.

SAM. I should like a little in advance
(*He makes a grab at the money playfully, runs back followed by*
MRS. WILLOUGHBY, *he dodges behind a chair.* MR. GIBSON *writes at table.*)

MRS. W. (*half hysterically, throwing herself into chair*). Oh, Sam, which that boy will be the death of his poor grandmother, he will.

SAM (*jumping over chair back, on which he perches, gives back money and kisses her.*) There, Granny, it was only a lark. (*Exit.*)

MRS. W. (*admiringly and affectionately*). Oh, what a boy you are! (*Exit.*)

MR. G. (*gives note to* BRIERLY). Here, young man, bring this note to my office, 25 St. Nicholas Lane, at ten o'clock in the morning. I've just discharged my messenger—we'll see if you are fit for the place.

BRI. Oh, sir!

MR. G. There, there, don't thank me. I like gratitude that shows itself in acts like yours to my wife. Let's hope your brother will repay me in the same coin.

MAY. Robert, the money has brought us a blessing already.
(*He takes her in his arms exultingly —music.*)

**CURTAIN**

# ACT TWO

SCENE: MR. GIBSON's *bill-broking office in St. Nicholas Lane. A mahogany railing runs up the stage, separating compartment L. (in which stand two large mahogany desks, set around with wire and a brass rail at the top to support books) from the compartment R. at the side of which is door leading to* MR. GIBSON's *private office. In front of the compartment runs a counter with a place for writing, divided off. A large iron safe stands near door which leads to passage and street. There is a small desk downstage. Two windows U.L. As curtain rises,* SAM *is discovered carrying ledgers through an entrance in the railing to compartment and arranging them on desks.* BRIERLY *is at counter, numbering checks in checkbook.*

SAM. There they are, all shipshape. I say, Bob, if Granny could see these big chaps *(Indicating ledgers.)* all full of pounds and me as much at home with them as Old Miggles with his terriers ... *(Puts books on desk and returns.)*

BRI. Only the outsides, Sam—fifty—fifty-one—

SAM. Everything must have a beginning. I'm only under-messenger, now *(Crosses to safe.)* at six bob a week, but it's the small end of the wedge. I intend to speculate—I'm in two tips already.

BRI. Tips?

SAM. Yes, *(Takes out betting book.)* I stand to win a fiver on Pollux for the Derby, and a good thing on the Count for the Ascot Cup—

BRI *(as* SAM *comes to him with the pens, he catches him by the collar and shakes him).* You young rascal! Now, you mark me, Master Sam, if ever I hear of you putting into a tip again, I'll thrash you within an inch of your life, and then I'll tell on you to Mr. Gibson, and he'll discharge you.

SAM. Now I call that mean. One city gent interfering with another city gent's amusements.

BRI *(bitterly).* Amusements! When you've seen as much as I have, you'll know what comes of such amusements, lad.

SAM. As if I didn't know well enough already. Lark, lush—a swell rig-out, and lots of ready cash in the pockets, a box at the races, and champagne lunch on the hill.

BRI. Ah, Sam that's the fancy picture—mine is the true one. Excitement first, then idleness and drink, and then bad companions—sin—shame—and prison.

SAM. Come, I don't want to be preached to in office hours.

BRI. Oh, my lad, take my advice, do. Be steady, stick to work and home. It's an awful look-out for a young chap adrift in this city.

SAM. Oh, I ain't afraid. I cut my eye teeth early.

BRI *(looking over check book).* You young rascal! You've made me misnumber my check.

SAM. Serves you jolly well right, for coming to business on your wedding day.

BRI. Oh, I've two good hours before I'm wanted for that.

SAM. I say, Bob, you don't mean to say that you've been to the bank for the petty cash this morning?

BRI. Yes.

SAM. And didn't leave the notes on the counter?

BRI. No.

SAM. And didn't have your pocket picked?

BRI. No.

SAM. Well, you *are* a cool hand. I've often wondered how the poor chaps at Newgate Prison managed to eat a good breakfast before they're turned off. But a fellow coming to office the morning he's going to be spliced—and when the Governor has given him a holiday, too—by Jove, it beats the Old Bailey by lengths! I hope I shall be as cool when I'm married.

BRI. You—you young cock-sparrow.

SAM. Yes I've ordered the young woman I want down at Birmingham. Miss Edwards ain't my style.

BRI. No, isn't she though? I'm sorry it's too late to have her altered.

SAM. She's too quiet—wants "go." I like high action. Now I call Mrs. Jones a splendid woman. Sam Willoughby, Esquire, must have a real tip-top lady.

BRI. Well, I wish you luck. But now, Sam, just trot off to the stationer's and see if Mr. Gibson's new bill-case is ready.

SAM *(vaulting over the counter, sees* MAY *through the glass door).* All right. Here's Miss Edwards a-coming in full tog. Psst—I ain't wanted. Quite correct.

BRI. Correct!

(SAM *puts his finger to his nose and exits. Enter* MAY *in wedding dress.)*

Ah, May, my darling! *(Takes her by hand and kisses her.)*

SAM *(looking in).* I saw you! *(Exit.)*

BRI. Hang that boy! But never mind his impudence, my own little wife.

MAY. Not yet, sir.

BRI. In two hours.

MAY. There's many a slip between the cup and the lip, you know. But I thought I might just look in and show you—*(Displays her dress.)*

BRI. Your wedding gown!

MAY. Yes. It's Mrs. Gibson's present to me—with such a kind note—and she's sent in the most beautiful cake, and flowers from their own conservatory. My little room looks so pretty.

BRI. It always looks pretty when you are in it.

MAY. There's only one thing I can't get off my mind.

BRI. What's that?

MAY. Mr. Gibson doesn't know the truth about you. We should have told him before this.

BRI. I'll tell him when I've been here long enough to try me, only wait a bit.

MAY. Perhaps you are right. dear. But you never said how you like my dress! *(Shows it.)*

BRI. I couldn't see the dress for looking at your bonny face—but it's a grand gown.

MAY. And my own making! I forgot, Mrs. Jones has come, and Mrs. Willoughby, too. They're going to church with us, you know. Emily looks so nice; she would so like to see the office, she says, if I might bring her in!

BRI. Oh, yes! The place is free to all the petticoats till business hours.

MAY *(calls at door).* Come in, Emily.

*(Enter* EMILY ST. EVREMOND.*)*

EMILY. Oh, Mr. Brierly!

MAY. While Robert does the honors of the office, I'll go and help Mrs. Willoughby to set out the breakfast.

MRS. W. *(calling outside).* Miss Edwards!

MAY. I'm coming, Mrs. Willoughby! Oh, dear, if I'd know the trouble it was to be married, I don't think I should have ventured. I'm coming! *(Exit.)*

EMILY *(who has been looking about her).* I did *so* want to see an office, a real one, you know. I've seen 'em set on the stage often, but they ain't a bit like the real thing.

BRI. They are but dull places.

EMILY. Yes, they are dull, but *so* respectable. Look so like money, you know. I suppose, now, there's no end of money passes here?

BRI. A hundred thousand pounds a day, sometimes.

EMILY. Gracious goodness! All in sovereigns?

BRI. Not a farthing—all in checks and bills. We've a few thousands that a queer old-fashioned depositor insists on Mr. Gibson keeping here. But except that—and the petty cash—there's no hard money in the place.

EMILY. Dear me! I thought you city people sat on stools all day shoveling sovereigns about. Not that I could bear to think of Jones sitting on a stool all day, even to shovel sovereigns about, though he always says something in the city would suit him better than the comic duet business. But he doesn't know what's good for him— never did, poor fellow.

BRI. Except when he married you.

EMILY. Well, I don't know about that, but I suppose he would have gone through all that property without me—he's so much the gentleman, you know.

BRI. He's coming to church with us?

EMILY. Oh yes! You know, he's to give the bride away. But he was obliged to keep an appointment in the city first; he wouldn't tell me what it was.

GREEN *(heard outside).* Two and six, my man. Very good, wait.

BRI. Here's your husband!

EMILY *(looking through door).* In a cab—and a new coat, and waistcoat and trousers! Oh Jones! Well, I shan't pay for them.

*(Enter* GREEN JONES *in a gorgeous new suit.)*

GREEN *(speaking off. He hands in parcels one by one.)* Hear, bear a hand.

*(He pitches parcels—hat box, gloves, clothes, etc.—to* BRIERLY *who pitches them to* EMILY *who deposits them on the counter.)*

EMILY *(as first bonnet box comes in).* Jones! *(As second bonnet box comes in.)* Green! *(As a case of Eau de Cologne comes in.)* Green Jones! *(Glove box comes in.)* Oh! *(Two bouquets in paper are given in.)* Gracious goodness!

GREEN. There—all out. Let's see—bonnets, Eau de Cologne, gloves, bouquets, seven-ten; two and six, the cab—my own togs, give ten— that's thirteen two and six in all.

EMILY. Jones, are you mad?

GREEN. Is your principal here, Brierly?

BRI. Mr. Gibson? No, it's not his time, yet.

GREEN. You couldn't advance me thirteen-two-six, could you?

BRI. What? Lend you the money? I'm afraid—

EMILY *(reproachfully).* Oh, Jones!

GREEN. Emily, be calm. It's not the least consequence. They can wait—the shopman. I mean. That is, the two shopmen and the cabby.

EMILY. Oh, he's gone crazy!

GREEN. The fact is, my love, I've had a windfall. Choker Black has struck it rich. He was put in a hole in California, and had to bolt to Australia. He struck an awfully rich pocket at the diggings and is paying off his old debts to me like an emperor. He let me in for two thousand, and has sent me bills for five hundred as a first installment.

EMILY. Five hundred! And you've got the money?

GREEN. I've got the drafts on his agent. Emily, embrace your husband. *(He kisses her.)*

BRI. I wish you joy, both of you. Mr. Gibson will discount the bills as soon as he comes in.

GREEN. But, I say, cash you know, no gilt certificates—no old masters or patent rights! I've had rather too much of that sort of thing in my time.

EMILY *(who has been peeping into bonnet box).* What a duck of a bonnet!

BRI. No, you're not among your old sixty-per-cent friends here. We only do good bills at the market rate.

EMILY *(who has opened glove box).* And what loves of gloves!

GREEN. That's your sort. I feel now the full value of commercial principle.

EMILY. Oh Green! But you'll be careful of the money?

GREEN. Careful! I'm an altered man. Henceforth I swear—you'll allow me to register a vow in your office?—to devote myself to the virtuous pursuit of money-making. I'm worth five hundred pounds with fifteen more coming in. Not one farthing of the money shall go in foolish extravagance.

EMILY. But how about these things, Jones?

GREEN. Trifles . . . a *cadeau de noce* for the ladies, and a case of Eau de Cologne for myself.

EMILY. Oh dear, Green. I'm afraid you're as great a fool as ever.

BRI. Nay, nay, Mrs. Jones—no man's a fool with 500 pounds in his pocket. But it's nearly business hours—band boxes and bouquets aren't quite business like, you know. You must carry these down to May.

GREEN *(loading EMILY with the parcels)*. Beg her acceptance of a bonnet, a bouquet, and a bottle of sweet scent—and accept the same yourself, from yours ever affectionately, G. J. *(Tries to kiss her over the parcels, but cannot.)*

EMILY *(from over the parcels)*. Oh, go along with your nonsense! I'll give you one downstairs. *(Exit.)*

*(Enter MR. GIBSON.)*

MR. G. *(rubbing his feet on the mat)*. Good morning, morning. Well, Robert, didn't expect you at the office this morning.

BRI. Here's a gentleman waiting for you, sir, on business.

MR. G. If you'll step into my room, sir?

*(Exit GREEN JONES into GIBSON's office.)*

BRI. I thought I might as well number the checks, sir, and go for the petty cash. Somehow, I felt I shouldn't like anything to go wrong today, sir.

MR. G. Well, that's a very proper feeling. I hope May likes my wife's present. She is a first-rate housekeeper, and I've every reason to be satisfied with you.

BRI. I'm right proud of that, sir.

MR. G. You won't mind my giving you a word of advice on your wedding day? Go on as you've begun—keep a bright eye and an inquiring tongue in your head. Learn how business is done, watch the market, and from what I've seen of you—the six months you've been here—I shouldn't wonder if I found a better job than messenger for you one of these days.

BRI. Mr. Gibson, sir, I can't thank you.

MR. G. In the city, there's no gap between the first rung of the ladder and the top of the tree. But that gentleman is waiting. *(Pauses, goes to the door.)* By the way, I expect a call from a Mr. Hawkshaw.

BRI. *(starting)*. Hawkshaw!

MR. G. Yes, the famous detective. Show him in when he comes. I've a particular appointment with him. *(Exit MR. GIBSON into his office.)*

BRI. Hawkshaw, coming here! The principal witness against me at my trial. Perhaps he won't know me—I'm much changed. But they say, at Portland, he never forgets a face. If he knows me, and tells Mr.

Gibson, he'll discharge me—and today, just when we looked to be so happy! It would break May's heart, but why should I stay? I'm free for the day—I will not wait to meet my ruin.

*(Enter* HAWKSHAW.*)*

HAWK. Is Mr. Gibson within?

BRI. Yes, sir, but he has a gentleman with him.

HAWK. Take in my name. *(Writes on card with pencil and gives it to* BRIERLY.*)*

BRI *(takes card and sees name on it, aside).* Hawkshaw, it is too late! Would you like to look at the paper, sir? *(Offers him one from desk.)*

HAWK *(as he takes it, gives a keen look of recognition at* BRIERLY, *who shrinks under his eye, but represses his agitation by an effort).* I've seen you before, I think?

BRI. I don't recollect you, sir.

HAWK *(carelessly).* Perhaps I'm wrong—though I've a good memory for faces. Take in my card.

*(*BRIERLY *goes off with card.)*

It's Dalton's pal—the youngster who got four years for passing forged Bank of England paper, the Bellevue Tea Gardens. I owe Master Dalton one for that night. Back from Portland, eh? Looks better for his schooling. But Portland's an odd shop to take an office messenger from. I wonder if his employer got his character from the last place.

*(Re-enter* BRIERLY.*)*

BRI. Mr. Gibson will see you in a moment, sir.

HAWK. Very well. *(Gives him a look.)*

*(Re-enter* GREEN JONES *from* MR. GIBSON's *room.)*

GREEN *(to* BRIERLY*).* All right! Market rate—and no old masters. I say, you must allow me to order a little dinner at the "Star and Garter" and drive you down—all right, you know. Carriage and pair, your wife and my wife. I want to show you the style G. J. used to do it in. *(Exit.)*

BRI *(aside).* He little thinks what may be hanging over me.

MR. G. *(appearing at door of his office).* Now, Mr. Hawkshaw, I'm at your service.

HAWK *(returning paper to* BRIERLY*).* Cool case of note-passing that at Bow Street yesterday. *(*BRIERLY *winces, aside.)* It's my man, sure enough. *(Exit to* GIBSON's *office.)*

BRI. He knows me—I can read it in his face—his voice. He'll tell Mr. Gibson? Perhaps he is telling him now. I wish I'd spoken to him, but they have no mercy. Oh, if only I'd made a clean breast of it to Mr. Gibson before this! *(*ROBERT *is writing at desk.)*

*(Enter* GIBSON *and* HAWKSHAW *from* GIBSON's *office.)*

MR. G. Robert!

BRI. Yes, sir.

MR. G. Before you leave, just step round into Glynn's and get me cash for this. You'll have time enough before you're wanted at the wedding.

BRI *(aside).* He knows nothing. *(Aloud.)* I'll be back in five minutes, sir.

> *(As* GIBSON *is about to give him the check,* HAWKSHAW, *who is standing between* GIBSON *and* BRIERLY, *interposes and takes check carelessly.)*

HAWK. Your messenger, sir?

MR. G. Yes.

HAWK. Had him long?

MR. G. Six months.

HAWK. Good character?

MR. G. Never had a steadier, soberer, better-behaved lad in the office.

HAWK. Had you references with him?

MR. G. Why, I think I took him mainly on the strength of his own good looks and his sweetheart's. An honest face is the best testimonial, after all.

HAWK. Hmmm—neither is always to be relied upon.

MR. G. You detectives would suspect your own fathers. Why, how you look at the lad. Come, you've never had *him* through your hands. *(A pause.)*

HAWK. No, he's quite a stranger to me. *(Turns away.)* Here's the check, young man. Take care you make no mistake about it.

BRI *(aside, going).* Saved! Saved! Heaven bless him for those words. *(Exit.)*

HAWK *(aside).* Poor devil, he's paid his debt at Portland. *(Aloud.)* Now to business. You say a bill drawn by Vanzeller & Co., of Penang, on the London Joint Stock Bank, was presented for discount here, last night, which you know to be a forgery?

MR. G. Yes. As it was after hours, the clerk told the presenter to call this morning.

HAWK. Bill-forging is tip-top work. The man who did this job knows what he's about. We mustn't alarm him. What time did the clerk tell him to call?

MR. G. At ten.

HAWK. It's within five minutes. You go to your room. I'll take my place at one of these desks as a clerk, and send the customer in to you. When the forged bill is presented, you come to the door and say—loud enough for me to hear—"Vanzeller & Co., Penang," and leave the rest to me.

MR. G. *(nervously).* Hadn't I better have assistance within call?

HAWK. Oh dear, no. *(He pushes* GIBSON *off.)* I like to work single-handed—but don't get too excited. Take it coolly or you may frighten the bird. *(Goes to desk.)*

MR. G. Easy to say, take it coolly! I haven't been thief-catching all my life.

> *(Exit* GIBSON *into his room. Enter* MOSS.)

MOSS *(at counter, getting out his bills).* Let me see—Spelter and Wayne. Fifty, ten three, thirty days after sight. That's commercial.

*(Examining another bill.)* For two hundred at two months, drawn by Captain Crabbs—accepted the honorable Augustus Greenway; that's a thirty-per-center. Better try that at another shop. *(Takes out another.)* Mossop and Mills—good paper—ninety-nine, eight, two at sixty days. That'll do here.

MR. G. *(at door of his room).* Mr. Hawkshaw!

HAWK. H—sh! *(Crosses, warns him against using his name, but obeys his call, goes in.)*

MOSS *(on hearing name).* Hawkshaw! *(With a quick glance as HAWKSHAW passes into MR. GIBSON's office.)* A detective here! *(Alarmed, but recovering.)* Well, I should like to know Hawkshaw's little game, and I shouldn't mind spoiling it.

*(Re-enter HAWKSHAW.)*

Mr. Gibson, if you please.

HAWK. He's in his office, sir.

*(As MOSS passes in, he recognizes him. Exit MOSS.)*

Melter Moss here? Can he be the forger? He heard my name. Dear, dear, to think that a businessman like Mr. Gibson should be green enough to call a man like me by his name.

*(Re-enter MOSS.)*

Here he comes. Now for the signal. *(Goes to desk, sits.)*

MOSS. All right. Thank you, Mr. Gibson!

HAWK *(aside).* No signal!

MOSS *(in front of counter).* If you'll allow me, I'll take a dip of your ink, young man, I've an entry to make in my bill book.

*(HAWKSHAW pitches him the pen.)*

Thank you. *(Crosses to table.)*

*(Enter DALTON, dressed as a respectable elderly commercial man, in as complete contrast as possible with his appearance in first act.)*

DAL. Mr. Gibson? *(Takes out bill case.)*

HAWK *(at desk).* You'll find him in his office, sir.

DAL *(aside).* That's not the young man I saw here yesterday afternoon. *(Aloud.)* Let me see first that I've got the bill. *(Rummages for bill.)*

MOSS *(recognizing DALTON).* Tiger here, in his city get-up. I'll drop him a line. *(Crosses to DALTON, hand on shoulder, and announces himself.)* Moss here!

DAL *(recognizing him).* Moss! *(Taking paper, reads.)*

MOSS. Hawkshaw is at that desk! Forewarned, forearmed!

*(Exit MOSS, MR. GIBSON appears at door of office.)*

MR. G. *(about to address HAWKSHAW again).* Mr.—

HAWK *(hastily interrupting him).* H'sh! A party wants to see you, sir, if you would step this way for a moment.

DAL. Would you oblige me, Mr. Gibson, by looking very particularly at this bill? *(Gives to GIBSON.)*

MR. G. "Vanzeller and Co., Penang." *(Glances at Hawkshaw, aside, who crosses and seats himself at desk.)* He don't stir! "Vanzeller and

Co., Penang." *(Aside.)* Confound it, I haven't made a blunder, have I? "Vanzeller & Co., Penang."

*(HAWKSHAW prepares handcuffs under the desk.)*

DAL. Yes, a most respectable firm. But all's not gold that glitters. I thought the paper as safe as you do, but unluckily, I burnt my fingers with it once before. You may not remember my presenting a bill drawn by the same firm for discount two months ago.

MR. G. Yes, Particularly well.

DAL. Well, sir, I have now discovered that it was a forgery.

MR. G. So have I.

DAL. And I'm sadly afraid, between you and me—by the way, I hope I may speak safely before the clerk?

MR. G. Oh, quite.

DAL. I'm almost satisfied that this bill is a forgery, too. The other has been impounded, I hear. My object in coming here yesterday was, first to verify, if possible, the forgery in the case of this second bill; and next to ask your assistance, as you had given value for the first as well as myself, in bringing the forger to justice.

*(HAWKSHAW looks up as if in doubt.)*

MR. G. Really, sir—

DAL. Oh, my dear, sir! If we city men don't stand by each other in these rascally cases! But before taking any other step, there is one thing I owe to myself, as well as to you, and that is, to repay you the amount of the first forged bill.

MR. G. But you said you had given value for it?

DAL. The more fool I! But if I am to pay twice, that is no reason you should be a loser. I've a memorandum of the amount here. *(Looks at his bill-book.)* Two hundred and twenty-seven-five. Here are notes— two hundreds. a ten, and two fives—seven—and one—two—three. *(Counting coppers.)*

MR. G. Oh, pray, sir, don't trouble yourself about the coppers.

DAL. I'm particular in these matters. *(Counting out coppers.)* Three, four, five. There, that's off my conscience! But you've not examined the notes.

*(HAWKSHAW pockets handcuffs.)*

MR. G. Oh, my dear sir.

DAL. Ah, careless, careless! *(Shakes his head.)* Luckily, I *had* endorsed them.

MR. G. Really, sir, I had marked that two hundred and twenty off to a bad debt a month ago. By the way, I have not the pleasure of knowing your name.

DAL. Wake, sir, Theopilus Wake, of the firm of Wake Bros., shippers and wharfmongers, Limehouse and Dock Street, Liverpool. We have a branch of the establishment at Liverpool. Here's our card. *(Gives card.)*

MR. G. So far from expecting you to repay the money, I thought you were coming to bleed me afresh with forged bill No. 2—for a forgery it is, most certainly.

DAL. Quite natural, my dear sir, my dear sir, quite natural—I've no right to feel the least hurt.

MR. G. And what's more, I had a detective at that desk ready to pounce upon you.

DAL. Not really.

MR. G. You can drop the clerk bit now, Mr. Hawkshaw.

(HAWKSHAW *comes down.*)

DAL. Hawkshaw! Have I the honor to address Mr. Hawkshaw, the detective, the hero of the great gold dust robberies and the famous trunkline transfer forgeries?

HAWK *(modestly).* I'm the man, sir. I believe . . .

DAL. Sir, the whole commercial world owes you a debt of gratitude it can never repay. I shall have to ask your valuable assistance in discovering the author of the audacious forgeries.

HAWK. Have you any clue?

DAL. I believe they are the work of a late clerk of ours. He got into gay company, poor lad, and has gone to the bad. He knew the Vanzeller's signature, as they were old correspondents of our firm.

HAWK. Is the lad in London?

DAL. He was within the week.

HAWK. Can you give me a description of him? Age—height—hair— eyes — complexion — last known address — habits — associates — *(Significantly.)* any female connection?

DAL. Unluckily I know very little of him personally. My partner, Walter Wake, can supply all the information you want.

HAWK. Where shall I find him?

DAL. Here's our card. We'll take a cab and question him at our office. Or *(As if struck by sudden thought.)* suppose you bring him here—so that way we may all lay our heads together.

HAWK. You'll not leave this office till I come back?

DAL. If Mr. Gibson will permit me to wait.

MR. G. I shall feel extremely obliged to you.

HAWK. You may expect me back in half an hour at the most. *(Leaving; returns.)* Egad, sir, you've had a narrow escape. I had the darbies open under the desk. *(Shows the handcuffs.)*

DAL. Ha, ha, ha! How very pleasant. *(Takes and examines handcuffs curiously.)*

HAWK. But I'll soon be down on this youngster.

MR. G. If only he hasn't left London.

HAWK. Bless you, they can't leave London. Like the moths, they turn and turn about the candle till their wings are burned.

DAL. Ah! Thanks to men like you. How little society is aware of what it owes to its detective benefactor.

HAWK. There's the satisfaction of doing one's duty—and something else now and then.

MR. G. Ah! A good round reward.

HAWK. That's not bad; but there's something better than that.

DAL. Indeed!

HAWK. Paying off old scores. Now, if I could only clinch the darbies on Jim Dalton's wrists.

DAL. Dalton! What's your grudge against him in particular?

HAWK. He was the death of my pal—the best mate I ever had—poor Joe Skirrit. *(He draws his hand across his eyes.)* I shall never work with such another.

MR. G. Did he murder him?

HAWK. Not to say murdered him right out. But he spoiled him— gave him a clip on the head with a blackjack, he did. He was never his own man afterwards.

DAL. You know this Dalton?

HAWK. Know him! He has as many outsides as he has aliases. You may identify him for a felon today, and pull your hat off to him as a parson tomorrow. But I'll hunt him out of all his skins; and my best night's sleep will be the day I've brought Jim Dalton to the dock!

DAL. Mr. Hawkshaw, I wish you every success!

HAWK. But I've other fish to fry now. *(Looks at card.)* Wake, Buckles Wharf, Limehouse. *(Exit.)*

DAL. Ask anybody for our office! *(Aside.)* And if anybody can tell you I *shall* be astonished. *(Following him and then returning.)*

MR. G. I'm really ashamed to keep you waiting, sir.

DAL. Oh, I can write my letters here. *(Pointing to counter.)* If you don't mind trusting me alone in your office.

MR. G. My dear sir, if you were Dalton himself, the redoubtable Tiger, you couldn't steal ledger and day books, and there's nothing more valuable here, except my funny old Miss Faddle's five thousand that she insists on my keeping here in the office in gold, as she believes neither in banks nor bank-notes. And—talking of notes—I may as well lock up these you handsomely paid me. *(Goes to safe.)*

DAL. Not believe in notes! Infatuated woman! *(Aside.)* I hope he'll like mine.

MR. G. *(locks safe)*. I'll leave you to write your letters. *(Exits into his office.)*

DAL. *(whistles low)*. Phew! That's the narrowest shave I ever had. So, Jack Hawkshaw, you'll be even with Jim Dalton yet, will you. You may add this day's work to the score against him. How the old boy swallowed my soft talk and Brummagem notes! It would be a pity to leave them in his hands—and five thousand shiners perhaps alongside of them. Come—I've my wax handy—never travel without my tools. Here goes for a squeeze at the lock of this safe. *(Goes to safe, and with picklock applies wax to the wards of the lock.)*

*(Music. Enter* BRIERLY.*)*

BRI *(hangs up hat)*. Clerks not returned. Hawkshaw gone? *(Sees* DALTON *at safe.)* Halloa, what's this? Tampering with the safe? Hold hard there. *(He seizes* DALTON, *who turns.)*

DAL *(aside)*. Brierly. Hands off, young'un. Don't you know a locksmith when you see one?

BRI. Who are you? What are you doing with that safe?

DAL. You ask a great deal too many questions.

BRI. I'll trouble you to answer them.

DAL. By what right?

BRI. I am messenger in this office, and I've a right to know who touches a lock here.

DAL. You messenger here? Indeed! And suppose I took to asking questions—you mightn't be so keen of answering them yourself, Robert Brierly!

BRI. You know me!

DAL. Yes, and your character from your last place—Port—

BRI (terrified). For mercy sake!

DAL. Silence for silence. Ask me no questions, and I'll press for no answers.

BRI. You must explain your business here to Mr. Gibson. I suspected you for a thief.

DAL. And I know you for a jailbird. Let's see whose information will go the farthest. There, I'll make you a fair offer, Robert Brierly. Let me pass, and I leave this place without breathing a word to your employer that you're fresh from a sentence of penal servitude for four years. Detain me, and I denounce you for the convict you are!

(A knock at the door.)

MRS. W. (outside). Mr. Brierly!

BRI. Hush! Coming, Mrs. Willoughby!

DAL. Is it a bargain?

BRI. Go, go—anything to escape this exposure! (Gives him hat from counter.)

DAL (at door). There's Moss, waiting for me outside. He shall blow the lad to Gibson. He may be useful to us, and I owe him for spoiling my squeeze. (Exits.)

(Enter MRS. WILLOUGHBY.)

MRS. W. Which, I've to ask pardon for intruding, not bein' used to an office, and knowing my place, I 'ope. But it's gettin' on for a quarter past eleven, Mr. Robert, and twelve's the latest they will do the weddin'. But whatever's the matter? You look struck all of a heap like!

BRI. Oh, nothing, nothing, it's natural, you know, a man should look strange on his wedding morning. There, go and tell May I'll be with her directly.

(Enter SAM.)

SAM. Come along, Bob, we're all tired of waiting, especially this child. I'm hungry!

MRS. W. (admiringly). Oh, that boy! If it ain't enough to make any grandmother's 'eart proud.

BRI. Go, go, I'll follow—I've some business matters to attend to.

SAM. A nice state for business you're in—I don't think. There, Granny. (Looks at BRIERLY.) That's what comes of getting married. If it ain't a awful warning to a young fellow like me!

MRS. W. Drat your impertinence.

SAM. But the party's waiting downstairs, and we're wanted to keep 'em in spirits, so come along, Granny.

*(SAM polkas out with MRS. WILLOUGHBY.)*

BRI. Known! Threatened! Spared by Hawkshaw, only to be denounced by this man.

*(Enter MOSS.)*

MOSS. Mr. Gibson, if you please?

BRI. He's in his office, sir—that way. *(Points to open door.)*

MOSS. I remember the young man now. A convict got himself into a respectable situation. It is a duty one owes to society to put this employer on his guard. *(Exit.)*

BRI. Yes—he's gone—I can draw my breath again—I was wrong to let him go. But to have the cup at one's lip, and see it struck away—I couldn't—even the detective had mercy. When we're married, I'll tell Mr. Gibson all.

*(Re-enter MOSS and MR. GIBSON from his office.)*

MOSS. You can question him, sir, if you don't believe me. Anyway, I've done my duty and that's what I look to. *(Exit MOSS.)*

BRI. Here's the money for the check, sir.

*(GIBSON takes money, BRIERLY starts to go.)*

MR. G. Robert.

BRI. Sir.

MR. G. Where are you going?

BRI. To dress for church, sir.

MR. G. Stay here!

BRI. Sir!

MR. G. You have deceived me.

BRI. Mr. Gibson—

MR. G. I know all—your crime—your conviction—your punishment!

BRI. Mercy! Mercy!

MR. G. Unhappy man!

BRI. Ah, unhappy you may well call me. I was sentenced, sir, but I was not guilty. It's true, sir, but I don't expect you to believe it—I've worked out my sentence: they hadn't a mark against me at Portland. You may ask them, here's my ticket-of-leave, sir. You know I've been steady and industrious since I came here. By heaven's help, I mean to be so still—indeed I do.

MR. G. I dare say, but I must think of my own credit and reputation. If it was buzzed about that I kept a ticket-of-leave man in my employment—

*(Enter GREEN JONES, MAY, EMILY, MRS. WILLOUGHBY and SAM.)*

MRS. W. Which, axin' your pardon, Mr. Gibson, we're all ready, and the cab a-waitin'.

SAM. And the parson getting cold.

MAY. Robert, why are you not dressed? What is the matter?

BRI. Heaven help you, my poor lass.

MAY. You are pale—tremble—are ill—oh, speak! What is it?

BRI. Bear up, May. But our marriage—cannot—be—yet—awhile.

ALL. The wedding put off!

EMILY. No bonnets!

SAM. And no breakfast!

GREEN. By jove!

MRS. W. Poor girl!

*(together)*

MAY. Am I dreaming! Robert, what does this mean?

BRI. It's hard to bear. Keep up your heart—I'm discharged. He knows all.

MAY *(to GIBSON)*. Oh, sir, you couldn't have the heart! Say it is not true.

MR. G. Sorry. You have both deceived me. You must both leave the place.

BRI. You hear—come, May.

MAY. I'll go, sir. It was I deceived you, not he. Only give him another chance.

*(Music until end.)*

BRI. Never heed her, sir. She'd have told you long ago, but I hadn't the heart—my poor lass—! Let her stay here, sir, I'll leave the country.

MAY. Hush, hush, Robert! We were wrong to hide the truth—we are sorely punished. If *you've* the courage to face what's before us, I have.

BRI. My brave girl! Thank you for all your kindness, sir. Goodbye, friends. Come, May, we'll go together.

**CURTAIN**

# ACT THREE

## SCENE ONE

SCENE: *The Bridgewater Arms. A large gaily decorated coffee room set with tables and benches. A bar crosses the corner of the room, with brightly painted hogs' heads above it, and beer engine. At head of bar, there is a door to street. Door to parlor is stage R. Windows are curtained. A trap-door to cellar (practical!) is upstage and near end of bar. Tables and chairs are in front, tables and benches in back.* MOSS, *with bags of silver, and* DALTON *are seated at a table.* MALTBY *is waiting upon them.*

MALT *(at back of table).* Pint of sherry. *(Putting it down.)* Very curious! Yes, Mr. Moss, it's a pleasure to see you, sir, at the Bridgewater Arms, though it ain't the Bellevue Gardens, worse luck.

MOSS. Ah, ups and downs is the lot of life, Mr. Maltby. You'll let me know when Mr. Tottie comes in?

MALT. Ah, yes, the contractor for the main sewer line in the next street. Such a noise and such a nuisance! Stops all traffic—

MOSS. But sends you all the business. The workers are taken on and paid here, don't forget.

MALT. Well, not aristocratic, but beery; we do four butts a week at the bar, to say nothing of the concert room upstairs.

DAL. So, they like music to their malt, do they?

MALT. Oh, yes, sir! I introduced the arts from the West End. Those roughs adore music. If you could only hear Miss St. Evremond touch them up with the "The Crimson Stain," the new sensation ballad, sold at the bar, price one shilling. Why, we've disposed of three dozen copies on a pay night—astonishing how it goes down!

DAL. With the beer?

*(Enter* EMILY ST. EVREMOND, *wearing a handsome evening dress under a shawl.)*

MALT. Here comes Mrs. Jones, gentlemen, this is the great and gifted creature.

EMILY. Go along with your nonsense!

MALT. Miss St. Evremond, the great sensation balladist, formerly of the Nobility's Concerts, and her Majesty's Theatre *(Aside.)* and the chorus line.

MOSS. Proud to make the acquaintance of so gifted an artiste.

EMILY. You're very obliging. *(Taking off her bonnet and shawl and smoothing her hair. To* MALTBY.*)* How's the concert room tonight?

MALT. Slow now—but wait till later—it's pay night, you know.

EMILY. Oh, Lord! I'd forgotten. *(Sighs.)* To think of Emily St. Evremond wasting her sweetness on an audience of sewer diggers!

DAL. Not aristocratic, I guess, but they are appreciative.

EMILY. Yes, poor creatures! They do know a good thing when they hear it!

DAL. If Miss St. Evremond would oblige us with a little ballad—

MALT. Yes, "The Crimson Stain," I was telling you about.

EMILY. But we must call my husband; he's so fond of hearing me sing. *(Goes to door.)* Come in, Green Jones, you're wanted.

*(Enter* GREEN JONES *with basket of trotters.)*

GREEN. In the trotter line, Emily?

EMILY. No, to listen to "The Crimson Stain." *(She starts to arrange her hair.)*

GREEN. Till you're ready, these gentlemen wouldn't like to try a trotter, would they? Penny a set, and this morning's boiling.

MALT. No, no, Jones, these are not *your* style of customers. They don't even know what a trotter is.

GREEN. Excuse me, Mr. Maltby. I'm aware trotters are not known in good society. *(Shows one.)* You see, gentlemen, the last leg joint of that tender creature, the lamb, a true delicacy, I assure you, with just a soupçon of pepper. I liked 'em as a swell before I was reduced to selling them.

MALT *(to* EMILY*).* Perhaps now you are ready?

EMILY. I can't do it without letting down my back hair!

GREEN. One word of preface, gentlemen! Scene, Criminal Ward, Bedlam! Miss St. Evremond is an interesting lunatic—with lucid intervals. She has murdered her husband—*(Finds basket in his way.)* Emily, if you'd just shift those trotters—and her three children—and is supposed to be remonstrating with one of the lunacy commissioners on the cruelty of her confinement!

EMILY. (SONG: *"The Crimson Stain"* *)

> You have held my heart so closely in your keeping,
> It was prisoned there forever at your call;
> I cannot take it from you even sleeping
> So I choose this way to go and end it all.
>
> I had dreamed we two would live in love forever,
> Then you gave the blow that caused the deadly pain;
> So the end of life alone the tie can sever,
> And between our lives there lies a crimson stain.

(ALL APPLAUD.)

MALT *(going off).* Now, look sharp, Miss St. Evremond. It's nearly time for the concert. *(Exit.)*

EMILY *(to* GREEN JONES*).* Bye, bye, dear, till after the concert. You know I can't be seen speaking to you while you carry that basket.

GREEN. True—in the humble trotter-man who would suspect the husband of the brilliant St. Evremond! There's something romantic

*Music on page 371.

in it—I hover around, I hear you universally admired, applauded, adored—oh, agony!

EMILY. Now, Jones, you are going to be jealous again! I do believe jealousy's at the bottom of that basket.

*(Exit* EMILY *and* GREEN JONES.*)*

MOSS. Now's our time—while the fools upstairs are having their ears tickled. Have you the tools ready for jumping that safe at Mr. Gibson's?

DAL. Yes, but tools won't be enough. I must have a clear stage and a pal who knows the premises.

MOSS. I've thought of that. Nobody sleeps in the place but the old housekeeper and her precious grandson.

DAL. He's sharp as a terrier dog—and bites, too, the young varmit. *(Threateningly.)* If I come across him—

MOSS. No occasion for that—you're so violent. I've made the young man's acquaintance. I've asked him to meet me here tonight for a quiet little game—his revenge, I called it. I'll dose the lad till he's past leaving the place. You drop a hint to the old lady—she'll come to take care of him—and the coast will be clear yonder.

DAL. And the five thousand pounds will be ours in the turning of a jemmy. If we had that young Brierly in on the job—he knows his way about the place blindfold. But he's on the square, he is, bent on earning an honest livelihood.

MOSS. But I've blown him wherever he's got work, and I'll blow him here. He *must* dance to our tune at last.

DAL. Ah! If you've got him in hand, work him into the job, and I'll jump the crib tonight.

MOSS. He's applied to be taken on here on the sewer job. Tottie, the contractor, is a friend of mine—

DAL. He's lucky!

MOSS. Not heavy interest, but no risk. A word from me, and he'll discharge any man on his gang. So, I've only to breathe "jailbird"—

DAL. Ah, nobody likes the Portland mark, I know. I tried the honest dodge, too.

MOSS. It don't answer.

DAL. It didn't with me. I had a friend, like you, always after me. Whatever I tried, I was blown as a convict, and hunted out from honest men.

MOSS. And then you met me—and I was good to you—wasn't I?

DAL. Oh, yes, you were very kind.

MOSS. Always allowed you handsome for the swag you brought, and put you into no end of good things! And I'll stick by you, my dear, I never drop a friend.

DAL. No, not until the hangman takes your place at his side. *(Presses his elbows in the attitude of a man pinioned.)*

MOSS. Don't be disagreeable. You give me a cold shiver. Hush—here comes someone.

*(Enter* HAWKSHAW, *disguised as sewer worker. He appears flustered with drink, goes to one of the tables, and assuming a country dialect, calls swaggeringly.)*

HAWK. Gallon 'o beer—d'ye hear?

MALT. A gallon?

HAWK. Aye, and another when that's done. I got my pay and I'm in brass tonight. Here, mates, who'll drink?

*(*DALTON *and* MOSS *ignore him. Enter* BRIERLY.*)*

Come, won't thou drink?

BRI. No, thank you. I've a poor head for liquor, and I've not had my supper yet.

HAWK. Sure it's not pride?

BRI. Pride? I've not much call for pride. I've come to try and get taken on at the works.

HAWK. Well, thou look'st like a tough 'un. There'll be room for you if can'st swing the anchor.

BRI. The anchor?

HAWK. Ha, ha! It's easy to see thou'st no banker—why the pick, to be sure.

BRI. Well, then, wish me luck with the pick. If I'm taken on, I'll buy.

*(Enter* MALTBY.*)*

MALT. Mr. Tottie's in the parlor, and wishes particularly to see you, Mr. Moss.

MOSS. I should think he did. Say I'm coming.

*(Exit* MALTBY.*)*

DAL *(aside to* MOSS*).* You look after Brierly—yonder he sits—and I'll drop a hint to the old woman. Stay, we'd better work from the old churchyard of St. Nicholas—there's a door opens into it from Gibson's office. I'll hide the tools behind one of the tombstones.

*(Exit* MOSS *into the parlor. Exit* DALTON *by street door.)*

HAWK. Here, landlord, take your change out of that! *(Flings money on the table and exits, staggering like a drunken man, after* DALTON.*)*

BRI. My last chance. I've tried every road to an honest livelihood, and one after another they are barred in my face. Everywhere, that dreadful word, "jailbird," sometimes in a letter, sometimes in a hint, sometimes a copy of the newspaper with my trial, and then it's the same story—sorry to part with you—no complaint to make, but can't keep a ticket-of-leave man. Who can it be that hunts me down this way? Hawkshaw spared me. I've done no man wrong. I wouldn't care for myself, but my poor wife—my brave, true-hearted May. I'm dragging her down with me! Ah, here she is.

*(Enter* MAY, *poorly dressed. She has a can and some food in a bundle.)*

MAY *(cheerfully).* Well, Robert, dear, I said I shouldn't be long. I've brought your supper.

BRI. Thank you, I'm not hungry. You've been out after work all day long. Eat—you need the strength most.

MAY. Nay, dear, what will become of me if you lose heart? But if you'll be good and take your tea *(Opens tin and takes bread from bundle.)*, I'll tell you a piece of good news.

BRI. That will be something new.

MAY. I've a promise of work from the Sailor's Ready Made Clothing House near here. It won't be much, but it will keep the wolf from the door till you get another situation. Have you tried to see if the contractor will take you on here?

BRI. Not yet. He's busy paying the men now. He'll send for me, but I scarcely dare to ask. Oh, May, lass, I've held hard onto hope, but it feels as if it was slipping out of my hand at last.

MAY. Robert, dear Robert, grasp it hard; so long as we do what is right, all will come clear at last. We're in kind hands, dear, you know we are.

BRI. I begin to doubt it, lass; I do, indeed.

MAY. No, no, never doubt that, or my heart will give way too—

BRI. And you that has had courage for both of us. Every blow that has fallen, every door that has been shut, every time that clean hands have been drawn away from mine, and respectable faces turned aside, I've come to you for comfort, and love and hope, and I've always found them.

MAY. Of course! It's hard weather tries women best, dear. You men aren't half so stout-hearted.

BRI. I'd not mind the misery so much for myself, but for you—

MAY. I don't complain, do I?

BRI. Never! But since Mr. Gibson discharged us, the plight that has followed me has reached you, too. The bravest, dearest and brightest lass that ever doubled a man's joys and halved his burdens. Oh—it kills the heart out of me—it drives me mad!

MAY. I tell you, 'twill all come clear at last if we are only true to ourselves—and to each other. I've been promised work, and perhaps you may be taken on here. I see bright days before us still.

BRI. Bright days! I can't see them through the prison cloud that hangs over me. Nay, I sometimes think I had better let it all go— run—make a hole in the water, anything that would rid you of me!

MAY. Oh Robert, that is cruel! Nothing others could do to us could hurt me like those words from you. We are man and wife, and we'll take life as man and wife should, hand-in-hand. Where you go, I will go; where you suffer, I will be there to comfort; and when better times come—as come they will—we will thank God for them together.

(SONG: *"Keep on the Sunny Side"*\*)

Keep on the sunny side
And let dull care pass you by.

*\*Music on page 370.*

Just figure out you're a long time dead,
Don't start to worry or sigh.
Weep, and you weep alone,
Don't give up hope till you've tried,
Don't join the crowds that walk under dark clouds,
But keep on the sunny side.

BRI. I'll try to hope.

MAY. There's a brave dear. Now I must go to the warehouse, but I'll be back soon. Goodbye, dearest. Remember, when the clouds are thickest, the sun still shines behind them. *(Exit.)*

BRI. Bless that brave, bright dear. She puts strength into me, in spite of the doubts that have got their claws about my throat. Yes, I *will* try once more.

*(Enter* MOSS *from parlor.)*

MOSS *(speaking off).* So, all paid at last?

*(Re-enter* DALTON *and after a short pause,* HAWKSHAW, *after him.)*

DAL. All right, the lad's coming. I've tipped the old woman and planted the tools.

HAWK *(taps* BRIERLY *on shoulder).* All the gang's gotten their brass. Tottie's ready to take on men now. Thou go in, and put on a bold face. Tottie likes chaps as speaks up to him. *(Goes to table.)*

BRI. If this chance fail, God help us both. *(Exit into parlor.)*

MOSS. There he goes!

DAL. It would be such a pity to let a ticket-of-leave man in among all those sober, well-behaved young men.

MOSS. Don't worry. I've done the work. He'll be at the end of his tether now and ready to listen.

*(Enter* SAM WILLOUGHBY.*)*

Here comes our young friend. *(Coaxingly to him.)* Ah, my dear, so you've come out for a little hanky-panky with old Moss. Sit down—my friend, Mr. Walker. What'll you have?

SAM. I don't care—I'm game for anything. Suppose we start with a brandy and soda, to cool the coppers?

DAL *(calls).* Brandy and soda, Maltby.

SAM. I had an awful go in of it last night at the balls and dropped into a lot of 'em like a three-year-old! *(Imitates billiard play, using walking cane for cue.)*

MOSS. Billiards! Lord, what a clever young chap you are!

*(*MALTBY *brings drink.)*

SAM *(sits at back of table).* Yes, I know a thing or two. *(Takes glass.)* I wasn't born blind. I rather think, but you promised me my revenge, you old screw. *(Drinks.)* Now fork out the pictures, old boy.

MOSS *(shuffling cards).* Oh, what a boy you are! What shall it be this time?

SAM. Well, a few deals of brag to begin with.

*(As he deals, enter* BRIERLY *from room.)*

BRI. My last chance, gone, gone!

HAWK. Well, my little flannel-back, has he taken you on?

BRI. No, he says all jobs are full—perhaps later—I know there was a job to be filled.

HAWK. Never mind, maybe next week, eh? Cheer up then, let's wet thy footing.

BRI *(recognizing* SAM*)*. Sam Willoughby, in this place, and over the devil's books, too. Oh, I hate to see this—his poor grandmother, if she only knew.

SAM *(calling)*. Best card! *(Shows it.)* First stake!

DAL. Stop a minute—ace of diamonds!

SAM. First stake to you. Hang it! Never mind. *(Deals.)* One can't lose much at this game. *(Puts a stake on cards.)*

MOSS. A shilling.

SAM. Five.

DAL. I stand.

MOSS. Ten.

SAM. A sovereign! Third stake. *(Shows cards.)* Pair royal, pair—ace of spades. Fork over the shiners.

MOSS. Oh dear! Oh, dear! I'm ruined—ruined. *(Pays sovereign.)*

SAM. Now, for my deal. *(He deals three cards to each.)*

*(*MALTBY *brings brandy.)*

MOSS. Best card? First stake. I stand.

SAM. I brag. Hang piddling with shillings—half a crown.

DAL. Five.

*(*MOSS *looks at* SAM*'s hand and signals to* DALTON*.)*

SAM. Ten.

DAL. A sovereign.

MOSS. Oh, oh, dear, what a boy it is! How much have you got in your pocket?

SAM. Lots! I'm paid quarterly now. Had my quarter today. *(Calls.)* Let's see—I'll hold on. *(Draws card.)* Thirty-four, overdrawn, confound it. Now, let's see your hand.

DAL. Three pairs—fives, trays, deuces, and the knave of clubs.

SAM. Hang it all! How is a man to stand against such cards?

BRI. How is a man to stand against such play? He was looking over your cards, and see *(Seizes a card from* MOSS*'s lap.)*—the ace of diamonds! Sam, if you won't believe me, believe your own eyes! You're being cheated, robbed. You old villain, you ought to be ashamed of yourself!

MOSS. Oh dear, oh, dear! To say such things to a man at my time of life.

DAL. We're not to be bullied.

SAM *(threateningly)*. You give me back my money!

*(*MALTBY *comes down.)*

MOSS. I shan't! Here, Mr. Maltby.

MALT. Come, be off. I can't have any disturbance here. Mr. Moss is a most respectable man, and his friends are as respectable as he is.

And as for you, if you won't leave the room quietly, you must be made to.

SAM. Who'll make me? Come on, *(Squaring.)* both of you! I'm not afraid.

*(Enter* MRS. WILLOUGHBY.*)*

MRS. W. It's his voice—which well I know it. Oh Sam, Sam, I've found you at last!

SAM. Well, suppose you have, what then?

MRS. W. What then! Oh, dear, oh dear. And I've run myself into that state of trimmle and perspiration, and if it hadn't been for the gentleman, I might have been east and west, and high and low, but it's at the Bridgewater Arms you'll find him, he says, and here I have found you, sure enough, and you come home with me this very minute.

MOSS. Ah! You'd better go home with the old lady!

DAL. And if you take my advice, you'll send him to bed without his supper.

SAM *(MRS. W. pushing him away).* I ain't a-going. Now, you give me my money—I'm not going to stand any nonsense.

MRS. W. And this is what he calls attending elocution class of a night, and improvin' of his mind, and me a-toilin' and a-moilin' for him—which I'm his grandmother, gentlemen, and him the only one of three. *(Still holding him.)*

SAM. It's no use, Granny. I'm not a child to be tied to your apron strings. You've no right to be naggin' and aggravatin' and coming after a chap, to make him look small this way. I don't mind. I shan't stir. There! *(He flings his cap on the table, sits on it, swinging his legs.)*

MRS. W. Oh, dear, oh, dear, he'll break my 'eart, he will.

BRI. Sam, my lad, listen to me, if you won't harken to her. The road you're on leads downwards. Trust one who knows. There's no working clear again. You may hold out your hand; you may cry for help; you may struggle hard; but the quicksands are under your foot, and you sink down, down, till they close over your head.

HAWK. Poor chap. He talks like a missionary, he do.

BRI. Go home, my lad. Go home with her. Be a son to her. Love her as she has loved you. Make her old days happy.

SAM *(who has betrayed signs of feeling).* I don't know—I feel so— well, don't look at me that way. *(Gets off table and goes to* MRS. W.*)* I've been a regular bad'un, Granny, and I'm sorry. I'll put on the curb, that is, I'll try.

MRS. W. Oh, bless him for those words! Bless you, my own dear boy. *(To* BRIERLY.*)* And you too, Mr. Brierly, which if the widow's blessing is worthwhile, it's yours, and many of them. Oh, dear, oh, dear! *(Cries, gets out her handkerchief, and in doing so drops her purse and keys.)*

*(*MOSS *picks up purse.* MRS. W. *catches his eye, as he does so.*

DALTON, *unobserved by all, picks up the keys.)*

BRI. Nay, don't thank me. It's late now. Go home. Sam, give her your arm.

*Caught in the acts of gambling and drinking, pugnacious Sam Willoughby defies his long-suffering grandmother. Bob Brierly, now a "ticket-of-leave" man, urges him to reform. Stephen Leutheuser as Bob Brierly, Rusty Myers as Sam Willoughby, Robin Taylor as Mrs. Willoughby.*

MOSS *(to* SAM*).* What, you won't stay and make a night of it?

MRS. W. I'll trouble you not to speak to my grandson. If ever an old man was ashamed of his grey hairs, it's you *ought* to be. Come, Sam.

MOSS *(aside).* Balked.

DAL. No—I didn't give her back her keys.

SAM *(turning to* MOSS*).* If I wasn't going to turn over a new leaf—oh, wouldn't I like to pitch into you!

*(Exit* SAM *and* MRS. WILLOUGHBY.*)*

HAWK *(pretending to be very drunk).* Sho should I, sho should I—*(Pretends to fall asleep with head on table.)*

MOSS *(to* DALTON*).* Honesty's bowled over at last! It's our game now. *(Hand on* BRIERLY's *shoulder.)* I say, my friend—

BRI. Eh? Yes—you. It's you. You're the man who told him.

MOSS. Oh, yes, but don't put yourself in a passion.

BRI. Only tell me—is it you who have followed me—turned all against me, kept me from earning honest bread?

MOSS. Yes.

BRI. But why, man, why? I had done you no wrong.

MOSS. Ask him. *(Pointing to* DALTON.*)* He's an old friend of yours.

BRI. I don't know him—yet—I've seen that face before. Yes, it is—Jem Downey! Villain! *(Seizes him.)* I know you now. You shall answer to me for all this misery.

DAL. Easy does it, Bob, hands off. And let's take things pleasantly.

BRI. Not content with leading me into play and drink and deviltry, with making me your tool, with sending me to prison, it's you that have dogged me—have denounced me as a convict.

DAL. Of course—you didn't think any one but an old friend would have taken such an interest in you.

BRI. Did you want to close all roads against me but that which leads back to prison?

DAL. Exactly.

*(BRIERLY turns to MOSS.)*

You see, when a man's in the mud himself, and can't get out of it, he don't like to see another fight clear. Come, honest men won't have anything to do with you—best try black sheep—we aren't proud.

*(ALL sit.)*

We've a job in hand will be the making of all three. *(Fills his glass.)* Here, drink, and put some heart into you.

*(BRIERLY drinks.)*

That's the sort—a lad of spirit—I said there was a real grit in him, didn't I, Moss?

MOSS. You always gave him the best of characters.

DAL. Is it a bargain?

BRI. Yes.

*(Enter MAY.)*

MAY *(crossing to table, in pain)*. Ah, Robert.

BRI. You here—lass?

MOSS. Oh, those petticoats!

DAL. You're not wanted here, young woman.

MAY. He is my husband, sir. He is not strong and drink will do him harm.

DAL. Ha, ha, ha! Brandy do a man harm! It's Mother's milk—take another sip. *(Fills BRIERLY's glass again.)* To your girl's health?

MAY. Robert, dear—come with me.

BRI. Have you got work?

MAY. No—not yet.

BRI. No more have I, lass. I went to see him, it was the old story—

MAY. Oh, Robert—come with me!

BRI. I shall stay here. Now, go home and don't sit up for me.

MAY *(imploringly)*. Robert!

BRI. I've my reasons.

DAL. Come, are you going?

BRI *(MAY clings to him)*. Stand off, girl. You used to do what I bid you—stand off, I say!

*(He shakes himself free from her.)*

MAY. Oh, Robert! Robert! *(Staggers back to table and sits.)*

BRI *(aside)*. I must—or they'll not trust me.

MAY. These men? To what have they tempted him in his despair?

They shan't drive me away. *(Aside.)* I'll watch. *(Exits after a mute appeal to* BRIERLY.*)*

*(*HAWKSHAW *lies head in hands as if asleep;* MOSS *rises.)*

MALT *(re-entering, shaking* HAWK *by shoulder).* Now, my man, we're shutting up the bar.

HAWK. Shut up. Shut up. I'm shut up. Good night. *(Lets his head fall.)*

MALT. It's no use. He won't go, and I'm wanted in the concert room. *(Exit.)*

MOSS *(to* DALTON, *suspiciously pointing to* HAWKSHAW.*)* What about him?

DAL *(shaking* HAWKSHAW*).* Eh? Hello there, wake up.

*(*HAWKSHAW *grunts.)*

MOSS. He's in a deplorable state of intoxication.

DAL. Yes, he's got his cargo—no danger in him now—now for business. First and foremost, no more of this. *(Pockets bottle. To* BRIERLY.*)* You've heard the job we have in mind?

BRI. Yes, but you have not told me where it is, or why you want my help.

DAL. It's old Gibson's office. The five thousand, you know—you know where it's kept.

BRI. Well.

DAL. And you'll take us to it?

BRI. Yes.

DAL. That's the ticket. Then we may as well start.

BRI. Now?

DAL. My rule is never put off until tomorrow the crib I can crack today. Besides, you might change your mind.

MOSS. One has heard of such things.

BRI. But—

DAL. Game?

BRI. Yes.

DAL. I'll get a cab. *(Going.)*

MOSS. And I'll get another—we'd best go single. *(Following him.)*

DAL. No, it wouldn't be polite to leave Mr. Brierly. *(Aside.)* I don't half trust him. Don't let him out of your sight *(Exits.)*

BRI *(aside).* If he'd only leave me for a moment.

MOSS *(crosses, sitting).* He's carried off the bottle, and the bar's shut up, or we might have a little refreshment.

BRI. Perhaps, if you went to the landlord—

MOSS. No, I'd rather stay with you. I like your company uncommon well, I do.

*(Enter* MALTBY *with wine basket and candle.)*

MALT. Here's Mr. Tottie standing champagne round to the Wisconsin Warblers, and the bar stock all out. I must go to the cellar myself—very humiliating. *(Goes to trap near bar.)* What with the light, and what with the liquor—I say, Mr. Moss, if you would lend me a hand.

BRI *(aside).* I might give *him* the information. *(To* MALTBY.*)* Let me help you, sir.

MOSS. Then I'll go too.

*(*MALTBY *opens trap.)*

BRI. The stairs are steep—two's quite enough.

MOSS. But I'm so fond of your company.

MALT. If you'll hold the light—*(*BRIERLY *takes it and* MALTBY *goes down.)*

BRI *(aside).* A word'll do it.

*(*MOSS *takes candle from* BRIERLY *and gets between him and* MALTBY.*)*

MOSS. Allow me. The light will do us all best in the middle.

*(*MOSS *descends.)*

MALT *(from below).* Now, then!

BRI *(rapidly closes the trap, and stands upon it).* Now's the time. *(Seizes pen that stands on bar, and writes, reading as he writes, quickly.)* To Mr. Gibson, Peckham. The office will be entered tonight. I'm in it to save the property and secure the robbers. R. Brierly. But who'll take it?

HAWK *(who has got up and read the letter over his shoulder).* I will.

BRI. You?

HAWK *(pulls off his rough cap, wig, and whiskers, and speaks in his own voice).* Hawkshaw, the Detective. *(Gives a pistol.)* Take this—I'll be on the lookout.

*(*HAWKSHAW *lets his head fall as* DALTON *reappears, beckoning at the door, and* MOSS *reappears from the trap with* MALTBY.*)*

DAL. Come along, you two, the cab is waiting.

MALT. Goodnight to you, gentlemen, and many thanks. *(Exits.)*

MOSS. A pleasure, sir, a pleasure. Come, Bob.

*(Exit* BRIERLY, MOSS, *and* DALTON. HAWKSHAW *goes to door and gives a peculiar low whistle. Enter* DETECTIVE *and* MALTBY. HAWKSHAW *gives note to* MALTBY.*)*

HAWK. Take the fastest Hansom cab you can find. Tear down with this to Dalton and the old gent behind Nicholas Lane. Say he'll be wanted to make a charge. There's a safe to be cracked. By the bye, lend me your barker.

*(*DETECTIVE *gives him pistol and exits.)*

James Dalton's a tough customer. I always feel rather ashamed to burn powder. Any fool can blow a man's brains out. *(Tries cap and charges.)* That lad's all square, after all. I had no idea that he tumbled to their game. He managed that letter uncommonly neat. Now for St. Nicholas Churchyard. When James Dalton planted his tools, he never thought they'd come up darbies. *(Shows handcuffs and exits.)*

**CURTAIN**

## SCENE TWO

SCENE: *The Churchyard of St. Nicholas with tombstones and neglected trees, wall at back. An iron railing separates the churchyard from the street. In flat is the wall of* MR. GIBSON's *office, with (practical) back door.* DALTON and BRIERLY *drop over the wall, followed by* MOSS.

DAL. All serene. Come along, Bob. *(Aside.)* Where could he have got that six-shooter from? Well, anyway, I unloaded it in the cab. Moss, you be crow—two whistles, if the coast is clear. We'll work the crib. Lucky I nailed the old woman's keys. *(Shows them.)* They'll save tools and time. *(To* BRIERLY.*)* Now, my lad, take care. I'm a man of few words. The pal who sticks by me, I stick by him, till death. But the man who tries to double on me had better have the hangman looking after him than James Dalton.

    *(Exit* DALTON *and* BRIERLY. *Enter* MAY.*)*

MAY. I've followed the cab as far as I could. I saw them get out, then lost them at the last turning. If I could only keep them in sight. If he could but hear my voice—Robert! Robert!

MOSS. I'm just taking a little walk before retiring for the night. They've gone on down to the Cave of Harmony—first turn on the left. There's a red lamp over the door, you can't miss it.

MAY. Oh, thank you—thank you! *(Exit.)*

MOSS. That's neat! Trust old Moss when anybody's to be made safe.

    *(*HAWKSHAW, *during the above, has dropped over the wall at back. He seizes* MOSS *from behind, stops his mouth with one hand and handcuffs him.)*

HAWK. Stir or speak and you're a dead man!

DAL *(appearing at back door)*. Hang that cloud. I can't see, Moss!

HAWK *(imitating)*. All serene!

DAL *(coming down)*. We've done the job. *(Calling to* BRIERLY.*)* Now, the box.

BRI *(inside)*. I'll bring it. *(Comes from door with cash box.)*

DAL. We'll share at the Pigeons in Duck Lane. The box! Quick!

BRI. A word or two first.

DAL. We can talk in the cab.

BRI. No, here. You were my ruin four years ago.

DAL. I've paid you back twice over tonight with this haul. Come, the box.

BRI. I suffered then for *your* crime. Ever since—you've come between me and an honest life. You've broken me down—you've brought me to this.

DAL. I suppose you mean you've a right to an extra share of the swag?

BRI. No, I mean that you're my prisoner, or you're a dead man. *(Seizes him and draws pistol.)*

DAL. Hands off, you fool!

BRI. Hands up! *(Snaps pistol.)*

DAL. You should have asked for the caps. Here they are. *(Holds them up.)*

BRI. No matter. Armed or unarmed, you don't escape me.

*(A struggle.* DALTON *strikes* BRIERLY *down as* HAWKSHAW *rushes from concealment.)*

HAWK. Now James Dalton! It's my turn!

DAL. Hawkshaw!

*(Fight.)*

*(Enter* MAY *followed by* SAM.*)*

MAY *(rushing on).* Robert! Husband!

SAM *(over* DALTON*).* Lie still, will you? You're a nice young man! *(Crossing and looking at* MOSS.*)* You're a pair of them!

HAWK. Now, James Dalton! Remember poor Joe Skirritt! I promised him I'd do it. I've done it at last.

*(Enter* MR. GIBSON *from back door of office.)*

MR. G. Here they are! The safe open! The cash box gone!

HAWK. No, saved. *(Gives him cash box.)*

MR. G. By whom?

HAWK. That young man bleeding yonder, Robert Brierly.

MAY. My husband—wounded. Oh, mercy! *(She kneels over him.)*

MR. G. Thank heaven, he's not dead. I can repay him yet.

HAWK. He's paid his score. Now he can hold up his head with honest men.

MAY. Look, he opens his eyes. Robert, speak to me—it's May, your own wife.

BRI *(getting to his feet carefully).* May—wife! Hush, dear, it's only a clip on the head. I'm none the worse. It was all my game to snare those villains. Mr. Gibson, sir, you wouldn't trust me, but I'm not ungrateful. You see, there may be some good left in a "Ticket-of-Leave" Man, after all.

**CURTAIN**

# Under Two Flags

A Melodrama in Three Acts
as adapted from a dramatization
of Louise de la Ramée's 1867 book

# CAST OF CHARACTERS

LADY VENETIA, the "Silver Pheasant"
THE COUNTESS OF WARMINSTER, an impoverished noblewoman, her
  mother
RENÉE BARONI, a forger's tool
CIGARETTE, Vivandière, soldier of France
BERT CECIL, alias Corporal Victor, "Beauty of the Brigade"
LORD JACK ROCKINGHAM, his longtime friend
RAKE, manservant to Bert Cecil
THE MARQUIS DE CHATEAUROY, Chasseurs D'Afrique
BARONI, proprietor of the bric-a-brac shop, and a forger
ENTAMABOULL, Arab sergeant
BEAU BRUNO, Arab soldier
YUSSEF, Arab soldier
TIGER CLAW, Arab soldier
SI HASSAN, a Bedouin
PAULETTE, a dancing girl of the "Ace of Spades"
BOUAMANA, another dancing girl

# SYNOPSIS OF SCENES

### ACT ONE

**Scene One:**  Baroni's bric-a-brac shop in London, late afternoon.
"Let us drink to the benefit of those we love—and to
the ruin of those we hate."
**Scene Two:**  Card room in Warminster Manor, the next evening.
"Very well, you have the money and the girl!"

### ACT TWO

**Scene One:**  Ace of Spades Wine Shop, Algeria.
"Tomorrow night then, at the Villa Aiyussa, at ten."
**Scene Two:**  Same, the following morning.
"It isn't wise to fool with Cigarette!"
**Scene Three:** Same, that evening.
"Ah, he shall have more company than he ever
expected!"

### ACT THREE

**Scene One:**  The Villa Aiyussa, later.
"Then man to man let it be!"
**Scene Two:**  Ace of Spades Wine Shop, the next morning.
"Cigarette, child of the Army, soldier of France."

*The first Cigarette: Lotta Crabtree created the role in an adaptation of* Under Two Flags *which was titled* Firefly, *at the Boston Theatre in 1868.*

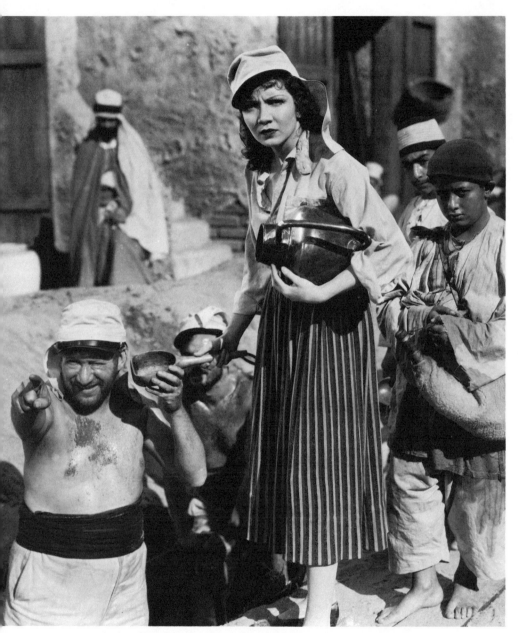

*The last filmed, and perhaps the most famous Cigarette —Claudette Colbert —in Twentieth Century Fox's 1935 film.*

# About the Play

*Under Two Flags* was first published as a novel. It was written in 1865 by Louise de la Ramée, one of the most prolific writers of the latter half of the 19th century, who wrote under the name of Ouida. She also wrote the popular stories, *Bimbi* and *Dog of Flanders*.

Early records indicate that *Under Two Flags* was first presented as a play under that title at the Southminister Theatre in Edinburgh, Scotland on April 29, 1872. However, Constance Rourke recounts in *Troupers of the Gold Coast* that Lotta Crabtree played at the Boston Theatre in 1868 in an adaptation of the Ouida novel, *Firefly*, and that she was advertised by manager Junius Booth as "Little Fairy Lotta, the Diamond Edition of Dramatic Delights." Of her performance as Cigarette, it was written:

> The play was considered daring. Lotta was a *vivandière*, a mascot, madcap, rebel, who wore her skirts six or eight inches from the ground, and smoked freely and gracefully. She afterwards insisted that she learned to smoke from Lola Montez; certainly it must have been from that daring example or from (Adah) Menken that she received the impulse to smoke on the stage; yet she seems to have kept an air which it was not their fortune to maintain, that of innocence, which carried her past the increasing rigor of the sixties. In *Firefly* she used dozens of reckless small pieces of business with her incalculable air of distinction."

The term "vivandière," incidentally, was used in France to describe a woman who accompanied troops to sell them food, supplies and liquor. Probably Cigarette's mother, who was captured by the Bedouins, was such a one, and it was thus that Cigarette came to join the soldiers who raised her and made her one of them.

The first recorded New York performance, an adaptation by Paul Potter, was produced at the Garden Theatre by Charles Frohman and David Belasco on February 5, 1901. Here, actress Blanche Bates as the vivacious Cigarette was dubbed "a gold-tipped Cigarette" in a review by Alan Dale.

The play continued in popularity with such favorite stars as Maude Adams and Helen Ware as Cigarette. In 1912, Thanhouser Pictures made the play into a silent film. In a 1916 movie, Theda Bara played the sultry Cigarette. The last filming, by Fox Pictures in 1935, featured Claudette Colbert in the lead, with Ronald Colman, Rosalind Russell and Victor McLaughlin.

*The evil Baroni gloats over the perfection of his step-daughter's enforced forgeries, as he plots to take away the rightful heritage of Bert Cecil. The Marquis de Chateauroy patiently bides his time, knowing that the fortune will then be his. John Storace plays Baroni, Nancy Duff is Renee, and Eldon Hallum is the Marquis in the Imperial's 1961 production.*

# ACT ONE

## SCENE ONE

SCENE: *Baroni's bric-a-brac shop in London. The room is cluttered with furniture and antiques; shelves contain old books. The shop is dimly lit. Old volumes are stacked on a worktable U.R. A candle is burning at the table.* BARONI *is moving about arranging shop items, dusting.* RENEE BARONI *is at the table going through books stacked in front of her. She is a young girl of about 20, attractive, with a plain hairdress that makes her look older than her age. She is dressed in a drab skirt and blouse.* BARONI *is in his fifties, greying at the temples. He walks with a stoop.*

BARONI. Ah, you'll do well to mind what your old papa says, my girl. It's not wise to burn your bridges nor make enemies of anyone, for you never know from day to day who's up and who's down.

RENEE. And little it matters to you, so long as you can turn your profit!

BARONI. That's just my point, Renee, and you're a wise girl to see it my way. I have an appointment in a little while with young Bert Cecil, heir to the fortune and title of our great, good friend, the Duke of Chateauroy—

RENEE. And what do you hope to get out of him now? Isn't it enough that you blackmailed the old man into leaving you these books? You'll make a tidy sum once I've finished making them into autographed editions. Isn't that enough for you?

BARONI. Now, my daughter, surely you don't mind turning your considerable talents into a little security for your papa's old age.

RENEE *(explosively)*. As though I had a choice! Had I known in the beginning what you were forcing me to do—

BARONI. Enough of that, now. *(Holds paper over candle as though drying it.)* Ha, there's nothing like coffee grounds for making parchment look old. *(Pause.)* Do you remember the bracelet of Marie Antoinette that the young Marquis de Chateauroy was admiring last week?

RENEE. Well, I guess he won't be buying it now that his uncle has left everything to Bert Cecil. No one could believe he would completely ignore the French branch of the family.

BARONI. But he did—and so now it's Mr. Cecil who's got the money to buy the bracelet—and probably the Lady Venetia along with it, since he's the heir.

RENEE. But you told me she was engaged to Chateauroy—

BARONI. She was *(He hangs papers up to dry.)*, but now watch and see what way the wind blows.

(BERT CECIL *and* LORD ROCKINGHAM *appear at door.*)
The old Countess will never see her married to a pauper—
*(Knock at door.)*
There he is now. Run along now, Renee. Go for a walk in the fresh

air; it will do you good. *(Pushing her toward the door.)* We have
business to discuss.

*(Exit* RENEE. *Enter* BERT CECIL, *a good-looking young man, well
dressed, with fine manners and speech, and* LORD ROCKINGHAM, *a
British gentleman in his mid-twenties, well dressed in morning
clothes.)*

BARONI. Ah, good day, gentlemen, good day.

BERT. I have come for the bracelet of Marie Antoinette.

BARONI. I beg your pardon, Mr. Cecil, but another gentleman is
interested in the bracelet, and has made me a higher offer, which,
you can understand—

BERT. Very well, how much is it now?

BARONI. Well, the other gentleman has offered me—

BERT. Never mind the act, Baroni. I have the money here. *(Pats
pocket.)* What is the price?

BARONI. A thousand pounds.

BERT. Robber! Well—go and get it.

BARONI. Ah, we understand each other. At once, Mr. Cecil, at once.
*(Bows and exits.)*

ROCK. That's a stiff price to pay for an engagement present, but if
you ask me, it's only a beginning with Venetia.

BERT. It's no use, Jack. My mind's made up.

ROCK. Listen to me, Bert, you're a fool. Do you think she dropped
Chateauroy and agreed to marry you because she's had some change
of heart? No, it's because you've had a great change of fortune!

BERT. I tell you, you're wrong there. She accepted me before I ever
told her about the will.

ROCK. Then you can be sure someone else told her before that.

BERT. Jack, I won't deny that her mother is grasping and ambitious, but Venetia's different.

*(Enter* RAKE, *manservant to* BERT CECIL. *He is tall and thin, about
ten years older than the other men.)*

RAKE. Ah, there you are, Master Cecil. I've been looking all over for
you. Have you changed your mind?

BERT. I wish you two would stop arguing with me. I've told you I'm
not going to join up with you now. That's all changed. I'm getting
married.

RAKE. What? Desert the two best friends a man ever had and jump
the best regiment in the world for a woman? I won't let you do it.

ROCK. That's what I've been telling him, Rake, but he's blind with
love and won't listen. As for me, since I've lost every cent I had, you
can count on me to join up with you.

RAKE. Well, that's some comfort, at least.

BERT *(to* ROCK*)*. You needn't enlist just because you've lost your
money. What's mine is yours and you might as well share my good
fortune as you have the bad.

ROCK. No, I can't stay here now.

BERT. Well, think it over. I'll wager you'll think better of enlisting.

ROCK. And you'll think better of marrying.

*(Enter* BARONI.*)*

BARONI. The bracelet, my lord. *(Hands him jewel case.)*

BERT *(looks inside, closes case, takes money from his pocket and hands it to* BARONI.*)* And here's your money.

ROCK *(to* RAKE*)*. Well, come along. There's no help for our friend, I'm afraid.

*(They start to exit. Enter* VENETIA, *"The Silver Pheasant," and her mother, the* COUNTESS OF WARMINSTER. VENETIA *is a pretty young woman, obviously upper class. She is impeccably dressed. The* COUNTESS *is an impoverished noblewoman. She has a most demanding air and expects to be catered to. She is elegantly dressed.)*

ROCK. Well, good day, Venetia. How do you do, Countess?

COUNTESS. Very well, thank you.

VENETIA. My mother wanted to do some shopping.

*(*RAKE *and* ROCKINGHAM *exit.* BERT *pockets the jewel case quickly.)*

COUNTESS. Ah, Mr. Cecil. How delightful to see you! I had no idea you were a collector.

BERT. Not a collector, really. I only came to look over some old books of my uncle's.

COUNTESS. Indeed! A bibliophile? Why, Venetia, I had no idea your intended had so many sides to his nature. Mr. Baroni, would you mind getting me a cup of tea?

BARONI. Tea?

COUNTESS *(very sharply)*. Tea!

BARONI. Tea. *(Exit.)*

VENETIA. I've often told you, mother—

COUNTESS. Yes, Venetia. But how fortunate to find you here. We've been wanting to reach you to invite you and your friends—Mr. Rockingham and—and—

BERT. And Rake?

COUNTESS. Oh, how stupid of me! I never can remember the names of servants except my own.

*(Enter* BARONI.*)*

Ah, here's my tea.

*(Exit* BARONI.*)*

BERT. Well, he isn't exactly a servant, you know—he's a friend.

COUNTESS. Of course. Well, I wanted to know if you and your friends could come to a small dinner party tomorrow evening.

VENETIA. Mother thought we could announce the engagement to a few friends.

BERT. How thoughtful of you, Countess. At what time?

COUNTESS. Let's say we'll dine about eight?

BERT. Fine.

COUNTESS. Then come, Venetia. *(Rising and going.)* We haven't time for shopping now, I'm afraid. I have an appointment with my attorney and—

VENETIA. Yes, mother, but if you will permit me, I would like to speak to Bert—

COUNTESS. Certainly, you two love birds must have many things to talk over and plan. I'll wait outside. Don't be long, dear— *(Exit.)*

VENETIA. I only wanted to tell you again how happy I am, Bert.

BERT. I pray that I may keep you so. Venetia, I have loved you for so long and yet I never dared to hope—

VENETIA. Everything is so different now—now that it's settled. It wasn't an easy thing, you know, after all my mother's hopes and plans with Chateauroy. She was so determined and we had such bitter words.

BERT. I know—I know, but I think she has come around now. At least, she's never been as cordial to me before.

VENETIA. You must forgive her, Bert, she has been nervous and worried about so many things—bills and creditors—not to mention the marriage of her only child.

BERT. I understand.

COUNTESS *(calling from outside)*. Venetia—Venetia!

VENETIA. Yes, mother. *(Rises. To BERT.)* Come see us to our carriage.

BERT. I would be delighted.

*(They exit. Enter BARONI. He goes to the table and spreads books out. RENEE enters from outside. She has a cape over her shoulders which she throws over chair, roses in her hands which she puts on table. BARONI goes to table and looks at flowers.)*

BARONI. What's this? Roses—did you spend money for these?

RENEE. You know I have no money.

BARONI. Roses—in November! And your father toiling for a bare subsistence. *(Lights candle.)*

RENEE *(crosses and takes chair from side of table, placing it at back)*. You'll gain nothing from telling me your troubles. Don't think you fool me, too. The money you make from forgeries alone will keep you comfortable the rest of your life!

BARONI *(threatening her)*. You know nothing—do you hear? Nothing! I've taken good care that you know nothing.

RENEE. It's true the only schooling you've ever given me was enough to spell the manuscripts I write for you and food enough to keep me alive while I execute them.

BARONI. Renee, it grieves me that you should say such things about your father.

RENEE. Stop it! My father? You are not my father! You've made me a forger—you've made me a thief—but you are not my father!

BARONI. Ah, yes, what a comfort it must be to remember that your own father could never bless you with his name.

RENEE. He blessed her with his love, all the love she ever knew. Fear and misery were your gifts to her!

BARONI. How thrilled the Cecils would be to welcome you into the bosom of their family, the aristocratic Cecil family. *(Laughs.)* Especially your brother Bert—your half-brother Bert.

RENEE. Don't say that! Don't ever say that!

BARONI. Why not? What will you do? Answer me. What can you do?

RENEE. I can do nothing! You killed my mother with your slimy, threatening tongue, but I'm too valuable—too valuable to kill.

BARONI. So you are, my dear. Your mother—that's another thing. She never was any credit to me. Fourteen years barren until he took her! Miserable slut, we're well rid of her.

RENEE *(crossing to him)*. Promise me you will never let Bert Cecil know?

BARONI. And would I be so foolish? Haven't I been kind enough to keep him near you? Don't we enjoy his purchases and the profits on them together, my girl? Now, so that you can do your work, we'll just throw these roses out the window.

RENEE *(rushes to protect them)*. Don't touch them!

BARONI *(laughs)*. I know—you didn't buy them. They were given to you. Given to you by Bert Cecil, "Beauty of the Brigade," as some fool women call him.

RENEE. The roses were thrown to me from a carriage by the Lady Venetia.

BARONI. Whom the "Beauty of the Brigade" is going to marry. *(He goes to door, locks it.)*

RENEE. How do you know? *(Aside.)* Ah, what is it to me, a slave, a drudge! *(To* BARONI.*)* Vex me once more tonight and I'll not write another line.

BARONI. What is the matter?

RENEE *(sits at desk)*. My eyes. They pain me so. Perhaps I need a stronger light.

BARONI. There, there, my dear. *(Gets candle from window.)* The pride of her old father's heart.

*(Knock at door.)*

Who's there?

CHATEAUROY *(outside)*. Chateauroy!

BARONI *(aside)*. The Marquis de Chateauroy? What is the matter now? *(Goes to door and opens it.)* Come in.

*(Enter* THE MARQUIS DE CHATEAUROY, *a young man of about 30, tall, slim, well dressed in morning clothes. He carries a hat and cane.)*

CHAT. Ah, the same old shop, the same old curios. It reminds me of the cave of the forty thieves—and there is only one. Have you got something to drink?

BARONI. I have some cider.

CHAT. Cider. Ugh. *(Crosses to table near* RENEE *who is seated, writing.)* Renee, my pretty girl, do you venture out in the streets at night? Are you afraid?

RENEE. Aye.

CHAT. Here. *(Throws coin on table.)* Brandy, and the rest for you. Your father and I have business. We are in no hurry.

RENEE *(rising and taking coin)*. You want me away? Why not say so like a man? *(Looks at coin, shrugs.)* Why not?—like a woman. *(Takes cloak and exits.)*

CHAT. So, your daughter grows rebellious, eh?

BARONI. Women are queer cattle.

CHAT. So they are, but men are stranger. Baroni, in the variety of your occupations, there is nothing I admire more than your talent for manipulating ordinary playing cards.

BARONI *(makes deprecating gesture).* So?

CHAT. And my cousin being of a liberal disposition, and always willing to cut the cards for a thousand or so, I have found the needle hole you make in the corner—to distinguish a low card from a high one—to my advantage.

BARONI. How many packs?

CHAT. Only one.

BARONI. One? *(Gets pack and gives it to him.)* And now?

CHAT. My cousin was here tonight.

BARONI. Yes.

CHAT. And bought the bracelet, the Marie Antoinette—

BARONI. Yes, for the Lady Venetia—

CHAT *(sits in chair at table, he picks up candle and holds it up close to his face, looking into flame as though reading fortune).* Baroni—there is money in this candle.

BARONI *(rising and coming near, his eye on the candle).* Money?

CHAT. Unlike most cavalry officers *(He moves the candle to the left.* BARONI *follows.)* I have not soaked my brains in absinthe. Having a head to plan, and your daughter's hand to execute, I think I see wealth for you.

BARONI. How much?

CHAT. I haven't settled on the figure. *(He moves the candle to the right.)*

BARONI. I would be interested in what figure you might settle on—let us say—

CHAT. Let us say about seven thousand pounds. *(He puts candle down on table.)*

BARONI. Seven thousand pounds?

CHAT. Yes, I think I will settle at that figure. *(Rises and follows* BARONI *who retreats toward chair at back of table.)* Sit down. Now, you knew how my uncle, the late Duke, took a fancy to my cousin Bert.

BARONI. Yes, they say he was in love with the young man's mother. He was at all times odd.

CHAT. But in spite of hearsay, he believed in me.

BARONI. He was decidedly odd.

CHAT. There were some who said that my uncle's moral sense was too strong to let him disinherit the French branch of the family, and that a later will would be found, in which he would treat me justly.

BARONI. Your riddle is still unsolved.

CHAT. He was a bookish fellow—took a fancy to those literary autographs of which your daughter's skill—pray accept my compliments *(He touches* BARONI's *shoulder with his cane.)*—has no difficulty in supplying. *(He tips* BARONI's *head with cane under chin.)* Now, when he died, he bequeathed to you a portion of his library. *(Hand on* BARONI's *shoulder.)* What then more natural than that, amongst the leaves of one of his rarest books, this later will has now been found.

BARONI. By you?

CHAT. Not I, but you, dear Baroni. You were the man to find it. *(Both laugh.* CHATEAUROY *rises to his full height, cane in hand.)*

BARONI. Oh, ho, ha, ha—no, no. There is only one improbability. You see, I didn't find it. *(Rises and confronts him.)*

CHAT. I foresaw the objection. *(Puts* BARONI *down again with his cane.)* And that is why I thought that the sum of seven thousand pounds, paid after delivery of the will, would make it clear that my uncle left his fortune to me and not to my cousin, Bert Cecil.

*(Enter* RENEE *with bottle of brandy, which she places on table and exits, returning at once with two glasses. She puts them on the table with the bottle, crosses to the table, sits, and begins to write, as if copying something.)*

BARONI. I am old and won't live very long. Renee must be provided for. But I—I am to run the risk. I must be well protected.

CHAT. Trust me. *(Takes out pocketbook, crosses to* RENEE, *takes out papers.)* Ah, Renee, my good girl. Here are a few papers. *(Places folded pieces of paper on table where she is writing.)* One of them a business form, this one a sample of handwriting.

RENEE *(looks at paper, then, to* BARONI). It's impossible—you can't! I won't! *(She rises.* CHATEAUROY *turns away.)*

BARONI *(pressing her).* Do it quickly or I promise our secret will be secret no longer.

CHAT. What's this?

BARONI *(soothingly).* It's nothing. Renee is tired; she has had a great deal of work to do.

RENEE *(writing).* Yes, a great deal. Forgive me.

CHAT. Now *(Watching her.)* see if you can—that's it, just like his own hand!

*(*BARONI *fills two glasses, hands one to* CHATEAUROY.)*

BARONI. Let us drink to the trade of literary autographs.

CHAT. Let us drink to the benefit of those we love and to the ruin of those we hate. *(They drink.)* And to my honored cousin, "Beauty of the Brigade!"

BARONI *(looking over* RENEE's *shoulder as she writes).* Bravo, my girl, Bravo.

*(He blows out candle. As candle goes out, the stage lights go down.)*

**CURTAIN**

## SCENE TWO

SCENE: *Card room in the winter palace of Warminster Manor, an elegant interior. Music, the March of the Foreign Legion, is heard softly at rise, becoming louder as scene progresses until bugle is heard.* RAKE *is seated at table playing solitaire, decanter of brandy and glasses on table. Enter* COUNTESS WARMINSTER. *All are in evening dress.*

COUNTESS. Why, for pity sake—Mr.—a—Mr.—

RAKE. They call me Rake, my lady. *(Rises.)*

COUNTESS. Well, whatever they call you—what are you doing sitting all alone playing cards at one of my parties?

RAKE. Oh, no offense meant, milady, and no discredit to your party, I assure you.

COUNTESS. Are you ill?

RAKE. Oh, no indeed—it's just that I'm not the sort—well, you see, I'm just more like myself when I'm *(Sound of bugle.)*—well—when I'm one of those.

COUNTESS. One of those—who are they?

RAKE. The Chasseurs D'Afrique, my lady. They start for Algiers tonight. *(On the words "D'Afrique," he stamps his foot.)*

COUNTESS *(looks at his feet, then at* RAKE*)*. They do? Oh, the poor fellows.

RAKE. Well, they're not poor fellows. They're a regiment of the Foreign Legion, the finest fighting outfit on the globe. I for one wouldn't mind joining them.

COUNTESS. Joining that bunch of ruffians? Are you then tired of Mr. Cecil's service?

RAKE. Tired of Mr. Cecil's service! *(Again he stamps his foot for emphasis. The* COUNTESS *stares.)* Tired of taking orders from the man who saved my life in Asia? That I'm not, and Mr. Cecil could keep on giving me orders as long as it was his pleasure.

COUNTESS. Then why would you want to join the Legion?

RAKE. Well—it's different than the life I'm used to, but I can't go back to the old outfit, for I was courtmartialed for walloping a corporal who walloped my dog. Master Cecil, bless 'im, got me discharged and took me in his service, but after he's married, I'll feel like a blooming fish out of water.

*(Enter* BARONI. *He is not dressed for the party, but wears a shabby coat over the outfit he wore in the shop.)*

BARONI. I beg your pardon, Countess.

COUNTESS. Why, Mr. Baroni—I'm terribly sorry, but I simply can't talk with you now. You see, I'm having a small supper in honor of Venetia's engagement, and I must return to my guests—do forgive me.

BARONI. My apologies for the interruption, but I have urgent business with Mr. Cecil that could not wait.

COUNTESS. Aha! You needn't be sly with me, Mr. Baroni. I think I have some idea that looking over books yesterday wasn't the primary purpose of his visit to your shop.

BARONI. You misunderstand me—please. I must see him at once.

COUNTESS *(moves close to him and speaks confidentially)*. Well, it's hardly proper to summon one of my guests . . . Couldn't you tell me, and I can convey your message to him later?

RAKE. Beg pardon, but if you wish, I can take a message to Mr. Cecil.

COUNTESS. Yes, of course, but no hurry, mind you, and don't disturb him if he's with Venetia.

RAKE. Excuse me, I'll see if I can find him. *(Starts to exit, stops.)* Ah, a perfectly lovely party, my lady. *(Bows and exits.)*

COUNTESS. What is it? Tell me at once!

BARONI. I really couldn't—well, you see, it's rather private, as it's bad news.

COUNTESS. Bad news? Well, good or bad, I've every right to know—after all, he's soon to become my son-in-law.

BARONI. Well, then, don't breathe it to a soul?

COUNTESS. Of course not—now tell me quickly—he'll be here—and I must know.

BARONI. A new will has been found, dated later than the other—

COUNTESS. And Bert Cecil?

BARONI. Is no longer the heir. The old man apparently had a falling out with him and a change of heart. The later will leaves everything to the Marquis de Chateauroy.

COUNTESS. Are you sure? How do you know?

BARONI. Only because I came across the will myself, put away in one of the old gentleman's rare volumes—

COUNTESS. And you have it? Are you certain there can be no doubt?

BARONI. None whatsoever. *(Takes out will and shows it to her.)* I have the document with me here—

COUNTESS *(backs up and pushes* BARONI *back.* BARONI *follows very closely)*. Oh, excuse me—I'll see if I can find Mr. Cecil. Oh, how terrible—for him, I mean . . . I'll send him right away. *(Exits hurriedly.)*

*(Enter* BERT *and* RAKE.*)*

BERT. You wished to see me, Baroni?

BARONI. Yes, my business is urgent—*(Indicating* RAKE.*)* and private.

BERT. He may hear anything you have to say to me.

BARONI. Very well.

BERT. Now to the point.

BARONI. A very disastrous point it is, Mr. Cecil. You know what a strange man your uncle the late Duke was.

BERT. Granted. Didn't he leave all his property to me?

BARONI. Yes, in the will he made three years ago.

BERT. And as he made no other?

BARONI. I am sorry, Mr. Cecil, but as you know, life has its accidents.

BERT. Accidents?

BARONI. I have discovered that the Duke did make a later will.

BERT. What?

BARONI. My dear Mr. Cecil, this evening, in looking over one of the old books left to me by your uncle, I discovered this later will bequeathing all his property to —

BERT. Stop! Don't give it to me all at once. Let me have it in driblets. It is not left to me, you say? Then who is the heir?

BARONI. The Marquis de Chateauroy. *(Pulls out documents.)*

BERT. Give it to me.

*(RAKE comes up to his side and looks over his shoulder.)*

BARONI. Now, cast your eyes over this. I came as soon as I found it in the old book your uncle left me.

RAKE *(looking at document)*. Fight it, sir. The estate is worth it.

BERT. Oh, damn the estate. It's given me nothing but trouble.

*(Enter COUNTESS, comes to BERT.)*

COUNTESS. Whatever is the matter?

BERT. A new will has been found and I am no longer the heir.

COUNTESS. Can this be true?

BARONI. Here's the proof. *(Points to document.)*

COUNTESS. If my sympathy —

BERT. Thank you, but I won't need it.

*(Enter VENETIA. BERT goes to her.)*

Ah, Venetia, I believe the next waltz is ours?

*(VENETIA looks at COUNTESS as if for instruction.)*

COUNTESS. The Lady Venetia was complaining of fatigue.

*(Enter CHATEAUROY. He comes to VENETIA.)*

CHAT. First strain of the waltz — may I?

COUNTESS. Oh, you do dance so well, I think my daughter's fatigue —

BERT. Is this your wish, Venetia?

VENETIA. I believe there is some mistake. The waltz after this one was ours, Bert. *(She takes CHATEAUROY's arm.)*

COUNTESS. Pardon a mother's enthusiasm, but I think they make the handsomest couple. Mr. Baroni, I believe we have finished our business.

BARONI. Yes, Countess. *(Exits.)*

COUNTESS. Mr. Rake.

RAKE. Yes, Countess. *(Exits.)*

COUNTESS. Mr. Cecil, as we are both people of the world, I may speak plainly to you. You have not the means to support a girl of Venetia's luxurious habits, and I am sure you are too much of a gentleman to hold her to an engagement that would bring only misery to you both.

BERT. Did Venetia wish to tell me this?

COUNTESS. Venetia's wishes have always been identical with —

BERT. Not another word! Is Venetia in accord with breaking faith with me?

COUNTESS. I understand your excitement and overlook the extravagance of your language, but Venetia desires me to tell you that she considers her engagement with you at an end. *(Exits.)*

(BERT *stands by table with head bowed. Enter* RAKE *with jewel case. He hands it to* BERT.)

RAKE. Mr. Cecil.

BERT *(taking case)*. There will be no need of this now.

*(Exit* RAKE.*)*

It was the token of our love. *(Sits in chair, head in hands.)*

*(Enter* ROCKINGHAM, *with a dish of salad, eating it. He sees* BERT.*)*

ROCK. What's the matter, Bert, not feeling well?

BERT. Never felt better in my life.

ROCK. Have some salad.

BERT. No, thank you, I'm not hungry. I'll try a drink of brandy. *(Pours and drinks.)*

ROCK. It will do you good.

BERT. I feel as careless and indifferent—

ROCK. What about?

BERT. And as for Chateauroy—

ROCK. What has he been up to now?

BERT. I'll do it. *(Pours and drinks again.)* In a week's time, we'll be back at the old stand, booted with light hose, and mounting guard.

ROCK. Not I. In a week's time, I will have vanished from the earth, known only as private so-and-so, Chasseurs D'Afrique.

BERT. Then you mean business?

ROCK. Indeed I do. I'm going to enlist tonight.

BERT. Count me in.

ROCK. What?

BERT. I am going with you.

ROCK. You mean she threw you?

BERT. No, not exactly.

ROCK. Her mamma then?

BERT. That's nearer—my fortune has gone up in smoke.

ROCK. How's that?

BERT. Another will has been found. Chateauroy gets the cash and Lady Warminster has informed me that my engagement with Venetia is at an end.

ROCK. And you would quit because of a mercenary old woman?

BERT. You were right, Jack. She's a chip off the old block.

ROCK. Well, I'm sorry, old chap, but I'm glad you found out in time. Either one of them would barter their immortal souls for cash.

BERT *(looking off)*. There's Venetia now, dancing with Chateauroy, all aglow with happiness, while I—*(Takes pocketbook from pocket.)* Well, this pocketbook contains every cent I have in the world.

*(Enter* CHATEAUROY. *He hears the last of* BERT's *speech, throws pocketbook on table.)*

CHAT. Are you in the mood for a friendly little game?

BERT. I don't understand you.

CHAT. We are cousins, after all our differences, you know. When I needed a thousand, you were always willing to cut the cards. If I won, you paid like the Bank of England. If I lost, you said nothing about it. Come—I'll cut the cards with you. How much is in the pocketbook?

BERT. Four hundred pounds.

CHAT. Let's cut four times, a hundred a cut—what do you say?

BERT. All right, get the cards.

CHAT. Here. *(Takes pack from pocket.)*

ROCK. Play carefully.

BERT. Never mind. I'm feeling lucky now.

ROCK. Well, take my advice. There's more in this than reaches the eye. (BERT *sits at table opposite* CHATEAUROY. *His pocketbook and the jewel case are on the table.)*

CHAT. Now, my dear cousin—remember I am lucky with cards—

BERT. At times—deal.

CHAT. I've occasioned some success with the ladies, too, you know. Lowest wins?

BERT. As you please.

> (CHATEAUROY *cuts the cards;* BERT *cuts, too.* CHATEAUROY *turns up a low card;* BERT *shows higher card.)*

CHAT. Mine!

> *(They both cut a second time, same business.)*

Mine again. What do you say, double or quits?

BERT. No, we agreed on four cuts.

CHAT. All right.

> *(Cuts again, same business.* CHATEAUROY *wins again.)*

How much is left now?

BERT. One hundred pounds.

CHAT. Once more then.

BERT. All right.

> *(Same business.)*

Well—you have it all now. *(Pushes pocketbook to him.)*

CHAT. I can't take it. I'll take your note instead.

> (ROCKINGHAM *has been watching and as soon as cards are released, he sits and spreads cards out looking at them carefully, but pretending to play solitaire.* CHATEAUROY *does not take pocketbook.)*

BERT. I can't owe you money.

CHAT. Haven't I owed you?

BERT. That's different.

CHAT. Well, if there is any feeling—*(Goes to table and extends hand as if to take pocketbook, stops, turns.)* No, damn it, Cecil, I can't.

BERT. You won it, you must.

CHAT. Look, Cecil *(Pauses and touches jewel case.)*, Baroni tells me you bought a bracelet at his shop yesterday. Now give me the bracelet and we'll call it quits.

BERT *(goes to table and takes bracelet).* You would lose by the deal. *(Hands him jewel case.)*

CHAT *(takes jewel case)*. I know how to double its value.

(CHATEAUROY *picks up pocketbook and hands it back to* BERT, *who puts it in his pocket. At this,* ROCKINGHAM, *who has discovered the cards are marked, strikes table with his fist.)*

ROCK *(seeing that he has attracted their attention)*. Solitaire—can't make it out.

*(Very busy with cards,* BERT *sits at table, lets head fall in hands.)*

CHAT. Aren't you feeling well?

BERT. Yes, I'm feeling well, all right.

CHAT. Our little game, I hope, is not responsible for your unpleasant feeling.

BERT. No, rather the reverse.

CHAT. Sentiment, then, perhaps. Well, if there is anything I hate it is sentimental memories.

(CHATEAUROY *tries to pick up the cards but* ROCKINGHAM *stops him. He then picks up the jewel case and exits.)*

ROCK. Bert—look here.

BERT. What is it, Jack?

ROCK. Press your first finger and thumb on the corner of that card.

BERT. Why, it has been pricked with a needle.

ROCK. What is it?

BERT. Three of clubs.

ROCK. And that one. *(Same business.)*

BERT. Smooth.

ROCK. What is it?

BERT. King of hearts.

ROCK. That one. *(Same business.)*

BERT. Ace of spades, pricked.

ROCK. So, there's the milk in the coconut. The lowest cards are marked.

BERT. But the pocketbook—why didn't he take it then?

ROCK. He wanted the bracelet.

BERT. The bracelet is of no use to him—of course! To give to—

ROCK. Precisely. *(Puts hand on his shoulder.)* This is a bitter bad job, a bitter bad job, Bert.

*(Enter* RAKE.)

Get ready and start for Algiers; that's all you're fit for now.

RAKE. Mr. Cecil, sir—

BERT. Rake—you know I'm beggared.

RAKE. What's the odds, sir, we're young, and there's lots of fun left in life yet.

BERT. Rich or poor, you've followed my fortunes. You'll follow them still?

RAKE. What trunk shall I pack, sir?

BERT *(rises and puts arm on* RAKE's *shoulder)*. Rake—Jack—we start for Algiers tonight.

ROCK. Agreed!

*(They shake hands.)*

RAKE. We're off for Algiers.

ROCK. And I'm off to pack. We'll meet at the station at midnight.

*(Exit* ROCK *and* RAKE. *Enter* VENETIA.*)*

VENETIA. There's no mistake now—the next waltz is ours.

BERT. Your mother gave me a message from you.

VENETIA. From me?

BERT. Yes, and I asked her if you had authorized it. You bring me proof that you have.

VENETIA. How?

BERT. On your wrist. The bracelet of Marie Antoinette, that I bought in Baroni's shop. *(She puts hand to bracelet as if to take it off.)* Don't take if off—Chateauroy won it from me, no matter how. *(She still tries to take it off.)* Pray, don't take it off. Venetia, hear me for the last time. You told me that you loved me; it was false. You told me you cared nothing for wealth—that was false, too. You told me you could never accept my cousin—false, all of it, false!

VENETIA. Bert—wait—hear me.

*(Enter* COUNTESS *and* CHATEAUROY.*)*

BERT. Your mother told me that you wish to end our engagement. Very well, I accept the decision. I renounce you gladly. And remember, Venetia, whatever the future has in store for me, I will never hear your name without contempt.

CHAT. Sir—Lady Venetia is my affianced wife.

BERT. Very well, you have the money and the girl. The game is not done, and when we meet again, it will be where you won't have a chance to mark the pack. *(Strikes cards with hand.)*

COUNTESS. Leave this house!

BERT. Oh, I am going, but before I go, I will have the satisfaction of declaring that this latest token of your daughter's engagement *(Points to bracelet on Venetia's wrist.)* was won from me by a gambler's trick.

CHAT. Sir!

BERT. Aye *(Takes cards and crosses to* CHATEAUROY.*)*, and a sharper at cards! *(Throws pack of cards in his face and exits.)*

**CURTAIN**

# ACT TWO

## SCENE ONE

SCENE: *Ace of Spades Wine Shop, Algeria, a fancy Moorish scene. There are large double doors, the upper parts of which are glass. Arab soldiers are seated at tables, jugs in front of them, drinking.* PAULETTE *and* BOUAMANA, *in belly dancing costumes with finger cymbals and head veils, are dancing as the soldiers watch, drinking, celebrating. The Arab soldiers are dressed in uniform, bloused full trousers, faded blue Foreign Legion shirts, sashed at waist with bright fabric sashes. All wear turbans, except* YUSSEF, *who wears a red fez.* SI HASSAN *sits at a table with his head in his hands, apparently asleep.*

BEAU BRUNO. Wine! More wine! *(Pours and drinks. To* ENTAMABOULL.*)* And may the wine be better than the dancing.

YUSSEF. Wine improves all things.

BEAU. Where's Cigarette? Her dancing would be more to our fancy, eh?

ENTAMABOULL. Pah! Cigarette! You'd think she was a goddess! I say she can't dance any more than she can fight. She has you all bewitched!

YUSSEF. Not us, Entamaboull, but the enemy.

ENTA. Bah! You're all in love with her and have lost your senses!

BEAU. Where is she? Do you know?

YUSSEF. Gone to meet Billabee, the letter carrier.

ENTA. Well, I for one don't wait on her. This is a celebration. Now, three cheers for our victory at Zeralia!

*(They cheer.)*

And the brave men of the Chasseurs!

*(They cheer.)*

We will sing the Marseillaise, and if any African dog refuses to sing the chorus, I'll split his nose with my fist!

*(They sing chorus of "La Marseillaise" in French.)*

Well done, my brave fellows. There's not in all France a troupe more brave.

*(All cheer.)*

TIGER CLAW *(points to* SI HASSAN*)*. There's one who didn't sing.

BEAU *(going to* SI HASSAN*)*. He sleeps—wake up, there.

*(*SI HASSAN *rises.)*

ENTA. Here—this cup to your lips *(Puts wine cup to his lips.)* and sing!

TIGER *(putting another cup to his lips)*. Aye, drink to our victory at Zeralia!

SI HASSAN *(puts up hands and pushes back cups)*. No, for the love of Allah—I am a Moslem. My faith forbids.

ENTA. Sacre—what is your regiment? Turko or Zephyr?

SI HASSAN. Neither, sire, I am a Bedouin.

*(General disorder.)*

ALL *(drawing guns, revolvers).* Shoot him—kill him! *(Etc.)*

TIGER *(gets in front of* SI HASSAN*).* Wait, lads, the new Colonel arrived today. He is a regular martinet, and if he hears of our killing Bedouins for their religion, it will go hard with us.

ENTA. Then we will give him the lash!

ALL. Yes, the lash!

ENTA. Fifty blows will break every bone in his body—it will come near killing him anyway.

*(Enter* CIGARETTE *with mail pouch strapped over her shoulder. She is a beautiful dark-haired, dark-skinned girl, dressed in Foreign Legion uniform, knee-high boots, embroidered skirt over trousers, Turkish fez hat. Her manner is bold and her voice full of command.)*

CIG. And I'll come near killing you—my prince of bullies!

ALL. Cigarette!

CIG. Aye, Cigarette! I'll teach you to whip a defenseless man. *(Takes whip and lashes* ENTAMABOULL *about the legs. To* SI HASSAN*.)* Go in peace.

*(*SI HASSAN *rushes to her, kneels and kisses hem of her skirt. She makes exclamation of anger and points to door. He starts to go; the men stop him. She rushes and lashes them about the legs. They let him go and he exits quickly.)*

CIG. Ah, who hates Bedouins more than I! This man was one against all of you. I'll not have you spoiling the victory at Zeralia at the bidding of a drunken chasseur. *(She strikes* ENTAMABOULL *about ankles with whip.)* Now, there's more important business. Billabee, the letter carrier, is dead, and I have brought these through for you.

ALL. Dead?

CIG. Yes, dead. I rode up in time to hear the shots. They shot him and left him to die, but he kept your letters. When I came up, he could hardly speak with the blood in his throat. "There are the letters, Cigarette," he said, and he just turned over and died. *(She shrugs and opens mail pouch.)* Beau, here is one from your mother. She doesn't know what a bad one you are. Entamaboull, a love scrawl for you. That girl doesn't know you, eh? *(To* TIGER CLAW*.)* And tobacco. *(Smells package.)* That girl knows you. She knows your passions go up in smoke. And here's another—*(To* YUSSEF*.)* papers, commission—Billabee forgot nothing, and Billabee is dead.

ENTA *(puts arm around her).* Well, I'm not dead.

CIG *(pushes him away).* It's time you were—why is it all the good men get killed, while you—

ENTA. And if I were Corporal Victor—

CIG. You would know better.

ENTA. That dandy, with the soft white hands.

CIG. Which he keeps in his own pockets. *(She pushes him.)*

ENTA. He treats you like a china doll, and will throw you out the window when he gets enough of you.

CIG. Never mind—I can take care of myself. I can shoot a louis from between your fingers at twenty paces.

ENTA. Not mine.

CIG. Ha—I thought so, coward!

*(Enter* BERT *in uniform of French Foreign Legion.)*

BERT. Let me hold the louis. *(Comes to her.)*

ENTA. Yes, let the brave Corporal Victor hold it—he has so much faith in your marksmanship!

BERT. Oh, I have more than faith, I have the louis. *(Takes coin from pocket, tosses it in the air, catches it.)* Where shall I stand? Here?

CIG *(draws pistol and aims. She flinches, unable to fire, hesitates; soldiers watch).* I can't. I can't!

YUSSEF *(goes and takes louis from* BERT*).* Here, let me hold the louis. *(*YUSSEF *holds it out.* CIGARETTE *shoots. He drops the coin.* BERT *picks it up. All cheer.)*

ENTA. I've seen enough of this—come on, all fall in for parade.

*(Bugle heard off. Soldiers line up and exit, talking noisily, calling to one another. All off except* BERT *and* CIGARETTE.*)*

BERT. Jack and Rake have been out all day. They'll soon be here and hungry. Is there food for them?

CIG *(gets bread and cheese, brings it to table, picks up pipe and match).* Do the women in your country smoke?

BERT. Well—they draw the line at pipes.

CIG *(takes pipe out of her mouth, looks at it and puts it on table. She wipes her hands on dress.)* Do they swear?

BERT. Very mildly.

CIG. Do they shoot Bedouins?

BERT. There are no Bedouins to shoot.

CIG. Well, do they cut off enemies' rings on the battlefields?

BERT. Really—that's a peculiar question.

CIG. Do they wear their dresses short like this?

BERT. It is not the prevailing mode.

CIG. I see. Did you leave a woman back there?

BERT. Little girl, enough of this. While you are worrying over such illusions, I shall have some food. *(He cuts bread and cheese and begins to eat.)*

CIG. I know what she is like. She is like a silver pheasant, strutting around all day in the sun and admiring herself in the glass. She has ribbons, laces and flounces, and she combs her hair. *(Runs her fingers through her hair angrily.)* Well, I hate her—do you hear? And if I ever meet her, I'll kill her! *(Puts hand on revolver in belt.)*

BERT *(puts hand over hers and returns revolver to belt).* Now, now— you keep your killing for the Bedouins. You're a brave soldier, and you won the day for us at Zeralia, by bringing your soldiers to my rescue.

CIG *(has cross on breast attached to ribbon. She raises it to her lips and kisses it).* My soldiers gave me this cross for it. I wanted it so much. But more than that I wanted—I wanted—

BERT. Yes—and now, my comrades will want their dinner.
*(She stamps her foot and turns away. Enter* ROCKINGHAM *in Foreign Legion uniform with bag on back. He does not see* CIGA-RETTE.*)*

ROCK. Well, Cecil?

CIG *(aside)*. Cecil?

ROCK. I've brought some potatoes for us. *(Takes bag to* BERT.*)*

BERT. Fine, we'll put them in the kitchen. Come, Jack, we'll go and get some wine.

CIG. But we have wine here.

BERT. Yes, but in honor of Zeralia, we'll drink champagne tonight, and the louis you shot shall pay for it. *(Throws coin to* ROCKINGHAM, *who catches it.)* Come, Jack, we'll find champagne.

*(They exit.)*

CIG. Cecil—his name is Cecil. And there is a woman! Am I so ugly? I'll see—I'll see. *(Runs and gets glass hanging on wall and looks in it. She studies herself in different positions.)* Why no, I'm not—really, I'm not. Yes, I am, but there's no reason why I shouldn't fix myself up. I will. I will. *(Puts glass on table and gets bucket from back, also curry comb and brush.)* Now, we'll see what The Silver Pheasant does. I can comb my hair as well as she. *(Takes curry comb and knocks it on chair, as if knocking dust out of it. Then she brushes it with a brush. This is an imitation of a man using a curry comb and brush when currying a horse.)* I can comb my hair. *(Repeats brushing.)* There. And she keeps her clothes clean. *(Brushes jacket and dress.)* And she blacks her boots every morning. *(Puts up foot and brushes boots with same brush. She brushes hair down, rolls it up, goes and gets small fez hat, and puts it on.)* She has a little cap that comes way down over her eyes, I know the kind. *(She walks as if imitating a grand lady, looks at herself in glass, shakes her head and lets her hair fall down around her shoulders again.)* No, it's because she has ribbons and flounces and a long train, trailing on the ground *(Stoops down and walks so low, her own short skirt trails. She walks, swinging it behind her as a train.)* Oh, I hate her, I hate her. I can't have those things. *(Pause.)* I have to be feminine. *(Sits and puts foot across her leg and lights match.)* No, the first thing—*(Pauses, realizes what she is doing. She lays down pipe, uncrosses legs, sighs, folds hands and lets head drop wearily to one side.)* That's the first thing—I mustn't swear. Mustn't loot Bedouins—mustn't smoke. *(Takes pipe, looks at it, kisses it, gets up and throws pipe on floor.)* There—there—there—I'll only smoke ciga-rettes.

*(Enter* RAKE *in uniform.)*

RAKE. Well, little lady, what's all this?

CIG. Rake, oh Rake, he really doesn't care for me. There's another woman in his life.

RAKE. Well, if the Lady Venetia—

CIG. There, you've said it.

*Cigarette (Georgia Loveless in the Imperial's 1971 production) contemplates how she might fix herself up and imitate her rival, "The Silver Pheasant." Most aggravating, she decides, is that she will have to give up her pipe and smoke only cigarettes!*

RAKE. That's the name of a yacht.

CIG. I don't like the name, do you?

RAKE. I tell you, it's the name of his yacht he used to have in other days.

CIG. Stop lying—I hate her.

RAKE. See here, Cigarette, you're off on the wrong track.

CIG. I'm not—he loved her—he loves her still.

RAKE. Why don't you make him jealous?

CIG. I don't know how—wait, I do, if you will help. You fall on your knees at my feet.

RAKE. Don't be silly.

CIG. Come on—he might come in and see you—and—shoot you. *(She moves close, coaxing him.)*

RAKE. No, thank you, I don't want to be shot, even for you, young lady.

CIG. Please, just this once. *(She tickles his stomach. He laughs wildly.)*

RAKE. Well, I don't want to be shot even once. Besides, it would look so silly.

CIG. No, it won't, not if you do it.

RAKE. Look, I want to help you, but I don't believe in this kind of nonsense. *(Suddenly thinking.)* Why don't you get a letter?

CIG. A letter? I've never had one. *(Goes to chair, kneels on it, hands on back.)*

RAKE. Yes, a letter from some Johnny.

CIG. What's that?

RAKE. Well, that's just some man that admires you.

CIG. Even if I did, I couldn't read it.

RAKE. Bless your little heart. *(He kisses the tip of her nose.)* You see, that's the point—get him to read it to you. Let him read the letter!

CIG. Oh, you dear man! *(She embraces him.)* Sit down and write it. *(She places him in chair R. of table, pulls up chair and sits, pipe in hand.)* Write something that will burn into his very soul.

RAKE *(sits and takes up pen)*. Burn in his soul—burn in his soul. Ah—I have it! *(Writes.)* "My dear Cigarette"—*(Pause.)*

CIG *(takes lock of hair and brings it down around her nose, twirls end of it)*. That won't burn him.

RAKE. Won't it? *(Writes again.)* "My own little girl"—

CIG. Say, that's all right—and—queen of my heart. *(Stands on knees in her chair.)*

RAKE. Don't you think that's a little ordinary?

CIG. The witch doctress uses it. *(Leans over table close to him as he writes.)*

RAKE. All right. *(Writes.)* "I love you." *(Kisses her cheek.)*—And it's true. *(Very quietly.)*

CIG *(not noticing. He returns to writing as she dictates)*. "You are the sweetest girl in camp." No, "on earth." "On earth" sounds better.

"Sounds better" is not part of the letter. "You are the sweetest girl
on earth. I will wait for you tonight."

RAKE *(she has dictated too fast for him to keep up with her).* Wait for
me now. *(He writes very fast.)*

CIG. Say, Rake, where will he wait for me?

RAKE *(writing).* I don't know.

CIG. At the Moorish ruins, of course.

RAKE *(writing).* Rather damp amongst the ruins.

CIG. We will exchange vows.

RAKE. Good—very good.

CIG. That will scorch him. I think that is good enough to write
twice.

RAKE. All right. *(Goes on writing.)*

CIG. No, scratch it out—it will take too long.

RAKE. Scratch out twice.

CIG. Yes. Now sign.

RAKE. Sign—sign what?

CIG. Rake—that's your name, isn't it?

RAKE. Yes, but Corporal Victor might object you know—

CIG. Well, then sign it—well, sign it—Adamond—

RAKE. Adamond.

*(BERT calls outside.* RAKE *quickly folds the letter and gives it to*
CIGARETTE. *He makes a quick exit into kitchen.* BERT *enters.)*

BERT. Rake—Rake—

*(CIGARETTE stands in center of room, letter over her heart.)*

What's the matter, little girl?

CIG *(comes to him, points to letter).* It's a letter. *(She puts letter in his
face.)*

BERT. So I see.

CIG. It's my first one—and I—I can't read it.

BERT. Your parents ought to have been whipped not to teach you.

CIG. Don't say that. My mother was a camp follower. Years ago the
Bedouins captured her.

BERT. I'm sorry—

CIG. They tortured her and tossed her from one drunken devil to
another, then cut her throat. I swore then to kill and kill and kill and
I have kept my word.

BERT. And your father?

CIG. Who knows? After my mother was taken, my soldiers brought
me up. But here—read the letter.

BERT *(reads).* "My own little girl."

*(CIGARETTE shows joy at the success of her plan.)*

Shall I go on?

*(She nods.)*

"Queen of my heart, I love you. You are the sweetest girl in camp, on
earth sounds better."

*(CIGARETTE starts as he reads this, then knowing it is* RAKE's *fault,*

*she shakes her fist at the door.* BERT *does not see this. When he looks at her, she composes her face.)*

*(Resumes reading).* "I will wait for you tonight at the Moorish ruins, rather damp among the ruins."

*(He laughs. She stamps her foot and mumbles cuss words.)*
"Twice—scratched—Adamond." *(He rises.)*

CIG *(goes to him and snatches letter).* You're not jealous?

BERT. Jealous?

CIG. Yes, that's what I said.

BERT. Of who, Adamond?

CIG. No, of Rake, your skinny, stupid friend. He wrote the letter. *(Tears it up and jumps on it.)*

BERT. Why, little girl, I'm heartbroken. Why didn't you warn me?

CIG. Because I wanted to see if Entamaboull spoke the truth.

BERT. What did he say?

CIG. He said that when you got tired of me, you would throw me out the window.

BERT. I'll knock his head off for that.

CIG. Then it isn't true?

BERT. Why, it's absurd.

CIG. Then there's no other woman?

BERT. Nonsense. *(Turns away.)*

CIG *(looking at him. He has turned his back, knowing that he is deceiving her. She stamps foot.)* Then I suppose you won't be hurt by what I've got to say about her.

BERT *(turning quickly).* About who?

CIG. About the Lady Venetia.

BERT. Venetia?

CIG. Yes, the woman Bert loved.

BERT. Where did you hear this?

CIG. I heard it from the Zouaves.

BERT. It's a lie! I'll call them out singly or six at a time to exterminate the whole brigade.

CIG. We're quits—quits—quits! I knew nothing. I picked up two names by chance. I fired in the air and the bullet went straight to your heart. *(Goes to door, stands looking off.)*

BERT. Little one, I know I'm a fool to behave like this, but if you only knew—if you only knew.

CIG. I know now—I do know. You told me you loved me, but you still love her! *(Stamps foot and exits.)*

BERT. Cigarette, wait—Cigarette! *(He follows her off.)*

*(Enter* ROCKINGHAM *with champagne. He takes it to table, brings glasses, has back to entrance when* VENETIA *enters. She is wearing soft, light dress, appropriate to the hot North African climate.)*

VENETIA. Pardon me, sir, but could you direct me to—

ROCK *(turns and sees her).* My God, Venetia, what are you doing here?

VENETIA. I was touring the Moorish ruins and lost my way. What are you doing in that uniform?

ROCK. Exactly what you would assume.

VENETIA. There was such talk after you disappeared. No one knew where you went—such guesses, such gossip. And Bert, what about Bert?

ROCK. Beg your pardon.

VENETIA. Bert Cecil—you know whom I speak of.

ROCK. Oh yes, dear old Bertie. I heard that, like me, he lost all his money. I wonder what became of him.

VENETIA. Don't you know?

ROCK. I suppose he went to the Klondike—America—or some other place.

VENETIA. When I saw you, I had hopes of seeing him again.

ROCK. I can't quite see why you should. But what brings you to Africa?

VENETIA. Our future was in danger. The old Duke's will provided that my husband must serve with the Legion, as the family has for generations.

ROCK. And Chateauroy consented to that?

VENETIA. He had no choice. He has just been appointed Colonel of the Chasseurs.

ROCK. Of the Chasseurs? Chateauroy—our Colonel?

VENETIA. Tell me honestly, do you know where Bert Cecil is?

ROCK. Come, Venetia, your husband will be missing you. Go to this next corner and ask the guard on duty there to take you to your hotel.

*(CIGARETTE is heard singing off.)*

Quick, someone is coming. You can't be seen here in this wine shop. Go in there.

*(He pushes her behind curtain. Enter BERT.)*

BERT. What is the matter with you?

ROCK. I had a sunstroke.

BERT. Well, you're as pale as if you'd seen a ghost.

ROCK. It's nothing—I'll be all right.

*(Enter RAKE.)*

RAKE. It's a woman. *(Pulls up curtain, revealing VENETIA's skirt.)* Jack's got a woman.

BERT. Jack, why didn't you tell us?

*(All laugh. VENETIA re-enters.)*

ROCK. The jig is up. Come, Rake.

*(They exit.)*

BERT. Venetia, my God!

VENETIA. Are you afraid? Why do you turn from me?

BERT. Why have you come here?

CIG *(enters D.R.)*. The Silver Pheasant! *(Exits D.R.)*

VENETIA. I have come with my husband. He could no longer avoid serving his time with the Legion and retain his fortune. He has just been made Colonel of the Chasseurs.

*A chastened and penitent Venetia pleads with her former suitor to forgive her mistake. Venetia is now the wife of the Marquis de Chateauroy, who has been appointed Colonel of the Chasseurs in North Africa. Kathleen Murphy as Venetia, Richard Rorke as Bert Cecil.*

BERT. The Chasseurs!

VENETIA. Oh Bert, he has made my life a nightmare. No sooner were we married than he began to torture me. You knew—you knew him. Why didn't you tell me?

BERT. You knew he was a gambler and a cheat. You knew it that night when I threw the cards in his face.

VENETIA. But he convinced us all that the charge was false.

BERT. Oh, easily, no doubt.

VENETIA. Some say I only got my just desserts, but if you only knew—

BERT. Venetia—I have tried to forget you. Let me. Through these past two years, the bivouac, the campfire, and the heat of battle—your face was always before me. At first, my only wish was that an Arab's spear would put an end to my life and I might die with your name upon my lips.

VENETIA. But now fate has brought us together again.

BERT. A fate I never should have wished for. *(Goes to her, embraces her.)* Venetia, you can't draw back now.

VENETIA. When shall it be?

*(Noise outside. Enter soldiers,* RAKE, ROCKINGHAM, *girls.)*

ENTAMABOULL. Wine! We want wine! Music!

*(General movement; men pour drinks, girls bring wine to them; there is loud conversation.)*

BERT *(aside to* VENETIA*).* Tomorrow night then.

VENETIA. At the Villa Aiyussa, at ten.

BERT. I will be there.

VENETIA. Don't disappoint me. Don't make me repent.

*(Embrace and she exits.* CIGARETTE *enters.)*

CIG *(aside).* Oh, God help me.

*(*CIGARETTE *looks at* BERT. *He retires and looks off as if watching.* CIGARETTE *takes off her uniform coat, goes C. and begins dance.\* The girls join her. At the beginning of the dance,* PAULETTE *gets up and goes to chair at R. of table and stands on it.* BOUAMANA *goes D.R. to* BEAU, YUSSEF *and* TIGER CLAW. *The dance becomes more and more desperate and frantic. All clap for* CIGARETTE *as she dances. She dances to* BERT, *who each time turns away. At the last of the dance, she throws her canteen to* ENTAMABOULL, *and then falls exhausted in a faint.)*

CURTAIN

*\*Music for* CIGARETTE's *Dance on page 371.*

## SCENE TWO

SCENE: *Ace of Spades, the following morning. Discovered are* ROCKINGHAM *and* RAKE. RAKE *is at couch,* ROCKINGHAM *pacing.*

RAKE. I tell you, Cap'n, you might as well save your shoe leather. There's nothing we can do.

ROCK. There is—there has to be. Why, if Chateauroy should get wind of this—

RAKE. Well, what could he do? All three of us got our discharges and we're out of it all tomorrow.

ROCK. Yes, out of the Legion, but I'd sooner go through Zeralia again than see Bert go back to Venetia.

RAKE. Well, there's no accountin' for tastes, as they say. As for me, I wouldn't put all the titles in the Empire up against that little girl. *(Gestures* D.R. *to indicate* CIGARETTE *is inside.)*

ROCK. Nor I. Well, at any rate, it's luck we had our papers signed before Chateauroy took command. If it had been left to him, we'd all be turned down.

RAKE. And sent to Timbuktu in the bargain, I'll wager.

ROCK. I know it's not our business, but we've got to talk to him. We must get some sense into his head.

RAKE. Then you'll have to do it. I never could.

*(Enter* TIGER CLAW, ENTAMABOULL, YUSSEF, *and* BEAU BRUNO.)

ROCK. Come along— I think we'll find him at the barracks—at least we'll try. *(Exit.)*

TIGER. So, our brave vivandiere fights Bedouins and kills like a tiger, but faints for love.

ENTA. Ah, he will soon tire of her and she will be back with us where she belongs.

YUSSEF. Tell me where all of you would be if it were not for Cigarette. Many's the time she's slashed us all out of a tight spot when we would have been killed or captured.

TIGER. The Bedouins say she's a witch.

BEAU. And well she may be, the way she rides into battle and comes out without a scratch.

*(Enter* CHATEAUROY, *in Colonel's uniform. The soldiers all rise to attention.)*

CHAT. as you were. Gentlemen, I am your new commander, Colonel Chateauroy, Chasseurs D'Afrique. I am searching for a young woman, whose bravery, I understand, turned the tide of battle at Zeralia.

YUSSEF. It did, sir. Two companies sprang at her bidding from the ground and turned defeat into victory.

BEAU. And on Columbus sands, she rode into battle with a raven on her shoulder and scattered the enemy like a mist.

CHAT. Who is this woman? I was told I might find her here.

*(Enter* CIGARETTE *with wine jug.)*

YUSSEF. Here she is—Cigarette—the bravest soldier in all Africa!

CIG *(puts wine jug on table, salutes)*. Colonel?

CHAT *(to soldiers)*. I would speak with this young woman alone.

*(Soldiers exit hurriedly.)*

I am Colonel Chateauroy, newly in command of the Chasseurs D'-Afrique. I have heard of your bravery since my arrival here two days ago and have come to offer my compliments and your country's gratitude. *(Offers medal.)*

CIG. I've had enough of medals, thanks.

CHAT. And, upon meeting you, I'd like to add that you're a very pretty girl.

CIG. Ah, sir, your compliments and interest please me, but I would ask a favor.

CHAT. Anything you wish, provided it is within my power.

CIG. I want one of your corporals locked in the guardhouse overnight.

CHAT. What? Have one of my men locked in the guardhouse to please a minx? Well, this is delicious. And what will you give me if I do?

CIG. My friendship—that's all—will you do it?

CHAT. He must be a very foolish man to earn the displeasure of Cigarette. What's his name?

CIG. Corporal Victor.

CHAT. What regiment?

CIG. Chasseurs D'Afrique.

CHAT. And what has he done?

CIG. He's tired of me.

CHAT. He's an idiot. *(He moves toward her.)*

CIG *(moving back)*. He wants to throw me out the window.

CHAT. I'll catch you. *(He moves to embrace her. She slips out of reach.)*

CIG. He met the woman he loved in former years.

CHAT. They have a way of turning up.

CIG *(mockingly)*. And hoped he might die with her name on his lips.

CHAT. How romantic.

CIG. I must prevent their meeting.

CHAT. They have arranged one?

CIG. Yes—on the Blidah road tonight—at ten.

CHAT. And where is the rendezvous to be?

CIG. The Villa Aiyussa.

CHAT. The Villa Aiyussa! And who is the woman, do you know?

CIG. I call her "The Silver Pheasant." Her name is Lady Venetia.

CHAT *(aside)*. My wife! *(Aloud.)* And the man—what was his name before?

CIG. He was Bert Cecil.

CHAT. Where can I find him?

CIG. I know a tumble-down shack in the Moorish ruins. I could bring him there.

CHAT. No, it would be best to take him red-handed at the Villa Aiyussa. *(Calls out.)* Sergeant!

*(Enter* ENTAMABOULL.*)*

Meet me at the Villa Aiyussa at nine tonight.

ENTA. Yes, Colonel. *(Exits.)*

CIG. You won't hurt him? No blows—no wounds—injuries?

CHAT. Well, my girl, I thought you wanted revenge. Very well, only enough persuasion to bring him into the guardhouse.

CIG. And will you turn him loose in the morning?

CHAT. Yes, and I shall bring him back to you myself—humble and penitent. *(Exit.)*

CIG. Ha-ha-ha, Master Victor. It isn't wise to fool with Cigarette!

CURTAIN

## SCENE THREE

SCENE: *Wine Shop that evening. At rise,* RAKE *and* ROCKINGHAM *are at table playing cards.* YUSSEF *is at back of table, looking on.*

ROCK. There, that's the fourth game tonight. You're careless.

*(Enter* BERT.*)*

Bert, take his hand.

*(*RAKE *rises and goes to window.)*

BERT *(pours drink).* No—I can't—I'll be going out soon.

ROCK. Is it a girl?

BERT. Yes.

ROCK. What kind of girl?

BERT. A female girl.

ROCK. Well, if you're going to meet Venetia—

BERT. Well, what if I am?

ROCK. Just this. You ought to be kicked from here to the Sahara, and if Chateauroy doesn't do it—

BERT. I've had enough of your good advice.

ROCK. Now see here, Bert, Chateauroy is a low-down blackguard, we both know that, but Venetia married him with her eyes wide open.

BERT. Jack—he has made the poor girl's life a hell. This is her only chance to escape from it, and I'm going to give it to her.

ROCK. Well, she can go anywhere she likes and take anything she wants, so long as she doesn't take you. Bert—it's Cigarette—I won't let you break her heart.

BERT. Ah, she'll soon forget. I'm not the only one and there'll be others.

RAKE. Master Cecil, sir, ever since you took me out of jail, I've been as true to you as a blooming shadow, but if you do this thing, I'll jolly well let you go to the devil in your own way.

ROCK. Those are my sentiments.

(RAKE *comes to him. They shake hands silently.*)

Good—good.

(RAKE *retires to window. Enter* CIGARETTE.)

CIG. Ah, you're all here. Yussef, my keg.

(*Takes off wineskin and throws it to* YUSSEF, *who exits.*)

As the cards are out and the whiskey here—

ROCK. I'm very sorry, Cigarette, but I promised to pitch quoits with Tiger. (*Goes to door, looks at* BERT *who is at the table, turns to* CIGARETTE *and puts his arms around her.*) Cigarette, do you know, you're a damn fine little girl. (*He circles to door. Aside.*) I'll pitch those quoits at the Villa Aiyussa. (*Exits.*)

CIG. You won't desert me, Rake?

RAKE (*getting up and going to door*). I must, Cigarette, I have to go and plant—well—I'm going to plant a banana tree. (*Aside.*) I'll plant it at the Villa Aiyussa. (*Exits.*)

BERT. Little woman, I've a confession to make.

CIG. I know—you're going to meet the Lady Venetia at the Villa Aiyussa at ten tonight.

BERT. How did you know that?

CIG. Oh, a convenient curtain—I heard it all.

BERT. Did you tell anyone?

CIG. Would it interest anyone?

BERT. No, I don't think it would.

CIG. She still loves you and you love her; why do you deny it? (*Goes to window at back.*) It's nights like this that bring back all the memories—nights in the desert seated on a rug outside your tent—

BERT. I've told you, Cigarette—it's over for both of us.

CIG. Yes, I know how foolish I am. I keep thinking you care. You didn't even ask me of my adventures on the sands this afternoon.

BERT. What happened? Were you hurt?

CIG. Nothing hurts me—not even being jilted.

BERT. Stop it, Cigarette. You promised we'd be friends.

CIG. Do you think I could share you?

BERT. Don't talk like this. It's all over between us. (*He starts out.*)

(CIGARETTE *runs between him and door.*)

CIG. No, you shan't go yet.

BERT. Don't try to stop me.

CIG. I mean—I mean—I don't want you to go yet. You have a whole hour. You will have plenty of time, and this is the last time I will ever see you. I'll have to give you up forever.

(*She buries her face in her hands and sobs. He holds her.*)

BERT. Cigarette, you can't do this. It's idiotic.

CIG. I know—I know—all love is idiotic, but I can't forget and I can't give you up. Remember that night on the desert—we were outside your tent, the regimental band was playing at the officer's quarters, not a cloud in the sky, your arms around me, music all around us, and you told me—you told me that you loved me!

BERT. Cigarette, believe me, whatever happens, I will never be that happy again.

CIG. I mustn't believe you again—yet I love to hear you say it! Say it, oh, say it again, please!

BERT. Little girl, when I first met you *(hands on her shoulders.)*, I had lost the woman I loved. I thought I'd had all the suffering a man could stand in his life, and living it was the same as being dead. It was you who brought me back again—you who taught me it was better to go on with the fight than run amuck on an Arab bullet.

CIG. And you would leave me now? You can't—you won't leave me to go back to the old rut. Oh, I was happy enough till you came. I knew nothing of life but the dancing, the Zouaves, and the rough men who are my soldiers. *(She goes to him, pleading.)* But now they sicken me. I want to get away—to live like you want me to. I can do better, I know I can. Help me—don't leave me! *(Falls at his feet weeping.)*

BERT *(raises her up, arms around her, kisses her tears).* I won't, little one, I won't. I didn't lie to you—God help me, Cigarette, I love you.

CIG. You mean it now, don't you? Oh, I'm so happy I can't believe it! Write to the silver pheasant and tell her. Rake will take the letter and tonight we'll march down to the barracks before them all. *(She dries her eyes, straightens her hair.)* Fall in.

*(*BERT *stands at attention.)*
Forward march!

BERT *(comes down in marching order).* Halt, eyes front!
*(Both click heels and face front.)*

CIG *(salutes).* Corporal Victor.

BERT *(salutes).* Full Private Cigarette.

CIG. Friends, comrades in arms. *(Runs to him.)* Lovers forever!
*(They embrace.* CIGARETTE *starts to door, turns and runs springing into his arms, arms about him. Then she runs off and is heard singing off.)*

BERT. Sing on, little woman, sing on. I've been a fool, but I'm a fool no longer. I'll write to Venetia and tell her and then I'll be free again, free as I've only been free with Cigarette. *(Sits and starts to write.)* No, I mustn't write and I mustn't send Rake. I'll go myself.
*(Enter* YUSSEF, *who hangs barrel on nail and stands at door.)*
Yes, I'll go to the Villa Aiyussa. *(Takes hat and exits.)*

YUSSEF. The Villa Aiyussa. *(Exits.)*
*(Enter* CIGARETTE.*)*

CIG. Now to pluck the feathers from The Silver Pheasant, and we'll do it too, won't we, Victor? *(Looks around and, not seeing him, exclaims.)* Where is he? Oh—why should he frighten me like this?

*(Runs to door and looks out, then to window and back.)* Could he have gone? No, I won't believe it. Victor—Victor! *(Calls out door.)*

*(Enter* YUSSEF.*)*

Where is Corporal Victor, Yussef? Where is he?

YUSSEF. Oh, mistress, he took his hat and went—

CIG. Where—where did he go? *(Goes to* YUSSEF *and catches him by the throat as though to choke the answer out of him.)* Answer me—where did he go?

YUSSEF. I heard him say—

CIG. What?

YUSSEF. I will go—

CIG. Where?

YUSSEF. Oh, mistress, he said to the Villa Aiyussa. *(She releases him.)*

CIG. To the Villa Aiyussa!

*(Exit* YUSSEF.*)*

To her—to The Silver Pheasant—after all he said to me. It was all a lie, a lie, a lie. Oh, he shall have company, more company than he ever expected. Liar! Liar! Liar! *(Exit, sobbing hysterically.)*

**CURTAIN**

# ACT THREE

## SCENE ONE

SCENE: *The Villa Aiyussa, in the garden of the desert villa. Lights down. Moon effect on water at back. Curtained doors under portico. U.R. Enter* CHATEAUROY, *followed by* ENTAMABOULL. CHATEAUROY *comes downstage, goes C. and looks off.*

CHAT. Stand by orders.

ENTA. Yes, my Colonel. *(Salutes.)*

CHAT *(looks at curtain door, peeps in, but does not disturb curtain more than is absolutely necessary).* Place a sentry at the door of the courtyard. Let anyone in, but challenge all who go out. Sergeant, you have nothing to do with this man's innocence or guilt.

ENTA. No, my Colonel. *(Salutes.)*

CHAT. I'll see to your advancement.

ENTA. Thanks, my Colonel. *(Salutes.)*

CHAT. Now, follow me.

*(He exits R.* ENTAMABOULL *follows. After a pause,* RAKE *peeps on, then disappears. The same business is repeated, and then he enters, looks around, and motions to someone outside. He stands at attention, while* ROCKINGHAM *enters slowly.* RAKE *salutes.* ROCKINGHAM *nods his head indicating the door which is curtained.* RAKE *salutes and goes to curtain, taps on door, returns C.* ROCKINGHAM *retires up a little. Enter* VENETIA *from curtained door. She is dressed in a full-length negligee, her hair loose over her shoulders, tied with a ribbon.)*

VENETIA. Bert—I—I—Rockingham!

ROCK. Yes—and as there's little time to lose, and I've no aspirations to join the heavenly choir, I'll get to the point. Venetia, your conduct won't wash.

VENETIA. And by what right do you judge my conduct?

ROCK. By my friendship for Bert and my fondness for cards. We had a little whist party, which you interrupted.

RAKE. And the jolliest little whist party, if you please, my lady.

ROCK. Scoot, Rake, I think I can handle this better alone.

RAKE. Yes, sir. *(Salutes and exits.)*

ROCK. A whist party, where the cordiality of the players compensated for the smallness of the stakes.

VENETIA. What is that to me?

ROCK. Just this. I don't propose to have it broken up. Bert has other interests now, and I'm going to prevent his running away with you, if I'm compelled to blow the top of his head off in the process.

VENETIA. How did you know?

ROCK. Never mind. Forewarned, forearmed. *(Exits, very slowly.)*

VENETIA. Other ties, other interests, he said. What can he mean? What if he is deceiving me? I can't believe it. I mustn't believe it. I'll force him to tell me the truth.

*(Enter* BERT. VENETIA *is downstage, she hears him, but does not turn.)*

BERT *(goes to her, extending hands).* Venetia—*(She remains motionless.)* have I offended you?

VENETIA. No, but I want to be perfectly frank with you. When we met in the wine shop, I was willing to follow you anywhere.

BERT. Well?

VENETIA. After coming here, I began to count the cost. I thought of the world's opinion, and I find I lack the courage to brave it.

BERT. Venetia, you have lifted a world of care from my conscience.

VENETIA. How is that?

BERT. Oh, I know I'd be a coward to carry out the plans we laid in the wine shop.

VENETIA. Have you relapsed into the gallantry of other days? Have you found another Guenevere or an Algerian Zu-Zu?

BERT. Not that, I swear, but for tonight enough that our senses are restored to us. Venetia, our love has never brought anything but misery to our lives. I wish—oh, God, how I wish—

VENETIA. Wish nothing.

BERT. Yes, I wish one thing. I wish that this hell, which is only a half step from heaven, may never come to us again. *(Extends hand.)* Goodbye.

*(She remains motionless.* BERT *exits hurriedly.)*

VENETIA. It's true—it's true, but who's the woman?

*(Enter* CIGARETTE *from over the balustrade.)*

Who's this?

CIG. Cigarette. *(Has pistol in belt; her hand is on it.)*

VENETIA. Come nearer, have no fear.

CIG. Fear? What fear have I of you, a bird of paradise that does nothing but spread its wings in the sun.

VENETIA. Why have you come here?

CIG. For two reasons: One is because I want to look at your clothes. *(She does so.)* They aren't like anything I've seen before. And the other is because I want to hurt you. *(Goes to her, puts up hands as if about to attack by taking her by the throat.)* If only I knew how. *(Retires back a step.)* All right, now that I've seen you—and although I hate you—I can't help saying that you are beautiful—very beautiful. I don't wonder men fall in love with you.

VENETIA *(taking a few steps forward).* What have I done?

CIG. You have stolen my Corporal.

VENETIA. Corporal?

CIG. Corporal Victor of the Chasseurs. *(She stands very straight.)*

VENETIA. The name is familiar.

CIG. Aye, you know him, you cannot deny it—Bert. *(She turns to* VENETIA.)

VENETIA *(starts).* Cecil.

CIG. Yes, until you slipped into the wine shop and saw him, he never looked at any girl but me—me—do you hear?

VENETIA. Then we are rivals?

CIG. Yes—yes.

VENETIA. I, daughter of the Lyonnesses of England.

CIG. And I—a soldier of France. *(Salutes.)*

VENETIA. Before so formidable a rival I must retire, but first let me tell you, your Corporal was here and went away.

CIG. Where do you meet next time?

VENETIA. Nowhere. We quarreled; is that not enough?

CIG. What did you quarrel about?

VENETIA. He had other ties.

CIG. Meaning me.

VENETIA. And as I had ties of my own—

CIG. What ties? *(Half turns to VENETIA.)*

VENETIA. Only a husband.

CIG. Husband? Who is he?

VENETIA. The Marquis of Chateauroy, Colonel of the Chasseurs— Good night. *(Exits into curtained room.)*

CIG. Chateauroy, Chateauroy—what have I done? *(Thoroughly frightened.)* Victor—he must be warned in time.

(BERT *enters R.* CIGARETTE *sees him, but he does not see her.)*

BERT. Strange. The sentry at the door of the courtyard asked me for the word, but I could not give it to him. *(Turns and sees* CIGARETTE.*)* Cigarette, you here?

CIG. Yes, but what—what is the matter?

BERT. It looks devilishly like a trap.

CIG. But who would betray you?

BERT. Why no one, but—*(Notices that* CIGARETTE *looks confused. He pushes her roughly.)* You? This is your loyalty—your love—you who would fight like a lion? You are a traitoress.

CIG. Victor, for God's sake, not that—not that. I did not know. I did not know that he was her husband. So help me, I did not know.

BERT *(embracing her).* There, there, it is all right.

CIG. And you forgive me?

BERT. There is nothing to forgive.

CIG. But the Black Hawk will accuse you.

BERT. He'll do that soon enough.

(A *shot is heard offstage.* ROCKINGHAM *and* RAKE *run on.* VENETIA *enters from curtained door.)*

CIG. Go in there, quick. *(Pointing to curtained door.)*

BERT. No, I'm not built that way.

CIG. Don't you see—remorse will kill me. Go, go—for God's sake— for my sake!

(*Enter* CHATEAUROY. BERT *goes in curtained door.)*

CHAT. What's this?

ROCK. Probably you don't remember me: Lord Rockingham, calling on the Lady Venetia.

CHAT. I don't remember you. *(To* VENETIA.*)* May I ask why you permit this rabble in my house?

VENETIA. There is no rabble.

CHAT. Do you wish me to tell you what I have to say?

RAKE *(starts to go)*. A family difference.

VENETIA. Rockingham.

CHAT *(to* VENETIA*)*. Where is your lover?

VENETIA. I need not reply to an insult.

CHAT. Where have you hidden him?

VENETIA. I have nothing to say.

CHAT. Then I must appeal to the informer. *(Pointing to* CIGARETTE*.)*

CIG *(coming down)*. That's all right. *(Salutes.)* Sir, I told you to lock Victor in the guardhouse over night. That's Cecil—because I thought he was in love with the silver pheasant—that's your wife. But I was wrong. He told me so on the way to the barracks, and he is in the barracks now.

CHAT *(to* VENETIA*)*. Do you confirm this story?

VENETIA. I do.

CHAT. And you, who I take is this fellow's friend?

RAKE *(salutes)*. The story is true.

ROCK. It is, sir.

CHAT. I regret to lay aside such a notable body of evidence, but I believe the girl is lying and it is my intention to have her flogged—flogged until she confesses the hiding place of her lover.

CIG. I'll see you in hell—

CHAT. Enough! *(Goes up.)* Guard!

*(Enter* ENTAMABOULL, *with whip.)*

Strip the girl!

ROCK. Chateauroy!

CHAT. Silence!

*(*ENTAMABOULL *comes to* CIGARETTE *and takes off her jacket.)*

Whip her until she confesses the trick she played on me, and I will send her paramour to the barracks. I'll have you treated for what you are, the lowest of camp followers!

*(*BERT *comes from behind the curtain in time to hear the last speech. He goes to* CHATEAUROY *and strikes him in the face, knocking him down.)*

BERT. Coward!

CHAT *(rising)*. I'll have your life for this—I'll have you court-martialed!

BERT. Too late, Chateauroy. Our discharge took effect at noon today! Now it's man to man.

CHAT. Then man to man let it be! *(To* VENETIA.*)* To your room, Venetia! *(She leaves.)*

BERT. Come, Cigarette.

*(He picks her up in his arms and they exit.)*

**BLACKOUT**

## SCENE TWO

SCENE: *The Ace of Spades Wine Shop the next morning.* RAKE *is alone onstage.*

RAKE. We've been together more than forty years and it don't seem a day too much. Well, I suppose they'll get married, settle down and be happy, God bless 'em.

(*Enter* ROCKINGHAM.)

ROCK. Ah, good morning, Rake.

RAKE. Good morning, where is Master Cecil?

ROCK. Hasn't he been here yet?

RAKE. No.

ROCK. Have you heard anything of the Lady Venetia?

RAKE. Yes, he sent her packing. She sailed on the Crocodile today at eight.

ROCK. Good riddance.

(*Enter* BERT.)

Ah, good morning, Bert, where have you been?

BERT. To the adjutants, getting our discharge papers. We are now three free men.

ROCK. What is the next move?

BERT. Well, the whole world is before us.

ROCK. And the little girl?

BERT. Well—I hadn't thought of that.

RAKE. Well, after you and the little girl have settled down—

BERT. I'm not sure about the settling down part.

ROCK. You wouldn't be such a scoundrel.

BERT. I want to do the right thing, but unfortunately—

ROCK. As sure as you are alive—

BERT. That's just it. In half an hour, I may cease to adorn this celestial sphere.

RAKE. What's that?

BERT. When my discharge was in my pocket, I went to the club. There was Chateauroy and when he saw me, he said, "Who let that fellow in? This club is for officers, not rankers." "Chateauroy," I said, "I'm no longer Corporal Victor La Farge of the Chasseurs D'Afrique, I am Bert Cecil, your cousin, and I have to tell you that you are a liar, a forger, and a thief," and with that, I chucked a brandy in his face.

RAKE. Bully for you, sir, bully for you.

BERT. Two officers of the Zouaves at once advanced to be my seconds. That shows you how much they hate him. The time and the place is to be named at ten.

ROCK. Chateauroy is the best shot in the army.

BERT. Can't help that.

RAKE. Never missed his mark, sir.

BERT. More's the pity.

RAKE (*looking off*). Ah, here she comes.

(CIGARETTE *enters.*)

CIG. My three comrades! Jack! (*Embraces* ROCKINGHAM *then goes to* RAKE *and embraces him.*) Rake! (*After this, she turns and extends hand to* BERT. *He goes to her and they embrace.*)

ROCK (*goes to door and seeing that* RAKE *is still standing looking at* CIGARETTE, *he calls to him softly.*) Rake.

> (RAKE *does not hear him.* ROCKINGHAM *goes to* RAKE *and touches him on the shoulder.* RAKE *starts and exits.* ROCKINGHAM *follows him.*)

CIG. How high does the goose hang now?

BERT. Well, at least I'm a free man once more.

CIG. Yes, free, and the "Silver Pheasant" has gone out of our lives forever. When you promised me, why didn't you keep your word?

BERT. I did. I went to her and told her everything.

CIG. Never mind. It's good to have you home again. Soon you will be quarreling with Jack in the same old way, and Rake will be trying to keep peace between you.

BERT. I'm afraid we won't quarrel here any more.

CIG. Why?

BERT. Jack, Rake and I have our walking papers. Look, little woman, I know what you've done for me, but suppose I were to drop out of sight—vanish?

CIG. I know—I know—the silver pheasant has gone, but she has taken your heart with her.

BERT. No—no.

CIG. Ah, you can't forgive me for betraying you—I can't forgive myself.

(*Enter* RAKE, *hurriedly.*)

RAKE. Mr. Cecil, sir, Jack is bringing in a half-blind girl picked up on the desert who says she is looking for you.

BERT. Who is she?

RAKE. I think that—

> (RENEE *enters.* ROCKINGHAM *helps her.*)

BERT. Renee Baroni!

RENEE. I took passage to Algiers. There was a storm—they put me off at Samula—

BERT. Yes—yes—

RENEE (*growing weaker and confused*). I set out alone—wandered for days—lost in whirling sand—but now I've found you—I've come to tell you—

BERT. Yes, to tell me?

RENEE. That it was I who cheated you out of your fortune—forged your uncle's will.

BERT. Impossible—you would never—

RENEE. Baroni forced me. But now he's dead and can never torture me again!

ROCK. Poor girl!

RENEE. The proof is here. (*Reaches inside cloak and brings out papers.*)

ROCK (*looking at papers*). The original will!

RAKE. Mr. Cecil, you will once more be Lord of Chateauroy Manor. Congratulations!

ROCK. Congratulations!

CIG *(aside).* Lord of Chateauroy Manor?

BERT. But why, Renee? Why would you come so far to find me?

RENEE. Because you are my—my—*(Faints on the end of the line.)*

BERT. Take her to the hotel. *(Picks her up and gives her to* ROCKINGHAM *who exits with her.)* When she is well, we'll take her back to Chateauroy Manor—

CIG. Chateauroy Manor?

RAKE *(quietly, to* BERT*).* The arrangements for the duel have been settled. Ten o'clock at the Moorish ruins. Good Luck, Mr. Cecil. *(Exits.)*

CIG. You will go back to Chateauroy Manor—and I? What would the ladies there think of me? I, who smoke, and sit on troopers' knees?

BERT. Cigarette, I'm called away, but in less than half an hour, I will return, and in the presence of everyone in that canteen, I will ask you to do me the honour of becoming my wife. *(Extends hand.)*

CIG. It's because you pity me. Don't speak—if it is not so, let me think you mean it just for a moment, Victor—Victor. *(Embrace.)*

RAKE *(enters).* All is ready, sir.

BERT. In a moment, Rake.

CIG. Goodbye—in half an hour.

BERT. Yes, even less. Goodbye.

*(He kisses her and goes to door.* RAKE *hands him a box.)*
Rake, keep her company until I return. *(Shakes hands with* RAKE *and exits.)*

RAKE. Ah, here we are, Cigarette. Here are some sandwiches we didn't finish. Come, let's have some lunch. *(Goes to shelf; takes down plate with bread and knife; goes to table and begins cutting it.)*

CIG. Rake, I feel as if I were going to cry.

RAKE. Cry? Pooh, pooh, I know a cure for that. There's a music hall song I used to sing. It goes—

*(*SONG*: "Underneath the Arches"\*)*

Underneath the arches, I dream my dreams away.
Underneath the arches, on cobblestones I lay.
Every night you'll find me, tired out and worn,
Happy when the daylight comes creeping, heralding the dawn.
Sleeping when it's raining, and sleeping when it's fine,
I hear the trains, rattling by above.
Pavement is my pillow, no matter where I stray,
Underneath the arches, I dream my dreams away.

*\*Music on page 372.*

CIG. Rake, did you notice anything strange about Mr. Victor when he went away? Come to think of it, he kissed me as if he were going away forever.

RAKE. Nonsense! Now there's a ballad runs a trifle livelier. *(Sings.)* That's called "Lily of Laguna". *(He dances U.C.)*

(SONG: *"Lily of Laguna"**)

She's my lady love,
She is my girl, my baby love,
She's the girl for sittin' down to drink,
She's the only girl Laguna knows

I know she likes me,
I know she likes me, because she said so,
She is my Lily of Laguna,
She is my Lily and my own.

CIG. Rake, you know where he has gone to?

RAKE. I—I—little girl—*(Backing away, more and more nervous; he takes out handkerchief.)*

CIG *(pressing him)*. Rake—you are nervous.

RAKE. I—I—I—

CIG. Yes, you are as nervous as I am.

RAKE *(aside)*. They should have met by this time.

CIG. Rake, there is something I have to tell you. I hardly dare tell. Victor promised to return in half an hour, to ask me to be his wife. His wife. *(Pause.)* Ah, you see the time is flying by. This absence isn't natural. *(She looks out.* RAKE *is by door.)* Rake—is that clock right?

RAKE. I think it is fast, Cigarette.

CIG *(looks around and notices that box is gone)*. His pistols are gone. He is fighting a duel!

RAKE. If you would know the truth, he had to clear the score.

CIG. With the Black Hawk whose aim means death! *(Starts to go.)*

RAKE *(trying to stop her)*. You mustn't go, Cigarette, you mustn't go!

CIG *(pushing him aside)*. Don't stop me—don't stop me! *(She exits and is heard calling in distance.)* Victor—Victor!

RAKE. I thought I liked the master pretty well, but before a love like that!

*(Two shots heard, a short pause between them.)*

It's over. *(Goes to window, looks out.)* There's a man running down the street. Can it be Cecil? *(Goes to door, opens it.)*

(ROCKINGHAM *runs in all out of breath.)*

ROCK. It's over, Rake.

RAKE. Was it Mr. Cecil?

ROCK. No.

*Music on page 373.

RAKE. The Black Hawk, then?

ROCK (*quietly*). No.

RAKE. Then who? (*Pause.*) My God—not—not?

ROCK (*nods head*). Yes. They drew lots. Cecil won and fired first. Chateauroy was fatally winged, but the devil's luck was with him as he pressed the trigger. (*Slowly turns to face* RAKE.) The little girl threw herself on Bert and received the bullet in her heart.

> (*Enter* TIGER CLAW, BEAU BRUNO, ENTAMABOULL *and* YUSSEF *who arrange chairs for bed.* YUSSEF *gets D.R. chair and puts it in front of couch.* BERT *enters from U.R. carrying* CIGARETTE. *He puts her on couch as others close in.* ROCKINGHAM *is at foot of couch on one knee.* RAKE *stands behind* BERT, *the Arab soldiers are behind* RAKE *in a line.* BEAU *is at* CIGARETTE'*s head. The Arabs stand to attention.*)

CIGARETTE (*rising on elbow*). Victor—Victor!

> (*He bends over her. She puts arm around him. He bows head.*)

Don't cry for me. It is better as it is. But I always loved you—ah, my soldiers, my soldiers.

> (ROCKINGHAM *and* RAKE *kneel in front of couch. Arabs do the same at back.*)

Think of me when I'm gone. Ah, Ma Belle, my flag!

> (RAKE *gets flag, hands it to* ROCKINGHAM, *who hands it to* CIGA-RETTE. ROCKINGHAM *holds staff.* CIGARETTE *wraps flag around her neck.*)

Let me have this when I am gone. (*Holds up one end of flag.*) Tell them in France I died for the flag. (*Becoming unconscious of her surroundings, as in a dream.*) The bugle is sounding for parade.

> (BERT *comes in front of couch.*)

I'll answer. Cigarette—child of the Army—soldier of France! (*Falls back dead.*)

> ("*La Marseillaise*" *plays softly.*)

BERT. Cigarette! (*Falls on knees and bows head, holding her hand.*)

> (*Arabs and* RAKE *salute.*)

**CURTAIN**

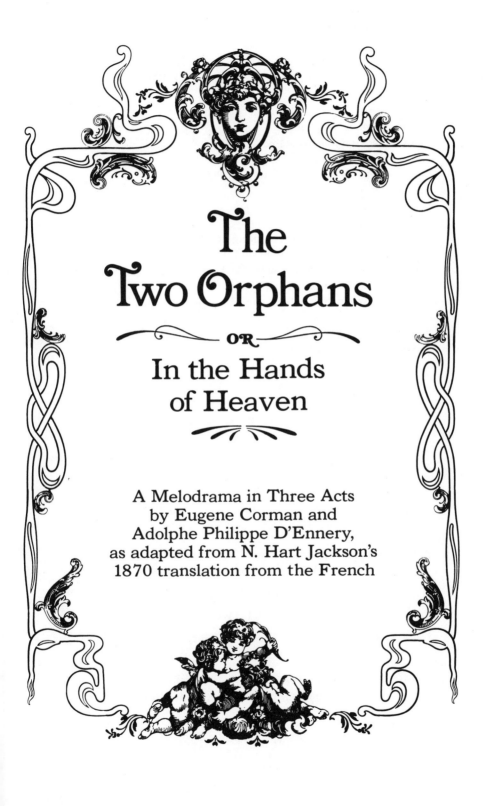

# The
# Two Orphans

## OR

## In the Hands
## of Heaven

A Melodrama in Three Acts
by Eugene Corman and
Adolphe Philippe D'Ennery,
as adapted from N. Hart Jackson's
1870 translation from the French

# CAST OF CHARACTERS

ANTOINE, in the service of the Marquis de Menton
PICARD, valet to De Vaudrey
JACQUES FROCHARD, from a line of outlaws
PIERRE FROCHARD, his brother
LA FROCHARD, mother of Jacques and Pierre
LOUISE, a blind orphan
HENRIETTE, also an orphan
JEANETTE, an outcast
BARON MAURICE DE VAUDREY, a young nobleman
COUNT EDMUND LEVANT, Minister of Police
COUNTESS DIANE LEVANT, his wife, her heart carries a guilty secret
DOCTOR, of the hospital and prison
SISTER GENEVIEVE, Sister Superior of the hospital
CLERK
POLICEMAN
MARIE MORAND, prisoner
JEANNE RAYMOND, prisoner

# SYNOPSIS OF SCENES

Time: September 1865                            Place: Paris

### ACT ONE

**Scene One:**   An open square near the Pont Neuf.
"You have fallen into good hands!"

**Scene Two:**   Apartment of Baron De Vaudrey.
"Miserable scoundrel—give me room!"

### ACT TWO

**Scene One:**   Office of the Minister of Police.
"I defend your honor against yourself."

**Scene Two:**   In front of the Church of St. Sulpice.
"Kill me, kill me if you like, but I love her."

**Scene Three:** Henriette's room.
"Take this girl to prison."

## ACT THREE

**Scene One:**  The prison courtyard.
"Punishment may purify a guilty soul."

**Scene Two:**  The hut of La Frochard.
"The rest is in the hands of heaven."

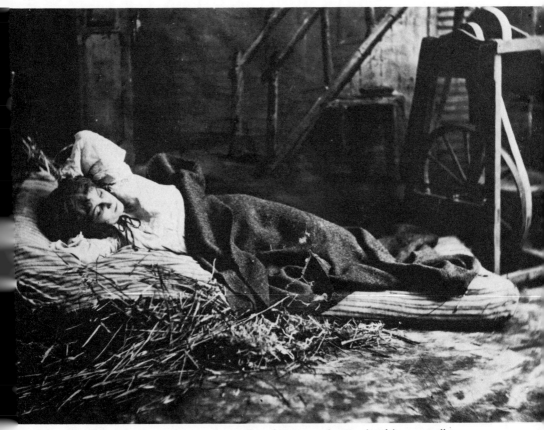

*Kate Claxton, shown here on her pallet of straw at the Frochards', eventually bought the rights to* The Two Orphans *and toured with it for several years. Legend has it that she wore a small bag of ice suspended down her bosom for the snow scene, so that she might shiver and weep more realistically.*

# PROGRAMME

# UNION SQUARE THEATRE.

VOL. VI.     NEW YORK, WEDNESDAY, FEBRUARY 24, 1875.     No. 135.

Proprietor,- - - - - **Mr. Sheridan Shook**

Manager,- - - - - **Mr. A. M. Palmer**

This and every evening this week, with Saturday Matinee at 1.30 P.M., the Grand Romantic Drama in Four Acts and Seven Tableaux, by ADOLPHE D'ENNERY (author of "Don Cæsar de Bazan," &c., &c.) and EUGENE CORMON, adapted expressly for this Theatre by HART JACKSON, Esq., entitled

## THE TWO ORPHANS,

with the following cast:

| | |
|---|---|
| CHEVALIER MAURICE DE VAUDREY, | MR. CHARLES R. THORNE, Jr. |
| COUNT DE LINIERES, Minister of Police, | MR. JOHN PARSELLE |
| PICARD, Valet to the Chevalier, | MR. STUART ROBSON |
| JACQUES FROCHARD, an Outlaw, | MR. McKEE RANKIN |
| PIERRE FROCHARD, the cripple, his brother, | MR. F. F. MACKAY |
| MARQUIS DE PRESLES, | MR. W. J. COGSWELL |
| LAFLEUR, in the service of the Marquis de Presles, | MR. H. W. MONTGOMERY |
| DOCTOR of the Hospitals St. Louis and La Salpêtrière, | MR. THOS. E. MORRIS |
| MARTIN, Citizen of Paris, | MR. LYSANDER THOMPSON |
| OFFICER OF THE GUARD, | MR. J. W. MATHEWS |
| CHIEF CLERK, in the Ministry of Police, | MR. W. H. WILDER |
| DE MAILLY, | MR. BOLTON |
| D'ESTRÉES, | MR. RAYNOR |
| ANTOINE, | MR. W. J. QUIGLEY |
| FOOTMAN, | MR. C. M. COLLINS |
| COUNTESS DIANE DE LINIERES, | MISS FANNY MORANT |
| LOUISE, } The Two Orphans | MISS KATE CLAXTON |
| HENRIETTE, } | MISS KITTY BLANCHARD |
| MARIANNE, an Outcast, | MISS MAUDE GRANGER |
| LA FROCHARD, Mother of | MISS MARIE WILKINS |
| SISTER GENEVIÈVE, | MISS IDA VERNON |
| JULIE, | MISS ROBERTA NORWOOD |
| FLORETTE, | MISS KATE HOLLAND |
| CORA, | MISS CORA CASSIDAY |
| SISTER THÉRÈSE, | MISS HATTIE THORPE |

Soldiers, Guards, Ladies and Gentlemen, Prisoners, Nuns, &c., &c.

### SYNOPSIS OF SCENERY.

ACT I.—TABLEAU I.   The Place Pont Neuf.
      TABLEAU II.   Illuminated Garden and Terrace at Bel-Air, near Paris.

ACT II.—TABLEAU I.   Private office in the Hotel of the Minister of Police.
      TABLEAU II.   The Place St. Sulpice.

ACT III.—TABLEAU I.   Henriette's Chamber.

ACT IV.—TABLEAU I.   Boat House on the Bank of the River Seine.

The Music incidental to the piece composed and arranged by MR. H. TISSINGTON.

During the evening the Orchestra will perform the following selections :

| | |
|---|---|
| OVERTURE—FRANZ SCHUBERT, | SUPPÉ |
| WALZER (New)—THEORIEN, | STRAUSS |
| POLKA (first time)—IL STACCATO, | BONNISSEAU |
| (Solo for the Cornet.) | |
| MEDITATION (first time)—FADED FLOWERS, | LANGE |
| ROMANZA—MAGIC BELLS, | JUNGENAN |
| GALOP—MADISON AVENUE, | PENELOPE |
| FANTASIE—SHINING LIGHTS, | H. TISSINGTON |
| (Introducing the Popular Song, Silver Threads among the Gold. Solo for the Xylo Calme Piano.) | |

| | |
|---|---|
| Treasurer | - Mr. E. H. GOUGE |
| Stage Manager | - Mr. J. W. THORPE |

| | |
|---|---|
| The Scenes all designed and painted by | - MR. RICHARD MARSTON |
| Music composed and arranged by | - MR. H. TISSINGTON |
| Properties by | - MR. W. HENRY |
| Gas and Lights by | - MR. CHARLES MURRAY |
| The whole production under the stage direction of | - MR. JOHN PARSELLE |

The costumes worn in this play, both by the Ladies and Gentlemen were made and designed by Mr. T. W. LANOUETTE, 830 Broadway.

SATURDAY, Feb. 27, 1.30 P.M., TENTH MATINEE OF THE TWO ORPHANS.

The Elegant Rustic Furniture used in this Play is from the Establishment of Messrs. Thonet Bros., Vienna, and 808 Broadway.

OPERA GLASSES TO HIRE IN THE LOBBY.

This Theatre will be perfumed every Friday Evening with THE CROWN PERFUMES, dispensed through OUTWATER'S EUREKA VAPORIZERS, from ATWOOD'S PHARMACY, 846 Broadway, adjoining Wallack's Theatre.

PIANOS USED IN THIS THEATRE ARE FROM THE WAREROOMS OF ALBERT WEBER.

The Church Organ used is from the Warerooms of Mason & Hamlin.

# About the Play

*The Two Orphans* was once praised by New York theatre impresario Daniel Frohman as being "the perfect play." It is one of the best written, most played and most durable plays of the 19th Century. Authored by Eugene Corman and Adolphe Philippe d'Ennery, it opened at the Porte St. Martin of Paris in January of 1874. From there it went to London stages and later was adapted by N. Hart Jackson for presentation at A.M. Palmer's Union Square Theatre in New York. There, with Kate Claxton in the role of Louise, it had 180 performances in its initial run. The play proved so successful that Miss Claxton took it on tour throughout the United States for approximately four years. She eventually bought the rights and made it her personal vehicle.

A particularly successful engagement featured Alice Dunning Lingard and her sister-in-law, Dickie Lingard, as the sisters at the California Theatre in San Francisco, where it netted $11,000 in seven performances, a record for that theatre.

*Alice Dunning Lingard, with her sister-in-law, Dickie Lingard, brought* The Two Orphans *to San Francisco in 1875. Dickie was Henriette, Alice was Louise.*

James O'Neill, the famous Irish actor, made his New York acting debut playing Pierre. An important New York revival in 1926 starred Fay Bainter, Henrietta Crosman, Robert Loraine and Wilton Lackaye. In 1922, D.W. Griffith used the play for his memorable silent movie, *Orphans of the Storm*, starring Lillian and Dorothy Gish. (See illustration on page 15.)

*Grace George and Margaret Illington played the sisters in a star-studded revival in New York in 1904. James O'Neill was also in the cast, as well as Clara Morris, one of Augustin Daly's famous stars, making her farewell stage appearance in this production.*

# ACT ONE

## SCENE ONE

SCENE: *Open square in a quiet section of Paris.* ANTOINE *is discovered seated at table with drink. He is middle-aged, a servant to the Marquis de Menton, crafty and obsequious. He is well-dressed, trying to look like an ordinary businessman. He glances nervously at his watch and looks off.*

ANTOINE. I might have known better than to depend on that popinjay Picard to arrive on time! If he's not after his masters' wallets, it's his wenches, and between the two it's a marvel he ever keeps an appointment. Ah, but I had little choice at that—he's the one valet in Paris who's been gentleman to the new Prefect of Police and knows the secrets of every nobleman at court. There's no one else discreet enough to assist me in this affair.

*(Enter* PICARD, *hastily. He is a young man, charming, intelligent and witty. He is dressed as a valet, and he removes his hat and bows with elegance.)*

PICARD. Auguste Picard! Valet-de-chambre to the Baron De Vaudrey, present and at your service, sir!

ANTOINE. And about time! Did you receive my message?

PICARD. I did, but it wasn't simple to get away. I have such an odd new master. At this hour, you'd think he'd be playing piquet at the club or dawdling with some young damsel—ahhhh! He takes his evening pleasures as any young nobleman ought to do, but he's up at dawn and he works, he actually works! He sits down and he reads and he writes, just as though he were some lawyer's clerk. He thinks peasants and common people should have rights just as he. Sometimes he talks to me and says, "Picard, the day is fast approaching when there will be no titles and privileges for the nobility of France." Now, what do you say to that?

ANTOINE. Strange! Strange talk indeed!

PICARD. That's what I tell him, but come, you said in your note you wanted my help.

ANTOINE. I do! Your help to serve a nobleman whose tastes are more akin to yours, I'll wager. You see, the Marquis—

PICARD. Ah, yes. I have heard rumors that a certain house of pleasure lies at the edge of the city—

ANTOINE *(looking around).* Hush, we must be discreet! The Marquis de Menton wishes Chateau du Bel Air to have only the reputation of serving the rather special needs of his friends at court—

PICARD. Most understandable! Admirable as well! The divertissements in the city are becoming more and more distasteful to young noblemen of taste.

ANTOINE. Exactly, and the new minister of police less and less understanding, so I've been told. So, the good Marquis is prepared to pay well to provide only the best for his guests. His salon boasts the fairest girls in France.

PICARD. Indeed! I understand.

ANTOINE. Modestly, Picard, I will admit to you, I Antoine, have occasionally assisted the Marquis. That is, previously, I have made some arrangements, and now there is another in prospect.

PICARD. A very special one, I suppose. And is the price good?

ANTOINE. You will be well paid for the little work you will do. Listen to me and don't interrupt. Time is growing short. The Marquis returned today from a visit to the country. On the road, his carriage passed a coach, in which he discovered a young treasure, a Normandy girl.

PICARD. Ah, one of those Normandy beauties! With caps six feet high, rosy cheeks and wooden shoes!

ANTOINE. You're at it again—remember she's for noblemen and not for you. Now listen: he made her acquaintance when the passengers alighted for refreshment. He discovered she was coming to Paris in company with her sister, where they have no relations, but have been recommended to the care of an old fellow whom they expect to meet on this spot.

PICARD. And what am I to do?

ANTOINE. Get the old fellow out of sight. Take him to a tavern and get him drunk. Tell him the coach has been delayed for two hours by an accident. When he is drunk enough, turn him over to the tavern keeper to be put to bed, and come back and help me. (Hands him money.) Here, that's enough for brandy and the barkeep, too.

PICARD. True. He may want bribing if he's to keep our friend out of sight. Now, when does the coach arrive?

ANTOINE (looking at watch). At six o'clock. (Points off.) There's the old fellow now. I'll wait for the coach inside and trust him to you. Go quickly. (Exits into cafe.)

PICARD. (SONG: "Gentleman's Gentleman"*)

> I'd rather be a gentleman's gentleman than a gentleman
>     on my own.
> I wouldn't want a title or a throne;
> Any time I'm feeling frivolous
> And amorous, too,
> I know lots of courtly ladies who
> Like my parlez vous;
> I couldn't count the no-account counts whose
>     countesses count on me instead,

*Music on pages 374–375.

I'm very careful not to lose my head;
And though they don't invite me over to dine,
I've got the key to the cellar where they store the wine,
I'm a gentleman's gentleman all the time.

I wouldn't care to be a marquis 'cause my life's a lark
    as it is,
What do I care about the social whirl?
If the duke can't do the duties that
The duchess requires,
I'm the guy the duchess calls to come
Over and light the fires,
I never mind when measuring suits or polishing boots
    or mending hose,
Where do you think I got this suit of clothes?
And if an English lord and lady pay a visit to Paree,
I can take the lady while the lord is taking tea,
I'd rather be
A gentleman's gentleman
Any time.

(PICARD *exits. Enter* LA FROCHARD *at rear. She is a woman in her early forties, street tough, but pretty. Her shabby dress is carefully planned to evoke sympathy. She goes to members of the audience and begs.*)

FRO. My good man, charity, if you please, for an old woman.

(FROCHARD *moves on down, muttering.*)

Mongrels! Pigs! Dogs! (*She assumes a pious whine, accosts someone else.*) Charity—charity for a helpless old woman with seven children at home!

(LA FROCHARD *continues on up and onto stage, muttering curses under her breath. At the same time,* PIERRE *enters at back with scissors grinding wheel. He is* LA FROCHARD's *younger son, a slight hunchback, who walks with a limp from an injury suffered as a child. His clothing is worn and shabby, but clean and neat. He crosses, puts down wheel.*)

PIERRE (*coming front*). Knives to mend—scissors to grind! (*Sees* LA FROCHARD.) Why, mother, is that you?

FRO. Yes, it's me. You lazy good-for-nothing!

PIERRE. Lazy? Why, mother, I do all the work I can!

FRO. Work? You call that work? Bah! Why did Heaven bless you with such an ugly face—such a beautiful deformity? Why, to earn your living by, you puny thing—and you work, when all you need to do is to limp, hold out your hand, and make your fortune with your ugliness.

PIERRE. Mother, I cannot beg. It is not possible.

FRO. Eh? Not possible, why not?

PIERRE. Mother, when I was an infant you carried me through the streets and taught me begging prayers I did not understand. They put money into your pocket and I knew no shame. But now it is different. You drove me out and bade me come here to beg. But when I knelt and held out my hand to ask alms, shame choked me, and I was overcome by anger at my own humiliation. No mother, I cannot beg—I cannot!

FRO. Undutiful son, you would rather leave your poor brother and me to starve.

PIERRE. My brother need not starve; he has health and strength and you support him in idleness.

FRO. Why should my beautiful Jacques work? My handsome boy, the very image of his poor dead father, that those scoundrels of the law robbed me of.

PIERRE. Our father suffered death for a murder of which they found him guilty.

FRO. And can I look to you to avenge him? No, no, my handsome Jacques will do that. He's no milksop, nothing frightens him!

PIERRE. No, not even the sight of blood.

FRO. Shut up! You are good for nothing but to be honest. I hate honest people, scum that imposes on the poor. *(She comes down to audience.)* Good people, charity, for the love of Heaven!

PIERRE. Perhaps she is right, I am good for nothing except to be honest. Alas, I never had any one to teach me. *(Returns to his wheel, starts away with it, but stops as he hears noise in cafe.)* Ah!

*(Laughter is heard in cafe.* JACQUES *comes out. He is dark and handsome. In contrast to* PIERRE, *he is warmly dressed.)*

JACQUES. Hello! Here is the old woman and her precious abortion of a son. *(To* LA FROCHARD.*)* Has Jeanette come yet?

FRO. Not yet, my son.

JACQUES. Never mind, she'll come in time.

FRO. My son, do you need money? Or have you found a purse?

JACQUES. No, but Jeanette has. *(To* PIERRE.*)* Come here.

*(*PIERRE *comes down L.)*

FRO *(admiringly).* Isn't he in a good humor?

JACQUES. Look ye! Good children always give an account of their earnings to their parents. Isn't that so, Mother?

FRO. Certainly, my lamb—you have excellent principles.

PIERRE. And when I give an account, you pocket it all.

JACQUES. Well, what if I do?

PIERRE. It is unjust—it is—

JACQUES *(threateningly).* That's enough. None of your fine speeches. I want your money. How much have you got?

PIERRE *(hands the money to* LA FROCHARD*).* Twenty-two livres, seven sous.

JACQUES *(taking money from* PIERRE's *hand).* And all this fuss about that! Why, what have you been doing for a whole week?

PIERRE. I have walked the streets from morning until night, with my wheel upon my back. I have lived on bread and water. I could do no more.

JACQUES. Well, your trade don't pay. I must find you something better.

PIERRE. Something better? You? No! No! *(Returns to his wheel.)*

FRO. I have saved three livres, eighteen sous. Put them with Pierre's. That makes—

JACQUES. Oh, never mind how much it makes. I don't want it particularly, but I'll take it on principle. *(Takes money from* LA FROCHARD.) Come, cripple, let's drink.

PIERRE. No—I don't like to drink.

JACQUES. Why, who would think we are brothers? You have the blood of a sheep in your veins. You're a disgrace to the family. I boast the blood of a Frochard, the Frochards who have been outlaws for one hundred and fifty years.

FRO. Ah, what a man! I love him—he's so like his father.

JACQUES *(takes* LA FROCHARD *by the arm).* Come along, then, if you love me. I'm thirsty. *(To* PIERRE.) Are you coming with us?

PIERRE. No, no, there's the Normandy coach has just arrived. I'll run and see if there's not a chance to earn a few sous.

*(Coach horn and clatter of horses' hoofs off R.* LA FROCHARD *and* JACQUES *exit into cafe. Exit* PIERRE R. ANTOINE *comes out of cafe and watches as* HENRIETTE *and* LOUISE *enter; then he slowly wanders off without being noticed by them.* HENRIETTE *is a very pretty girl of about twenty, in peasant dress of the Normandy countryside.* LOUISE *is slightly smaller and younger; her dress is similar to* HENRIETTE's *but in different colors. She is obviously blind; she clings to* HENRIETTE, *who guides and cares for her. Both girls are dressed for travel. They wear gloves and carry suitcases.)*

HENRIETTE *(comes to bench).* Here, Louise, sit here!

LOUISE *(sitting).* I am surprised that Monsieur Martin is not here to meet us!

HENRIETTE. Oh, he'll come soon! Ah, Louise, Paris is beautiful! My poor sister, if you could only see its wonders!

LOUISE. Tell me what you see! Where are we?

HENRIETTE. In an open square on the bank of a river and there's a beautiful bridge further down, which has a magnificent statue in the middle.

LOUISE. That's the Pont Neuf—papa used to speak of it!

HENRIETTE. And on this side I can see two great towers—it must be Notre Dame Cathedral.

LOUISE. Notre Dame. *(Sadly.)* How I wish I could see it. It was on that spot I, a helpless infant, was left to perish. There your dear father found me! But for him I should have died of cold and hunger—perhaps, perhaps that would have been better!

HENRIETTE. My darling sister, why do you say so?

LOUISE. I should not have lived to become blind and unhappy!

HENRIETTE. Louise, do not speak thus. Our dear parents loved us both alike. You were their consolation and happiness, and it was their first grief when Heaven deprived you of your sight.

LOUISE. Misfortune pursues me, sister. Scarcely had this affliction befallen me when we were left orphans and without help of friends.

HENRIETTE. No, no, dear Louise! Not without friends, I hope! I have turned all we possessed into money and have come to this great Paris, where there are skillful doctors who will soon restore my poor Louise's eyes to their old-time brightness! Come, do not be sad! Remember when we were little ones, remember how I could always comfort you when you were hurt—remember the happy tunes our dear father taught us to sing together?

*(They sing,* HENRIETTE *leading off,* LOUISE *joining.)*

HENRIETTE &

LOUISE          (SONG: *"If I Had a Wish"*\*)

If I had a wish I'd wish for things,
No one ever thinks that wishing brings:
Something kind of odd, like a silver goldenrod
That would disappear when I nod.

If I had a wish, I'd wish to find,
Carved upon a tree with hearts entwined,
Names of all the beaus that the future holds
So that we could guess our betrothed.

Everyone wants to meet a wise man
Like the books reveal.
He would say magic words and then
Your wish would start being real.

If I had a wish I'd wish for you
Anything to make your wish come true.
What would be the fun when the wish were done
If it only came true for one.
If it only came true for one.

LOUISE. But where can Monsieur Martin be? Why doesn't he come for us?

HENRIETTE. Perhaps he is waiting in the cafe—I'll go in and see. *(Enters cafe, leaving* LOUISE *seated on bench.)*

*(The voices of* JACQUES *and others are heard laughing boisterously in the cabaret.* JEANETTE *enters at back, pale and staggering. She is an outcast, a girl of the streets. She is young, but*

\**Music on page 376.*

*shows signs of her difficult life. Her dress is gaudy but pretty, and she knows that she dresses to attract the attention of men.)*

JEAN *(listens for a moment).* Yes, it is his voice, singing and laughing. Aye, drink and carouse. Forget her whose heart you have broken. Enjoy yourself while the victim of your brutality seeks the only refuge left to her—death! One plunge and it will all be over. *(She goes up to the quay.)*

*(Re-enter* HENRIETTE.*)*

May my dying shriek of despair ring in your ears as a never-ending curse! No, it is not yet dark enough. I might be seen and perhaps saved.

HENRIETTE *(to* LOUISE*).* He is not there!

LOUISE. And you do not see him here?

HENRIETTE *(anxiously looking around).* No, not yet. But what can be the matter with that woman? *(*JEANNETTE *falls.)* She has fallen; she must be ill.

LOUISE. Go to her! Speak to her, Henriette!

HENRIETTE *(going to* JEANETTE*).* Pardon me, madame; can I do anything for you?

JEAN. Nothing—nothing!

LOUISE *(to* HENRIETTE*).* She said that with a voice full of misery and despair.

HENRIETTE. Madame, have confidence in us. We are not rich, but if we can help you—

JEAN. I have already told you I want nothing and that I cannot be helped. There are griefs that cannot be consoled; sufferings that cannot be alleviated. I only wish to—to—

LOUISE *(rising and joining them).* You wish to die.

JEAN *(rises).* Who told you so? How do you know I want to die?

LOUISE. I feel it while I listen to you. Do you not know that we who are blind can listen with our whole being?

HENRIETTE. Tell us your troubles.

JEAN. I cannot—I am pursued by officers of the law. I have no strength to fly further; they will arrest me.

HENRIETTE. What have you done?

JEAN. I have stolen.

*(*HENRIETTE *and* LOUISE *recoil a moment.)*

Stolen money confided to my care. All the meager savings of a poor workman. I did not steal it for myself, but for *him*, for a wretch whom I despise, but whom, alas, I love!

*(Loud voices heard in cafe—laughter.)*

JACQUES *(in the cafe).* Come—order anything you want—I'll stand it.

JEAN *(crosses to L.).* Listen—that is his voice. He is there, wasting in debauchery the money purchased by my crime. When I am away from him, reason returns, and I hate his baseness. Alas! But when he speaks to me—touches me—my hate disappears. I tremble at his touch and am his slave. I steal for him.—I almost believe I would kill at his bidding! You see, it is better that I should die! *(goes R.)*

HENRIETTE *(stopping her)*. You cannot atone for a fault by taking your life.

JEAN. If I am found, they will arrest—imprison me.

LOUISE. When you have left the prison, you will have paid the debt you owe to man.

HENRIETTE. And repentance will pay the debt you owe to Heaven.

JEAN. I cannot believe that there is a Heaven for an outcast like me.

LOUISE. Oh, unhappy woman!

HENRIETTE *(pointing to the river)*. See where such a belief would lead you. Listen and believe us. You can redeem your past and your future will be happier. *(Slips money into her hand.)* Take this!

JEAN *(refusing)*. No, no!

LOUISE. Do not refuse, I implore you.

JEAN *(weeping)*. Ah, you are right. There must indeed be a Heaven, for has it not sent two angels to succor and save me? *(She takes their hands and weeps over them.)*

HENRIETTE. Courage, courage!

JEAN. Yes, yes, I will have courage. I'll fly from Paris—from him. Have I the strength? I do not know! I only know I wish I could give my life for you.

(JACQUES *appears at door of cafe.)*
May Heaven bless you. Farewell! *(Crosses to R., goes to exit.)*

JACQUES *(calling after her)*. Jeanette?

(JEANETTE *stops suddenly; does not turn.)*

LOUISE *(to HENRIETTE)*. What is she doing?

HENRIETTE. Alas! She stops!

JACQUES. Where are you going?

JEAN *(with averted head)*. Away from you—away—and I hope never to see you again.

JACQUES *(coming out and going to her)*. Bah! You don't want to see me? *(Takes her hand.)* Then why did you stop when I called? What makes your hand tremble?

JEAN. It does not tremble. I have found strength to resist you. I am ashamed of the life I lead, and of the infamy into which you have plunged me.

JACQUES. Pooh! Pooh! Put all that stuff out of your head and follow me.

JEAN *(disengaging hand)*. I will not!

JACQUES. You must—enough of this foolishness. Come! Do you hear?

JEAN *(hesitates)*. I—I—*(Looks at girls and gains courage.)* Yes, I hear and I refuse. I will not obey you.

JACQUES. Do you want me to persuade you in the usual way?

JEAN. You shall not. Never again.

JACQUES *(threateningly)*. We'll see! *(Rushes upon her.)*

*(At the same moment a policeman enters L. JEANETTE, looking around for some means of escape, sees him.)*

JEAN. Ah, you *shall* see! *(To OFFICER.)* Monsieur, arrest me! I am a thief!

OFFICER. Arrest you? Who are you?

JEAN. My name is Jeanette Girard. Officers are in search of me. I escaped from them an hour ago. Now I wish to deliver myself to justice.

JACQUES *(goes up to hide himself)*. She has gone crazy.

*(OFFICER takes paper from his belt and looks at it.)*

OFFICER. Jeanette Girard. Yes, accused of theft.

JEAN *(looking at JACQUES)*. Of which I am guilty.

OFFICER. Well, if you confess it, I must take you to prison.

JEAN *(to OFFICER)*. Come! *(She takes his arm. As they pass JACQUES, she stops.)* My expiation begins. Pray Heaven that I may complete it. I said I would escape this time. You see—I keep my word!

*(Exit JEANETTE and OFFICER.)*

JACQUES. She is a fool! Humph! *(He exits into cafe.)*

*(Singing and noise continue.)*

LOUISE. Henriette.

HENRIETTE. You are frightened, sister.

LOUISE. Yes, yes, I am, indeed.

HENRIETTE. And night is falling fast.

LOUISE. Why doesn't Monsieur Martin come?

*(Enter ANTOINE.)*

ANTOINE. Here I am, Mademoiselle.

HENRIETTE *(with joy)*. Ah!

LOUISE. At last!

HENRIETTE. We began to be very anxious!

ANTOINE. You must excuse me, for I live a great distance from here.

HENRIETTE *(astonished)*. A great distance?

LOUISE. Why, we were told your house was but a few steps from the bridge.

ANTOINE *(aside)*. A mistake. *(Aloud.)* Yes, yes, indeed it was—that is, I did live but a short distance from here, but you see, I have moved. Come, come, let us go, mademoiselle!

HENRIETTE *(shrinking from him, in doubt)*. You have moved?

ANTOINE. Yes, yes, only yesterday.

LOUISE. And you said nothing of it in your letter.

ANTOINE. No, I did not write it because—because—in short, I didn't know I was going to move. But if you doubt me, here's a neighbor of mine—a good, honest citizen—he will vouch for me.

*(ANTOINE makes a sign and PICARD enters.)*

HENRIETTE *(crossing and looking at him)*. Honest citizen?

LOUISE *(extending her hands)*. Henriette, do not leave me.

*(The men seize HENRIETTE, place a handkerchief over her mouth and carry her off.)*

HENRIETTE *(as she is carried off).* No! No! Help, help!

LOUISE *(alone).* I hear nothing. Henriette, where is that man? Sister, why do you not answer me? *(With terror.)* Henriette, Henriette! Speak to me. Speak one word. Answer me. Henriette! *(With despair.)* No answer!

HENRIETTE *(heard in distance with stifled voice).* Louise!

LOUISE *(screaming).* Henriette, Henriette! Ah! 'Tis she! They have dragged her away from me! Oh, what shall I do? Alone! Alone! Abandoned! What will become of me? Alone in this great city, helpless and blind? *(She breaks down weeping, after a pause. She gropes her way up the stage and reaches the stone coping of the quay over the river. Just as she does so, she stumbles as though about to fall into the river.)*

*(PIERRE, entering at R., catches her in his arms just in time to save her.)*

PIERRE *(brings her down C.).* Great Heavens! What were you going to do?

LOUISE *(trembling with fright).* Nothing, nothing. What was it?

PIERRE. Another step and you would have fallen into the river.

LOUISE. Oh, save me, save me!

*(Enter LA FROCHARD from cafe.)*

FRO. Why, what is the matter? What are you doing there, Pierre?

LOUISE. Ah, madame, do not leave me! I beg you, I entreat you, do not leave me here all alone.

FRO. What is it? Have you lost your head?

LOUISE. Alas! Madame, a few minutes ago my sister was here with me, and they have stolen her away from me.

PIERRE. Stolen her?

FRO. Well, you must let your parents know.

LOUISE. Our parents? Alas, madame, we are orphans!

PIERRE. You have acquaintances—friends—

LOUISE. We have only just arrived in Paris and I know no one here.

FRO. No one? No one at all?

PIERRE. Were the people who took your sister away gentlemen or common people?

LOUISE. How can I tell?

FRO. You could see their clothes.

LOUISE. Alas! Madame, I am blind!

PIERRE. You are blind?

FRO. Blind, without relations, friends or acquaintances in Paris. *(Looks at her.)* And young and pretty.

PIERRE *(aside and low).* It is true, young and pretty.

FRO *(to PIERRE).* Go! Leave me alone with her; I'll take care of her.

PIERRE. Yes, mother. We must help her to find her sister.

FRO. That's all right. I know what to do. You clear out.

*(PIERRE crosses to wheel.)*

LOUISE *(uneasily).* You will not leave me, madame?

FRO. Never fear, my dear, I'll not leave you.

PIERRE *(goes up and takes his wheel).* Blind! So young and pretty. *(Laughing sadly to himself.)* Pretty! What is that to you, wretched one? *(Exit L.)*

FRO. Come, come, my pretty child, don't be downcast.

LOUISE. Alas! To whom shall I go for help?

FRO. To me. I am an honest woman, mother of a family. I'll give you a home until you find your sister.

LOUISE. Ah! Madame, you are very good to have pity on me. But we will find her, won't we?

FRO. Oh yes, certainly, in time. *(Aside.)* And we'll take plenty of time! *(To LOUISE.)* Come, then come along with me.

LOUISE. I trust myself to you, madame.

FRO. You couldn't do better. You have fallen into good hands. Come!

CURTAIN

## SCENE TWO

SCENE: *The beautifully furnished apartment of* BARON DE VAUDREY, *with satin drapes and elegant decorations. The lights are low. It is early evening. As the curtain rises,* ANTOINE *and* PICARD *carry* HENRIETTE *into apartment and place her on couch. They are arguing.*

PICARD. I tell you, my master may return at any moment.

ANTOINE. And what of it? She'll come around and we'll be on our way in no time.

PICARD. How is she? Is she coming to?

ANTOINE. No, curse her! She's still as death! Think of something, Picard—how do you revive such a one? Oh, I've never had such troubles with any of them before!

PICARD. What if my former master, Count Levant, the new Minister of Police, finds out about this? He'll put me in the Bastille for sure! Since he's taken this new post, he's hard as stone and cold as a fish. Why, he even plans to put a stop to everyone's amusements, and if he knew about the Marquis de Menton's place and these abductions— oh, oh, look at her, she's going to die on us!

ANTOINE *(fans her frantically, rubs her wrists).* No, no! Oh, how did I know she'd be ill and faint? I thought these peasant girls were supposed to be strong and sturdy. You know, we couldn't keep her in the streets in this state.

PICARD. I know—I know, but why did we bring her here? Oh heaven, this is the end of me! My master will discharge me, Count Levant will chastise me, and there isn't a gentleman in Paris will engage me once it's known I've been caught in such an affair! Ah, I remember, the master has some smelling salts! I'll get them.

*(He goes off and returns with vial, hands it to* ANTOINE. *Both bend over her. Enter* BARON MAURICE DE VAUDREY, *a young nobleman. He has an air of wealth and privilege.)*

DE VAUDREY. Picard!

PICARD. Wait a moment, master! Let me explain—the young lady has fainted!

DE VAUDREY. So I see!

PICARD. And my friend here is trying to revive her.

ANTOINE *(interrupting).* Your valet has accommodated me, sir. I was on my way to take this young lady to the residence of your friend, the Marquis de Menton. She became ill and faint, and so I brought her here.

DE VAUDREY. Ah—de Menton. Yes, I understand. Well, do what you can for her and get her out of here.

PICARD. But master, what if she wakens here? She will remember the place and will expose you.

DE VAUDREY. Expose me? And who would she be to expose me? I am tired of the pretense of these willingly abducted maidens! When the proper moment arrives, she will awake and go through it all. "Where am I?" "Why have you brought me here?" *(Laughs.)* And then by slow degrees this profound and virtuous despair, which commenced in a torrent of tears, will be drowned in—a flood of champagne!

*(*DE VAUDREY *turns his back during this speech.* HENRIETTE *gradually comes to, raises herself.)*

HENRIETTE. Am I mad? Do I dream?

DE VAUDREY. Now, that is singular. Something of an improvement, at least.

HENRIETTE *(rises and speaks to* ANTOINE *in a decisive tone).* How has this outrage been committed? Is this your house?

ANTOINE. Ah, mademoiselle, you do me honor! It is not for myself—

HENRIETTE. Not another word, sir. I wish to return this very instant to the place where my sister awaits me. Come, take me back at once.

ANTOINE *(firmly).* Mademoiselle, after all the trouble I have had, you can scarcely suppose we will let you go. No, I shall take you to the Chateau du Bel Air.

*(He grabs her arm. She gasps, jerks free from him.)*

HENRIETTE. Listen, sir! I see the horrible trap you have laid for me. But you, vile as you are, can scarcely understand the extent of your own villainy. You have separated me from a poor child whose only help in life I am, whose misfortunes command the respect of criminals even worse than yourself. She is dependent on me alone. Without me she cannot take a single step, for she is blind!

ALL. Blind?

HENRIETTE. Yes, blind, and alone! Alone in Paris, without money, without help, wandering through the streets, sightless, homeless, wild with despair. What will become of her? She is blind! Do you hear me? She is blind!

ANTOINE *(trying to placate her, keeping his eye on* DE VAUDREY*)*. Compose yourself, mademoiselle. I will have a search made for her to-morrow. I will find her and bring her to you.

HENRIETTE. Bring her—my little sister Louise to the Chateau du Bel Air—to a house of sin! No—no—never! Is this the only answer you have to my prayer? Are there no more gentlemen then of honor in Paris?

*(*DE VAUDREY *turns suddenly in anger, crosses to her.)*

DE VAUDREY. Take my hand, mademoiselle. I will conduct you to safety.

HENRIETTE. Oh, thank you, monsieur!

ANTOINE *(quickly bars the way)*. Excuse me, sir, but you cannot do this. I have promised the Marquis and if I am further delayed—

DE VAUDREY *(coldly)*. Miserable scoundrel—give me room!

ANTOINE *(pulls pistol)*. Even though you are the Baron De Vaudrey, you do not take my bread!

DE VAUDREY *(knocks pistol from his hand, trips him and knocks him to the floor)*. Picard! If you are my man and not the tool of this filth, tie him and hold him here!

*(*PICARD *comes and begins to tie* ANTOINE*.)*

Come, mademoiselle, later I shall attend to your abductor! And, if I'm not mistaken, the Marquis may also live to regret the day he sent you off on this errand!

**CURTAIN**

# ACT TWO

## SCENE ONE

SCENE: *The private office of the Minister of Police.* COUNT EDMUND LE-VANT *is discovered seated at table R.C. He is in his late fifties. His carriage and appearance indicate that is is accustomed to authority. He is well and formally dressed. His table is covered with papers which he is in the act of signing, hastily reading them over.* CHIEF CLERK *is at the table, standing in a respectful attitude.*

LEVANT. I regret that my recent accession to the position of Minister of Police compels me to occupy so much of your time.

CLERK. I am entirely at your service, my lord.

LEVANT. I am desirous that a stop should be put to the scandals which disgraced the preceding administration. *(Taking up paper and rising.)*, I have here a report which needs explanation. How is it possible that a young girl could be abducted in the open street at eight o'clock in the evening, and there should be no one to oppose such an outrage?

CLERK. There are scoundrels in Paris audacious and dexterous enough to do anything, sir.

LEVANT. Where were the police?

CLERK. The police have discovered the abductor and compelled him to confess; however, the chief actor who planned the affair has never been apprehended.

LEVANT. Three months have elapsed since this most daring outrage, and the really guilty one, you say, has not been punished?

CLERK *(in a very meaning tone).* That is due, my lord, to certain circumstances.

LEVANT. What circumstances? To whom does this Chateau du Bel Air belong?

CLERK. To the Marquis de Menton.

LEVANT. De Menton! An ancient and illustrious family, whose last scion would nonetheless stake all its glories on the cast of a die—a worthless rake! But the girl—what became of her?

CLERK. She was carried off—by—by—by—well, a person unfriendly to the Marquis.

LEVANT. His name—speak, sir.

CLERK *(after a pause).* The Baron Maurice De Vaudrey.

LEVANT *(astonished).* My nephew! H—mm. I appreciate the sentiment that caused you to hesitate, but for the future, sir, remember that justice is no respecter of persons.

CLERK. Do you wish, my lord, that this affair should be entered in the secret archives of the police?

LEVANT. The secret archives of the police? Do such records really exist?

CLERK. Certainly, my lord. The secret and complete history of every noble family in France may be found there. You have but to mention a name and in five minutes the desired volumes will be in your hands.

LEVANT. Very well, then. If the history of the house of De Vaudrey is there, let that history be complete!

CLERK. I shall obey you, my lord! *(He salutes and exits.)*

*(PICARD enters.)*

LEVANT *(seated).* Ah, Picard! I am glad to see you. I wish to speak to you of your master. How is he behaving himself?

PICARD. With all respect, my lord, his conduct is scandalous, perfectly scandalous.

LEVANT. Am I to understand that you wish to leave his service?

PICARD. Yes, my lord! The Baron, your nephew, has principles which I can no longer accept. Although the Baron thinks it proper to compromise his nobility, I cannot compromise my livery.

LEVANT. Very well, I will take you back into my service!

PICARD *(joyfully).* You will? Ah, my lord, you have relieved me, and I resume my personal dignity.

LEVANT. On one condition. I wish you to remain for a time with my nephew. It is important that I should know his movements. I could employ the police, but I have already learned too much from them, and through you, who are attached to him, I desire to know the rest.

PICARD. The rest? What has he been doing? You frighten me. What do the police know?

LEVANT. They know that after the duel—

PICARD *(starts).* The duel! What duel?

LEVANT. Do not pretend that you do not know that he dangerously wounded the Marquis de Menton in a duel about a woman!

PICARD *(bewildered, still pretending innocence).* He fought a duel and dangerously wounded his antagonist, and about a woman? Oh, the sly dog, and I wanted to leave him!

LEVANT. No, no, not yet. I desire that you remain with him and discover where he hides himself.

PICARD. I only know, sir, that he advises me he will not need my services for days on end. He spends his evenings, many of them, quietly at home, and alone, sir. But perhaps there's hope—perhaps there is a woman. I'll discover the saucy little beauty for whom he neglects all of his friends. Of course she must be little and saucy— that's the style I like!

LEVANT. Oh, indeed!

PICARD *(with relish).* Doubtless he has done everything in good style—has taken some elegant, quiet little house, rooms hung with velvet, all that sort of thing—

LEVANT. Why, at that rate, you will ruin your master.

PICARD *(assuming the airs of a gentleman).* Bah! If she is worth the trouble, where is the harm in a little ruin?

LEVANT. There, that will do for today!

*(The* COUNTESS DIANE LEVANT, *wife of* COUNT LEVANT, *and aunt to the* BARON MAURICE DE VAUDREY, *appears at the back. She is a very attractive woman in her mid-forties, well and carefully dressed. Her education and good breeding are apparent.)*

Go, and do not forget my orders.

PICARD. I will obey them, my lord! Baron, you are a sly dog, and I thought you a saint! *(Salutes the Countess as she enters. Exit.)*

COUNTESS. Monsieur, I am informed you wished to speak with me.

LEVANT. I was about to come to you, but you have anticipated me. I desire to speak with you on the subject of your nephew, the Baron De Vaudrey, and to ask you to prepare him for a marriage which His Majesty—

COUNTESS *(sadly).* Wishes to impose upon him. *(Sits.)*

LEVANT. Impose on him? A mangificent alliance which will complete the measure of the distinguished honors with which his Majesty deigns to favor me.

COUNTESS. What miracle has worked this change in you? You, whose life passed so quietly at our dear home in Dauphine, far from the intrigue of the court. *(Looking him steadily in the face.)* You have become ambitious—and of what?

LEVANT. Yes, I am ambitious.

COUNTESS *(sadly).* I cannot believe it!

LEVANT. Diane, my wife, I have vainly sought every means in my power to dispel the melancholy which has never left you since the first days of our marriage. Share with me the glorious task I have undertaken. Is it not a noble privilege to have the power to seek out and console those that weep, to assist the suffering, to relieve the misery of the unfortunate? Can you not share my ambition with me to do good?

COUNTESS *(shrinking from him).* Ah! I did not think of the limitless power placed in your hands, a power before which all doors are opened, a power that can penetrate all secrets—perhaps, enable you to discover—

LEVANT *(astonished).* Discover? What?

COUNTESS *(recovering herself).* The extent, as you say, of the misery in this great city.

*(Enter* DE VAUDREY *at back.)*

Ah, Maurice!

DE VAUDREY. My dear aunt!

LEVANT. Baron! I am glad to see you. The Countess and myself have an important communication to make to you.

DE VAUDREY. I regret that I should have been detained.

LEVANT. My dear Maurice, his Majesty did me the honor to receive me yesterday, and he spoke of you.

DE VAUDREY. Of me?

LEVANT. He takes a great interest in your welfare. He wishes you to accept a position at the court, and desires at the same time that you should marry.

DE VAUDREY. Marry?

COUNTESS. My dear nephew, have no fear that his choice will do violence to your feelings. The lady whom he has chosen has youth, beauty and fortune.

LEVANT. In proof of which I have only to tell you that his choice is Mademoiselle —

DE VAUDREY. Do not name her.

LEVANT. Why not?

DE VAUDREY. I refuse to marry.

LEVANT. Before committing yourself irrevocably, Maurice, reflect. This marriage is an honor which his Majesty desires to confer upon you, and when he speaks —

DE VAUDREY. I will go to him. I will thank him for his goodness, I will place my services at his disposal; my devotion, my life, if need be, are his, but my affections are my own, and I wish to remain — free.

LEVANT. Free! Free to lead a life of dissipation which you may not always be able to hide from the world.

DE VAUDREY. There is nothing in my life to hide.

LEVANT *(severely)*. Are you sure of that, Baron?

DE VAUDREY. Monsieur!

COUNTESS *(rising anxiously and interfering)*. Maurice! *(To LEVANT.)* My husband! Defer this for the present — permit me —

LEVANT. Very well, we will return to this another time. *(*DE VAUDREY *attempts to answer him.* COUNTESS *makes a mute appeal to him and he refrains.)* I leave you with the Countess, and I hope that your respect and affection for her will lend more weight to her counsel than you are disposed to give to mine. *(Exit.)*

COUNTESS *(crossing to* DE VAUDREY*)*. Who is this woman you love? What obstacle prevents the avowal of your affection?

DE VAUDREY. Ah! Where shall I find a heart like yours? You have divined my secret. I love a young girl, as charming as she is pure. I love her, yet my lips have never sought hers. I adore her, yet I have never dared to whisper my passion.

COUNTESS. Her name? Her family?

DE VAUDREY. She is born of the people. She is an orphan and lives by the labor of her hands.

COUNTESS. And you would make such a one your wife?

DE VAUDREY. Do not judge her until you have seen her. Consent to see her; then advise me.

COUNTESS. In such a marriage there can be no happiness for you, and for her only misery.

DE VAUDREY *(with force)*. Can *you* tell me that? You who have been the victim of a blind obedience which has sacrificed your life?

COUNTESS *(uttering a cry)*. How do you know? Who has torn aside the veil from my secret?

DE VAUDREY *(taking her hand)*. There was but one soul in all this world tender and noble enough to appreciate and sustain your own in its trials. Your dearly beloved sister! My mother! In her last moments she exacted from me the promise to devote myself to you, should misfortune ever come, and I gladly gave my word.

COUNTESS. Ah, yes. I was young and mad—I loved and was loved without knowing wrong. I consented to a secret marriage with a man beneath me in rank. They thought him my lover and killed him almost under my very eyes—and I was a mother. Family honor demanded that my child should disappear, because my hand was promised to the Count Levant. I consoled myself with the hope that perhaps I should see her again some day. Alas! The days have passed into months, the months into years, and all my prayers are in vain.

DE VAUDREY. My poor aunt. They were indeed cruel.

COUNTESS. So cruel that often I ask myself if it would not have been better had they killed me, too. And my child. May she not cry out from the depths of her despair, "Accursed be my unnatural mother!" I hear that cry always—it pursues me in my prayers, torments my dreams—I hear it always, always!

(LEVANT *enters at back and stands unobserved.*)

DE VAUDREY. Then do you, who have suffered so much, who suffer still, counsel me to obey? Would you have me chain my life to one woman, while my heart is filled with the image of another? Will you advise me to do this?

COUNTESS (*very emphatically*). No, no, never! (*Turns and sees* LEVANT, *speaks to him.*) Ah, Monsieur, have pity on him, do not ask him to stifle the cry of his conscience.

DE VAUDREY (*unobserved by* LEVANT *and in a low voice*). Take care!

(*The* COUNTESS *checks herself and stands in dejected attitude before her husband.*)

LEVANT (*severely*). Madame! To whom do you refer? Of what are you speaking?

COUNTESS (*trembling*). I meant—I spoke of—

DE VAUDREY. Monsieur, the words of the Countess are but the echo of those she just heard me utter. They are but the irrevocable revolt of my heart against the marriage and the suffering you would impose upon me.

LEVANT (*coldly*). Madame, had your words no other meaning?

COUNTESS. No, no. I am agitated, Monsieur; I am ill.

LEVANT. That is evident. Maurice, conduct the Countess to her carriage.

(DE VAUDREY *bows to* LEVANT, *offers his hand to the Countess and both exit, followed by the gaze of* LEVANT. *When they reach the exit,* LEVANT *speaks.*)

And return immediately. I desire to speak with you.

(*Exit* COUNTESS *and* DE VAUDREY. LEVANT *goes to his desk, writes on a paper, and rings a bell.* CHIEF CLERK *appears.*)

LEVANT. Take this to the keeper of the secret records, and return with what he gives you.

(DE VAUDREY *re-enters.* CLERK *salutes and exits.*)

LEVANT. Baron, you can readily understand that propriety and considerations for my own dignity induced me to accept the explanation made by you on behalf of the Countess.

DE VAUDREY. Monsieur!

LEVANT. You also understand that that explanation did not satisfy me.

DE VAUDREY. Well, sir, what are you pleased to think?

LEVANT. I think, sir, that the Countess wept not for you, but for herself. You spoke of her early life, which is shrouded in some dark secret, and which is the torment of her life and mine. Speak, Baron, what is it?

DE VAUDREY. Monsieur Levant?

LEVANT. I command you to speak.

DE VAUDREY. I know nothing, sir.

LEVANT. Very well—you choose to forget all you owe to me. Twice today you have refused obedience—nevertheless, I will know the secret which you refuse to disclose.

DE VAUDREY. I am ignorant of the secret to which you refer.

(CLERK *returns with a large folio in his hand, which he gives to*
LEVANT, *salutes and exits.*)

LEVANT. Then we will learn it together.

DE VAUDREY. What are you going to do?

LEVANT. Here—here in the archives of the Police are entered the secrets of every noble family in France. Here I will learn the secret of Diane De Vaudrey, Countess Levant!

DE VAUDREY *(while* LEVANT *is turning over leaves).* Why, that would be shameful! Infamous!

LEVANT. Hmmm—yes, here it is. House of De Vaudrey, and each member has a page. Ah, Diane Eleanor, daughter of the Count Francois De Vaudrey.

DE VAUDREY *(crosses rapidly towards the table and places his open hand on the pages).* Monsieur, that you must not read!

LEVANT *(starting up).* What do you mean?

DE VAUDREY. I mean that the act you are about to commit is unworthy of you—you must not, you shall not!

LEVANT. Who will prevent it?

DE VAUDREY. Your own honor, which will revolt against such treason. Ah, sir, if your own honor does not speak loud enough, I will!

LEVANT. You?

(DE VAUDREY *crumples up the page under his hand, tears it from the book and puts it in his bosom. Puts his hand to his pistol.*)

DE VAUDREY. I warn you, sir, that you can only wrest this paper from me with my life. You shall kill me before I part with it. Remember, sir, that it is not alone her secret I have saved you from violating; 'tis your own dignity and self-respect. I defend your honor against yourself. (LEVANT *bows his head.*)

**CURTAIN**

## SCENE TWO

SCENE: *The open square in front of the Church of St. Sulpice, including church portico and steps. The ground is lightly covered with snow.* PIERRE *is discovered seated on a stool.*

PIERRE. Nearly twelve o'clock; they will soon be here.
(JACQUES *enters at back.*)
JACQUES *(to* PIERRE*).* The women have not come yet?
PIERRE. No, not yet.
JACQUES. They ought to be here. The service will soon be over and they will miss the charitable idiots.
PIERRE. Ah, you need not worry about them. Jacques, I have a favor to ask of you.
JACQUES. If it is money, I haven't got any!
PIERRE. No—it is not money. Look, Jacques, when you are angry with me, curse me, beat me, if you want to, but do not call me "cripple"—not—not when Louise is present.
JACQUES *(surprised).* Ah—ah, indeed! We must speak to Monsieur respectfully—take off our hats, I suppose.
PIERRE *(supplicatingly).* Jacques!
JACQUES. So it hurts your feelings to be called cripple, does it? Well, look at yourself.
PIERRE. I know I am ugly—almost deformed—and yet, who, when I was an infant, beat me and twisted my limbs?
JACQUES. That is enough. As you don't want to be called "cripple" any more—I'll rechristen you "Cupid."
PIERRE *(discouraged).* Do as you like.
JACQUES. Now I come to think of it, it is only when Louise is about that you object to being called cripple. Perhaps you are in love with her.
PIERRE. What do you mean?
JACQUES. You are not so stupid, after all. She is blind and does not know the difference between a handsome man like me and a miserable abortion like you. Oh, ha! You're in love, in love with a blind girl. Ha, ha, ha!
PIERRE. I? I? In love?
JACQUES. Why then are you ashamed of being called cripple before her? Afraid she'll find you out?
PIERRE. I want to think there is one in the world who does not regard me with disgust. But—in love with her—she who is beautiful enough, good enough, to be an angel!
JACQUES. I don't know or care anything about her goodness. I know that her eyes are more use to her now than if she could see with them. *(Goes up.)*
PIERRE *(to himself.)* Yes, yes, she is blind, but her face is so sweet that it would move a stone to pity. And her great beautiful eyes seem to look at me so truthfully that I almost fear she can see me.

JACQUES *(coming down L.).* Come along, I want you, Cupid.

PIERRE *(rousing himself).* No, I won't.

JACQUES. Rebellion, eh! Now do as I order you or look out for a beating.

PIERRE. Jacques, you're straight and strong and I must submit to you, but when I see the use you make of your strength, I am satisfied with my miserable weakness.

(JACQUES *shrugs his shoulders. At the same time* LOUISE *is heard singing outside.)*

JACQUES. Ah, here they are at last.

(LOUISE's *song continues approaching.)*

That voice ought to be worth a louis a day at least.

(Enter LOUISE *led by* LA FROCHARD. LOUISE *is miserably dressed in rags and bits of clothing. She is pale and wan, and walks with faltering steps, continuing her song.* LA FROCHARD *goes around to people near stage.)*

FRO. Pity a poor, unhappy, blind child. Charity, if you please. Ah! there's nothing to be got from these miserable common people. They will stop and listen to the singing quick enough, but when you ask them for a sou they clear out. *(Takes* LOUISE *by the arm.)* Come, come, let's be moving.

LOUISE. I am very tired, Madame. We have walked so much today.

FRO. Well, didn't you want to walk? Didn't you say you wanted to look for your sister?

LOUISE. Yes, but you always walk in the same part of the city.

FRO. Bah! How do you know? You can't see.

LOUISE. I know that, madame, but when you found me you prom-ised—

FRO. I promised to help you look for your sister. Still, you have to earn your bread. You sing and I'll do the begging.

LOUISE *(weeping).* I'll sing, madame, if you wish it.

JACQUES. Yes, but how do you sing? Like a mourner at a funeral.

LOUISE *(weeping).* I sing as well as I can. But when I think of what I am—of what I am doing—I—I—*(Breaks down entirely, sobs.)* I am so unahppy—so miserably unhappy.

PIERRE *(starts forward).* Louise!

JACQUES *(pushing him).* Hello, what are you up to, Master Cupid?

PIERRE. Nothing, nothing. *(Aside.)* I am so helpless.

JACQUES *(looking at* LOUISE*).* She is pretty when she cries.

FRO *(to* LOUISE*).* Come, come. Enough of that. Let us be moving.

LOUISE *(tries to wipe her eyes).* Very well, madame. I will.

FRO *(stops her).* Don't do that. What! Wipe away real tears? Why, that is just the thing to catch the soft-hearted fools.

(A man crosses, sees LOUISE, *stops a moment, slips a coin in her hand, and exits into church.* LA FROCHARD *takes the money.)*

Go on singing. Have pity on a poor blind child. Charity, good people, if you please.

*(LA FROCHARD and LOUISE exit R., JACQUES and PIERRE L. Organ music begins. DOCTOR enters from the church. Middle-aged and very dignified, he is the doctor of the hospital and prison. He is professionally garbed, carries a doctor's bag. His manner is warm and concerned. Enter COUNTESS from L.)*

COUNTESS. Ah, Doctor, I am glad to see you.

DOCTOR. Because it is not a professional visit, I suppose?

COUNTESS. No, I am always happy to receive you as a friend.

DOCTOR. And not as a physician. I understand, Countess. Will you then permit me, as a friend, to advise you?

COUNTESS. Doctor, I assure you I am not ill. You are mistaken.

DOCTOR. Very well then, Madame, I will concede that you are in perfect health. Pardon me for speaking thus plainly to you, but I have already been consulted by —

COUNTESS *(startled)*. My husband?

DOCTOR. The Count Levant has imparted to me the great anxiety he feels for you.

COUNTESS. What did he say?

DOCTOR. That you are wearing yourself out with a secret grief.

COUNTESS. Alas! Yes. What am I to do?

DOCTOR. Address yourself to the Great Physician. *(Pointing to church.)* There you will learn that the heaviest burden is easier borne when shared by one who has the right to know your inmost thoughts.

COUNTESS. You mean my husband. Impossible!

DOCTOR. No, no! Not impossible. A generous heart like his will appreciate your confidence. Seek strength here, madame! *(Leads her to church.)*

COUNTESS. I thank you, doctor. Ah! If one such friend as you had been given me years ago, I might have been spared this anguish. *(Exit into church.)*

DOCTOR. Ah! What a strange thing is human nature.

*(Goes up C. As he starts to go, LA FROCHARD and LOUISE appear R.)*

FRO. Pity for a poor blind child, if you please, charity.

DOCTOR. Blind? Who? This young girl? *(Coming forward.)*

FRO. Alas! Yes, my good sir, pity.

DOCTOR. Poor unhappy child, at your age. Let me look at your eyes.

FRO *(harshly interposing)*. What for?

DOCTOR. Come here, my child. Let me see your eyes. I am a doctor!

LOUISE *(joyfully)*. A doctor?

FRO *(to LOUISE)*. Come along. *(To DOCTOR.)* They can't be cured; it is no use.

DOCTOR. But I insist.

FRO. Well, then, see for yourself if she is not blind. *(Passing LOUISE across. Aside.)* Curse him, I know him; he is that whining doctor at the hospital.

LOUISE *(as DOCTOR comes to her)*. Oh, sir, if you are a doctor —

DOCTOR *(after examining her eyes)*. You have not always been blind, my child, have you?

LOUISE. No, monsieur. I was fourteen years old when this misfortune befell me.

DOCTOR. Fourteen? And you have had no treatment?

LOUISE *(quickly)*. Monsieur—

FRO *(interrupting)*. We are so poor, good doctor, we have not the money to—

LOUISE. Oh, monsieur, is there any hope for me?

DOCTOR. Calm yourself, my child, calm yourself. *(He takes* LA FROCHARD *aside L.)* Come here!

FRO *(pushing* LOUISE *back and crossing to* DOCTOR*)*. What is it, doctor?

DOCTOR. Listen, you must not excite her; you must not tell her too suddenly what I hope. Bring her to me at the hospital St. Louis.

FRO. Yes, yes, I know, I have been there often.

DOCTOR. I thought I recognized you. Let me see, you are called Mother—

FRO *(indignantly)*. Widow Frochard, monsieur.

DOCTOR. Yes, I remember. Well, when she is calmer, tell her gently that I think there is hope for her.

FRO. Yes, yes, I will. I'll tell her gently.

DOCTOR *(crosses to* LOUISE*)*. Here, my poor child. *(Giving her a piece of money.)* Courage, my dear, I will see you again. *(Exit R.)*

FRO *(following him to exit)*. May Heaven bless you, good doctor. Heaven bless you. *(After his exit.)* Curses on you for an intermeddling old fool! *(Returns to* LOUISE.*)*

LOUISE. What did he tell you, madame?

FRO. He said it was not worth the trouble. There is no hope for you.

LOUISE. No hope! No hope! Alas! What am I to do?

FRO *(aside)*. If I bring her here every day he will see her again. *(Aloud to* LOUISE.*)* Look you, child, I am a good woman. You have been complaining that I always take you to the same places; now tomorrow we will look for your sister in some other part of the city.

LOUISE. Oh, madame, I thank you. I have now but one hope left, to find my dear sister, my dear Henriette.

*(*PIERRE *enters.)*

FRO *(to* LOUISE*)*. Look you, they will be coming out of the church soon; now sing loud. No laziness, mind you; I'll be watching you. *(Exit* LA FROCHARD.*)*

LOUISE. Yes, madame. *(She sings.)*

LOUISE. (SONG: *"If I Had a Wish"**)*

> If I had a wish I'd wish to find,
> Carved upon a tree with hearts entwined,
> Names of all the beaus that the future holds
> So that we could guess our betrothed.

*Music on page 376.

Everyone wants to meet a wise man
Like the books reveal.
He would say magic words and then—

*(She breaks down in sobs.)*

LOUISE *(sits on steps and tries to cover herself with her rags)*. I am so cold.
*(PIERRE takes off his coat, snow begins to fall.)*
I am so very cold.
*(PIERRE puts his coat on her shoulders.)*
Ah, is that you, Pierre?

PIERRE. Yes, mamselle.

LOUISE. Yes, it must be you, Pierre. You are the only one who is kind to me. *(Touches his coat.)* But this is your coat! What will you do without it, Pierre?

PIERRE. Oh! I'll do very well, indeed mamselle. I have my jacket, and my woolen waistcoat, and my—oh, that is only my overcoat. *(He shivers.)*

LOUISE. Pierre, without you I should die.

PIERRE *(seating himself beside her)*. I know they make you wretched, but I am helpless. I can do nothing.

LOUISE. Is your sympathy, your compassion, nothing? *(She touches coat on her shoulders. She gives her hand to him, which he grasps eagerly. She touches his shoulder with the other hand and discovers that he is in shirt sleeves.)* Oh, how selfish I am! *(She takes off coat and offers it to him.)*

PIERRE. No, no!

LOUISE. Pierre, do, do, my dear Pierre, for my sake. *(He takes coat, kisses her hand, and puts arm around her shoulders.)* I am not cold now. Did they not leave me in the cold garret to starve because I refused to beg?

PIERRE *(looking around)*. Have you never thought of escaping? I can help you. Let me inform the police and they will protect you.

LOUISE. No, no, you must not. I have thought of it, but that would deprive me of the only chance of finding my sister. They would shut me up in an asylum for the blind. Besides, I have an idea which sustains me. If they take me from one quarter to another, perhaps some day my voice may reach my sister's ears. I will sing the songs we learned together and when I finish I will cry out, "Henriette, 'tis I, your sister Louise. Do you hear me, Henriette, sister?"
*(Organ heard playing softly.)*

PIERRE. Hush. Mother may hear you! She will be coming back any minute to watch you. *(Rises and helps her up.)*

LOUISE *(rising)*. You are right. If she does not hear me singing, she will beat me.

PIERRE. I'll not be far away. *(Exit L.)*

*(*LOUISE *sings same ballad as before. The* COUNTESS *comes out of the church and stands on the steps.)*

COUNTESS. I have prayed to Heaven to restore to me my child. Will my prayer be answered?

*(*LOUISE *sings.* COUNTESS *starts off and is arrested by the sound of* LOUISE*'s voice.)*

What a voice! How tender, how sad! *(Approaches* LOUISE.*)* My child, can you not see me?

*(Enter* LA FROCHARD *quickly. She stops and looks on.)*

LOUISE. No, madame!

COUNTESS. Poor child! You have relations—a mother?

LOUISE. Mother!

FRO *(seizes* LOUISE *by the wrist).* Yes, my beautiful lady. She has a good mother, if I do say so.

COUNTESS. Is this your daughter?

FRO. The youngest of seven that Heaven has blessed me with, my lady. *(Tightens her grip threateningly on* LOUISE, *who bows her head.)* Isn't that so, my dear?

COUNTESS. She seems to be ill and suffering.

FRO. Ah! Good charitable souls, like you, my lady, have pity on her. She has a nice, good home. Haven't you, my darling? *(Aside, threatens.)* Speak out! *(Twists her arm.)*

LOUISE *(with great effort).* Yes, yes.

COUNTESS *(gives her money).* Give this to your mother and pray for me. *(Exit.)*

LOUISE. I will, madame.

FRO *(seizes* LOUISE*'s hand and snatches the money.)* Ah! A louis, another gold piece! A good day, after all. Come on and sing out, sing.

*(She heads* LOUISE *upstage.* LOUISE *sings as she walks off R.* PIERRE *enters L. and starts across, is about to follow them when* JACQUES, *entering from L., follows him and strikes him heavily on shoulder.* PIERRE *turns.)*

JACQUES. Stop. I have a word to say to you.

PIERRE. What is it?

JACQUES. I forbid you to follow Louise.

PIERRE. What? You forbid?

JACQUES. Yes, and I forbid you to even think of her.

PIERRE. Jacques, I cannot help it. You would not be so cruel. No, no, Jacques. Why are you so cruel?

JACQUES. Never mind why, I forbid you, that is enough, and if you disobey me, I'll twist your miserable legs again, Cupid!

*(As* JACQUES *speaks, he places both hands on* PIERRE*'s and forces him to the ground on his knees.)*

PIERRE. Ah, kill me, kill me, if you will, Jacques. *(Aside.)* But I love her and you cannot forbid that!

**CURTAIN**

## SCENE THREE

SCENE: HENRIETTE's *room, a plainly furnished chamber.* HENRIETTE *is discovered seated at table, sewing.*

HENRIETTE. Three long months since the dreadful day that robbed me of my darling sister. The Baron De Vaudrey promised he would come today and tell me if he had learned anything. Ah! How I try to cheat myself into the belief that he may bring me news of Louise. I cannot doubt that he loves me, and I madly indulge in dreams of happiness, while my poor Louise is wandering helpless in the streets of this great, heartless city.

*(A knock is heard at the door.)*

Come in! *(She runs hastily and opens the door.)*

*(Enter* BARON DE VAUDREY.*)*

DE VAUDREY. Henriette! *(He takes her hand, looks at her steadily a moment. They come downstage. She is agitated.)* Have you heard anything? You seem agitated.

HENRIETTE. I was expecting you. *(Recovering herself.)* I mean I thought, perhaps you would bring me news of Louise.

DE VAUDREY. No, I have heard nothing. Yet you know I have occupied myself unceasingly for the past three months in vain endeavors to ascertain her fate. But, today, Henriette, I wished to speak to you of something else—of myself.

HENRIETTE. I know, monsieur, all that you would say to me. I know that you rescued me from frightful peril, that you fought to defend me, and believe me, I am not ungrateful.

DE VAUDREY. Henriette, do you feel no other sentiment than gratitude? Do you not understand my heart? Until yesterday I was bound in honor to impose silence on my lips. Circumstances have released me, and today I can dare avow with pride—I love you.

HENRIETTE *(grasping the back of chair to support herself)*. Oh! This is wrong—wrong. I have known all that your heart was striving to hide from me, and I have been guilty in allowing it to distract me from the only duty I have in life. You should not compel me to confess my weakness.

DE VAUDREY. Henriette!

HENRIETTE. When Louise is restored to my arms, I shall have earned the right to be happy. Then tell me you love me, and I will listen.

DE VAUDREY. Henriette! Henriette! Dear Henriette!

*(She gives him her hand; he kisses it warmly. The door opens suddenly and* PICARD *appears.)*

PICARD. Don't disturb yourselves.

HENRIETTE *(with a cry)*. Ah!

DE VAUDREY. Picard?

PICARD. Yes, monsieur. Picard—only Picard.

DE VAUDREY. What do you want? What brings you here? *(Crosses to* HENRIETTE, *who is at table folding her work.)* Do not be frightened, Henriette. Picard was most ashamed of the affair, and I'll warrant will never get mixed up in another like it, eh?

PICARD *(to* HENRIETTE*).* Believe me, mademoiselle—I never knew—that is, it never occurred to me—

HENRIETTE. Never mind. *(To* DE VAUDREY.*)* I must take my work downstairs, they are waiting for it. *(She goes toward door.)*

DE VAUDREY *(following her).* You will return?

HENRIETTE. Yes, in a few minutes. *(Exit.)*

PICARD *(To* DE VAUDREY*).* So—this is the young man who is studying philosophy!

DE VAUDREY. Well, we are alone now. What brings you here?

PICARD. I took the liberty of following you, monsieur . . .

DE VAUDREY. Following me, you scoundrel!

PICARD *(delighted and aside).* Scoundrel is good—very good. Now he is something like a master.

DE VAUDREY. What do you say?

PICARD. I was saying, monsieur, that scoundrel is not half strong enough, particularly when I come to find out that, after all—

DE VAUDREY. After all? What?

PICARD *(aside).* Good, go on. He will kick me in a minute. *(Aloud.)* You must know, monsieur, that I had become so disgusted with your good conduct that I begged your uncle to relieve me of the duty of serving you any longer, and if he had not insisted on my remaining and watching you—

DE VAUDREY. So, you have become a spy, Master Picard, have you?

PICARD. Yes, sir, a spy on you. *(Aside.)* Now he will kick me. *(Turns and waits.)* No? *(Aloud.)* Why, monsieur, if I had not, how should I have found out that the reason you rescued the little beauty was not to save her—but to save her for your own! You're a gallant—a roué—after all!

DE VAUDREY. Gallant! Roué! *(Laughs.)* Well, how did you find that out?

PICARD. By obeying the instructions of your uncle. I follow you to the house of your inamorata, expecting to find you in the arms of some dark enchantress, and I discover you with this simple country lass.

DE VAUDREY. Believe me, you are quite mistaken in all you have surmised.

PICARD. Oh, you have the fairest of excuses. She is as pretty as—

DE VAUDREY *(interrupting quickly).* Look you, Master Picard, another word and I'll throw you out of the window.

PICARD *(crossing to window and looking out).* Oh, that is going further than I had bargained for. Thrown out of a six-story window.

DE VAUDREY. Listen to me, sir.

PICARD. I am all ears, monsieur, but please to remember that we are very high up.

DE VAUDREY. Return at once to the Count Levant, and tell him that, after having dogged my footsteps day by day, you have found me at last in the presence of the woman I love, and you may inform the count that she is to be my wife.

PICARD *(astounded)*. Your wife? Impossible!

DE VAUDREY. Silence! Ah, Henriette!

*(Enter* HENRIETTE *hurriedly and weeping. She throws herself upon a chair, at table.)*

HENRIETTE *(weeping)*. Shame! Shame! I am sure I do not deserve to be so insulted.

DE VAUDREY. Who has insulted you?

HENRIETTE. I am ordered to leave this house.

DE VAUDREY. Ordered to leave this house! Why?

HENRIETTE. Alas! Monsieur, they tell me that a young girl living alone has not the right to receive the visits of gentlemen such as you.

DE VAUDREY. Such as I—I who have always treated you with the respect due a sister!

PICARD *(aside)*. Just now she was his wife—now she is his sister! Oh, it's all right.

HENRIETTE. The mistress of the house, who until now has been so kind to me, says she cannot permit me to remain, for she has a good name to protect, which my conduct scandalizes.

PICARD. Poor thing! Monsieur, I say this is unjust, this—is—

DE VAUDREY. Shameful!

PICARD *(to* HENRIETTE*)*. Certainly, it is shameful! Mamselle, I will go to see that woman myself. I'll tell her you are not—

*(*HENRIETTE *looks up astonished; he becomes abashed and stammers.)*

That is—I mean that you—that he—that—I don't know what I mean.

DE VAUDREY. Henriette, dry your tears! You shall leave this house to enter mine! Not mine alone, but yours as well, for you shall enter it on the arm of your husband!

HENRIETTE. Your wife! No! No! That is impossible. Think of the immeasurable distance which separates us. How can I defy the will of your family? They are rich and powerful—a marriage with me would entail their enmity.

DE VAUDREY. If my family will not *give* their consent, I will find means to compel them.

PICARD *(very energetically)*. Certainly—we'll compel them!

DE VAUDREY. Picard, my hat, we must go!

*(*PICARD *gets hat and hands it to him.)*

PICARD. Yes, monsieur, we must go.

DE VAUDREY. Henriette, I go to find the means of assuring our happiness!

HENRIETTE. Farewell, monsieur, farewell!

DE VAUDREY. No, Henriette, I will not say farewell. I cannot part with all my hopes. I need them to give me courage—au revoir!

HENRIETTE *(gives her hand and forces herself to smile)*. Au revoir!

*(Exit* PICARD *and* DE VAUDREY. HENRIETTE *throws herself on a chair.)*

No, I have not the strength to continue this conflict between love and duty. I am justly punished. Insulted, driven from this house. I must go where I shall never see him again!

*(During the last lines, she rises and begins to search for her things as though preparing to go. Knock is heard and the door opens. Enter* COUNTESS LEVANT.*)*

COUNTESS. Mademoiselle Henriette de Gaul, I believe.

HENRIETTE *(surprised)*. That is my name, madame.

COUNTESS. You have been warmly recommended to me, mademoiselle.

HENRIETTE. Recommended to you, madame?

COUNTESS. Yes, I am the Countess Levant. I have known for some time the attachment which exists between you and my nephew, and I have defended him against the wrath of my husband. But reflection has shown me my duty to you both. The opposition of his family renders this marriage impossible.

HENRIETTE. Madame, I had determined my course before seeing you. The path of sacrifice and duty.

COUNTESS. I shall not prove ungrateful. I am rich and powerful.

HENRIETTE *(looking up, interested)*. Powerful?

COUNTESS. And if at any time I can show my appreciation of your noble conduct—

HENRIETTE. Madame, you can; now—at this very instant—you can.

COUNTESS. How?

HENRIETTE. Use your power to find the poor child who has been torn from my protection. Do I ask too much?

COUNTESS. No, no. I promise you not alone my aid, but that of the greatest power in Paris. Give me her name, her age and description.

HENRIETTE. A description, alas, madame, too easily given. She is but sixteen and blind!

COUNTESS. Blind?

HENRIETTE. Her name is Louise.

COUNTESS *(with feeling)*. Louise! That name is very dear to me. Be comforted, my child, we will find your sister.

HENRIETTE. She is not my sister, Madame.

COUNTESS. Not your sister?

HENRIETTE. No, madame, but I owe her the love and tenderness of a mother and sister combined, for she saved us all from misery and want.

COUNTESS. How could a poor child do that?

HENRIETTE. From poverty so terrible that my father had not even bread to give us. Anxious to save at least the life of his child, he took me and set out toward Notre Dame. There he stood weeping and irresolute, when suddenly he heard a plaintive cry. He approached and saw a babe half buried under the snow. He took her to his breast to warm her, when the thought came to him that, as this child would have died had he not arrived in time to save it, so his own might die before help could reach her. "I will leave neither of them," he said, and he returned carrying both infants in his arms.

COUNTESS. Oh! Go on, mademoiselle, go on.

HENRIETTE. Entering his home, he said to my mother, "We had only one child, Heaven has sent us another." Heaven rewarded his generous action, for on opening the clothing of the child, a roll of gold was found, with these words written on a scrap of paper, "Her name is Louise, save her."

COUNTESS (struggling with herself). Ah!

HENRIETTE (astonished). Are you ill, madame?

COUNTESS (trying to be calm). No! No! I—it is nothing! Then the infant fell among good and worthy people?

HENRIETTE. Ah, madame, I cannot tell you how we loved her.

COUNTESS. Now I know why Maurice loves you. I will love you, too!

HENRIETTE. Then you will help me to find her?

COUNTESS (with force). Help you? (Rises.) All Paris shall be searched from end to end. (Crosses.) But—she is blind! How is that? And how did you lose her? Tell me all.

(The voice of LOUISE is heard faintly at a great distance, gradually approaching. As HENRIETTE speaks, she grows more abstracted, listening to the voice.)

HENRIETTE. Yes, madame—it—was—one evening—

COUNTESS. Go on—my child—

HENRIETTE (listening). About—about two years ago.

COUNTESS. Two years ago. Well?

HENRIETTE. Yes, two years ago. Louise was then—

COUNTESS (astonished at the abstraction of HENRIETTE). Go on.

HENRIETTE. Louise was then—fourteen.

(Voice approaches nearer.)

We were playing together one evening, when—

(Voice is now quite close under the window; HENRIETTE screams.)

Ah!

COUNTESS. What is it?

HENRIETTE. Hush—sh, listen! It is she, madame, it is she! (Rushes to the window.)

COUNTESS. She? The poor little beggar whom I just left on the steps of the church?

LOUISE (outside, after finishing her song). Henriette! Henriette! Do you hear me?

HENRIETTE. Louise! I am coming. I am coming!

LOUISE (outside). It is I, Louise, your sister! (Then cries out as though she had been checked.) Ah!

HENRIETTE *(frightened)*. Ah, what is that?

COUNTESS. Come, come!

   *(As they reach the door, it is violently thrown open and* LEVANT *enters, followed by an* OFFICER. COUNTESS *stops suddenly.)*

My husband!

HENRIETTE. Gentlemen, gentlemen, do not stop me!

LEVANT *(to* OFFICER*).* Do your duty!

   *(*OFFICER *seizes her.)*

HENRIETTE. In the name of heaven, let me go! Take pity! Let me go or I shall lose her again!

LEVANT. Take this girl to prison!

HENRIETTE *(screams).* Ah! No! No!

   *(*OFFICER *takes her out, struggling.)*

COUNTESS *(tries to go out).* At least let me go! I must go!

LEVANT *(takes her by the arm).* You will remain where you are, madame. You have not told me what brought you here.

COUNTESS. Later, monsieur, I will tell you everything. But now let me go before she—

COUNT. Of whom are you speaking, madame?

COUNTESS. Of—of—of—my—

   *(*LEVANT *looks at her sternly and threateningly. She screams and faints.)*

Ah!

   *(The voice of* LOUISE *is heard faintly in the distance.)*

**CURTAIN**

*The Count Levant detains his wife in Henriette's room after she has discovered that the blind orphan Louise is her daughter. VanAnn Moore plays the Countess; John Masterman plays her husband, the Count Levant, Minister of Police.*

# ACT THREE

## SCENE ONE

SCENE: *Prison courtyard surrounded by leafless trees. At back, a wall, over which can be seen the dome of a church. There is a grated gate in the wall, a door leading to dormitory, a door to the hospital. Several prisoners are discovered kneeling in prayer with* SISTER GENEVIEVE, *Sister Superior of the Hospital. She is dressed in a nun's habit with hood. The gate opens and* DOCTOR *enters,* SISTER GENEVIEVE *rises, dismisses the girls who exit into dormitory.*

SISTER G. Ah, Doctor, I have been waiting impatiently for you.

DOCTOR *(looking at his watch).* I am not late, I believe.

SISTER G. No, but you led me to hope that when you came today you would bring me —

DOCTOR. Good news? Yes. Well, I have done everything in my power. I have spoken of the interest you take in this unfortunate woman, of her sincere repentance.

SISTER G. Then you have succeeded?

DOCTOR. Completely!

SISTER G. Ah, Heaven be praised! *(Calling.)* Jeanette, come here, my child!

JEAN *(coming in from dormitory).* Do you want me, Sister?

SISTER G. Yes, hurry, we cannot keep the doctor waiting. Here is the good doctor, who will tell you what he has done for you.

JEAN. For me?

DOCTOR. You must thank Sister Genevieve, not me. Touched by your repentance, she has solicited and obtained your pardon and release.

*(DOCTOR hands two official papers to SISTER GENEVIEVE.)*

JEAN. My benefactress! My Mother!

DOCTOR. No, your release is granted to the good Sister Genevieve. To that good and noble woman, who, born within the walls of this prison, has never consented to cross its threshold; who has made this prison her country and its unfortunate inmates her family; who brings to you all her daily blessings of consolation and prayer, so that even the vilest here respect and love her.

*(JEANETTE kneels and kisses SISTER GENEVIEVE's hand.)*

I did not intend to make you weep, Jeanette. Come, come, I shall be crying, too, in a minute. *(He helps her to her feet.)*

*(Bell is heard striking.)*

SISTER. It is time to go in. Come, my child. This evening you will be free. *(Gives her one of the documents which the DOCTOR brought.)* Do not forget that I am responsible for you. Society sent me a guilty woman; I return it a repentant one, I hope, Jeanette.

JEAN. I hope so, Sister. *(Loud noise is heard outside in the hospital.)*

HENRIETTE *(outside).* Leave me, leave me! Let me go!

SISTER. What is the meaning of those cries?

(HENRIETTE *appears at door, held by policeman with whom she is struggling.*)

HENRIETTE. You shall not keep me! I must go! I tell you I must!

JEAN *(looking at her).* Good heavens! *(Goes up.)*

HENRIETTE *(runs to* SISTER GENEVIEVE*).* Oh, madame! If you are mistress here, have pity on me! Order them to set me free! I ask you on my knees!

SISTER *(gently).* Be calm, my child. You are ill.

DOCTOR. Certainly you are. Why have you left your bed without my permission?

HENRIETTE. But, monsieur, I am well now. Now that you see I am quite well, you will tell them to let me go, will you not?

DOCTOR. That is impossible. To release you from this place requires a far greater power than mine.

HENRIETTE. This place? Why, what is it? Is it not a hospital?

DOCTOR. A hospital and a prison.

HENRIETTE. A prison! Ah, I remember. Yes, I remember the soldiers who dragged me thither, and he who commanded them. "To the Hospital of La Salpetriere," he said, the prison for *(Looking round her.)* unfortunate women. Oh! My God! *(Goes to bench at back and weeps.)*

DOCTOR *(to* SISTER GENEVIEVE*).* Sister, this is not a case for my care. You must be the physician here. *(Crosses and exits into hospital.)*

SISTER. I have seen many guilty women, but this one—

JEAN. Is not guilty, Sister.

SISTER. Do you know her?

JEAN. When I came here, I told you that on that very day I had been prevented from adding the crime of suicide to my many sins by two young girls, angels of virtue and goodness. This is one of them.

SISTER. How is it possible that she should be here?

JEAN. Misfortunes may have overtaken her, but I am sure that vice has never sullied her life.

(PICARD *appears at the gate, speaks with* SISTER GENEVIEVE *and shows her a paper. After a few words, he is admitted.* JEANETTE *goes to* HENRIETTE *and brings her forward.*)

SISTER. Courage, my child. Look up.

JEAN. Look at me, mademoiselle. Do you not know me? Do you not remember the woman who wished to drown herself?

HENRIETTE *(looking up slowly).* You—you? Ah, yes, I remember you too well. *(Despairingly.)* Alas! We were together then. You saw her, my poor sister.

SISTER. By whose orders were you sent here?

PICARD *(comes down).* By the order of the Count Levant, madame.

SISTER. Who are you, sir?

PICARD *(with importance).* First valet-de-chambre to his Excellency, the Minister of Police.

SISTER. Then it is by his order that this poor child is—

PICARD. Alas! Madame, the honor of an illustrious house must be protected.

HENRIETTE. You are witness that I refused the hand of the Baron De Vaudrey!

PICARD. If Madame the Superior will allow me to inform the young lady of the further wishes of His Excellency the Minister of Police, I think I can make her understand.

SISTER. You may do so. *(To* HENRIETTE.*)* Have courage, my child, trust in heaven. *(Kisses her on forehead, crosses. To* JEANETTE.*)* Jeanette!

*(*JEANETTE *precedes her as they exit D.R.)*

HENRIETTE. We are alone. What new misery do you bring me?

PICARD. Come, come, mademoiselle—can you never forgive me? That is too bad, to have you reproach me, too. Because the master I deceive is the Minister of Police.

HENRIETTE. But Baron De Vaudrey, what of him?

PICARD. He refused to obey his uncle, and—and yesterday he was sent to prison, too.

HENRIETTE. He too is a prisoner, then?

PICARD. Yes—he made me swear to come here and tell you that if, at the worst, they decided to send you into exile to Cayenne—

HENRIETTE. Exile! Cayenne! Why, that would be death!

PICARD *(in an undertone).* Wait a little, mamselle. If my pretended master comes to that decision, he will release my real master from prison, and once he gets out of there, why, off he goes, followed by your humble servant. We overtake the guard having you in charge. With the gold with which we take care to be provided, my real master will bribe the guards, and if they should be incorruptible, that is, if we have not enough money with us to buy them, why, then we will share your exile, and we will be happy in spite of the treachery of my other master.

HENRIETTE. You speak to me of happiness? Who then will search for my sister, Louise?

PICARD. Do I count for nothing? Do you suppose that a member of the secret police of His Excellency the Minister of Police is going to fold his arms quietly? No—come, come, mademoiselle, I will arrange everything.

*(*OFFICER *appears at gate.* SISTER GENEVIEVE *enters with* JEANETTE *and opens gate.)*

HENRIETTE *(pointing to* OFFICER*)*. Good heavens! Look there!

OFFICER. Sister Superior, I have the honor to hand you this list of prisoners, who by the order of His Excellency the Minister of Police, are condemned to exile. Permit me to order them assembled here and we can proceed to identify them. *(Hands papers to* SISTER GENEVIEVE.*)*

SISTER. You may do so, monsieur. I will follow you.

*(*OFFICER *salutes and exits.)*

The list! I dread to look at it. *(She opens the paper hesitatingly, and *reads. Looks at* HENRIETTE, *and cries out.)* Ah!

HENRIETTE. Madame, why do you look at me so? Answer me, for pity's sake! Have mercy!

SISTER. Ah, my poor child!

HENRIETTE. I see it. Alas! I am condemned. I am lost, lost!

*(Enter* DOCTOR.*)*

PICARD *(aside to* SISTER GENEVIEVE*)*. Madame, is this true?

SISTER *(showing the list)*. Henriette de Gaul.

> (HENRIETTE *screams and falls weeping into the arms of the* DOC-
> TOR *and* JEANETTE, *who led her to the bench.* SISTER GENEVIEVE
> *stops and looks at her pityingly for a moment and exits.)*

PICARD. They are going to send her off immediately. Today! I will go to the prison and inform the Baron, my master, that my other master has villainously deceived me—that he has had the indelicacy to actually suspect my fidelity. Ah! He shall pay for that!

HENRIETTE *(to* JEANETTE, *coming forward)*. Ah! Now I understand why one may wish to die!

JEAN. Do not speak so, Mademoiselle. Remember the words of hope you spoke to me.

HENRIETTE *(to* DOCTOR*)*. Ah! sir, exile has no terrors for me. I do not weep for my own misfortunes, but for my sister's. I had found her at the moment they arrested me. I heard her voice; I saw her. She was covered with rags. She was being dragged along by a horrible old woman, who I know ill-treats her, beats her, perhaps.

DOCTOR *(trying to recall)*. Wait a minute, my child. I believe that I have met that very young girl.

HENRIETTE. You, monsieur?

DOCTOR. Yes, yes. A young girl led by an old woman who called her Louise.

HENRIETTE. Yes, yes; that is her name!

DOCTOR. I know the old woman, too; she is called La Frochard.

PICARD. La Frochard? The old hag who goes about whining for alms in the name of Heaven and seven poor children. Where does she live?

JEAN *(aside)*. Jacques' mother! She must be saved from their vile hands. *(Aloud)*. She lives in a hovel by the river side; it was formerly used as a boathouse, but has long been occupied by thieves and the worst criminals. There is a secret entrance from the Rue Noir, but it is difficult to find, and it is always carefully guarded.

PICARD. Never mind that. The police of Paris can find secret entrances. If not, we'll capture the main one. First to release my master—then for the boathouse! *(Exit.)*

HENRIETTE. You are sure she lives there? Then we will go at once. I have found her again. *(Recollects herself, utters a cry.)* Ah! I am to be sent away, away far from her.

JEAN. No, no, mademoiselle—you need not—you shall not be sent away. *(To* DOCTOR.*)* Doctor, have pity on her and consent to help me.

*(Enter* OFFICER.*)*

OFFICER. I need another prisoner to complete the list, Henriette De Gaul.

JEAN *(advances very quickly to* OFFICER*)*. Here, monsieur.

HENRIETTE *(low)*. Ahhh!

DOCTOR *(seizes her arm)*. Silence!

JEAN *(to* OFFICER*)*. Permit me, monsieur, to bid her a last farewell!

*(*OFFICER *makes gesture of consent and exits.* JEANETTE *crosses to* HENRIETTE.*)*

HENRIETTE. No, no! I cannot, I will not consent!

JEAN. Hush! It is not you whom I save, Henriette, it is myself. If I remain, Jacques will find me again, and once in his power I shall be lost. You will remain, you will find Louise, and we will both be saved.

HENRIETTE. Louise?

JEAN. Here, take this.

*(*JEANETTE *gives* HENRIETTE *the paper which* SISTER GENEVIEVE *has given her.* HENRIETTE *hesitates and looks at* DOCTOR.*)*

DOCTOR *(behind* HENRIETTE*)*. Take it. Your sister's fate depends upon it.

*(*HENRIETTE *takes the paper and embraces* JEANETTE, *weeping. Enter* SISTER GENEVIEVE *and* OFFICER.*)*

Ah—the Sister Superior!

OFFICER *(to* SISTER GENEVIEVE*)*. Madame, will you please verify this list and identify the prisoners who are intended for exile?

SISTER. I am ready, monsieur!

OFFICER *(reading from list)*. Marie Morand?

*(As each name is called, one of the girls comes from hospital, head down, face averted.* SISTER GENEVIEVE *looks into the face of each one as they pass.)*

SISTER. Yes.

OFFICER. Jeanne Raymond?

SISTER. Yes.

OFFICER *(turning to* JEANETTE*)*. Henriette de Gaul?

JEAN. Here, Mother! *(Crosses to* SISTER GENEVIEVE *and kneels.)*

SISTER. You?

*(*DOCTOR *points to* HENRIETTE *with appealing gesture.* SISTER GENEVIEVE *looks from one to the other and seems greatly agitated.)*

JEAN. Mother! Mother! Have pity, Bless me and let me go, for this exile will purify a guilty soul and save an innocent one.

OFFICER. Well, Sister?

*(*SISTER GENEVIEVE *takes* JEANETTE'*s head in her hands, stoops and kisses her forehead, and then, with a firm voice and eyes uplifted to heaven.)*

SISTER. Yes. *(Aside.)* Ah, Doctor—my first falsehood.

TABLEAU

CURTAIN

In the prison "La Salpetriere," Jeanette volunteers to take Henriette's place as one of the prisoners sent into exile at Cayenne. Sister Genevieve verifies the falsehood, as she silently asks Heaven's forgiveness. Jeanne Miclot is Henriette; Sheila Stanker, Jeanette; Nancy Holt, Sister Genevieve; and Herb Prizeman, the Officer.

## SCENE TWO

SCENE: *The hut of* LA FROCHARD. *The stage represents an old and dilapidated boathouse. At the back C. are two large and heavy doors opening
down, which are closed with a bar across resting in heavy socket and
secured by padlock. Beyond doors, when they are forced open, are discovered steps leading down to the river. Across river can be seen views of
Paris by starlight. At L. is a staircase leading up to a garret with door
opening down. Door has lock and bolt. In room is a crude bed, a table
with knife-grinding machine. At rise of curtain,* LOUISE *and* PIERRE *are
discovered,* LOUISE *asleep upon miserable straw bed,* PIERRE *seated on
stool at foot of bed.*

PIERRE. Poor child! So young, so weak, so lovely, and yet condemned to so hard a fate. Ah—and I can do nothing. Jacques sus-
pects and watches me. If I were to make a step toward her release,
Jacques would discover it and kill me. (*He rises and looks at her.*)
Ah—she shivers in her sleep, she must be ill!

LOUISE (*half rising*). Who is there?

PIERRE. It is I—mamsélle, Pierre!

LOUISE. Ah, Pierre! I am glad it is you. I may sleep a little longer,
may I not?

PIERRE. Sleep, mamselle, sleep—don't be frightened, I will not
leave you.

LOUISE. I am so tired—thank you, Pierre, thank you. (*She lies down.*)

PIERRE (*looking at her*). Yes, sleep, poor child, and forget your misery. (*Pauses.*) Jacques has forbidden me to think of her, but I will
think of her—aye—and save her, too, even if it costs me my life. I can
weaken these bolts, and Jacques will not discover it. (*He goes to
wheel, takes a screwdriver and works at screws in heavy bolt across the
door.*) What am I doing? Alas! I shall pay for this with my life. No, no,
I cannot!

LOUISE (*sighs in her sleep*). Henriette! Sister Henriette!

PIERRE (*running to her side*). She dreams of her sister—a smile
lights her face. (*Thoughtfully.*) Ah! If I help her to escape and her
happy dream were to become a reality, she might remember me
with pity, perhaps with love. (*Goes up.*) I have begun my work and I
will finish it.

(PIERRE *returns to doors at back and is about to commence work
when* LA FROCHARD *enters from door under staircase.*)

FRO (*brings in carrot and turnip, which she puts on table and scrapes
through dialogue which follows*). Hello, master knife-grinder! What
brings you home so early? No work outside, eh?

PIERRE. It is growing dark. I have brought my work home with me.

FRO. So as to be near to Mamselle Louise. Oh, I have my eye on you.

PIERRE. It would be better to have your eye on Jacques. But you
never find fault with him.

FRO. Why should I? He is the oldest, and master here.

*(Enter* JACQUES *by door under staircase.)*

JACQUES. There, that will do for today. *(Takes off apron and throws it.)* No more work for me. I'm tired of it. *(Crosses and sits on a stool.)*

FRO. It is tiresome, isn't it, my son?

JACQUES. Ugh! Disgusting. *(Sees* PIERRE.) Hello, Master Cupid. *(Looking at* LOUISE.) What is this? Asleep. Why isn't she at work?

FRO. That is what I want to know, sleeping instead of working for her living.

JACQUES *(looking at her).* Why, she is so used to it that she cries when she sleeps.

PIERRE *(looking at* LOUISE). Is she crying?

JACQUES *(stops him).* What's that to you?

FRO. She is obstinate, lazy and a hypocrite. This morning I had to push her along to make her walk at all, and as to singing, she has no more voice than a crow.

JACQUES *(sitting).* I will make her sing.

PIERRE. You will kill her. Can't you see she is ill?

FRO. Nonsense—she is shamming—I know her tricks.

JACQUES. What is the matter with her now?

FRO. She has got some new notion in her head—I can't tell what.

PIERRE. I can. You remember the night of the snowstorm. After finishing her song, she cried out at the top of her voice, "Henriette, my sister."

FRO. Yes, and I stopped her mouth pretty quick, too.

PIERRE. Yes, yes, you twisted her arm until you nearly broke it.

FRO. Well, why didn't she mind me?

PIERRE. You're killing her.

FRO. I can't afford to support her idleness. She has to work, and if she won't—

JACQUES. I'll find a way to make her sing—

PIERRE. You, what would you do?

JACQUES *(crossing to* PIERRE). That is my business.

FRO *(goes to* LOUISE). Come, get up, my fine lady. No more airs. You must go out and make your living.

*(She makes* LOUISE *rise.)*

Give me that shawl. *(Throws shawl on bed.)* Take off this scarf; it keeps you too warm. *(Takes off scarf and puts it on her own neck.)* You'll shiver more comfortably without it.

LOUISE. I don't wish to go out, madame.

FRO *(to* JACQUES). Eh? What next? You hear that? She don't wish to go out.

JACQUES. We'll see about that. *(Crosses to* LOUISE *and goes to take her hand.)* Come here, my little beauty.

LOUISE *(recoils from his touch).* I forbid *you* to touch me.

JACQUES. Oh, ho! Then we're no longer friends?

LOUISE. Friends? You? You're cruel wretches! Both of you.

*Pierre sits by helplessly as his brother Jacques attempts to push the blind Louise out to beg once more. La Frochard looks on with admiration at her son's consistent cruelty and heartlessness. Lynn Bradley is the evil La Frochard; Allen Fearon, Pierre; Mary Stevens, Louise; and Joe Maltsberger is Jacques Frochard.*

JACQUES. Yet you were glad enough to share our home when we picked you up in the streets.

LOUISE. Yes; I was grateful to you then, because you offered me shelter. Alas! I learned too soon it was not pity for my misfortune that moved you. No, no, you wanted to make use of my affliction. You have starved, tortured, *beaten* me; but now—weak as I am—my will shall be stronger than your violence! *(Straightening herself up.)* I will beg no more!

PIERRE *(terrified)*. Louise!

JACQUES. Ah! When her blood is up, she is superb!

FRO. Oh, well, well, that is all mighty fine; but where is the bread and butter to come from?

LOUISE. I care not!

PIERRE *(crossing to* LA FROCHARD*)*. Do you hear? Do you know what she means? She will starve rather than beg.

FRO. Nonsense, she will get tired of that soon enough.

LOUISE. Never!

FRO. Well, we'll see if locking you up in that garret won't bring you to your senses.

LOUISE. If I enter that place, you know I will never leave it alive.

JACQUES. Why, she is magnificent. I'd never have believed she had so much spirit. *(Advances towards her.)* Why—I love you! *(Seizes her and attempts to kiss her.)*

LOUISE. Ah! *(Screams and escapes from him.)*

PIERRE *(angrily)*. Jacques! *(Loudly, coming down on his L.)*

JACQUES. Well, what is it? You don't like it, I suppose, Master Cupid. Well, forbid it, why don't you?

PIERRE. I do! *(Looks at* JACQUES *who eyes him sternly and he cowers U.)* Oh, miserable, cowardly wretch that I am! *(Breaks down sobbing, goes to wheel.)*

FRO *(crosses to* LOUISE*)*. Come—come along. You're strong enough when you want to be. Up into the garret with you.

*(She leads* LOUISE *to the foot of the stairs.* LOUISE *falls on steps.)*

JACQUES. Yes, that is right, mother, take her up there out of the way. Here—I want to speak to you.

*(LA FROCHARD *crosses to* JACQUES; *they whisper.)*

PIERRE *(going to* LOUISE, *at foot of steps, and speaking in a low tone, very rapidly)*. You can escape, I have unscrewed the lock; the key to the door to the street is under your mattress. Trust to heaven to guide you. Nothing worse can happen than threatens you here.

JACQUES *(aloud to* LA FROCHARD*)*. Lock her up securely. I have my reasons for distrusting Master Cupid here!

FRO. Yes, yes, I understand.

JACQUES. Come with me and keep your whining for this blind beauty till another time. Come along, I say!

*(He pulls* PIERRE *off R.)*

FRO *(sitting)*. Ah! What a splendid fellow he is. The very image of his dear father. There was a man for you. They cut off his head. *(Turns to* LOUISE *and takes bottle from her pocket, from which she drinks.)* Ah! That warms my heart! *(To* LOUISE.*)* Yes, Jacques is right. We must break your obstinate spirit.

*(*LOUISE *has sunk down on steps.* LA FROCHARD *goes to her.)*
Ah! Shamming again. Get up and come with me!

*(*LA FROCHARD *forces her to rise and they go up the stairs.)*
LOUISE. Oh, Madame, have you no soul, no pity? Do not kill me!

FRO. I don't intend to. You're too valuable. There, get in with you. I'll see you safe inside.

*(They exit into garret.* LA FROCHARD *closes the door. After a moment's pause, the door under the stairs opens and* PICARD *enters.)*

PICARD. Ah! At last I've found a door that leads to something and somewhere. *(Looks about him.)* There's nobody at home! *(Sees brandy bottle, takes it up.)* Hello, what's this? Brandy! *(Smells it.)* Bad brandy; very bad brandy! What is my best course? Let me see. *(Examines C. doors.)* These doors must open on the river. Good. That is the point for the police. Now to return through the half-mile dark passages to the Rue Noir where I left Mamselle Henriette; then to the Baron, liberated by his uncle on the assumption that Mamselle Henriette has been sent to Cayenne. And now, if I have not earned my promotion, my name is not Picard. *(Exit understairs, slamming door.)*

*(Enter* LA FROCHARD.*)*

FRO *(opening door of garret)*. Hm! Eh! What's that? *(Comes down quickly.)* I thought I heard someone. Jacques, is that you? No, there is no one here. I'm an old fool to be so easily frightened—it's my nerves. *(Drinks.)*

*(Knock at door.)*
Who's that?

*(Knock heard again.)*
Who can have found their way here? *(She hides the bottle and goes to the door.)* Who is there? What do you want?

HENRIETTE *(outside)*. I am looking for someone—for Madame Frochard.

FRO. What do you want of her?

HENRIETTE *(outside)*. I must speak with her.

FRO. Are you alone?

HENRIETTE. Yes, I am alone.

FRO *(cautiously opens the door and looks behind* HENRIETTE*)*. Well, if you are alone, you may come in.

*(Enter* HENRIETTE *looking around her, affright.* LA FROCHARD *closes door and comes down.)*

HENRIETTE. How imprudent I was to leave the spot where Picard left me. I have lost him and wandered here by accident. Great heaven! Can this be the place?

FRO. Well, well, young woman, you want to see Madame Frochard.

What have you got to say to her? Do you expect to find anyone here?

HENRIETTE (*looks around searchingly*). Yes, yes, I am looking for the person who lives here with you.

FRO. What person?

HENRIETTE. A young girl.

FRO. I don't know anything about any young girl.

HENRIETTE (*astonished*). You don't know her?

FRO. No!

HENRIETTE. Am I mistaken? This house answers the description and your name is Frochard, is it not?

FRO. Euphemie Frochard—what then?

HENRIETTE (*Sees* LOUISE's *shawl on the bed and utters a loud cry*). Ah!

FRO. What is the matter?

HENRIETTE (*seizes the shawl*). This shawl! I know it—it is hers, it is hers, I tell you!

FRO. Not a bit of it. It is mine. (*Attempts to recover the shawl.*)

HENRIETTE. And the scarf around your neck?

FRO. Well, what of it?

HENRIETTE. It was made for her by my own hands. (*Tears the scarf from* LA FROCHARD's *neck.*) Ah, wretch, you have lied to me.

FRO. Well, well, if you must know the truth, I'll tell you. When you came in, you were so excited and frightened that I didn't dare tell you all—

HENRIETTE. What? Speak quickly.

FRO. One evening, about three months ago, I met the girl you are looking for wandering about in the streets. I had pity on her and brought her home with me, where I took good care of her. But you see, the poor child wasn't very strong, and what with the life we lead and the sorrow she felt, she could not stand it. She broke down entirely, and that was the end of it. For two days now she has been gone.

HENRIETTE. Dead! Louise—dead! (*She faints.*)

FRO. Ah! fainted. What am I to do with her? Oh, if Jacques were only here. I must go for him. But if she were to come to and see the other one. No, no, I'll fix that. (*She goes up the stairs, locks the garret door, takes the key with her.*) There, there is nothing to fear now; I'll go and call Jacques.

> (*She exits at door L. and is heard to lock the door on the other side after her. As soon as she is off, the door of the garret is seen to move, at first gently, then with more force. Finally the lock tumbles off, the door opens and* LOUISE *appears.*)

LOUISE. They are all gone. Pierre told me the truth, the lock would not hold. (*She comes down.*) If I can find my way to the street, through that long passage—(*She gropes around and passes very close to* HENRIETTE.) Where is the door? Ah, here. (*She tries the door L.*) Locked, locked; what shall I do? Ah—I remember, Pierre told me he had made another key for it. (*She gropes her way rapidly to the bed, feels under the mattress and finds the key.)* Ah, good, brave Pierre, now I will go at once. *(She crosses the stage with rapid steps and stumbles against* HENRIETTE. *She recoils frightened, then advances and stoops, feeling with her hands.)* A woman! *(She touches* HENRIETTE's *hand.)* Oh, Heaven! They have committed some horrible crime and fled. *(She raises* HENRIETTE's *head to her knees and puts her hand on her heart.)* Madame, madame, speak, speak to me.

> *(The door is heard to unlock and* LA FROCHARD *and* JACQUES *enter quickly.)*

FRO. How is this? Together!

JACQUES. Separate them at once—quick!

FRO *(dragging* LOUISE *away from* HENRIETTE*)*. What are you doing here? How did you get out?

LOUISE. I—madame—I!

JACQUES *(seeing* HENRIETTE *recovering)*. Quick, get her out of the way—quick, I tell you—the other one is coming to.

> *(*PIERRE *appears at door.)*

LOUISE. But this woman who is lying here!

> *(At that moment* HENRIETTE *opens her eyes and sees* LOUISE.*)*

HENRIETTE *(screams)*. Louise! Louise!

> *(*JACQUES *puts his hand over her mouth.)*

LOUISE *(stops)*. That voice? I know it.

FRO. Go on—I tell you—get in with you!

HENRIETTE *(pushing* JACQUES' *hand away)*. Louise! Sister!

> *(With an effort,* LOUISE *pushes* LA FROCHARD *aside and runs down the stairs.* HENRIETTE *disengages herself from* JACQUES. *They meet C. and embrace.)*

LOUISE. Henriette! Henriette! It is you!

HENRIETTE. Louise, Louise! My sister!

PIERRE *(joyfully)*. Her sister! She has found her! Now I would gladly die—now that she is happy.

HENRIETTE. Oh, my Louise, my poor Louise! What have they done to you? Miserable wretches that you are! I will have you punished.

> *(*JACQUES *goes to door L.)*

Let us go at once! Let us go!

JACQUES *(barring the passage)*. No, you shall not go! You cannot leave here.

HENRIETTE. I will cry out—I will call for help!

JACQUES *(backing them to R.)* Try it, and see what good it will do! Besides, I warn you we come of a family that kills! *(Seizes* LOUISE, *dragging both of them to C.)* She is mine and I will keep her!

LOUISE *(screams)*. Ah!

> *(*PIERRE *rushes in between* LOUISE *and* JACQUES, *forcing* JACQUES *to release* LOUISE, *and he faces* JACQUES.*)*

JACQUES. You dare to interfere against me?

PIERRE. I dare!

JACQUES. Against me!

PIERRE. Against you! I have acted the coward long enough. I thought, because you were big and strong, that you were brave—but you are not! You fight women—you are a coward! In their defense, my courage will be more than a match for your strength!

LOUISE. Brave Pierre!

JACQUES *(advancing to him)*. What do you want?

PIERRE. Let these two women go!

JACQUES. Indeed! Suppose I refuse, what then?

PIERRE. What then? What then? Well, you have said it—we come from a family that kills.

FRO *(on steps)*. Pierre!

PIERRE. Lay a hand on either of them *(Runs to his wheel and takes up knife.)* and I plunge this knife into your heart.

*(JACQUES recoils as though in spite of himself.)*

JACQUES. Your life shall pay for this!

PIERRE. Or yours!

FRO. Remember you are brothers!

PIERRE *(bitterly)*. Yes, brothers—the sons of Adam—only this time Abel will kill Cain!

JACQUES. Very well, if you will have it.

*(He takes knife from PIERRE; they fight, and JACQUES wounds PIERRE in the shoulder.)*

HENRIETTE. He is wounded.

PIERRE. No!

JACQUES. Isn't that enough, cripple?

PIERRE. No; cut again, for while she is in danger, you may slash my flesh to ribbons. I shall feel nothing.

*(They fight again. PIERRE wrests knife from JACQUES and stabs him. He falls dead. PIERRE stares at him in horror.)*

Yes, he was right, we do come of a family that kills!

FRO *(crossing to PIERRE in fury)*. And for this, I shall kill you! You have killed my strong, handsome son, and you shall pay with your worthless life!

*(During this speech she takes knife from PIERRE who gives it up without a struggle. HENRIETTE comes forward.)*

HENRIETTE. No! No!

*(As LA FROCHARD raises knife to stab PIERRE, door is thrust open violently. DE VAUDREY enters, grabs LA FROCHARD and takes knife away from her.)*

DE VAUDREY. What's this? Would you kill this one who stands here defenseless?

FRO. Who are you to interfere? He is my miserable, misshapen son—and he has killed my handsome Jacques! *(Screams.)* I will kill him—I will!

*(She attacks PIERRE. DE VAUDREY pulls her away and protects PIERRE.)*

HENRIETTE. Oh, sir, you have come just in time—this lying hag would have killed us all!

*(Noise is heard beyond door and voice of* PICARD.*)*

PICARD. Open, open in the name of the law!

*(The noise of a battering ram is heard against the door. The bar falls; doors open and enter* PICARD *with* OFFICER *with drawn pistols.)*

PICARD. Ah, master, thank Heaven you are here!

DE VAUDREY. Yes, and in good time, Picard! Murder has been done here, and but for me, the old woman would have committed yet another! Officer—take that boy to prison!

LOUISE. No, no, he deserves no punishment! He killed in self-defense! But for him I should not be alive—he has been my only hope, my only defender against these evil ones! They have starved me, and only Pierre stood against them!

DE VAUDREY. My uncle, the Minister of Police will decide his fate, Henriette—but for now, he must go to prison.

PIERRE *(to* LOUISE*).* Do not grieve, mamselle. I shall not mind, now that you are saved. *(To* OFFICER.*)* I will go with you.

*(During this speech,* LA FROCHARD *attempts to escape unnoticed. When she has almost reached door,* PICARD *wheels and catches her.)*

PICARD. Ah, no, you don't get off so easily, old woman! You shall go with your son and answer for your crimes.

FRO *(turning to audience).* Charity—charity, good people, for a poor old woman—please—have pity on a poor mother with seven children at home.

*(*PICARD *motions to* OFFICER, *who grabs* LA FROCHARD *and drags her off, kicking, biting and cursing. As he leaves,* OFFICER *calls to* PIERRE.*)*

OFFICER. Come along, you!

PIERRE. I will come. *(To* LOUISE; *he takes her hand.)* Farewell, mamselle.

LOUISE *(weeping).* Oh, dear, dear Pierre—*(She kisses him on cheek.)* I promise we will make them understand how brave you are!

*(*OFFICER *calls from outside.)*

OFFICER. I say there—come along!

PIERRE *(as he joins* OFFICER *at exit).* Brave—she said I was brave!

DE VAUDREY. Henriette, my love!

HENRIETTE. A second time I owe my life to you! Louise, my darling sister, thank your preserver.

LOUISE. Ah, monsieur, you do not know from what a frightful fate you have saved us!

DE VAUDREY *(to* PICARD*).* And now, monsieur le capitaine, how are we to get away from this hole of a place?

PICARD. Monsieur le Baron, I have provided for everything. The Minister of Police promised to follow me here, with your aunt, the Countess, as soon as possible.

HENRIETTE. The Minister of Police coming here? Let me go with my poor Louise at once.

DE VAUDREY. Stay, Henriette! I have restored your sister to your arms, to replace your care by the endearing protection of a mother.

*(The* COUNT LEVANT, COUNTESS *and* DOCTOR *enter.)*

HENRIETTE *(bewildered).* Mother?

LOUISE *(joyfully).* My mother!

*(*DE VAUDREY *meets* COUNTESS *and brings her down.)*

DE VAUDREY. Your mother, the Countess de Levant.

COUNTESS *(embracing her).* My child, my Louise!

HENRIETTE *(sadly).* I have found her, only to lose her again!

LEVANT. Not so, mademoiselle. It is only within the past hour that I have learned the truth. The Countess has confessed the secret which has clouded our married life!

DE VAUDREY. Picard, you may unpack my trunks. I shall not go to Cayenne.

PICARD. No necessity for it, monsieur. We found our Cayenne in Paris, and for a few minutes as hot as we wanted it.

*(*COUNTESS *comes down with* LOUISE *and* HENRIETTE. PICARD *and* LEVANT *are engaged in whispering through the last two lines.)*

LOUISE. Monsieur, we are all so happy; yet you must not forget poor Pierre. Noble, brave Pierre!

COUNT. My dear, I promise you we shall not forget Pierre! If what Picard has told me is true, he will be pardoned.

LOUISE. Oh, I could never thank you enough. Henriette, how can we ever reward these kindnesses?

DE VAUDREY *(to* HENRIETTE*).* Henriette, is my reward to be delayed longer?

HENRIETTE. To be near Louise, my sister, and to be your wife, seems too great a joy.

LOUISE *(to* COUNTESS*).* Ah, mother, if I could only see you!

DOCTOR. Ah! That is my affair.

COUNTESS. And do you think you can restore her sight, doctor?

DOCTOR. I can be the instrument! The rest is in the hands of heaven!

TABLEAU TO HEAVEN

AND

CURTAIN

# After Dark

## OR

## Pardon—for a Price

A Melodrama in Three Acts
as adapted from
Dion Boucicault's 1868 script

# CAST OF CHARACTERS

CHANDOS BELLINGHAM, a fugitive from justice
OLD TOM, a man without a name
GEORGE MEDHURST, a reckless and disillusioned youth
SIR GORDON CHUMLEY, Captain of the Dragoons, a man of honor
POINTER, a minion of the law, a division policeman
ELIZA, George Medhurst's wife
ROSE EDGERTON, a young woman to whom duty dictates
DICEY MORRIS, gambling house keeper, proprietor of the Silver Bell
SALLY CRUMPETS, denizen of the London underground
JACK CRUMPETS, another London outcast
DEALER at the Silver Bell
BARMAID of the Silver Bell
SERVANT

# SYNOPSIS OF SCENES

Time: 1868                                      Place: London

## ACT ONE

**Scene One:**   DICEY MORRIS' gambling hall, the Silver Bell.
"You will, of course, expect the lion's share?"

**Scene Two:**   GEORGE and ELIZA's garret apartment.
"We cannot part like this."

**Scene Three:** DICEY's gambling hall.
"Of course, it is for the best."

**Scene Four:**  Street in front of gambling hall.
"I do not forget our bond."

**Scene Five:**  Street on way to the waterfront.
"Please, which way to the bridge?"

**Scene Six:**   On bridge under arches.
"It is for his sake — for his sake!"

## ACT TWO

**Scene One:**   OLD TOM's lodgings.
"I feel ashamed to own who I am."

**Scene Two:** MEDHURST's villa and garden.
"Checkmate! You have mistaken your profession."

**Scene Three:** ROSE's boudoir.
"I can never ask forgiveness of her."

### ACT THREE

**Scene One:** DICEY's gambling hall.
"I have frustrated your villainy."

**Scene Two:** The underground railway.
"After dark the light will come."

## About the Play

The prolific Irish playwright, Dion Boucicault, adapted freely from an earlier French play, *Les Bohemiens de Paris*, when he created his play *After Dark*, transferring the action from the streets of Paris to the well-known haunts of London. He stirred recognition in British audiences with his references to Ruppert Street, Silver Hell, Blackfriar's Bridge, and the recently completed underground shown with the train rushing through it. The play first opened in London on August 12, 1868, where it enjoyed a long, successful run.

As with many of Boucicault's other adaptations, *After Dark* became a New York and travelling troupe favorite. It also enjoyed long runs in the California Theatre and the Opera House in San Francisco in the late 1860's. During the 1890's, several enterprising managers conceived the idea of featuring well-known prizefighters in favorite melodramas to bolster the plays' lagging box office receipts. During this period, Gentleman Jim Corbett was, for a time, cast in *After Dark*.

Christopher Morley, in partnership with Cleon Throckmorton, enjoyed a long run with a revival of the play in Hoboken, New Jersey in 1928 and 1929. At this time, apparently the reputation of melodrama had deteriorated to the point that they chose to present it as a burlesque, with overacting, top hats and twirling moustaches. (See page 16.)

# ACT ONE

## SCENE ONE

SCENE: DICEY MORRIS' *gambling hall, the Silver Bell. The bar, C.R., has a screened exit behind it; table and chairs are at C., chairs U.R. An enclosed entryway, U.L., has a door facing out.* DICEY, *a pretty woman in her mid-thirties, with an elaborate coiffure, richly dressed with heavy jewelry and makeup, is busily stacking chips at the bar, tidying up. Enter* BELLINGHAM, *a sleek, well-dressed man-about-town.*

DICEY. So—I thought you would come crawling back! *(She laughs sarcastically.)* I see the horses didn't mend your fortune after all!

BELLINGHAM. True, Dicey, true! I backed Lady Elizabeth and she let us all down. I am a ruined man, a ruined man—ruined, I tell you.

DICEY. Well, now you've emptied your pockets, perhaps you're not too proud to listen to my plan. It's only a thousand pounds, mind you, not guaranteed to make you rich, but if you will help, your share will keep your creditors quiet for a month or two.

BELLINGHAM. And you, of course, will expect the lion's share?

DICEY. Come, why not be fair? If it is my idea, and you take only a small part of the risk—You're lucky that I'll let you in at all, Richard Knatchbull!

BELLINGHAM. Quiet, Dicey! *(He moves toward her quickly to silence her.)* Never call me by that name again! Someone will hear! You know I am now called Chandos Bellingham.

DICEY. How elegant! And my, how jumpy you are! No one will hear—I've seen to that. I've cleared the place for an hour or two—I'll lock the door. Customers who come this time of day never spend a penny, anyway. Only a bunch of sidewalk pigeons looking for a place to roost!

BELLINGHAM *(sits in chair at table).* So they are, Dicey. Now, what's the scheme?

DICEY. It's this! *(She produces newspaper.)* Right here in the second column—the sensation column!

BELLINGHAM *(reads).* "George Medhurst—Fifty pounds reward will be paid to anyone giving information of this gentleman. He is said to have emigrated to Canada or Australia in 1856. Apply to G.C., Grosvenor Hotel, Pimlico." What does this mean, Dicey? Do you know the man?

DICEY. It means money, Chandos, and I can turn up the man at a minute's notice. I could have had him transported three years ago.

BELLINGHAM. What has he done?

DICEY. He's done forgery, that's what, put his father's name to a worthless scrap of paper.

BELLINGHAM. But what is this to you? Do you hold the note?

DICEY. Of course I do—I've held it now for three years. You never know when such a thing may come in handy, especially when the forger is to come into a title and a fortune. It was a gamble, but that's my business!

*(She puts dice in cup and rattles them, then throws them out on the table.)*

BELLINGHAM. But does the young man know of this?

DICEY. Not a bit of it. Wait, I'll show him to you. *(She crosses to the door and calls.)* Hello—come here, cabby—come here!

*(Enter* MEDHURST, *whip in hand. He is an attractive young man in his mid-twenties. He wears working clothes covered by a fingertip-length cape.)*

MEDHURST. Well, what do you want?

DICEY *(at table; she takes paper).* What do I want? Don't tell me you've forgotten me?

MEDHURST. Forgotten you, Dicey? No! *(Sullenly.)* Not since that day when you took up my note at Haymarket and I came like a dog to your call! So, now that you have me, what do you want of me?

DICEY. There's gratitude for you! I want you to take a look at this. *(She offers him the paper.)*

MEDHURST *(with paper).* "Fifty pounds reward—George Medhurst." What does this mean?

DICEY *(snatches the paper back).* It means the police want to find out about your forgery, but I won't tell them. I'll see them and get them off the trail. Come back tonight and I'll have news for you.

MEDHURST. I will come, don't doubt. *(Aside.)* For I must.

DICEY. Tell me, where are you living now?

MEDHURST. Five hundred twelve Campton Mews.

DICEY. In the same place. And how is your wife? Is she well?

MEDHURST. She is, thank you.

DICEY. Fine—fine.

*(Exit* MEDHURST.*)*

There! He's the heir to a baronetcy and six thousand pounds a year. And what do you think of that—driving a night hack and picking up a living in the streets! I don't much think he'll go near "G.C." or the Grosvenor Hotel!

BELLINGHAM. But what are you going to do with me, Dicey? What do you want with me, when you have him in your power? It's not like you to take me in as a partner and show up a good thing to me without security. Come—what's your game?

DICEY. Well, Chandos, you do remember that eight years ago, when you were transpor—I mean, when you emigrated to Australia—you were living in Pentonville, with such a great lady—and a little girl.

BELLINGHAM. Of course, and I asked you, if anything should happen to me, to take care of the child.

DICEY. And I did take care of her! I brought her up like a lady—like a lady, do you understand? And when she grew up, I put her in as one of my barmaids.

BELLINGHAM. Then what became of her?

DICEY. Why, my young friend you just met fell in love with her—and she married him!

BELLINGHAM. Married him?

DICEY. Yes. That's what I'm getting to. He married your child—and now he's the heir to six thousand a year.

BELLINGHAM. But she was not my child!

DICEY. Not your child! Oh, then, I'm sorry. It's all off—all off. I don't need you in this business after all!

BELLINGHAM. What? Of all this you only see your way to a thousand pounds? You hold in your hands the fair fame and honor of an old county family, and you cannot plan to squeeze more than a paltry one thousand pounds out of it? Dicey, I was wrong, you do need me—you are a fool!

DICEY. I know, I know. But she's a good girl, and she's his wife. So, I'd only figured to take good interest on my money—a thousand pound's my price.

BELLINGHAM. One thousand pounds! How about five thousand?

DICEY. Five thousand—it's too much!

BELLINGHAM. You're a foolish woman, Dicey. Leave the game to me. I'll get five thousand for you. Then you can close the Silver Bell and buy a house in Kearney Street.

DICEY (*sits and begins to play with cards*). All right—if you think it's worth five thousand, you go see this "G.C." at the Grosvenor Hotel. Come back when you've seen him. I'll be here.

(*Exit* BELLINGHAM. *Enter* OLD TOM, *about 40, but he looks 50. He is unkempt, stooped and drunk. He staggers under the weight of a billboard he is wearing.*)

DICEY. So this is the way my advertising is done! A fine advertisement for a respectable place! Put down my sign this minute! I'll report you—you—you—oh, what is your name?

TOM. I don't have a name!

DICEY. Come—that won't do with me! Of course, I remember now! You're called Old Tom!

TOM. Sure, old Tom! I live on Old Tom!

(*Enter* BARMAID *with tray, bottle and whiskey glass. She is young, attractive, dressed in evening clothes, and heavily made up. She goes to* TOM.)

Old Tom for breakfast, Old Tom for dinner—Old Crow for supper—

(*He takes up the glass, drinks, puts glass back on tray.*)

Ha! It keeps the rain out and I don't feel hungry. Whiskey—good strong whiskey—give us a copper for half a quart!

DICEY. Poor fellow—poor old fellow! I pity him—I actually do.

(BARMAID *crosses to table and puts tray and glasses down.* DEALER *enters U.R., sits on high stool, stacks chips and shuffles cards. He wears black pants, a white shirt open at the neck, black garter armband, open vest & green visor eyeshade.*)

TOM. You pity me? You? Dicey Morris that keeps the Silver "Hell"

on Ruppert Street pities me? I've not forgotten you. I lost my last
sovereign over your tables, and my last sixpence over your pewter
bar. And *you* pity *me*? You, who picked me up out of the gutter, and
clothed me in the rags you keep for your customers—the livery of sin
and degradation. I must be the meanest wretch in all the town to
deserve pity from *you*!

DICEY. No use making a row about it. There's a shilling—go drink
it. (*She gives him shilling.*)

TOM (*taking it, he holds it up*). A shilling! A shilling taken over your
tables may be the last drop of some poor devil's blood, or only the
coin of some shop-boy, stolen from his master's till. Ah, take it from
you, Dicey? No, it would choke me!

(*He throws down the shilling;* DICEY *retrieves it.*)

DICEY. Won't take a shilling? It's shocking what drink will bring a
fellow to. In all these years, I've never seen such a one.

(SONG: *"Hooray for Gambling"* *)

DICEY (*steps out and recites first line*). Deal the cards!

| | |
|---|---|
| DEALER. | Stack the chips! |
| TOM. | Gamblin' is a sin! |
| DICEY. | I'll deal anything, boys— |
| BARMAID. | I'm in— |
| DEALER. | I'm in— |
| TOM. | I'm in! |

| | |
|---|---|
| BARMAID. | Although you make a thousand bets, |
| DEALER. | You cannot win them all— |
| BARMAID. | I'll take a pair— |
| DICEY. | I'm standing pat— |
| TOM. | I'll take a bushel, Joe! |
| ALL. | Hooray for gambling and bravo for vice! |
| | We're thankful for poker and thankful for dice. |
| | It may be a sin, but we'll pay the price, |
| | Hooray for gambling and bravo for vice. |
| DICEY & | |
| BARMAID. | Three cheers for women whose virtue is spent! |
| | We may be forsaken, but we pay the rent. |
| | And though we won't make it to Paradise— |
| ALL. | Hooray for gambling and bravo for vice! |

(*At the end of song,* TOM *takes another drink from* BARMAID's *tray
and sits at table, slumped.* BARMAID *picks up tray and glasses and
exits.* DEALER *stays at table, picking up and stacking chips.* TOM
*continues to slump as the scene progresses, until he slides down
and goes to sleep.*)

*Music on page 377.

All: "Bravo for vice!" Dicey is Patricia Gamble; Bert Hood is Pointer; Marvin Hall is the Dealer; and David Rosario is Chando Bellingham alias Richard Knatchbull.

In this production, Bellingham and Pointer took part in the song; Old Tom and the Barmaid were not in the scene.

(Enter BELLINGHAM with GORDON CHUMLEY and ROSE EDGERTON. GORDON CHUMLEY is a young nobleman in his late 30's, very properly dressed for the city, with top hat and cane. ROSE is an attractive young woman, about 20 years old, also well dressed, obviously of good breeding and well educated.)

BELLINGHAM. I wish to present to you a long-time acquaintance— Mrs. Morris—one who has been a great friend to Mr. Medhurst in adversity. (To DICEY.) These are friends of our dear George.

DICEY. Well, friends of Mr. Medhurst—welcome!

ROSE. Oh, yes, we are cousins and were brought up together in childhood.

DICEY. I should have known it by the likeness.

BELLINGHAM (aside). Remember your manners, Dicey! (Aloud to DICEY.) And this is Captain Gordon Chumley.

CHUMLEY (aside). She looks like a hard one to me. As for the other, I can't make him out. I have seen his face somewhere before. (Aloud.) I think, Mr. Bellingham, that we have met. Was it in India or the Crimea?

BELLINGHAM (as if relieved). Neither.

CHUMLEY. Then were you ever in Australia?

DICEY (aside). Only for seven years!

BELLINGHAM. Never!

CHUMLEY. Ah, it's very odd, I beg your pardon.

BELLINGHAM. Don't mention it. But we are forgetting our friend Medhurst.

ROSE. I bring news to him. Our dear Sir John has died.

DICEY. His father dead?

ROSE. Yes, but George will be happy to learn that Sir John at the last forgave him.

DICEY. Forgave? What had he done to forgive?

ROSE. I never really knew, for he was reluctant to speak of it. The rumor was that as a youth he gambled—but it little matters now— since he has his father's complete forgiveness.

CHUMLEY. Yes, but only on condition. Remembering the wildness of his youth, he imposes upon him a proviso. He must marry to gain the estate.

DICEY. That's easily arranged—he's . . .

(BELLINGHAM nudges her.)

BELLINGHAM. Hold your tongue! (Aloud to CHUMLEY.) On that condition, eh?

CHUMLEY. Yes, on the condition that he marries his cousin. If he refuses, all the property goes to her. A most painful position for the young lady, very painful.

DICEY. I don't see why—she's safe to have hers!

BELLINGHAM (aside to DICEY). Will you keep quiet!

CHUMLEY. It is not probable that Mr. Medhurst will rebel against such a condition.

BELLINGHAM (to ROSE). They say there is no husband like the reformed rake. I trust George will prove no exception to the rule. Madam, your servant! We will go and be the first to break the good fortune to George. (He takes DICEY aside.)

DICEY. I'll tell them—it's impossible.

BELLINGHAM. No—no—it's better than we hoped.

DICEY. But his wife—

BELLINGHAM. His wife must disappear.

DICEY. She'll do no such thing! If there's money to be had, the girl's to share it!

BELLINGHAM. Fool! Of course, she'll share it—her price to set him free.

(DICEY *and* BELLINGHAM *exit.*)

CHUMLEY. Ah, it's awfully hard on me, Rose, to have to see you for the last time and say goodbye.

(OLD TOM *goes to sleep.*)

ROSE. You are not going to leave me all alone in London?

CHUMLEY. Yes, Rose, I must. George will soon come to claim his bride.

ROSE. Oh, when we tell him all, that I—I—I—

CHUMLEY. You love me? I had feared as much, while I hoped. You might have spared me that. My task—our task—was hard enough before.

ROSE *(moving toward him, pleading).* Yes, Gordon, I—I suppose I've always loved you, but I never knew how much till now. You were my only comfort when my mother died—and now with Sir John gone, I would have none to turn to save for you. Oh, must I do this thing my whole heart bids me not to do?

CHUMLEY *(putting his arm around her).* Yes, Rose. Your uncle has pointed out the only way to restore George Medhurst to his true position in the world. None could aid him save a wife like you.

ROSE *(takes his hand in hers).* Then stay with me and strengthen me to do what is right, and do not leave me until all is done.

CHUMLEY. So much is duty—and pleasant so far. But to part from you will be so much the harder, now that I know your heart.

(OLD TOM *approaches him.*)

What do you want?

TOM *(very drunkenly).* I saw you talking with them—them! *(Jerks his hand in* BELLINGHAM'S *direction.)* Don't have nothing to do with them! Nothing to do!

CHUMLEY. Why, the man's drunk!

TOM. Eh? It's Gordon Chumley!

CHUMLEY *(amazed).* You know me!

TOM *(aside).* He has forgotten me. No wonder! I have almost forgotten myself. *(Pathetically.)* Never mind, never mind!

(*Enter* POINTER, *a young policeman, dressed in traditional British bobby's uniform and hat. He carries a nightstick.*)

POINTER. Come, move on; this won't do. *(Pushes* OLD TOM.)

TOM *(whining).* What's wrong? I wasn't begging.

CHUMLEY *(to* ROSE). Stay! I know him now. He was an old brother-officer of mine.

POINTER *(to* OLD TOM). Come, be off.

TOM. I'm a-going, ain't I? Ain't I?

CHUMLEY. Stay! I know you, don't I? You are—

TOM *(screams).* Ah, don't speak it, don't speak it! Don't say my name! *(Whining)* I am Old Tom, Old Tom!

POINTER. Be off with you!

(*Pushes* OLD TOM *off and follows him out.*)

CHUMLEY. Poor old Frank! Has he come to this? What a depth of misery! Look, Rose! He used to be the handsomest and gayest in the regiment, the pride of the mess. It is to save George from a fate like that, that we are working. For his sake, we must keep our word!

CURTAIN

SCENE TWO

SCENE: GEORGE *and* ELIZA MEDHURST's *garret apartment. It is small and poorly furnished, but very neat. A door leads into another room. A bonnet and shawl hang on a small clothes rack U.R.* MEDHURST *enters.*

MEDHURST. Eliza! Eliza!
  *(Enter* ELIZA, *a pretty young woman, plainly dressed. She carries a lighted candle.)*
MEDHURST. Has anyone been here?
ELIZA. No. Why, what brings you home so early?
MEDHURST. I have had an accident with the cab.
ELIZA. An accident! Are you hurt, George?
MEDHURST. No, I am not hurt. Come here, Eliza. I am compelled to leave London this night. Even now there may be hunters on my track. I must go to see Dicey, who will assist me in my escape.
ELIZA. Dicey? My old employer, Dicey? Oh, George, don't trust her!
MEDHURST. I must, Eliza. I have no choice!
ELIZA. Oh, my husband, what have you done?
MEDHURST. What I have never had heart to tell you. That's why I have been forced to go creeping out after dark, driving a night cab, for fear I would be seen, leading a dog's life, which you consented to share!
ELIZA. What better have I ever known? You found me a nameless child! And I never asked more than to have you my own! And you are my own, George. *(Embraces him.)*
MEDHURST. In the depth of my misery, there was a deeper still which I have forborne to confide to you. Forgive me for having deceived you.
ELIZA. You have not deceived me in your love! What do I care for the rest?
MEDHURST. I hear steps by the door. None but my pursuers could be coming here at this hour! Shade the light!
ELIZA *(goes to window).* There are men below who seem to be looking up here. Oh, George, what have you done that men hunt you in the night?
MEDHURST. I cannot tell you now. I must escape by the other way. Gain what time you can. Put out the light.
  *(*ELIZA *puts out the candle, turns down the gas.)*

Footsteps on the stairs! *(Embraces her.)* Farewell, Eliza! This may be our parting kiss. Goodbye, goodbye.

*(Exit* MEDHURST.*)*

ELIZA. Tell me what to do, George!

*(She goes to the door. Enter* BELLINGHAM.*)*

BELLINGHAM. Where is your husband?

ELIZA. He has not yet returned from work.

BELLINGHAM. That is false, for he was here not ten minutes ago. I will see if he is concealed on the premises. He has escaped by the backyard, and will be soon at Dicey's. You can light the candle again. *(Picks up candle.)* He's safe enough. You see that I know more of your husband's doings than you do. *(He lights candle.)*

ELIZA *(taking candle from him and holding it up to his face).* Who are you? Friend or foe? Richard Knatchbull!

BELLINGHAM. No longer Dick Knatchbull, but Chandos Bellingham. I see you have not forgotten me.

ELIZA. No, I have not forgotten the man who left my mother to die in the workhouse.

BELLINGHAM. And not forgiven me?

ELIZA. She forgave you, long since, but I never shall. *(She goes to door.)*

BELLINGHAM. This is dutiful language to hear from a daughter.

ELIZA. You insult me, sir! You are not my father.

BELLINGHAM. Ah! You know that? Then why did you not marry George Medhurst under your own father's name? Or did you know who your father was!

ELIZA. Because my mother had implored me with her latest breath not to bear the name which you had tried to disgrace.

BELLINGHAM. It would be well if George Medhurst had not succeeded with a similar experiment on his own.

ELIZA. What do you mean?

BELLINGHAM. That he has committed a forgery and may be forced to fly. What would you do to save him?

ELIZA. He is my husband. I would lay down my life for him.

BELLINGHAM. Less would do. Give me your hand. *(She offers her right hand.)* The other—the left. *(She holds it out.)* Would you lay down this ring—this wedding ring—for his sake? He has committed forgery; the money cannot be obtained, but to secure his safety, you must sacrifice yourself.

ELIZA. Oh, I cannot. I—I do not understand.

BELLINGHAM. It is necessary that he should marry again. Your marriage was made under false names. You need only go abroad and forget him.

ELIZA. Forget him!

BELLINGHAM. Oh, you can name your terms. As long as you live, he will be at your mercy.

ELIZA. I see it now. You want him to deceive some innocent girl, to induce me to join you to commit a bigamy! Has George agreed to this?

BELLINGHAM. He had no choice. The man whose head is in the jaws of Newgate is not particular to a shade.

ELIZA *(aside).* This is the depth of infamy which he was afraid to confide in me.

BELLINGHAM. You consent?

ELIZA. No! Whatever he may have done, he is my husband. I will share with him, but I will not help him to commit a new crime!

BELLINGHAM. And this is what you call love? You would rather see the man you love consigned to a convict's cell than let another woman make him happy.

ELIZA. I would die for him, but I will not live in guilt.

BELLINGHAM. Ahem! He has no alternative.

ELIZA. But I have! *(She turns her back on him.)*

BELLINGHAM. Will you be silent, at least?

ELIZA. He has cast me off! I shall be silent as the grave.

BELLINGHAM. He does not ask for your approval. He will be content with your silence.

ELIZA. My silence! *(Aside, bitterly.)* My silence! *(Points to the door.)* There's your way. Good night!

BELLINGHAM. Good night. *(Exit.)*

ELIZA. Merciful Heavens, what have I done? He said that might be our parting kiss. No, I cannot part from him like this. I cannot aid him to commit a wrong, but I can remove the consequences of his fault. I will go to the Silver Bell and wait for him. Oh, I must see him again. Where is my bonnet and shawl? . . . Yes, I shall see him again, and then—oh, George! *(Sobbing.)* Oh, George! *(She takes bonnet and shawl from rack and is putting them on as the scene is blacked out.)*

BLACKOUT

SCENE THREE

SCENE: DICEY's *gambling hall. Discover* DICEY, *impatient, and* DEALER *at table. Enter* MEDHURST.

MEDHURST. I am followed!

DICEY. Of course, you are. It's only right you should be looked after since you've come into a fortune. I've iced champagne to celebrate your return to society. *(She pours for him.)*

MEDHURST. It's so long since I drank champagne, I scarcely know the taste of it.

DICEY *(joins him at table).* Well, I've seen the gentleman—

MEDHURST. What gentleman? Do you not hold the note yourself?

DICEY. Oh, no! I had a run of winners and was forced to pay off with your note. Now the gentleman's insisting that unless I make it good, he'll go to the police. But I've persuaded him to give you time—give you time. Now that you've come into your fortune—

MEDHURST. Did you say I've come into my fortune? Then my father is—is dead?

DICEY. Yes, it's fortunate I had the news today and could persuade my friend to be patient.

MEDHURST. How do you have the news? Oh, if only he would have consented to see me once more. If he only could have known how I have changed and forgiven me!

DICEY. He did forgive you—of course, he did—or you wouldn't be coming into his fortune.

MEDHURST. Oh, if only he had relented sooner—

DICEY. Come, what's done's done! You're Sir George now—as good a name as was ever known, and 6,000 pounds a year!

MEDHURST. So—I see now why you were being kind to me! What is your price for that paper?

DICEY. My friend has decided to ask half the income.

MEDHURST. Three thousand pounds!

DICEY. Yes, isn't it disgraceful! I did my best to get him to take less, but he knows the value of the name. And my advice to you is pay it! What use would the fortune be if he brings you to trial? Better half the money than all and you go to Newgate!

MEDHURST. I believe you still hold the document yourself!

DICEY. I've kept you out of prison all these years—and now, you turn to accuse me! I tell you I had to let it go.

MEDHURST. To redeem my name. I suppose I must consent. *(Aside.)* I am in their power. Oh, then I will be free! Free!

DICEY. Come, it's not so bad. You've spent more over these tables than this man asks to clear your name. What will you have—more champagne? Money? *(Gives him notes.)* Five pounds—ten—fifty? Come. *(Hands him dice.)*—Renew an old acquaintance!

MEDHURST *(aside).* Fifty pounds! Fifty devils!

DICEY. Come—throw the dice—you're sure to win! Once your luck changes, you always win!

MEDHURST *(going to dice table).* Another pair of dice. *(Throws dice on the table; then picks them up and examines them. Through the following,* MEDHURST *continues to play and win.)*

DICEY. It will be all right. If only Chandos has persuaded Eliza to take the money and give him up. What's keeping him? *(To* MEDHURST.*)* See? The weather's always fair when you've a fortune to back you up. That's the way to enjoy yourself. Ah, I hope you can settle this matter in a few days, and I'll see you in a week or two driving a carriage in the park with that lovely girl by your side.

MEDHURST. What do you mean?

DICEY. I mean Miss Edgerton, your cousin. The property won't come to you unless you marry her.

MEDHURST. Then it was left on condition? You know I cannot do that. I am married to Eliza.

DICEY. There's where you both made a mistake—but if you provide for her, she'll give you no trouble. The marriage was made under false names—I can witness that. But you've not had a fair taste yet—here—some more champagne. You'll see the thing in the right light yet.

DEALER. He still wins!

DICEY. Still the winner! *(Aside.)* I wonder what keeps Bellingham! Ah, here he is.

*(Enter* BELLINGHAM.*)*

BELLINGHAM. You have him here? He seems sprung!

DICEY. Only a little—I didn't give him too much until you'd be here. How did you get on with Eliza? Did she see the money was worth more than this man who will gamble away his income as fast as it comes in?

BELLINGHAM. I have seen her—she will hold her tongue. Good evening, Sir George! Allow me to congratulate you upon coming into your title!

MEDHURST. Who is this man?

DICEY. This is the gentleman who holds the forged paper—Mr. Bellingham!

BELLINGHAM. I have explained to Eliza your position, and she recognizes the necessity of her secrecy. If you will pay her, she consents to disappear and trouble you no more.

MEDHURST. Disappear?

BELLINGHAM. That is, go abroad.

MEDHURST. Eliza consents to go from me?

BELLINGHAM. Of course. You see, I know her better than you do—or that is, I know women.

DICEY. I hoped she would consent.

BELLINGHAM. She sees the difference in your stations. How would you like to have her pointed at in your lordly mansion, by her swell friends of the Silver Bell?

DICEY. Of course, it's for the best. You'll pay her liberally, and she'll live very well without any annoyance to you. Now again, sir, at the game. *(She pours more champagne and hands it to* MEDHURST.*)*

MEDHURST *(half-aside).* I can never love anyone as I love her.

DICEY. Here, Sir George, some more champagne!

CURTAIN

### SCENE FOUR

SCENE: *The street in front of the gambling hall, with a backdrop of old buildings and with a lamppost. Enter* ELIZA.

ELIZA. He could not take our love so lightly! Surely he will not consent to marry another. He cannot have grown so cold. I must help—help him. He has not come out yet. Patience! Patience!

(*Enter* MEDHURST, *drunk.*)

MEDHURST. I'll get a bed at some hotel for the night, see a tailor in the morning, pass my head through Truefitt's hands, and emerge in the Parks as a new man, leading a new life.

ELIZA. George! Don't be angry at my being here. I could not think of parting from you as I did. Oh, why did you not tell me? I would have fled London with you. We could have gone abroad—away—

MEDHURST. I would not ask you to share such a life—forever fleeing justice. There is but one way to clear my name.

ELIZA. No, not this way—not to give you up forever! George, if this is true (*Grabs him and pleads with him.*), give yourself up—pay the price. I'll wait for you, I'll wait, no matter how long the time!

MEDHURST. It is too late. I beg you, Eliza, to save me from a felon's fate. You shall have everything you require—money, jewels—far more than I have ever given you.

ELIZA. George, not money; do not pay me for my love. (*She goes to him, caresses his back.*) Take me to your arms and ask me to lay down my life for your happiness, and I will do it. Your embrace will give me strength, and your kiss will seal my lips forever.

MEDHURST. There is no other way, Eliza. (*He moves away from her.*) And though we part, I shall never care for anyone but you.

ELIZA (*aside*). There is no use! (*To* GEORGE.) I never loved you more than now, when we must part forever.

MEDHURST. Not forever, Eliza.

ELIZA. Yes, forever! I do not forget our bond, "Till death do us part." Farewell—kiss me—kiss me, George! It is for the last time.

MEDHURST (*kisses her*). How cold your lips are!

ELIZA (*half aside*). They will be colder by morning. God bless you! God bless you!

(SONG: *"There's Nothing We Can Say"*\*)

There's nothing we can say but just goodbye.
My breaking heart forgives him, but can I?
Don't shame me with a bribe I cannot take.
Our sacred bond your words can never break.

Come, take of me your life of wealth and fame,
You may regret me walking in my shame.
Don't tell me that you love me, or promise to think of me—
There's nothing we can say but just goodbye.

(*Exit* ELIZA.)

\**Music on page 378.*

MEDHURST. How strange she is. I could not believe she would have taken it so kindly. She never said a hard word to me. Yes, Bellingham is right. She would never fit the society of Sir George Medhurst. It is better so, and she will soon forget. Money has mended many a broken heart. Still, no one can ever love me as she has done. *(Exits.)*

BLACKOUT

## SCENE FIVE

SCENE: *A dark street on the way to the waterfront. In the background, you can see old houses. A lamppost is U.R. Enter* CHUMLEY.

CHUMLEY. I cannot rest until I have seen Frank. What can have brought him to such a pitch of misery? I appointed to meet a policeman at Temple Bar—and here he comes.
*(Enter* POINTER.*)*
POINTER. He lives, sir, at the Dry Arches, but he is to be found under the bridge. He works on the river by night.
CHUMLEY. Can you guide me there?
POINTER. Well, sir, it's hardly the place to take a gentleman. The nightbirds of London roost there.
CHUMLEY. I don't care.
POINTER. Well, sir, put your watch-chain in your pocket, button up your coat. If you have anything in your coat pockets, take it out.
CHUMLEY. All right. Will that do?
*(*POINTER *nods. Enter* ELIZA.*)*
ELIZA. Which is the way, please, to Blackfriar's Bridge?
POINTER. Fifth turning on the right. We're going that way. Will you have our protection?
ELIZA. Not for the world! *(Runs off.)*
POINTER. I don't like the look of the girl!
CHUMLEY. Do you know her?
POINTER. No, sir, she's not an unfortunate—you can see that by her face. She is after no good. Come on, sir. Step out, sir.
*(Exit* POINTER *and* CHUMLEY.*)*

BLACKOUT

## SCENE SIX

SCENE: *Street leading to Blackfriar's temporary bridge, with view of the Thames and St. Paul's in the distance. Moonlight.* JACK *and* SALLY, *waterfront bums, are huddled asleep under the arch U.R. Enter* POINTER *and* CHUMLEY. POINTER's *lantern is lit.*

POINTER. This is the place, sir. I don't see that girl, though it's sure she passed us. She must have given us the slip.

CHUMLEY. Perhaps gone over the bridge.

(JACK and SALLY CRUMPETS *stir, waken and slowly stand. She leans on him drunkenly. He pushes her playfully. They are both dressed in rags, with rough woolen caps.*)

POINTER. Not likely, sir. I'll try and find the person you seek.

JACK. I say, pals! Here's a lark! Here's a broken-down swell come to beg a night's lodging of Crumpets.

POINTER. No, he don't, he's a gentleman, only come down to look around.

JACK. Well, then, the gentleman ought to stand something for his footing! (*He puts out his hand for money.*)

POINTER. You'd better give him a little something, sir.

CHUMLEY. Do people live here?

JACK. Rayther! Should think they does! Vy, this is Bankside Hotel, unlimited; airy rooms and the water always laid on. (*He makes a grand gesture toward the water.*)

POINTER. Have you seen Old Tom?

CHUMLEY. He went along the foreshore a moment ago.

JACK. You'll find him in the boat.

(*Exit* POINTER.)

More like at the bottom of it, drunk.

CHUMLEY. Here's half a crown for you. (*Gives coin.*) Here comes Dalton. I want to speak with Old Tom—an old friend of mine. If you'll keep it quiet here while we have our talk, there'll be another half crown for you.

JACK. Very good, sir. (*He exits.*)

(*Enter* POINTER.)

POINTER. Here he is, sir!

(*Exit* POINTER. *Enter* OLD TOM.)

CHUMLEY. Dalton!

TOM. Ah! Is it for this I have been brought here? To be insulted by your commiseration? Well, you see how low I have sunk. You have seen what I do by day; at night I sell bills at the doors of the theatres and eke out my living after midnight by helping a man who trawls for the dead—when I am sober enough to think of such things!

CHUMLEY. Have you no friends?

TOM. Friends? I have friends? Look at me! I don't want any.

CHUMLEY. You know what true comrades we were to one another. We shared the same meals, the same tent, and when I lay for dead under the cannon on the field, it was you who flew to lift me up and carry me back to our lines, where we arrived, you dripping with the blood from a shot in your shoulder. Dalton, do you think I forget?

TOM. No! But I must! Oh, Gordon, don't harrow me with memories of the past! Don't rouse up the devil within me, that I try to drown with drink!

CHUMLEY. Would you leave me if you found me in the mire without a helping hand? You had a wife—what has become of her?

TOM. What! You have not heard what became of the lovely Fanny Dalton? Ha, ha!

CHUMLEY. I see. She died!

TOM. You remember how she clung round my neck when we were ordered off to the Crimea—and how I used to weep at her letters, and the postscript that she guided our little child's hand to write to me? You called me a fool and laughed at me. You were right. For even then she was the prey of a designing villain. When I returned home, I found that she had fled with him. He was a convicted felon, and when justice seized upon him, she was left in the workhouse.

CHUMLEY. And your child?

TOM. No one knows what became of her, no one but that villain, whom the cares of the Government keeps from my vengeance. Oh! My bitterest curses light on every letter in the name of Richard Knatchbull!

CHUMLEY. Knatchbull! Why, that is the name of a convict that I met in Van Dieman's Land. *(Aside.)* Ah, that face I saw at the railway station today. Impossible! Oh, if he may have come back?

TOM. Well, you have had your say, and I thank you. I will go back to my work—though I am unfit for any work tonight.

CHUMLEY. Goodbye, Frank.

TOM. Goodbye. *(Exit.)*

CHUMLEY. I was afraid to offer him money. He might have been offended. It was better not.

*(Enter* JACK *and* POINTER.*)*

CHUMLEY. Here's the half-crown I promised you. Have you found her?

POINTER. No, she must have crossed the bridge. Mr. Jack, mind you look after your lodgers. If any of the workmen's tools are missing, we shall have to break up your nest! *(Exit.)*

JACK. All right, Sergeant! There's nobody frequents my establishment but members of the h'upper ten! What a horful draft comes in here! Crumpets should really ordter hang up curtings in the arch— I'll spile my voice next.

*(Enter* ELIZA, *cold and shivering.)*

ELIZA. Heaven help me understand and forgive what he has done! Today my faithful husband and tonight I know him not. Oh, my mother, why were you not spared to counsel me tonight—tonight when I need you so! And my father—does he live? Does he wander the earth this night searching for me as I now search for him? But I must not question—I must not be sad—in a few months George has given me all those things for which a woman lives—his love, faith, devotion—such a love as I had never dreamed! Merciful heaven, forgive me for what I do! Farewell, George, farewell! It is for his sake, for his sake! *(She jumps.)*

JACK. What's that?

*(Enter* POINTER *and* CHUMLEY.*)*
CHUMLEY. Where? What?
JACK. Something in the water. It's a woman!
POINTER. Hunt up a rope somewhere!
*(Enter* OLD TOM, *rushes to bridge, around pillar, U.R.)*
TOM. It's all right, I am here!
*(He jumps to save her.* ALL *cheer.)*

CURTAIN

*Old Tom: "Can you take the demon in that bottle and strangle him?" (Charles Johnson played Old Tom in the Imperial's 1956 production.)*

# ACT TWO

## SCENE ONE

SCENE: OLD TOM's *lodgings, an arched vault under the street, gas up. A cot is U.R., a rough bench, an oil lantern; clothes are hung on the wall.* ELIZA *is sleeping on the cot.* OLD TOM *is seated, drinking.*

TOM. I wonder who she is? She is not a servant-girl; her hands do not show signs of work. She is not a seamstress; her fingers show no marks of the needle. I wonder what made her do it?

ELIZA *(in her sleep)*. George! Come back, George!

TOM. Ah! That's it! George is at the bottom of it, whoever he is. Ever since nine days ago when I picked her out of the Thames, nothing save that name "George" has passed her lips.

*(Enter* CHUMLEY.*)*

CHUMLEY. Dalton, I received your message, and I have come.

TOM. You are come to my mansion.

CHUMLEY. Do you live here?

TOM. Now they let me. At first I was worried out of it by the overseer of the parish, but whenever I came out of prison, I came back to here. I told him he would get tired of it before I did. So here I am.

CHUMLEY. Well, do you want me to assist you?

TOM. No, not me! I've called to see if you can help that poor girl there. Nine days ago I fished her out of the Thames and she has lain there ever since. It was not love that drove her to it, for there is her wedding ring on her finger. It was not want, for she had one pound seven odd in her pockets.

CHUMLEY. What can I do for her?

TOM. I don't know. I thought that you might know of some situation for her.

CHUMLEY. Without a character? I have no knowledge of her but such as you give.

TOM. I'm a nice-looking article to recommend anybody!

CHUMLEY. Stay! Now I think of it, I do know a lady who is want of a person; she is about to be married.

TOM. Not to you, I hope?

CHUMLEY. No!

TOM. That's right.

CHUMLEY. I wish she was, for I love her!

TOM. And you think she will take her?

CHUMLEY. Yes, I shall see her today, and if your charge will come to her—here's her address *(Hands him a card.)*—I am pretty sure she will not have to return. And now, Dalton, can I do nothing for you?

TOM. No! I want nothing. I have nothing to live for.

CHUMLEY. Not even your daughter?

TOM. I have buried my last hope of ever finding her.

CHUMLEY. Then I will dig it up—and revive it! I have not been idle since I last saw you. I remembered that I had seen a convict of the name of your wronger in Australia. I inquired about him and found that he escaped. I traced him from place to place, till I found that he was in New Orleans, where he joined the Confederate Army in '63. The record says that he fell among the killed at the battle of Harper's Ferry.

TOM *(bitterly)*. Ah! He died like a brave soldier—while I shall perish like a dog.

CHUMLEY. No. He was not killed. Among the Southern officers who sought refuge in London, I know one General Freemantle. I went to him. He remembered Knatchbull, who had been in his corps, attached to him. In the action, the two had been thrown down by the explosion of the same shell, but both rose unhurt, save that Knatchbull lost a portion of his left ear!

TOM. Fate set the felon's mark on him, after all.

CHUMLEY. If I am not much mistaken, he is at this moment in London. If so, do not fear. I am in the same cage as the reptile, and he cannot escape. Leave him to me, and I'll give you a good account of him. *(Exit.)*

TOM. Knatchbull alive! Knatchbull here! Here? I may have passed him in the street, looked him in the face! Oh, if I had his throat within the grip of these fingers as now I grasp this pewter measure, I would—No, I didn't mean to spoil you, old fellow. Pah! A gorilla could have done as much. Can you take the demon in that bottle and strangle him? Yes, I can. I'll—I'll give up drink.

*(ELIZA gradually wakes, pushes hair from her eyes.)*

I—I mean I will try. I'll—I'll do it! *(Raises bottle.)* I will, by degrees. *(About to drink.)*

ELIZA. Oh, sir! Don't! *(Seizes bottle.)*

TOM. Leave go! *(Struggle.)* I must have it!

ELIZA. Don't, you hurt me.

*(OLD TOM lets go bottle; she flings it off.)*

TOM *(falls into seat, shaking fearfully)*. I am a brute.

ELIZA. No!

TOM. I am a brute.

ELIZA. No, you are not. You have a good heart under these rags. I esteem you now, but I should love you if—if—

TOM. If I did not drink?

ELIZA. I cannot feel for you all the interest that you deserve, but I hope to see you worthy of more than my gratitude some day.

TOM. I was speaking to a friend about you, my girl, and he has given me this address as one useful to you.

ELIZA *(takes card)*. "Miss Edgerton, the Lilacs."

TOM. That lady will take you into her service, I hope. There you will find a home. This place is not for such as you—I did not pick you up out of the Thames to make you the drudge of a drunken beggar. Pack up your things, my girl, it is a good way off, and you must be there this afternoon. You will write me sometimes?

*Old Tom: "Someday, when I shall have other clothes, if I come to you, you will see me sometime?" (Charles Johnson, Karen Duke)*

ELIZA. Oh, often!

TOM. What name will you go by?

ELIZA. It little matters now that he has deprived me of the one he gave me. You can call me Fanny Dalton.

TOM *(with emotion)*. Fanny Dalton! What! Is that your name?

ELIZA. It seems familiar to me—it must have been that of one that I held dear in my childhood.

TOM. Your mother—does she live?

ELIZA. No, she died in the St. Pancras Work House, ten years ago.

TOM. And your father—your father?

ELIZA. I never knew him. I only know the man who stole my mother from him—only to let her die in misery.

TOM. How was he called?

ELIZA. Richard Knatchbull.

TOM *(aside)*. Richard Knatchbull! It is my own child!

ELIZA. Why do you look at me like that?

TOM *(aside)*. My child! and I feel ashamed to own who I am. I am afraid to ask her to come to the arms of this drunkard, clothed in rags! Ashamed, ashamed!

ELIZA. What is the matter?

TOM. Oh, don't be frightened. I shall not hurt you again! Go on your way. I will follow you—but at a distance. You shall not be disgraced by the company of me.

ELIZA. Oh, never!

TOM. Some day, when I shall have other clothes, if I come to you, you will see me sometime? You have pity for me now, but in time you will learn something better—you will learn to love me—as if I were indeed your father?

ELIZA. You deserve that name!

TOM. Not yet, not yet! But by the help of Heaven, I will work to gain it.

ELIZA. After the darkness the light will come.

(SONG: *"After the Darkness."*\*)

> After the darkness, the light will come—
> After the clouds, the sun—
> After the years, with their sorrows and
>     tears,
> Gladness is sure to come.
>
> Though you have travelled the road of
>     regret,
> Always the end is in sight.
> After the nighttime, the dawn will
>     break through—
> After the darkness, light!

TOM *(suddenly kisses ELIZA's hand)*. Go on—I will follow you! Go on, go on! *(Kisses her on cheek.)*

*(Exit ELIZA.)*

*(TOM sings.)*

> Though I have travelled the road of
>     regret,
> Always the end is in sight.
> After the nighttime, the dawn will
>     break through—
> After the darkness, light!

She was right. After dark—the light *has* come. *(Exits.)*

**CURTAIN**

\**Music on page 377.*

## SCENE TWO

SCENE: MEDHURST's *villa and garden. Enter* BELLINGHAM *and* DICEY. *She is dressed in a very well-tailored suit, with matching hat and gloves, very proper.*


BELLINGHAM. This is the place. What do you think of it, Dicey?

DICEY. And what a fine place it is.

(*Enter* SERVANT.)

BELLINGHAM. Is Sir George Medhurst at home? Take in my card.

(*Exit* SERVANT.)

DICEY (*walking around, admiring*). Well, look at this! Isn't he in clover? And what a beautiful garden!

BELLINGHAM. Ah—I feel at home here—born to this sort of thing. (*He peeks in window.*) I expand with each breath of air.

DICEY. Come, Chandos, you forget yourself—born to this, indeed! You may fool some, but don't forget I first saw you picking pockets at the county fair twenty years ago. You've never worked a day nor earned a honest shilling in your life. (*She sits on bench.*)

(*Enter* MEDHURST.)

MEDHURST. So you have penetrated to this place of peace? You have come to me. What do you want?

BELLINGHAM. We come now because we did not like to wait longer. It is best to see you on the eve of your marriage.

MEDHURST. I know what you would say—but go on.

BELLINGHAM. Here is an order for your banker to sell out the stock he has in his hands to the amount of your indebtedness to us. All you need do is sign it.

MEDHURST (*takes paper*). I cannot give you the answer now—

BELLINGHAM. Oh, any time before the ceremony. We are in no hurry. Besides, we can take advantage of the interval to make the acquaintance of your charming bride. (*He bows low.*)

MEDHURST. Never! There is some excuse for your accosting me in my own house, but there is none to pollute by your presence the lady who is to be my bride.

BELLINGHAM. What madness makes you speak like this!

MEDHURST. Not madness. It is remorse that makes me speak.

BELLINGHAM. Remorse! The word of a fool! What has remorse to do with a man who has had all obstacles swept from his path? And has inherited a fortune?

DICEY (*to* BELLINGHAM). Let him have his remorse. All we want is his signature. Don't waste time. Give him the paper, Chandos.

BELLINGHAM (*takes the paper from pocket*). Here it is. Sign it and be free.

MEDHURST. Yes, I shall be free from you, but how can I be free from *her?* She is dead—she died—as much murdered by me as though my own hands had thrust her into her grave. In the night I see her again, and I hear from her icy lips, in a cold breath like that of the dead: "For your sake, George, for your sake." Poor Eliza!

BELLINGHAM (*sneering*). Poor Eliza! Pah! Are you going to hang remorse around your neck like a chaplet forever? Pshaw, man, it's your change in living!

(MEDHURST *falls seated on garden chair, his face in his hands.*) It's your digestion out of order!

DICEY. I'd think it would be enough to upset the stomach to go from a night cab and a rat-ridden garret to this!

BELLINGHAM. You are behind the age. Science has done away with all such ancient delicateness. You must not think of remorse: it is simply nausea.

MEDHURST. I am in no mood to speak with you. Leave me now. I will meet you in the garden later on.

DICEY (*to* BELLINGHAM). I've had enough of his moods. Have him sign the paper!

BELLINGHAM (*to* DICEY). Let him sulk. He will come to terms. He is a whining cur, and we'll be lucky to have done with him. (*To* MEDHURST.) We will expect you shortly.

(*Exit* BELLINGHAM *and* DICEY.)

MEDHURST. I have made my own taskmasters and heavy as is the debt, alas, it must be paid.

(*Enter* ROSE, *dressed in light, summer clothing, suitable for the country estate.*)

ROSE. Dear George, you look sad. You are not displeased with me? I wish I could be more kind.

MEDHURST. You unkind, Rose? You could never be unkind to any creature.

ROSE. You seem to see the approach of our marriage with regret. Might it not be arranged that I should not be your wife?

MEDHURST. No, no! Believe me, I do not shrink from it. On the contrary, I wish you to be my wife. Love me, Rose, love me even more, and (*Aside.*) perhaps she whom I have wronged will forgive me for your sake.

(*Enter* CHUMLEY.)

I must—I will try to throw off my gloominess. (*He embraces* ROSE.)

CHUMLEY (*aside*). There they are. I asked Rose to be more kind to him, but she is carrying out my instructions with more fidelity than I could wish. (*He comes down.*) I am not intruding?

MEDHURST. Certainly not.

CHUMLEY. I have obeyed you, and brought that bracelet. (*Gives* ROSE *jewel case.*) You will see what a good likeness of George it contains.

ROSE. Oh, how beautiful! (*To* MEDHURST.) Oh, have I again to thank you for something? (*To* CHUMLEY.) Now, you never give me anything.

CHUMLEY (*sadly, aside*). Have not I? (*Aloud.*) Well, I will give you something. You were in need of a servant. Has anybody in the neighborhood made an application?

ROSE. No.

CHUMLEY. Then there will be one come today whom I will leave to your kind heart.

ROSE. What is she?

CHUMLEY. I know nothing of her, except her misfortune, which must have been great.

ROSE. Oh, George, can we take such a person into our house?

MEDHURST. What, Rose? A poor creature has lost her way in the storm and comes to our door, and shall we refuse to let her in because the night is too dark, and she is too poor to enter our splendid house? No, take her in, and we shall not repent it.

CHUMLEY. Then she may depend upon having the situation?

ROSE. Yes, and I shall be glad of her services. My rooms are so overcrowded with wedding finery that it has overflowed into the parlor, and thence to the library *(Laughing.)* from which places you are duly warned, under penalty of crushing a crinoline or sitting down on a bonnet. *(Exits.)*

CHUMLEY. I wanted to speak with you, George. A man and a woman passed me at the railway station. They came this way. Have they called? I hope you have shaken them off.

MEDHURST. I cannot. I am in their power.

CHUMLEY. I feared as much. May I be so bold as to inquire?

MEDHURST. You may know all. Tempted by Dicey Morris, in her gambling house, in a fit of drunken desperation, I forged my father's name.

CHUMLEY. And these rascals hold the forgery?

MEDHURST. Yes. Here is a paper which I have but to sign to have the evidence of my guilt restored to me.

CHUMLEY *(takes paper)*. You shall do no such thing.

MEDHURST. Eh?

CHUMLEY. Leave me to deal with them. You shall not be ruined by them.

MEDHURST. What have I done to deserve your interest?

CHUMLEY. You? Nothing. But I wish her life to be shared with a man whom no one will be able to reproach. I wish her unclouded happiness—for I love her!

MEDHURST. You!

CHUMLEY. Yes, George, I love her, and with a love so pure that no better proof of its spotlessness can be given than my fearlessness to tell it to you. We are rivals!

MEDHURST. Rivals! And yet you would save me from the consequences of my own crime?

CHUMLEY. Yes. She says that "I gave her nothing." But I shall give her your name, cleared forever from disgrace.

MEDHURST. Oh! It shall never be disgraced again!

CHUMLEY. For her sake, George, I expect you to keep your word.

MEDHURST. I will, by Heaven, I will!

*(They shake hands.)*

But I must go with you. Dicey would keep her word, but this Bellingham—I do not like the look of him, and it might be best if there were two of us—one to witness—

CHUMLEY. No, I shall do this thing alone.

MEDHURST. All right, since you insist. But if you do not return, I shall come to your aid. Depend upon it. *(Exits.)*

*(Enter* ELIZA.*)*

CHUMLEY *(aside)*. Now, how am I to deal with these villains?

ELIZA. I beg your pardon, sir, but I found the garden gate open and I came in. Can I see Miss Edgerton?

CHUMLEY *(aside)*. This is she. It is an honest, suffering face. *(Aloud.)* The lady will see you at once. I beg you to be seated.

ELIZA. I beg pardon, sir, I am not the person that you take me for.

CHUMLEY. Nay, I never make mistakes on such things, I hope. I always recognize the gentlewoman, however misfortune may disguise her.

*(Enter* ROSE.*)*

This is the person of whom I spoke. *(To* ELIZA.*)* This is the lady. *(Exits.)*

ROSE. Poor girl! You look very wearied and dusty.

ELIZA *(faintly)*. I have walked all the way from Waterloo Bridge. I have been ill, and I am not yet strong.

ROSE. You wish to enter my service; what can you do?

ELIZA. I can be faithful, obedient and grateful.

ROSE *(smiles)*. You have evidently not been accustomed to service.

ELIZA. No, madam, I—I—never was—ah! I am faint!

ROSE. Oh! *(Supports* ELIZA.*)* How thoughtless of me. Don't cry! There is something in your manner that assures me that you will be invaluable to me—oh! Do not give way to tears thus.

ELIZA. How can I thank you? Such kindness from the hands of strangers makes the coldness of those who were dear to me in times past seem all the more painful by contrast.

ROSE. Dry your tears. Come with me—you must not be seen in this dress.

ELIZA. I have no other.

ROSE. Oh, I beg your pardon. Never mind, we'll find some of my dresses to replace those poor garments of yours.

*(Exit* ELIZA, *leaning on* ROSE. *Enter* OLD TOM.*)*

TOM. I have seen her in. Bless her that took her to her. I followed her all the way down here. And now to work! Till I can feel like her father. What a nice place! How good it smells! How I envy the birds that flit about from tree to tree, and even the vermin that lie out under the shade. Eh? I see two figures coming this way. Surely that can't be Dicey! Dicey Morris here? *(Hides himself.)*

*(Enter* BELLINGHAM *and* DICEY.*)*

BELLINGHAM. He's a long time coming about that paper.

DICEY. I hope you won't mind my asking, but since this is my plan, and you seem to have taken it over, suppose you explain how you intend to manage it?

BELLINGHAM. There's no difficulty. I present the check and get the money.

DICEY. But five thousand pounds is a big hatful of money! It's not that I don't trust you, but it might be enough to make a man like you forget he has a partner—could that be?

BELLINGHAM. Pshaw!

DICEY. Well, just to be on the safe side, suppose you tear the check in half. Then we'll each keep a piece and paste it together when we get it cashed . . . All right?

BELLINGHAM. Where in the geological formation of my character do you see any evidence of the vein of green that you are apparently in the thought of mining?

DICEY. Look here, Chandos Bellingham, don't be putting on airs with me! You'll agree to what I say or I'll take every penny. Don't forget who holds the forgery—I do!

BELLINGHAM. My dear Dicey—allow me to open your eyes. You hold the forgery? *(Produces paper.)* I beg your pardon; here is the document. *(Keeps it out of* DICEY's *reach.)*

DICEY. You don't tease me like this! That document is not the forgery, for I put it in the hands of my banker for safety.

BELLINGHAM. Of course you did—by *my* suggestion.

DICEY. I'd thought of it myself, but it had slipped my mind until you—*you did* suggest it! But even so, you didn't rob the bank, did you?

BELLINGHAM. No.

DICEY. Well, that's a consolation.

BELLINGHAM. I simply presented myself at the bankers, said I was Sir John Medhurst and wanted to pay an overdue bill of mine. I paid the money and obtained the bill—quite in the regular way of business. And you tried to make me a junior partner. Why, damned, I constitute the whole firm!

DICEY. You're quite right, Chandos. Why, I don't know what I'd ever do without you. We're such old friends. Remember, we were friends before you ever travelled to Australia—surely you wouldn't want to harm so strong a friendship as this!

BELLINGHAM. All right, Dicey, that's enough—go to the station. I'll meet you there to leave for London.

DICEY. Then don't be long. I don't like to be kept waiting.

BELLINGHAM. It won't be long. Go, for I see him coming.

*(Exit* DICEY. *Enter* CHUMLEY.*)*

CHUMLEY. Good-day, sir.

BELLINGHAM. I expected to see Sir George Medhurst.

CHUMLEY. I know it. But you see me instead.

BELLINGHAM. It was a matter private and important.

CHUMLEY. I know that, but still I believe Sir George will not lose by my intermediation.

BELLINGHAM. I should say not.

CHUMLEY. I act just as if it were himself. Can you spare me five minutes?

BELLINGHAM. Five minutes? No more, for I must catch the train that leaves for town in ten minutes.

CHUMLEY. I will be as brief as I can. Sir George has told me by what means he is in the power of Mrs. Morris and yourself.

BELLINGHAM *(half-aside)*. The more fool he!

CHUMLEY. Perhaps we shall alter our opinion on that point before our conversation is finished.

BELLINGHAM. You know the terms?

CHUMLEY. Yes, but we will pay only double what is on the face of the note.

BELLINGHAM. Mrs. Morris would never listen to such a proposition.

CHUMLEY. Then Mrs. Morris mistakes the value of the paper. I rely upon you to undeceive her.

BELLINGHAM. Upon me? Your confidence does me honor!

CHUMLEY. You flatter me.

BELLINGHAM. Not at all. I'll listen to you.

CHUMLEY. I do not forget your perspicuity as shown on other occasions.

BELLINGHAM. "On *other* occasions?" I beg your pardon.

CHUMLEY. Yes. Seven years ago, I was stationed at Melbourne. I was ordered out to assist the constabulary in the arrest of a notorious bushranger, one Richard Knatchbull!

BELLINGHAM. *Richard* Knatchbull! Ah! And you—ah—caught him?

CHUMLEY. Ye-es! We caught him. And while we held him in custody, curiosity impelled me to inspect the wild beast!

BELLINGHAM. And I suppose you think him like me?

CHUMLEY. Yes, very like you! The first time I met you since, at the railway station, I recognized—

BELLINGHAM. His features on my face. Ah, poor Dick! (CHUMLEY *is amazed.)* My elder brother, sir. He has been my ruin. His reputation has blasted mine and caused me to live under a false name. So you caught him? You hung him, of course!

CHUMLEY. No, he escaped.

BELLINGHAM. Did he, indeed! Ah, he has as many lives as a cat.

CHUMLEY. I beg your pardon, Mr. Bellingham. I really thought that you were the fellow and meant to use that belief as a weapon on you.

BELLINGHAM. I saw you did! But never mind apologies. It is my misfortune, not your fault!

CHUMLEY. I am very sorry that you are not the other scoundrel!

BELLINGHAM. Don't mention it.

CHUMLEY. But to business. Sir George will give five thousand pounds to be released.

BELLINGHAM. My partner would never think of such an idea!

CHUMLEY. Six thousand?

BELLINGHAM. It is hopeless.

CHUMLEY. Eight thousand?

BELLINGHAM. It is useless to mention it.

CHUMLEY. As a last sum, ten thousand?

BELLINGHAM. You are losing time, and I shall miss the train. I have but five minutes to reach the station.

CHUMLEY *(his watch out)*. You have lost it. Your watch is stopped.

BELLINGHAM *(puts watch to right ear)*. No.

CHUMLEY. Why do you test it by your right ear? Because Richard Knatchbull lost his left ear at Harper's Ferry.

BELLINGHAM. Checkmate! The game is yours! You have mistaken your profession.

CHUMLEY. I am a soldier.

BELLINGHAM. Nature has richly endowed you for that of a detective officer. Well, I think you mentioned ten thousand pounds?

CHUMLEY. Sir George would never think of such an idea.

BELLINGHAM. Eight thousand?

CHUMLEY. It is useless to mention it.

BELLINGHAM. Six thousand?

CHUMLEY. Quite hopeless, I assure you.

BELLINHAM. Then what are your terms?

CHUMLEY. Double that on the face of the note.

BELLINGHAM. If I accept them, you will make no use of the secret in your hands?

CHUMLEY. Safety for safety! When and where shall I have the pleasure to see you?

BELLINGHAM. At the Silver Bell, in the Broadway, Westminster, tonight.

CHUMLEY. I will come. *(Exits.)*

*(Enter DICEY.)*

BELLINGHAM. Ah! You here! You have overheard?

DICEY. Every word!

BELLINGHAM. He will come to the Silver Bell. He will bring the money with him. You can have nobody within your doors but those you can depend upon.

DICEY. I know, a private benefit—no one without a ticket. Done! *(Exit.)*

BELLINGHAM. And till then, Mr. Gordon Chumley, I'll not lose sight of you! *(Exit)*

*(Enter OLD TOM.)*

TOM. And I of you, Richard Knatchbull! *(Exit.)*

**CURTAIN**

### SCENE THREE

SCENE: ROSE's *boudoir. A love seat is stacked with clothes boxes, trousseau clothing, hat box.* ROSE *is seated at a dressing table.*

ROSE. She has told me all. And what a story! What are my sorrows compared to hers? Poor soul! So unused to kindness that one gentle word melts her to tears.
(*Enter* ELIZA, *wearing one of* ROSE's *expensive gowns, hair dressed, decorated with flowers.*)
Oh, Eliza! What a change! Who could make a servant of that? Why, you look as much of a lady as I do—a good deal more, I dare say.
ELIZA. I shall try to be more humble.
ROSE. I don't mean that.
ELIZA. I am not accustomed to this life, madam.
ROSE. Anyone can see that. Do you write a good hand?
ELIZA. I believe so. I used to copy music when I was employed in a French printing office.
ROSE. Do you speak French?
ELIZA. Oui, madame.
ROSE. Moi aussi. Je parle un peu francais.
ELIZA. Tres bien, madame.
ROSE. Comment il faut? And to copy music you must understand it?
ELIZA. I have not practiced for a long while.
ROSE. And, pray, have you any other accomplishments?
ELIZA. I can read a little Italian.
ROSE. Dear me! I can't have one for a servant who would smile at my attempts to murder Mendelsohn, and who is, I daresay, more familiar with Moliere and Dante than I am with Marshall and Snellgrove. Oh, what am I to do with her? Where am I to put her?
ELIZA. Oh, don't send me away!
ROSE. Send you away! Oh, you great goose! No, you shan't be my servant, except to the household in appearance; but when we are together, as now, you shall be my friend. Yes, we shall be friends, shan't we? (*Makes* ELIZA *take chair. She kneels beside her.*) In the first place, I am going to be married. Isn't it dreadful? (*She sits.*)
ELIZA. I wish you much joy.
ROSE. And my husband—I hope you'll like him. I think you will, for he is much like you—I mean, in manner. He is so grave and reserved. He's my cousin, and we have been betrothed almost since childhood. Poor George!
ELIZA (*starts*). Is his name George?
ROSE. Yes, George. Don't you like it? Oh, he's so generous to me. Only look at all the things I have! See here! I wonder how you would look in it. (*Puts necklace around* ELIZA's *neck.*) Oh, beautiful! The diamonds look like petrified tears! What's that? Off again? You are crying. Oh? Look at this—nice bracelet, isn't it? (*Gives bracelet to* ELIZA *while she arranges veil upon her.*) There's his likeness in that.

See if you find the secret spring.

ELIZA. No, I cannot find it.

ROSE. Do you see the ruby heart? Press on that, and the loving giver will appear. *(ELIZA starts opening bracelet.)* Well?

ELIZA. Oh! Who is this?

*(A crash chord.)*

ROSE. My husband, Sir George Medhurst!

*(Another crash chord. ELIZA hangs her head. Enter SERVANT.)*

SERVANT. Captain Chumley wishes to speak to you, ma'am, before he leaves for London.

ROSE. Tell him that I will be with him presently.

*(Exit SERVANT.)*

Stay here, dear. I shall not be gone long. *(Exits.)*

ELIZA. My husband here! I am under his roof! And she, for whom I have been discarded—she has been kind to me. Oh, I must leave this place at once. I will go and change this dress for my old clothes, and—is this window open? Yes. I—ah! Someone approaches. Oh! My husband!

*(Crash chord.)*

Oh, oh!

*(MEDHURST enters, comes down, keeping his shadow on ELIZA until she rises.)*

MEDHURST. Oh, Rose, dear Rose! I have come to tell you what I can keep hidden no longer. You were right when you said that I saw the approach of our wedding day with aversion. I do not love you—for another has possession of my heart. I ask forgiveness of you—but oh! I can never ask forgiveness of her. She is gone—I have murdered her.

ELIZA *(faintly)*. Spare me, oh, spare me!

MEDHURST. And not until that time did I know how she loved me. How did she love me? To the greatest, for she died for me. Oh, can you forgive me?

(SONG:*"I Promised to Protect Her"*\*)

> I promised to protect her years ago,
> When we stood at the altar side by side.
> And though our paths have parted here below,
> I can't forget this girl who was my bride.
> And though she treads this empty vale of tears,
> I'll try to do my duty to her still.
> God be witness to this vow, I cannot forsake her now!
> I promised to protect her, and I will!
>
> *(Enter ROSE.)*

ROSE. George!

MEDHURST. Rose! You here? Who then is this?

*(ELIZA rises and he recedes to let light fall on her.)*

Oh, my wife!

\**Music on page 379.*

# ACT THREE

## SCENE ONE

SCENE: *The gambling house.* DICEY *is pacing;* DEALER *is at table.*

DICEY. What keeps Bellingham? He'd never dare skip out on Dicey Morris. Not with all the information I have on him! Still—what keeps him?

(*Enter* BELLINGHAM.)

Here at last! I waited at the station, but when you didn't come, I could hardly keep pacing the platform.

BELLINGHAM. I'm sorry, Dicey, the business with Chumley took longer than I intended. He—ah—it took him a while to see my point, but now all is settled. (*Looking at* DEALER.) Can you trust this man?

DICEY. Never mind him. He's been "in trouble," too. Another of my "faithful" ones—faithful since he has no choice, as you should know, Chandos, eh?

BELLINGHAM. No need to emphasize your point, Dicey. We understand each other. Now—I have asked Mr. Chumley to meet us here. (*He goes to the door, locks it.*)

DICEY. He'll bring the police at his heels!

BELLINGHAM. No, he will not let the police into the secret. That would be betraying Medhurst.

DICEY. And what do you mean to do once he's here? Will we get the money?

BELLINGHAM. Yes, Chumley will bring the money with him. He shall have the paper, but he shall not go away with it.

DICEY. What do you mean?

BELLINGHAM. Last year you concealed Jem Morgan on these premises when the police were hot after him.

DICEY. What's that to do with him?

BELLINGHAM. How did you conceal him?

DICEY. There was a hole in the wall leading to the tunnel of the underground railway. It only needed a little work to make it big enough for him to creep out.

BELLINGHAM. Is that hole there still?

DICEY. Not likely. I had it all bricked up again.

BELLINGHAM. Then it must be opened once more.

DICEY. I don't understand.

(BELLINGHAM *takes up a glass from the table, pours from a vial into it; then he turns the glass around to coat the inside with the liquid.*)

What are you doing?

BELLINGHAM. This is a solution of morphine. Do you see these drops?

DICEY. I can't say that I do.

BELLINGHAM. I have spread it over the inside of the tumbler.

DICEY. Yes, now I see.

BELLINGHAM. He will have a glass with us before parting. In an instant the drug will set to work. He will be benumbed and fall insensible into our power.

DICEY. Then what will we do?

BELLINGHAM. Little, yet much. There will appear in the newspaper tomorrow an account of the fatal accident on the Metropolitan Railway—a gentleman who had wandered from the street, in a state of intoxication, was found dead on the line.

DICEY. You can't. I'll have nothing to do with it. Why, you put me in a cold shiver.

(OLD TOM *opens door.* DEALER *stops him.*)

TOM *(drunkenly).* Who won't let me in? Isn't this a public place? I will come in.

(*Scuffle. Enter* OLD TOM.)

Now then, who's going to stop me? Who'll turn me out?

DICEY. Now look at that. How shall we get him out of here without causing a fuss? What will we do with him?

BELLINGHAM. Is he one of us?

DICEY. No, we must get rid of him.

(OLD TOM *is caught by* DEALER *who carries him to chair.*)

BELLINGHAM. Just give him some liquor. He's more than half drunk already. Another glass will make him put his shutters up. Then he won't be in the way.

(DICEY *gives* TOM *liquor. He drinks and slumps into chair mumbling.* CHUMLEY *appears at door.* DEALER *goes to bar his entrance.*)

DICEY. It's all right. Let the gentleman come in. He's expected.

(*Enter* CHUMLEY.)

CHUMLEY. A curious place for our appointment.

BELLINGHAM. Yes, but it belongs to my friend here, who refuses to let the document out of her possession. By the way, it's the custom for strangers to spend something for the good of the house. I can't recommend the wine, but the brandy is prime. Dicey, clean glasses!

(DICEY *clears the table, but she returns the glass which* BELLINGHAM *has poisoned.* DICEY *sits at table with* CHUMLEY *and* BELLINGHAM.)

Here is the document. *(He produces paper.)*

CHUMLEY. May I examine it?

DICEY. Certainly. It's all regular.

BELLINGHAM. Yes, all in order, as you will see.

(ALL *drink.* CHUMLEY *coughs several times during following, as if the liquor hurt his throat.*)

CHUMLEY. It looks genuine enough. *(Coughs.)* Ah! All right. There is your money.

(BELLINGHAM *counts money.* DICEY *watches closely.* CHUMLEY *gets sleepy, rubs forehead.*)

BELLINGHAM *(aside).* So far, so well.

(BELLINGHAM *puts up notes.* CHUMLEY *puts the paper in pocket-book and then in breast pocket slowly.* BELLINGHAM *drinks.)*

A pleasure to do business with a gentleman. To our next merry meeting!

CHUMLEY. I hope not.

BELLINGHAM. As you please. Now let Sir George Medhurst know at once. Don't deprive him of the news that he is free.

CHUMLEY *(rises).* I think I must—I think I must—I must go! I—I—I feel strangely—give me a glass of water—water, please. *(He supports himself on chair.)*

BELLINGHAM *(beckons to* DEALER*).* Here—glass of water for the gentleman!

(DEALER *brings glass.* CHUMLEY *hardly drinks.* DEALER *takes glass away.* CHUMLEY *falls into chair, his hat rolling under table.)*

Cover me, Dicey. *(He bends over* CHUMLEY *to take his pocketbook.)* All right—*(Flourishing book.)* it's safe in my possession.

TOM *(starts up, snatches book from* BELLINGHAM*).* Safer in mine!

(BELLINGHAM *and* DICEY *strike attitudes of astonishment.)*

DICEY. Drunkard! What does this mean?

TOM. It means that I have frustrated your villainy!

BELLINGHAM. Are you mad?

TOM. No, but you must be. This is one of the crimes so frequent now—not the open robbery in the day, but done in some foul den, after dark. But I have spoilt your work.

BELLINGHAM. Give it back—come, will you give back the pocketbook or not?

TOM. No, I shall hand it over to the police.

(OLD TOM *starts to leave.* BELLINGHAM *and* DICEY *block door.)*

Stand aside. Would you attempt to detain me in a public place?

BELLINGHAM. Return the book! Give it now or you'll not live to tell the tale.

TOM. Never! *(Turns to* DEALER, *who sits with head over cards.)* Sir—these two would commit robbery—murder! You must help me!

(DEALER *ignores him.)*

So, he disregards me! I am in a nest of thieves!

BELLINGHAM. Are you satisfied now? Return the property.

TOM. No, there are houses close by. My voice will attract notice. Help! Help! Police! Police!

(BELLINGHAM *and* DICEY *sing loudly.* DEALER *joins them and hammers on stage with pool cues, fists, etc.* OLD TOM's *voice is drowned.)*

BELLINGHAM. You will have it!

(OLD TOM *grapples him.* DEALER *brings bag from behind the table, puts it over* OLD TOM's *head, and carries him out struggling.* CHUMLEY *has fallen under the table, insensible. There is a knock at the door.)*

BELLINGHAM and DICEY *(whispering).* The police!

DICEY. Quick! Put those glasses away! *(Goes to door.)*

POLICE. What's all the row about?

BELLINGHAM *(pointing at* CHUMLEY*)*. Nothing out of the ordinary, sir. My friend here has been dining out and—ha, ha, wanted to fight, but he's quiet now.

DICEY. It's all right, officer. We've only been helping out a friend who's had too many. I'll quiet it down now, depend upon it.

POLICE. See that you do, or I'll have you padlocked for disturbing the peace. *(Exit.)*

DICEY. Yes, officer, yes. *(To* BELLINGHAM.*)* That was a close one. Now, what do you plan to do?

BELLINGHAM. Come with me. You'll see.

*(Exit* BELLINGHAM *and* DICEY.*)*

CURTAIN

SCENE TWO

SCENE: *The Underground Railway.* TOM *is peering through opening in the wall.*

TOM. Caged, trapped by those villains! Oh, Gordon Chumley, what have they done with him since they dragged me here? Where am I? Oh, the fiends! After I had dogged Knatchbull to this place, then to lose him at the hour of triumph. Is there no escape from this place?

*(There is a whistle, the sound of a train approaching.)*

What's that? A long dark street with green and red lights. Oh, I know it! I know it now! It's the underground railway. What's that?

*(Light appears.)*

Someone is coming. Surely that is Dicey's voice!

*(*BELLINGHAM *and* DICEY *enter, carrying* CHUMLEY *between them.)*

DICEY. I tell you, Chandos, I have gone as far as I will. Heaven knows I have no love for the man, but I refuse to—

BELLINGHAM. You refuse—don't make me laugh! With the forgery back in your pocket, you're in as deep as I. Tie the rope, Dicey!

*(*BELLINGHAM *starts tying* CHUMLEY *to the track.)*

TOM *(aside).* The fiends! I must get out of here!

DICEY. Never! I never blushed at making an honest shilling. I'll even admit to taking a few more than my share a time or two—but murder, no! If you do this thing, you do it alone, Chandos Bellingham.

*(She begins to move off during this line, as* BELLINGHAM *is busy securing the ropes.)*

BELLINGHAM *(jumping up).* Ah, no, Dicey! You don't desert me now! *(Pulls revolver.)* If I swing for this, you swing by my side! Give me that paper!

> (DICEY *screams and runs off down the track.* BELLINGHAM *shoots after her.)*

Damn, I've missed! But she shall join me yet! *(Exit.)*

TOM. Gordon, Gordon! Oh, what have they done! What's this? What's under my hand? A bar—I will—I can break through. *(Pounding, he breaks through.)* Gordon! Gordon! I am here!

> *(Bell rings loudly, whistle, sound of train approaching begins and is continued through speech.)*

I will save you! (OLD TOM *pulls switch, and the light of the train turns to other track.* OLD TOM *frees* CHUMLEY *and rolls him from track.)* Courage, Gordon, you are saved!

> *(Sound of train fades in distance.)*

CHUMLEY *(reviving slowly).* Where am I? Why are you here? *(He falls back.)*

TOM *(attempting to revive him).* That foul Knatchbull sought to murder you and keep the forged paper.

> *(Enter* MEDHURST.*)*

MEDHURST. Am I too late? Have they killed the one who would redeem my name?

TOM. No, he only suffers from the poison they administered. I have foiled their murderous plan, but they have escaped.

MEDHURST. Which way did they go? I shall go after them!

TOM *(pointing).* Down the track. They cannot have gotten far. I must stay with Chumley.

MEDHURST. Stay and aid him. I will go and I shall not rest until Richard Knatchbull is behind bars. *(Exit.)*

TOM. Gordon! *(Helps him to his feet.)* Can you stand? Are you all right now?

CHUMLEY. Yes, thanks to you, old friend. But the fiend who tried to kill me—where is he?

TOM. Escaped! But Sir George has followed him.

> *(Enter* POINTER *with* ROSE *and* ELIZA.*)*

POINTER. Have you seen George Medhurst? He is missing and these ladies have asked aid of the police to find him.

CHUMLEY. He has gone in pursuit of Chandos Bellingham, who doped me, tied me to these tracks, and tried to murder me! But this brave man risked his life and I am saved!

TOM. Stay with the ladies, Gordon. *(To* POINTER.*)* Come, sir, we must find George Medhurst. He will need our aid.

> *(Exit* TOM *and* POINTER.*)*

ROSE *(goes to* GORDON).* Gordon! Gordon! Who has done this thing? Tell me—tell me, quickly! Are you hurt?

CHUMLEY. No, only weak from the poison given me. Oh, my own dear Rose. *(Embraces her.)*

ROSE. How ever were you involved in such an affair?

CHUMLEY. I cannot tell you now. Only believe that what I did was honorable and for your sake.

ELIZA. Oh, Mr. Chumley, I feel it has to do with George. I know of the shadow that hangs over his head, and I am prepared to share his fate, whatever it may be. Only let me know—I—I am his wife.

CHUMLEY. His wife!

ROSE. Yes, Gordon. This girl, who in her sorrow consented to be my servant, is Lady Medhurst now. The lawyers, having learned that she was already his wife, have agreed to release the estate, and I am free from my promise.

CHUMLEY. Free? Oh, can this be true? Ah, say then you will marry me!

ROSE. Yes, yes!

(Enter BELLINGHAM in custody of MEDHURST.)

MEDHURST (to Chumley). Summon the police, Chumley, here's our man!

BELLINGHAM. Wait! You are mistaken! The person responsible for this foul play is a woman—not a man. Find Dicey Morris and you will know who blackmails and plots murder.

(Enter DICEY.)

DICEY. He lies! I held George Medhurst's note—and only meant to pick my profit from his gain! But he would murder to satisfy his greed! He tried to murder me! And would have, too, had I not found a hiding place!

BELLINGHAM. Pah, Dicey, who would take the word of a harridan like you?

DICEY (to CHUMLEY). Tell them—you know who brought you to my place! (She points to BELLINGHAM.)

BELLINGHAM (to CHUMLEY). If you appear against me, you consign me to death. You pledged your word you would not use the secret in your hands.

CHUMLEY. You have my word. I shall not appear against you.

BELLINGHAM (relieved). Right! Then there is none to appear against me.

(Enter TOM and POINTER.)

TOM. I will!

BELLINGHAM. Who are you?

TOM. Frank Dalton! The husband of your victim and the father of this girl. (Goes to ELIZA.)

ELIZA. Father! Oh, you truly are my father!

TOM. Yes, my child, you may call me so now. (To DICEY.) Now, Dicey Morris, will you bear witness against this fiend?

DICEY. I will. I knew him to be a convict and a thief, but now that he has added murder, I will speak.

BELLINGHAM (to OLD TOM). Dalton, there is that between us which you can never forget nor forgive.

*Pushed against the wall, convicted criminal Chandos Bellingham prepares to cheat the law of its prey as he drinks poison in the final scene of* After Dark *in London's underground railway. Left to right: David Rosario as Bellingham; Karen Duke as Eliza; Charles Johnson as Old Tom.*

ELIZA. My father will not be your judge.

BELLINGHAM. No, Eliza, he is my executioner. I confess I rendered Chumley insensible with poison, and then Dicey left me when I tied him to the track. She is innocent of attempted murder. But still guilty of extortion and she will not relent, since she still holds the forgery.

MEDHURST *(to* DICEY*)*. The note! Give it to me! I will pay all!

DICEY *(takes forgery from pocket)*. Here it is, and you owe me nothing. Richard Knatchbull *(Pointing to him.)* has already extracted too great a price!

POINTER. Richard Knatchbull!

BELLINGHAM *(to* POINTER*)*. Yes, officer, I am Richard Knatchbull, escaped convict! *(To* CHUMLEY.*)* I thank you, Mr. Chumley, for your kindness, though it was useless—there are too many here to give evidence against me. *(Pulls vial of poison from pocket, keeps it concealed until end of speech and then drinks it quickly.)* There is five hundred pounds reward offered for my capture, by the authorities at Hobartstown *(Drinks.)*, but you shall never collect it, nor shall any of my enemies. *(He falls and dies!)*

POINTER. He has done my work. Come, Dalton, we will carry him away!

TOM. Yes, away—away to the end of that crooked lane where the guilty find their steps barred by the gates of justice.

POINTER. Come, Dicey Morris, I must take you to the police. *(Exit.)*

DICEY. I will go. I will pay the price for such crimes of which I am guilty, but if I have friends among you, do not let them charge me with attempted murder. I am innocent of that, at least!

TOM. I will witness to that. Come along, and may the courts be as kind to you as you have been to many a sodden soul.

*(Exit DICEY. OLD TOM and POINTER carry out BELLINGHAM.)*

MEDHURST. Eliza, my own Eliza! Can you ever forgive me for all you have suffered for me? If only you will take me back, I promise that you will never have cause to be ashamed that you are Lady Medhurst!

ELIZA. Oh, George, have I ever been ashamed of you? Never! I love you and I shall always be your faithful wife. I know you will never give me cause to regret my devotion.

*(Re-enter OLD TOM. He stands looking at ELIZA and MEDHURST.)*

MEDHURST. Never, Eliza, and we shall be together till death do us part.

CHUMLEY. Rose tells me you did not know where or who your father was when you married. Let us have a double ceremony and Frank Dalton shall see his daughter married, and his honor restored.

TOM *(sings)*.

> After the darkness, the light will come—
> After the clouds, the sun—
> After the years, with their sorrows
> and tears,
> Gladness is sure to come.
>
> Though I have travelled the road
> of regret,
> Always the end is in sight.
> After the nighttime, the dawn will
> break through—
> After the darkness, light!

CURTAIN

*Music on page 377.*

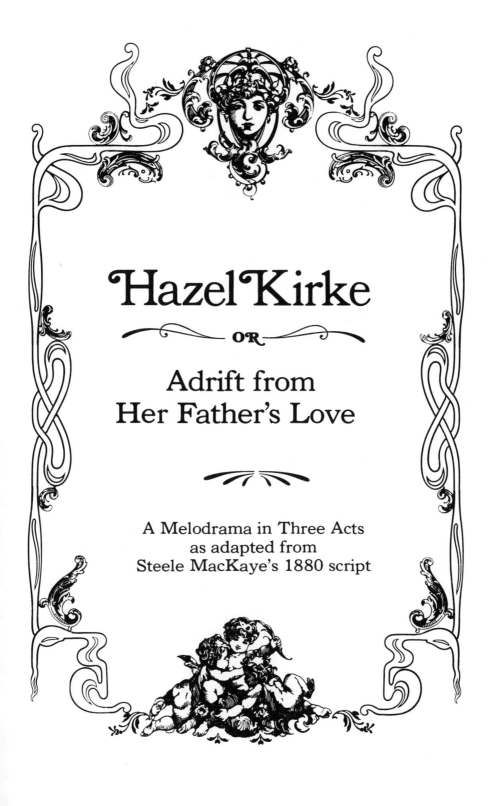

# Hazel Kirke

## OR

## Adrift from
## Her Father's Love

A Melodrama in Three Acts
as adapted from
Steele MacKaye's 1880 script

# CAST OF CHARACTERS

DUNSTAN KIRKE, a dour Scottish miller
MERCY KIRKE, his wife
HAZEL KIRKE, their daughter
DOLLY DUTTON, Hazel's cousin
MET MIGGINS, an orphan girl in the care of the Kirke family
AARON RODNEY, country gentleman and friend of Dunstan Kirke
PITTACUS GREEN, who was born a baby
ARTHUR CARRINGFORD, a young lord (Lord Travers)
EMILY CARRINGFORD (Lady Travers), his mother
BARNEY O'FLYNN, Lord Travers' valet
JOE, mill hand
INSPECTOR, from Scotland Yard

# SYNOPSIS OF SCENES

Time: Early spring, 1880                              Place: Lancashire

### ACT ONE

Exterior of Blackburn Mill.
          "Stand back, she is lost to thee forever!"

### ACT TWO

LORD TRAVERS' villa at Fairy Grove.
          "May Heaven forgive you all."

### ACT THREE

**Scene One:**   The Kitchen of Blackburn Mill, evening.
          "Oh, God, this is thy punishment!"

**Scene Two:**   Same, the following morning.
          "Peace after pain, and after sadness, mirth."

*Then, as now, actors and actresses often found their metier in a given role and wished to continue playing it for long periods of time. Effie Ellsler played Hazel Kirke with Charles Couldock as Dunstan in the first New York production in 1880. They repeated their success in San Francisco in 1881.*

## About the Play

*Hazel Kirke*, under its earlier title, *An Iron Will*, was first produced at Low's Opera House in Providence, Rhode Island, on October 27, 1879, and subsequently it was taken on tour to Philadelphia, Baltimore, Washington and other cities. The first New York production took place on February 4, 1880 at the Madison Square Theatre, where Charles Couldock created the role of the dour Scotsman, Dunstan Kirke, and Effie Ellsler played the title role. The play proved very popular, with 486 performances during the first run in New York, followed by 1,500 with a travelling troupe.

Although the play continued to enjoy phenomenal success for close to 30 years, the playwright received only a salary of $5,000 for two years, during which time the profits amounted to $200,000. Miss Ellsler and Charles Couldock starred again in an 1881 production at the California Theatre in San Francisco. The famed Laurette Taylor appeared in a later revival at the New Third Avenue Theatre in Seattle, Washington, in September of 1907.

*In the 1954 production of* Hazel Kirke, *Met Miggins (Isabel McClung, far right) delivered the coup de grace as she hit Aaron Rodney (Dieter Kiebel) and rendered him senseless in the final scene. Watching are* (left to right) *Pittacus Green (Tom Rea), Dolly (Norma Loy), Mercy (Beth White), Arthur (Bill McCarthy) and Hazel (Shirley Strain).*

# ACT ONE

SCENE: *Exterior of Blackburn, Dunstan Kirke's mill. At R., the exterior of house opens onto a courtyard. At L. is a large gateway. The walls to the courtyard are covered with vines. There is a view of the mill-wheel in the background. D.R. stands a bench; D.L., a rustic table with two chairs. A pile of empty bags is U.C., a broom on the porch. As the curtain rises,* JOE, *a mill hand in his forties, is discovered marking bags for market and* MET MIGGINS, *an orphan girl of about 25, is blowing a musical pipe.* JOE *is dressed in rough workman's clothing,* MET *in somber dress with scarf over her hair.*

DUNSTAN *(offstage).* Hey there, Dan, watch where you're loading that grain! *(He appears behind wall.)* Joe, you dolt, more bags, more bags! We hadn't got all day. *(Disappearing behind wall.)* Be off, boys, and bring another cart 'round. Will ye move your curs'd hides and look alive!

> *(Ad-lib from others offstage: "We're hurryin' as good as we kin." — "I can't find no more bags." — "Whoa, hold still, will ye?"*

MET *(mimicking Dunstan).* More bags — more bags for market!

JOE. Drat it! Give me time to mark 'em, can't ye?

MET *(blowing her pipe).* Oh, I don't care how long ye take, but old man Kirke is gettin' into one of his tempers.

JOE. Oh, his tempers be hanged! I'm doin' my best, no man can do more. *(He stands.)* Met Miggins — if you don't stop blowin' that frightful pipe o' yours, I'm goin' t' take the stick to ye!

MET. You wouldn't dare! If Miss Hazel found out, she'd see you off this place, and then where'd you go?

DUNSTAN *(offstage).* Hoorry, you dolts, or we'll never get loaded!

JOE *(to Met).* Seems to me y'd be a bit less ornery considerin' all Maister Kirke's done for ye since y' kin had the impudence t' die and leave you homeless. Y've growed up the mischievous booby ye are, and nobody c'n do a thing with ye, 'cept Mistress Hazel.

DUNSTAN *(offstage).* Hi there, Joe! Are ye never coomin' with those bags?

JOE. Aye — I'm coomin'! Drat that miller. If he don' beat the devil hisself. *(To Met.)* I'm warnin' ye, girl; bein' an orphan don' give ye the right to run 'round here like a half-wit mountain goat!

DUNSTAN *(offstage).* Are ye never coomin', ye lazy dolt?

MET *(teasing Joe).* You better hurry, Joe, or we'll all be killed. *(Starts blowing pipe again.)*

JOE. Ahh — h! You're as loony as they coom! *(yelling offstage.)* I'm coomin', I'm coomin'!

> *(Exit* JOE *U.L.* MET *follows blowing pipe). Enter* MERCY KIRKE *U.R. A Scottish country woman, middle-aged, in working dress with apron and mob-cap, she speaks with a thick accent.)*

MERCY. Dolly! Dolly, child!

DOLLY *(inside).* Aye, aye, aunt.

MERCY. Hoorry! Bring the bundles for market into the courtyard, lass.

DUNSTAN *(offstage).* Bags, more bags, Joe!

JOE. Here ye are, I'm bringin' the rest up now.

MERCY. Dolly! Dolly lass, what's keepin' ye?

*(Enter* DOLLY DUTTON, *niece to* DUNSTAN *and* MERCY KIRKE, *employed as maid of all work at Blackburn Mill. She is in her middle to late twenties, dressed in servant clothing. Her speech is that of an uneducated country girl, without the heavy accent of* MERCY *and* DUNSTAN.)

DOLLY *(entering with bundles).* Here I am, Aunt Mercy.

MERCY *(rising).* Has thee got the homespun, lass?

DOLLY. Aye, here 'tis, bundled and ready to go.

MERCY. That's a good child. Here, tie it up wi' the rest o' these.

DOLLY *(tying bundles).* La, Aunt Mercy! Is Uncle Kirke going to take all these to market wi' him?

MERCY. Aye, girl—times be hard, and money must be had for Hazel's wedding day.

DOLLY. Hazel's wedding day?

MERCY. Aye, child, that'll be soon now. Her father has decided that Hazel must marry Squire Rodney within three months.

DOLLY. Oh! How I hate that Squire Rodney!

MERCY. Hate him? What for, pray?

DOLLY. For stealing our Hazel away from her happiness.

MERCY. What dost mean, girl?

DOLLY. You're going to make Hazel marry Squire Rodney for gratitude, but it won't do, Aunt Mercy. Gratitude is not the stuff to make a happy marriage of. Can't Uncle pay off the money and let Hazel decide for herself?

MERCY. That he can't—for it takes all he can make to keep the mill a-goin'. Besides, Squire Rodney won't hear of it. He's bound Hazel will keep her promise and be his wife.

DOLLY. But what does Hazel say?

MERCY. She's not mentioned it for weeks. But she's been reared to honor her parents, and I know she'll never go against a promise made to her father. Hazel knows his iron will and harsh ways.

DOLLY. As who doesn't since he drove John—his own brother—from the mill, with a curse on his lips and anger in his heart, simply because he wouldn't be a miller all his life, as Dunstan thought he should.

MERCY. Peace, lass, peace!

DOLLY. La, Aunt Mercy! Thee'd say peace to the wicked one himself, if he were here.

MERCY. I think he be here indeed, Dolly, in thy temper.

DOLLY. Temper! Well, who has a better right to a temper? My mother was thy husband's sister, and all the world knows that Dunstan Kirke has the worst temper in all Lancashire!

DUNSTAN *(offstage, in a rage).* Coom! Coom! Off wi' ye—don't lollop around here all day! Hoorry to market, and don't loaf, for I'll be after ye wi' the young colt, as fast as ever I can.

DOLLY. Listen to Uncle Kirke, raging like a maddened bull.

MET *(enters, running across stage, frightened).* Hi! Look out, he's comin'! *(Exit D.R.)*

(DUNSTAN KIRKE *enters excitedly. He is a middle-aged, hard-working miller who has worked outdoors in all kinds of weather all his life.)*

DUNSTAN. Drat em! Drat 'em! I say! They're enough to make a devil o' a saint, so they are!

MERCY. There, there, dear heart, *(She crosses to him.)* Have patience, patience.

DUNSTAN. Patience! I am patient—patient as an angel. Confound 'em. It's taken me all day to get 'em off.

(HAZEL KIRKE *is heard singing outside. As he listens,* DUNSTAN'*s anger passes away, and he sinks into a chair).*

Ah! that does me good! That does me good! My Hazel's a lass, bless her, to gladden a feyther's heart—as modest as a girl should be, and as accomplished as any lady i' the land.

(*Enter* SQUIRE AARON RODNEY, *a country gentleman in his late forties, well-dressed.)*

MERCY. Yes, she's well eddicated, now.

DUNSTAN. Thanks to Squire Rodney, God bless him. T'was he got her the larnin'.

DOLLY. And he'll be well paid for it, too, when she's his wife.

DUNSTAN. Weel, that'll soon be now— that'll soon be now.

(MERCY *and* DOLLY *exit into house D.R.)*

RODNEY *(advancing).* I'm not so sure of that.

DUNSTAN. Ah! Maister Rodney, here at last! An' what's that ye're not so sure on?

RODNEY. That Hazel will ever be my wife.

DUNSTAN. Not be thy wife! Why, man, what's coom 'o thee, to say so strange a word? Didn't ye save me from ruin, and the whole mill from changin' hands, four year ago, and didn't Hazel promise then to be your wife, and didn't ye send her off to school, that she might learn to be the lady o' Rodney Hall?

RODNEY. True, Dunstan, but she was only fourteen then. There's many a slip 'twixt the cup and the lip, ye know.

DUNSTAN. Why! whatever do ye mean, man?

RODNEY. Why, I mean accidents may happen, and a young girl's heart may change.

DUNSTAN. Be careful what ye're sayin'! My Hazel—

RODNEY. Since you saved young Carringford from drowning, and brought him here, I've seen a change in Hazel. You don't see with my eyes, Dunstan—you don't see what I see.

DUNSTAN. And what dost see, sir?

RODNEY. I see an idle, handsome man lying ill and helpless. I see a lovely girl waiting upon him—nursing him. I see him looking at her, talking to her, touching her, and I know well what this must come to soon.

DUNSTAN. Maister Rodney, there is a holy book, that my bairn reads to us every day. Dost think that she can ever forget that that book commands us to keep our faith?

RODNEY. Ah, yes, Dunstan, but I warn you—the man bears watching. I've been a man of my word, sir, and I shall expect you to keep yours. You will remember that four years ago when you were on the brink of ruin, I did not at first take kindly to loaning the money.

DUNSTAN. I never did understand what made ye change yer mind.

RODNEY. Only the dictates of a kind heart, Dunstan. No one else would have loaned you money on a crumbling mill and the promise of a young girl's hand. And now that I've expended so much on the girl's education, I mean that she shall keep her promise.

DUNSTAN. That she will! A promise be a promise! If my child were to break her word, I'd drive her out as I would a scorpion on my hearth. Everybody knows the metal I'm made on. What I say, I'll do! And I tell thee now, Aaron Rodney, that this day three months, Hazel Kirke shall be thy wife!

RODNEY. Three months is too long—with young Carringford under your roof; you cannot know what turn events may take. I insist that the marriage shall take place within the week.

DUNSTAN. Why, man! Within the week!

HAZEL (offstage). Thanks—I've found them—I'll go myself.

RODNEY. Hush—that's her voice. We'll speak of this later.

(Enter HAZEL KIRKE, daughter of DUNSTAN and MERCY KIRKE. She is a beautiful young girl, well-dressed, and shows the effect of having been educated away from Blackburn Mill. Her clothes are quiet and tasteful, and her speech has no trace of her parents' accents.)

HAZEL (entering). Here, father, are some letters I want you to post. You won't forget?

DUNSTAN. Nothing that thee can ask, lass—not while thy face shines as bright wi' innocence as it does now! But look, child, there's Maister Rodney, child.

HAZEL. Good morning, Mr. Rodney.

DUNSTAN. Nay, lass, don't mind me. Give him your hand to kiss and a good hearty, honest girl's curtsey.

HAZEL (laughing). That's something I've never refused him yet.

(She does so. RODNEY attempts to embrace her, but HAZEL breaks away.)

Now, here, father, is the list of things for you to get.

DUNSTAN (gathering up bundles on table). A'reet, girl.

HAZEL. And here are my letters. Be sure you don't forget to post them.

DUNSTAN. No, girl, I shan't forget anything. I am not the forgettin' kind. (Starts to go; sees RODNEY and returns to HAZEL.) Ah! But I'm forgettin' one thing now, to ask after Maister Carringford. How is he this mornin', lass?

HAZEL. Better, I think.

DUNSTAN. Ah! He better be. He's been here more nor a month. He's a long time getting well.

HAZEL. But think how horribly he was hurt!

DUNSTAN. Aye, but I've seen older bones sooner mended. It's time he were well and off to his work; this is no place for idle hands. Give him a hint, girl—and here, my darling—gi' me a partin' kiss. God be wi' ye, child, and keep ye always the blessin' that ye are. Coom, Squire, see me to my colt.

(*Exits with* RODNEY.)

HAZEL. Ah! thank heaven he cannot see the wickedness in my wretched, wretched heart.

JOE (*offstage*). Get out of this!

MET (*offstage*). Hi! Hold on! Take that!

(*Crash is heard.*)

HAZEL (*starting*). What's that?

MET (*enters running*). Save me! Save me!

HAZEL. And now what have you done?

MET. Not a thing, Miss Hazel; I was only a-standin' blowin' my pipe.

HAZEL. But I've told you to stay out of Joe's way—he has no patience with your foolishness. Now, come with me—

MET. Are ye goin' to Mr. Carringford?

HAZEL. Why do you ask that?

MET. Because if you are, I won't go. I—hate him!

HAZEL. Hate him? What for?

MET. Because you love him so.

HAZEL (*severely*). How dare you say that!

MET. Because it's true.

HAZEL (*with mock severity, extending her hand*). Met, come with me this instant.

MET. Where?

HAZEL. To pick some flowers.

MET. Oh! Then I'll go, mistress—then I'll go.

(HAZEL *and* MET *exit.*)

RODNEY (*entering*). There she goes—the fairest lass to ever stroll the moors, and within the week she'll be mine! Her beauty would be prize enough, but the secret I've carried for four long years makes me heir to even more. Who would have dreamed that Dunstan's worthless brother—John—whom he drove out so many years ago, could have amassed so impressive a fortune in diamonds? And to think I nearly turned it down, the richest opportunity of my life! When Dunstan came to me four years ago, begging to be saved from ruin (*Taking letter from pocket inside coat.*), I laughed at him—and then this letter came. (*Reads.*) "Squire Aaron Rodney, Rodney Hall, Lancashire. My dear Sir, We have to hand the last will and testament of John Richard Kirke, brother of Dunstan Kirke, with whom I believe you are acquainted. It seems that because of an old family quarrel, John Kirke does not want his brother to know that before his untimely death in Africa, he had amassed a considerable fortune which, by his will, he leaves to his niece, Hazel Kirke. The estate is to be left with this firm, in trust for her, until she is of age. However, from the estate, funds have been provided for her education, with the further provision that the estate be placed in her hands only if she leaves her father's mill. If you will come to London, we believe it can be arranged for you to carry out his wishes regarding her education. Trusting you will hold this matter in strictest confidence—." And so, I went to Dunstan with my generous offer, asking no security save the opportunity to educate his lovely daughter. That Dunstan would discover all has oft caused fear to grip my heart; but his iron will doth blind him to the cunning of my ways. And now with Dunstan's promise to hasten Hazel's wedding day, the time is near when both her beauty and her fortune will be mine. One threat remains: Young Carringford! I must arrange that inquiries be made to crush his fondest wish!—But soft, someone comes. *(Exit.)*

*(Enter* DOLLY, *followed by* BARNEY O'FLYNN, LORD TRAVERS' *valet. His dress is rather formal, his Irish accent heavy.)*

DOLLY. Here is the house and here is the mill you're asking after.

BARNEY. Thankee! Thankee! So there's the mill-dam, where my master was drowned about six weeks since.

DOLLY. And now, who are you, and who did you want to see?

BARNEY. I'm Barney O'Flynn, Miss—the lackey of my lord.

DOLLY. And who's he?

BARNEY. One of your lodgers, I believe.

DOLLY. A lord lodging here? Ye're wrong—man—this is no place for lords.

BARNEY. True enough, darlin', true enough, but still my lord is here.

DOLLY. Will you give me the lie in my own house?

BARNEY. Hould now! Hould! Sure, here's his own direction in my own hand this minute: Lord Travers, at Dunstan Kirke's mill—Blackburn, Lancashire. Isn't this Lancashire?

DOLLY. Yes.

BARNEY. And isn't this Blackburn and the mill o' Dunstan Kirke?

DOLLY. Yes.

BARNEY. Very well, then, Lord Travers is here, just as sure as I'm Barney O'Flynn, and there's the proof of it—a letter calling Master Arthur home to onst.

DOLLY. Arthur, Arthur Carringford?

BARNEY. Yes, of course he's Lord Travers, and my master.

DOLLY. Mr. Carringford a lord!

BARNEY. Of course he's a lord—and I've been down from London to take him home in a howl of a hurry, too. Where is he?

DOLLY. There in the house.

BARNEY. Oh, he is, is he? Now ain't you ashamed of yourself, and you were going to drive me out! "Will ye give me the lie in my own house?" Never mind, darlin', I forgive ye, I forgive—

DOLLY. Get out of here, you fool! *(She chases* BARNEY *off left with a broom.)* Mr. Carringford a lord! And in love with Hazel, too—aye, I know he is—I can see it in his face every time he looks at her. Ah! If poor Hazel were only free, she might be Lady Travers, rich and grand! He has her heart already, aye, and except for Mr. Rodney, he'd have her hand as well. Ah! If I were Hazel, I know what I'd do. *(During speech* DOLLY *has been sorting vegetables from a basket. She holds a carrot through much of the next scene.)* I'd marry the man I loved in spite of all the world. *(She sits.)*

> *(Enter* PITTACUS GREEN, *behind the low stone wall U.R. A slight man, well-dressed as a country gentleman. He doffs his plaid wool hat as he appears.)*

GREEN. Stand where you are! You are the sweetest picture of surprise, that ever yet has blessed my eyes! Oh, 'tis true, and on my soul I swear it! *(He vaults the low stone wall.)* Will you permit me?

DOLLY *(standing).* Permit you what?

GREEN *(coming to her).* To change the situation—thus. Ha! Ha!

DOLLY *(backing up).* Who are you, sir?

GREEN. A hunter of heroes.

DOLLY. What brings you here?

GREEN. A tyrant called Curiosity.

DOLLY. La, the man is mad!

GREEN. No, I grieve to say I am not. I wish I were—madmen are monsters, everything monstrous is fascinating, but I, alas, am not a fascinating man, am I?

DOLLY. La, man, I don't know what ye are.

GREEN. You may not believe it, but I once was born—a baby too! Oh, I tell you, funny things have happened to me. At the early age of one minute, I howled to see the world. Luckily, my father made a handsome fortune in lemonade, by aid of which ade, I'm glad to say, I am enabled now today to see the world and have my way! That way, remark, is this: I go where I please, see what I please, say what I please, and please where I can, do you understand?

DOLLY. No, not a single word you say.

GREEN *(seating himself).* That's just what I supposed. Then I will be plain with you. I will be plain. A monster or a hero, I adore; ordinary mortals I detest; they are too much like Pittacus Green.

DOLLY. And who is Pittacus Green?

GREEN. The humble and devoted slave now gazing into those lovely eyes. *(He crosses to her, gazing into her eyes.)* Will you permit me to relieve you of that ponderous vegetable that cumbers those lovely hands? *(He takes the carrot from her, puts it down with other vegetables.)*

DOLLY. And so you are Pittacus Green?

GREEN. That is my distinguished name, Pit-ta-cus Green, or, as I'm called for short, Pitty Green. You may not believe it, but they say I'm cracked.

DOLLY. I knew it.

GREEN. Don't be alarmed. It's lovely to be cracked!

DOLLY. Lovely to be cracked!

GREEN. Of course, convince men that you are cracked, and they will let you do the oddest things. They'll smile instead of frown, and to gain a smile from lips like yours, I'd pay any price. Do you understand me now?

DOLLY. I think I do, and I like you, too, and here's Dolly Dutton's hand to prove it.

GREEN. You may not believe it, but you're an angel! Will you permit me? *(Takes her hand.)*

DOLLY. Anything that's honest.

*(He kisses her hand.)*

GREEN. 'Tis honest. Fair exchange is no robbery.

DOLLY *(sits)*. Now tell me truly—what is it that brings you here?

GREEN. As I said before, a monster or a hero I adore.

DOLLY. And do you expect to find a monster here?

GREEN. Yes, one in particular, one Dunstan Kirke, the miller of Blackburn Mill. He is the monster I mean—the rarest monster ever seen. A monster of goodness, who, during the last ten years, has saved from death by drowning at least forty souls, with their bodies attached.

DOLLY *(rises and crosses D.L.)*. And so, you are here to see my surly old uncle, who saves other folks, perhaps while he destroys his own daughter!

GREEN. Destroys his own daughter? Superb! Does he do it often? I mean, is he taken so frequently? Do sit down, make yourself at home; I do.

*(DOLLY sits.)*

Tell me all about it. *(He draws up a stool and sits beside her.)*

DOLLY. You've heard of the many he's saved; have you heard of the one he's sold?

GREEN *(rises, leans toward her)*. No, someone sold? Delightful! Who was it?

DOLLY. The pride o' this family, sir, my cousin, Hazel Kirke, she's the one that's sold.

GREEN. Indeed, poor thing, I sympathize; I've sold myself. Who sold her?

DOLLY. Her own feyther, Dunstan Kirke, your hero!

GREEN. Dear me! Why did he do it?

DOLLY. Because he loves his old mill more than anything else in the world. Four years ago, the bank that held my uncle's savings broke, and the old man was about to lose the mill, when Aaron Rodney loaned him the money without interest or security.

GREEN. He was a jolly old idiot! What was his little game?

DOLLY. "Sir," said the Squire, "You have a daughter, whom I admire; give me leave to send her off to school, have her taught, and then become my wife and the lady of Rodney Hall."

GREEN. Ah-ha! I smell a rat! Rodney goes to her, makes love to her, fills her mind with gaudy pictures, chromes and thromes, tells her of the good his wealth will do, and so she, a thoughtless child, makes a rash promise to please her father—which promise is sure to play the dev-Mephistopheles with them both.

DOLLY. Why, man, how did you know that?

GREEN. Quite simply, I guessed it.

DOLLY. Well, then, ye're not so much of a fool as I took ye for.

GREEN. Bless you for those kind words. Tell me what became of your cousin.

DOLLY. Four years ago she was sent to school; six months ago she returned.

GREEN. She is awfully fond of old Rod, of course?

DOLLY. She's proud and silent, sir, but I, who love her, read her heart. I know that she could not love Aaron Rodney.

GREEN. Egad! The situation inspires me! What would you say if I were to help you clear your cousin Hazel of her bargain?

DOLLY. I'd say ye were the best man that ever crossed the threshold of Blackburn Mill.

GREEN. That being the case—what would you give to have it done?

DOLLY. Anything I've got.

GREEN. Even your heart?

DOLLY. La, man! I haven't got any.

GREEN. Haven't you? Well, then would you give this fashionable substitute? *(He indicates carrot.)*

DOLLY. Oh, yes, if ye'd care to take it.

GREEN. Hmm! It's a little moldy, mildew-y, miller-y—the soil of honest labor, I mean. Yes, this is romance, and I'm the Roman. I'll be your best man—I'll outwit old Rod or die.

DOLLY. But how, man, how?

GREEN. You may not believe it, but once I had a mother; funny things have happened to me. That mother, she never could wind a yarn without making a snarl, and I never could undo the snarl without telling a yarn.

DOLLY. What of that?

GREEN. I have great faith in the power of a yarn to undo a snarl. Now there's a snarl in this family; give me leave to tell yarns enough, and I'll guarantee to undo the snarl. Why, bless me, it's perfectly delightful! There's the stern father, Dunstan Kirke; the heavy villain, old Rod; the pretty victim, Hazel Kirke; the scheming cousin, that's you; the good-natured, idiotic busybody, that's me; and—

DOLLY. Why do you stop?

GREEN. Confound it, there's something lacking! We'll imagine here's our Andromeda chained to a rock, about to be devoured by a dragon, a real dragon—wanted: the hero, Perseus, to deliver her. Where shall we get a hero? I have it—we'll advertise! Hello! How's this? Who's that?

DOLLY. Only one of my uncle's patients.

GREEN. Who is he?

DOLLY. Here he comes—find out for yourself.

GREEN. Fate, I thank thee! The conquering hero comes!

(*Enter* ARTHUR CARRINGFORD, *a young nobleman, Lord Travers. He is handsome and his speech and manner reveal his class and education. He is dressed in rough country clothing that has been loaned to him since his accident at the mill.*)

ARTHUR. Have you seen my dog? Ah, Miss Dolly!

DOLLY. She went off with Met a while ago. Shall I find her for you?

ARTHUR. You're very kind. If it isn't too much trouble, I should be glad of a little of Miss Hazel's company, if she's at leisure. You know I must soon leave this dear place.

DOLLY. I'll try and find her, sir.

GREEN. Ye great god of war.

ARTHUR. Ha—what idiot is this?

GREEN. It is! It is! By the bolts of Jove, it is!

ARTHUR. Indeed! Is it—what is?

GREEN. You is—either I'm a cow, or this is Lord Travers.

ARTHUR. Who is Lord Travers? You—

GREEN. You is—am—are. Look at me sharp. Don't you remember P.G.? Have you forgotten our tiger hunt in India? Ah, there was a monster worth meeting! He met you and treed you, too. Can't you recall your old comrade of the jungle, Pittacus—the mouse that freed you, the lion? Why, it was the proudest shot of my life!

ARTHUR. On my life—is it possible—you here?

GREEN. Of course I am! And (*They shake hands.*) bless my soul, how glad I am to see you.

ARTHUR. Hold on—the arm you are torturing is only half mended.

GREEN. Gracious! What do you mean?

ARTHUR. That this is a broken arm but slightly convalescent.

GREEN. A broken arm, forgive me! Travers, I'm a brute! Take that indigestible vegetable and crack my skull.

ARTHUR. Thanks, dear boy, it's cracked enough already.

GREEN. Precisely; I see your vengeance is complete.

ARTHUR. Now tell me how you found me out?

GREEN. By accident—the usual way. How did you get here?

ARTHUR. Came to Lancashire to escape the tiresome nonsense of town—went shooting with my dog—attempted to cross the stream by a tree that lay over it, just above the dam—there.

GREEN. Then what?

ARTHUR. Slipped like a fool, fell, broke my arm in falling and sank unconscious into the water.

GREEN. Merciful powers!

ARTHUR. My dog sprang in and held me above the surface. Kirke, the miller, caught sight of us and jumped in, pulled me out and lodged me here, where I've had the best of care for six weeks.

GREEN. Great fortune! I see it all. It's the saved and the sold, side by side, beneath the same roof; she is the sold and you are now the saved, two hearts with but a single stock. Travers, my dear boy, you may not believe it, but there's more than accident in this arrangement.

ARTHUR. Undoubtedly, but your exclamations are somewhat obscure.

GREEN. Look here, old man, let's get to business. Time flies. I helped you when you were in a pickle; now you must help me.

ARTHUR. With pleasure! How can I do it?

GREEN. By falling desperately in love.

ARTHUR. Oh, falling in love! Why, that's your business; you know you are always falling in love.

GREEN. And why not? As the poet says, come live with me and be my love. I love to live and I live to love.

ARTHUR. Eccentric dog! You always manage to make logic and delight agree.

GREEN. Oh, Travers, I've met my fate at last!

ARTHUR. Nonsense, you are always meeting your fate—who is she this time?

GREEN. Dolly Dutton, the miller's niece.

ARTHUR. You'll find her rather a lively fate, I fancy.

GREEN. Precisely! I know I shall, that's the way I like 'em. She's a perfect monster.

ARTHUR. Monster?

GREEN. Yes, a monster of beauty and goodness—but come—will you do me a favor and fall in love?

ARTHUR. Certainly. I find there's nothing easier than to fall; I've tried one element, I've no fear to try another. With whom must I fall in love?

GREEN. An angel in a fix; Hazel Kirke, the miller's daughter.

ARTHUR. Stop, sir, I shall not tolerate nonsense that touches her good name. Understand this at once.

GREEN. Capital! I'm more than satisfied! I'm ecstatic. You're in love with her already.

ARTHUR. Sir! Green, Miss Kirke is coming. I'm known here simply as Arthur Carringford, you must not betray my title; it would only raise a barrier between me and the golden hearts to whom I owe so much.

GREEN. Travers, I honor your sentiments, and will respect your wishes.

DOLLY *(entering).* Here she is, Maister Carringford.

*(Enter* HAZEL *and* MET.*)*

HAZEL. Now, Met, go to Mother Weedbury's cottage and carry some wood for the poor thing and stop there till I come. Tell her I will be there to help her with the children in the morning.

MET. All right, Miss, I'll go; but mind it's for you and not for the old woman. *(Exits.)*

HAZEL. Good morning, Mr. Carringford.

ARTHUR. Miss Hazel, I'm glad to have a glimpse of you at last.

GREEN. Have mercy! Why don't you present me to the lady?

ARTHUR. Miss Kirke, permit me to present a very dear old friend, Mr. Pittacus Green.

HAZEL. He's doubly welcome, as your friend, and for his own sake.

GREEN. Ah! Miss Kirke *(Kisses her hand.)*, I'm a very old-fashioned young fool. You will permit me? I am your slave. Pittacus, there's no use, you're an assassin from this hour; the one dear purpose of your life is to get Squire Rodney cremated without delay.

HAZEL *(offers flowers)*. Let me share my treasures. There—what do you say to that?

GREEN. I say nothing, nothing! I am dumb with delight, decidedly, Old Rod is a doomed man.

HAZEL. Will you accept a flower?

ARTHUR. Thanks. Miss Hazel, I know I sent for you, but if you will permit me, I'd like to retire to my room with my friend Mr. Green for a talk of old times.

HAZEL. Of course. Sorry to lose you.

*(ARTHUR exits U.L.)*

GREEN. My dear Miss Kirke, you may not believe it, but by the justice of Jove, we'll meet again.

*(HAZEL exits U.L. GREEN begins to hum snatch of a song.)*

DOLLY. Stop! Stop! Look here, you've promised to help me free my cousin Hazel from her bargain with the Squire. When are you going to begin?

GREEN. Dear Dolly Dutton: I've just begun, and you must help. First, you must see her mother and tell her you know that Rodney is not the man Hazel loves.

DOLLY. I'd never dare do that!

GREEN. What? You can't desert me now—I'm forming plans and you must help. So, courage, speak, and your cousin will be blessed! Here her Aunt comes, I'll leave her to the tender mercies of your tongue. Madam, will you permit me? In the words of the immortal bard of Avon, I humbly take my leaf. Madam, if all the world were right, you and I would never be in the wrong!

*(Exit U.L. MERCY enters from house.)*

MERCY. Dolly, who be that?

DOLLY. A man named Pitty Green.

MERCY. Pitty Green. An odd name, and he seems a bit off *(Taps her head.)* here!

DOLLY. That's all right, Aunt, so long as he is sound here. *(Hand to her heart.)*

MERCY. Aye, that's true, Dolly, that's true.

DOLLY. Aunt Mercy—

MERCY. Well, Dolly?

DOLLY. Did ye mark the look in Hazel's face this morning, after her father told her Mr. Carringford had been here long enough?

MERCY. What sort o' look, girl?

DOLLY. A pale, suffering, frightened look. Aunt, she's in love with Mr. Carringford, as sure as I'm a living woman.

MERCY *(with a start)*. My heart, child! Does thee mean what thee says? *(Stands.)*

DOLLY. Indeed I do.

*(Enter HAZEL.)*

HAZEL. Mother dear, be sure to let me know when father has finished his supper and settled his accounts. You won't forget?

MERCY. Where are thee going, child?

HAZEL. I'm going to Mother Weedbury's cottage to fetch Met home.

MERCY. Thee can wait a bit. I've a word to say to thee. Dolly, thee'll find work in the house. Leave us.

DOLLY. All right, aunt. *(Exit D.R.)*

MERCY. Hazel, child, come here and kneel at my feet as thee did when a little one, and I taught thee to pray. My child, many in this world may say they love thee, but none'll ever do it as I do. Thee may have friends and lovers, too, but thee can never have but one mother. Well, child, can't thee trust her?

HAZEL. Trust her? Have I ever distrusted her?

MERCY. Aye, thee's distrustin' her now. There's that in thy heart she ought to know.

HAZEL. Why, mother, what do you mean?

MERCY. Oh, thee knows well eno' what I mean. I've been foolish, child, and blind. I forgot the danger o' youthful blood, and I felt too sure o' thy promise to be Aaron Rodney's wife. But my eyes are open now. I've discovered thy secret, girl. And I must speak to thee.

HAZEL. Oh, mother—spare me—it is too late! It is too late!

MERCY. Too late! What dost mean, child? Speak! Lift up thy head and look me in the face.

HAZEL. Mother!

MERCY. Ah! It's a'reet, ye can look me i' the eye still, like an honest girl. But oh, I see it all now. That Maister Carringford be a bad man—a bad man.

HAZEL. Mother!

MERCY. There's no use, Hazel—I know all thee'll say for him! But thy feyther saved his life and cherished him in his house, and this is his gratitude, to make love to thee—the plighted wife o' another man.

HAZEL. No, mother, you wrong him. He has never spoken a word of love to me in his life.

MERCY. An' has thee been won then wi'out wooing?

HAZEL. Oh,how can I tell? All that I know is that day by day his voice grows sweeter, his words wiser. I did not realize how empty my life would be without him till now the time has come for him to go. It seems as if the shadow of death were upon my heart—it has grown so dull and heavy!

MERCY. Does thee say that he has never told thee that he loves thee?

HAZEL. Never! And yet I know he does. When my back is turned, I can feel his eyes upon me—I saw them once by accident in the glass. I knew all then, for I saw in them my own misery, my own love. *(She goes to* MERCY's *arms.)*

MERCY. My poor child! But we must do right, if it kills us. There's but one remedy for this, the short and sharp one. *(She starts to go.)*

HAZEL. Where are you going, Mother?

MERCY. He must leave this house at once. *(Crosses D.R. to go.)*

HAZEL *(stops her).* No, it is not for you to send him away; that is my duty. It will be less of an insult to him and less agony to me.

MERCY. Thou hast not the strength to do it.

HAZEL. I will find it. Send him here to me, and I promise you I will tell him we must part at once.

MERCY *(speaks as she goes).* Aye, it's better so. Perhaps thee'll fret less if thee send him away. Thee shall have thy way, Hazel child.

*(*HAZEL *comes to her and she kisses her.)*

Courage, lass, be strong i' the battle today, and thou'lt be rich i' the triumph tomorrow. *(She exits.)*

HAZEL. What am I going to do? Drive away the happiness that heaven sends me? Insult the man I honor most—and all for what? To keep the rash promise of a silly, thoughtless girl? *(She sits.)* Oh, I must not think of it, or I shall rebel.

*(Enter* ARTHUR*)*

ARTHUR. Why, Hazel, what's the matter?

*(She rises coldly.)*

Pardon me, Miss Kirke, you wished to speak to me?

HAZEL. Mr. Carringford, I have sent for you to say that which may sound strangely coming from me—but you must leave this place at once.

ARTHUR. Leave? May I know why?

HAZEL. No. Not from my lips.

ARTHUR. Do you wish me to go?

HAZEL. Yes, yes, go—and quickly!

ARTHUR. You are right—I will go.

*(Unseen by them,* RODNEY *enters U.L.)*

*(Extends his hand to her.)* Bid me farewell.

*(She turns away, holding her hand out toward him. He kisses it tenderly. She falls sobbing in chair.)*

You must have mercy upon me and let me speak.

HAZEL. No. I beseech you, leave me—in kindness, leave me without a word.

*(He turns to go;* RODNEY *steps forward.)*

RODNEY. Stay, Mr. Carringford, one word with you. I know all; I have seen how you have come into this house and made light with the affections of Miss Kirke.

(HAZEL *draws back.*)

I see how you have tried to win her from me—but you know she is my plighted wife.

HAZEL. You need say no more, Mr. Rodney—Mr. Carringford is leaving.

RODNEY. But I would say more. Mr. Carringford, I know who you are. I have taken the precaution of writing to your mother—you know the pride of your race, sir. Your mother would never consent to your marriage with this miller's daughter.

HAZEL. I beg you—stay your words—I do not understand their meaning, but Mr. Carringford is leaving at once. I cannot help the past, but I can be brave for the future. I can do my duty and keep my promise.

ARTHUR. No, Hazel! Your promise of the past was clouded in the innocence of childhood. Your duty to the future is to marry the man you love!

RODNEY (*steps toward* HAZEL, *she recoils*). And I—Mr. Carringford— claim to be that man!

ARTHUR (*stepping between them*). What demon would desire the plighted love of a righteous girl knowing full well that time alone and only the bower of true womanhood may bestow such a gift? I tell you, sir, your intentions are dishonorable!

RODNEY. I warn you, Carringford, you tread on treacherous ground. (*Backing off.*) I leave you to your fond farewells. Should you remain when I return, I'll demonstrate what sort of demon you defy! (*Exit.*)

(ARTHUR *starts after him but is stopped by* HAZEL.)

HAZEL. No, Arthur! Let him go. My father must never know the love I promised one man has been given to another. That secret must be kept, though it tear our lives apart! Until you came I never dreamed the sweetness such a love could bring. (HAZEL *goes to him, puts her hands up to his chest and looks in his eyes.*) Your eyes, your voice, your words have brought a singing to my heart! That song will last forever. (*She turns away, dropping head.*) I must not ask for more.

ARTHUR. Ah, Heaven! (*He takes her hand.*) This is the bitterest and sweetest moment of my life!

(*Enter* DUNSTAN *with bundles.* HAZEL *and* ARTHUR *separate.*)

DUNSTAN. Ah, lass, and here's thy bundles.

HAZEL. Father! But how quickly you've returned!

DUNSTAN. Aye, lass, there was a letter at post, so I hurried home. They said it was for me. Here, lass, read it for me. Let me hear what it says.

(*He hands her the letter; she opens it and starts.*)

Well, lass, and what says the letter?

(HAZEL *becomes faint. He assists her to a chair.*)

My heart, child, what be the matter? There, sit down, sit down;

what's the trouble? Is it bad news? Out with it. Who's it from? Let's hear.

HAZEL. It is signed "Emily Carringford."

(ARTHUR *starts.*)

DUNSTAN. What ha' she got to say to me? Read it, lass; what does she say?

HAZEL (*aside*). There's no use. I shall be forced to read it. "Dunstan Kirke, Esq., Dear Sir, I have been startled by learning of my son's presence in your home, deeply pained by hearing of his conduct with your child—"

DUNSTAN. Eh? What be that? What be that?

HAZEL. "I have besought him to return to me instantly. If he refuses, I call on you to add the force of your commands to my prayers."

DUNSTAN. Aye, aye, it's gettin' clearer, it's gettin' clearer. Go on child, what more does she say?

HAZEL. "I cannot describe my indignation at the thought of my son's love for—"(*She breaks down.*)

DUNSTAN. That's enough! Stop there, girl—ya need read no more! Mr. Carringford, I'd been warned and thought y' more of a man than ye are! I've only one child in all the world, and God knows I love her, better than my life. Well, sir, I'd rather bury her with my own hands than have her faithless to her word. Now, ye know she's the plighted wife o' Aaron Rodney. Well, then, are ye a serpent I've cherished in my breast to bite me and mine? Have ye dared to think o' making love to Hazel Kirke?

ARTHUR. Fate threw me helpless at her feet. 'Twas these hands (*Holding her hands.*) nursed me back to life. Well, sir, I confess what I could not wish to help—I learned to love her!

DUNSTAN. Hazel, thee hears what he says, and thee knows the duty o' an honest girl. Bid him be gone at once!

HAZEL. No, Father, I cannot.

DUNSTAN. What's that thee says?

HAZEL. If he must go, I should go, for I too am guilty.

DUNSTAN. What! My child avows dishonor?

HAZEL. Father—Father, hear me!

DUNSTAN. Hear thee! No, no! (*Advancing toward her.*) I've heard too much already. I could take thy shameless heart out.

(HAZEL *with a cry of fear, draws back into* ARTHUR's *arms.*)

ARTHUR (*shielding her*). Stand back, sir, stand back!

DUNSTAN. What! In his arms! Before my very eyes? Out upon thee, thou foul disgrace! Hear thy father's curse!

(*Enter* MERCY *and rushes to him, pleading,* DOLLY *follows her and stands watching.*)

MERCY. No, no, she is thy child, thine only child!

DUNSTAN (*throws her off*). Begone! Thou misbegotten bairn, begone! I cast thee out adrift, adrift forever from they feyther's love, and may my eyes no more behold thee!

HAZEL. Mother! Mother!

(MERCY *starts toward* HAZEL. DUNSTAN *comes between them.*)

DUNSTAN. Stand back! She is lost to thee forever!

TABLEAU. HAZEL *in* ARTHUR*'s arms, arms outstretched toward* MERCY *and* DUNSTAN; MERCY *silently pleading with* DUNSTAN; DOLLY *dropping her head in dejection.*)

CURTAIN

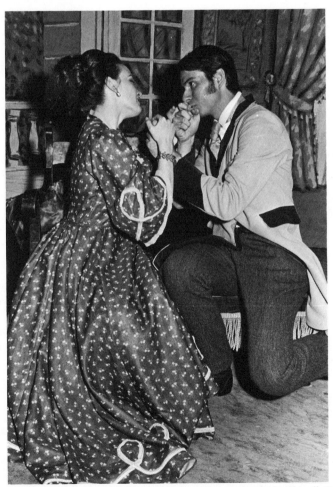

*Arthur. "May all our troubles end like this—in smoke and a kiss." (In Act Two—with Cynthia Montilla as Hazel and William Halliday as Arthur.)*

# ACT TWO

SCENE: *Interior of* LORD TRAVERS' *villa at Fairy Grove; a room bright with sunlight. On a table L. are cigarettes and matches, also a bell; water and glass are on a stand R. At rise of curtain,* AARON RODNEY *opens the door quietly and peers about. Seeing no one, he steps inside. Outside,* MET *can be heard blowing her pipe.*

RODNEY. Ha, no one about! So this is the nest where Carringford has hidden her all these months from the shame of a pretended marriage too hideous to serve the fine and noble manners of his titled race! I have had the devil's own time finding her myself while I kept the lawyers from locating her to give her the estate. Fortunately, the fools believed me when I told them that she had had a serious illness, was travelling on the continent, and could not be reached, but I surely cannot hold them off much longer. Time is of the essence and I must act with haste! Now—if only Carringford is not about, I shall bring his mother, Lady Travers, here to tell Hazel that this marriage to her son was a fraud. That done and Hazel in tears—I shall offer my forgiveness, agree to marry her in spite of her ah—sin, and she cannot fail, in gratitude, to allow me free rein with her fortune! Ssst—someone comes. *(Exit.)*

*(Enter* BARNEY.*)*

BARNEY. There's that worthless girl blowin' the pipe again, instead o' mindin' the kitchen. Why did Mr. Carringford ever let that ninny here!

*(Enter* MET *carrying flowers.)*

MET. I say, where's the mistress, Barney?

BARNEY. And what would you be wantin' of her now?

MET. Here's some flowers I've been picking for her. Where is she?

BARNEY. Oh, about some'res—cryin', I suppose.

MET. Cryin'—What do you mean?

BARNEY. Well, if you was half as witted as ye seem, ye'd know that for the past three days, she's been mighty put out about somethin'.

MET. What could be the matter with her?

BARNEY. Lonesome, I suppose. She goes nowheres, sees nobody, and for more'n a week Lord Travers has been gone. There's something wrong between 'em, Met. Do you know what it be?

MET. How should I know?

BARNEY. Well, you know the missus before she came here—she brought you here.

MET. No, she didn't bring me here; I followed her, and I'd follow her to the other end of the earth if she'd let me. She's a lady, she is, every inch of her, and she's too good for him!

BARNEY. Too good for my master—watch what ye say, girl!

MET. Well, look at the way he treats her. Why is it he brings no one here to see her. Why is it his mother and none o' his folks don't never come here at all?

BARNEY. How should I know?

MET. Well, ye know more'n you're tellin', to be sure. There she be on the shore of the Park Lake. I'll take her the flowers. *(Plays pipe.)*

BARNEY. Hold on, Met, tell me first—

MET. I'll tell ye nothin', and that's more than ye desarve. *(Exit U.R.)*

*(RODNEY enters U.C.)*

RODNEY. I say, man, is this place called Fairy Grove?

BARNEY. Yes, sire, that it is.

RODNEY. And is your master at home?

BARNEY. No, sir, that he's not.

RODNEY. And your mistress?

BARNEY. You mean Mrs. Carringford?

RODNEY. Is she called that here?

BARNEY. Indeed she is—for that's her name, sir! Did you wish to see her?

RODNEY. No—no—but I would speak with you. Have you been in service with the Carringford family for long?

BARNEY. Iver since my lord was a boy—and my father before me.

RODNEY. Ah, then, you will understand what a disgrace Lord Travers has brought upon his name.

BARNEY. An' what would ye be meaning?

RODNEY. I mean his—ah—presumed marriage to the common daughter of a miller.

BARNEY. What do you know of it? And by whose leave do you come around askin' questions?

RODNEY. My good man—I am an old friend of the Carringford family and have known Lady Travers for many years. I know that it would break her heart if she knew that her son lives in sin—

BARNEY. In sin, sir? *(Aside.)* How much does he know?

RODNEY. Yes, it has come to my attention that their marriage was falsely performed, and that young Lord Travers practiced the deceit, knowing that the marriage was not legal. Now, I should like to ask a favor of you for which I am willing to pay you well.

*(He takes bills from his pocket and holds them toward BARNEY.*

BARNEY *reaches;* RODNEY *withdraws them.)*

BARNEY. Yes?

RODNEY. Yes. I would like you to say, when you are asked, that you were with them when the ceremony was performed. *(Holding the money in front of him carelessly.)*

BARNEY. But I was, sir!

RODNEY. So much the better—I want you to swear that they were married in a Scottish ceremony on the English side of the border.

BARNEY *(aside).* How could he know? I'd swear no one knew. *(To RODNEY.)* Well, now, I don't know about that.

RODNEY. Come now, if you will do as I say, it will be worth a hundred pounds to you.

*(Extends bills. BARNEY grabs them and counts quickly.)*

BARNEY. Oh, no, ye don't do that to Barney O'Flynn! There's only fifty here.

RODNEY. I'll pay you the rest when his Lordship has gotten rid of this peasant girl!

BARNEY. Well, then, I'll do it. *(Pockets the money.)* Sure, it's not for the money, you understand, but for the honor of the family I sarve. *(Pats his pocket.)*

RODNEY. Of course, of course. *(Aside.)* They're all alike—the greedy thieves! Now mind you don't say a word until you're asked. I'll be back within the day to see what turn events have taken. *(Exit.)*

BARNEY. Now, who could he be to be so interested in Lord Travers affairs? Ah, well, I've got the fifty pounds, and I'll decide myself who and what I'll tell!

*(Enter ARTHUR D.R., with overcoat over arm.)*

ARTHUR. Well, Barney! *(Tosses overcoat to BARNEY.)*

BARNEY. Master, ye frightened me, sure, sir, I'm glad ye're back.

ARTHUR. Where's my wife?

BARNEY. Your wife, sir?

ARTHUR. Certainly, my wife.

BARNEY. Oh, yes, certainly, she's in the garden, I believe.

ARTHUR *(sits at table).* Let her know that I've arrived.

BARNEY. All right, sir. *(Aside.)* He's in one o' his quare moods again. *(Pacing.)* He's gettin' tired of this already. I knew it! I knew it! He'll end it sooner than I thought he would. Ah, there's nothing like a Scottish marriage on the wrong side of the line to save the trouble of divorce and chate the lawyers. *(Exit.)*

ARTHUR *(reads from letter).* "My dear Travers, your mother is in a very dangerous condition. Today she arose for the first time in months, laboring under some strong excitement that is giving her temporary strength. She asks the most searching questions concerning you. She gets more impatient every day for your marriage with 'Lady Maud'." *(Folds letter.)* I had hoped for good news. Ah, will this never end? How long must I conceal my marriage to Hazel? Shall I never be able to show the world the noble woman who is my wife? *(Sinks into reverie.)*

*(HAZEL runs in. Seeing ARTHUR, she creeps up behind him and puts her hands over his eyes. He exclaims.)*

HAZEL. Ah, you are back at last, my darling!

ARTHUR. Apparently.

HAZEL. Oh, I'm so glad, so glad! I've been almost dead with loneliness.

ARTHUR. Have you really missed me so much?

HAZEL. More than you will ever know or care, I fear.

ARTHUR. Oh, I love to have you miss me.

HAZEL. Of course you do—you wouldn't love me if you didn't.

ARTHUR. And you're not tired yet of these iron bonds of matrimony?

HAZEL. I call them golden bonds.

ARTHUR. And so they are, and so they are, darling. May they always hold us heart to heart.

HAZEL *(sadly)*. Heigh ho!

ARTHUR. Heigh ho? Well, well, what does this mean?

HAZEL. Oh, only a silly thought. I'm superstitious; too much happiness is dangerous, sometimes, you know, that's all.

ARTHUR *(taking her hand)*. Little woman, do you know I'm not blind—there's something troubles you. What is it?

HAZEL *(imitating him)*. Big man, do you know I'm not blind, and there's something troubles you? What is it?

ARTHUR. Come, come, dear, I'm in earnest.

HAZEL. And so am I, dear. For the last few weeks, whenever you're at home, you've been so silent and moody. Oh, Arthur, can't you trust me with your sorrows as well as your joys? Come, dear, tell me what troubles you.

ARTHUR. Business, that is all. But you, Hazel, you have no such cause for sadness.

HAZEL *(laughing, she rises)*. I sad? Why, I'm the gayest creature in the world.

ARTHUR *(holds her hands)*. You try to be—before me—but when you've supposed me absent, I've seen you in tears. Have I not done all that I could to make you happy?

HAZEL. Oh, indeed you have!

ARTHUR. Then why have I failed?

HAZEL. Failed! You have not failed. You have made me too happy. My happiness startles me sometimes; I so little deserve it. I confess at moments I am haunted.

ARTHUR. Haunted by what, dear?

HAZEL. I hardly know—a vague, uncertain dread. This last year has been so strange, the way we met, our secret marriage in Scotland—

ARTHUR. Yes, but you know why our marriage had to be so secret.

HAZEL. Yes, because your mother had set her heart upon another woman for you.

ARTHUR. My mother has been determined to make me the husband of Maud Wetherby; she has been very ill for years. To have acknowledged my marriage with you would surely have been to kill her. So I was forced to have our marriage take place in the way that offered the least risk of discovery by her.

HAZEL. Oh, my darling, I do hate this hiding! How much longer must it last?

ARTHUR. I have been hoping every day that my mother would have grown strong enough to learn the truth, but I am disappointed; she is no better, I even fear she is growing worse.

HAZEL. Your mother deceived! My father broken-hearted! Oh! It is horrible, I cannot stand it.

ARTHUR. What a fool I've been!

HAZEL. What do you mean?

ARTHUR. I've been stupid enough to fancy that my love—my devotion—might suffice to make you forget—to make you happy.

HAZEL *(going to him)*. And so they do, dear. I was wrong to confess these foolish fears to you. Say you forgive me?

ARTHUR *(embracing her)*. Forgive me that I have not rendered you the open honor that was due you as my wife. *(He turns his head away.)*

HAZEL. How strangely you say that! What can you mean?

ARTHUR. No matter now, dear. *(Affecting gaiety.)* Away with gloomy thoughts! All's well that ends well! Where are my cigarettes—no objection to my smoking, dear?

HAZEL. No, on the contrary, I'll light one for you.

ARTHUR. Thanks, that will be delightful.

*(She lights it—draws and coughs.)*

HAZEL. There—take the horrid thing.

ARTHUR. Horrid thing! *(Puts his arm around her.)* Why, I declare it's the most delicious cigarette I've ever smoked in all my life. Thanks, little woman, may all our sorrows end like this, in smoke and a kiss.

*(He kisses her; she smiles up at him. Meanwhile, PITTACUS GREEN has appeared at the window and observed. He enters C., laden with sporting traps, a sun umbrella over his head. He coughs.)*
I declare—at last, it's our dear old Green.

GREEN. Tis true, 'tis Pitty, and pity 'tis, 'tis true. You may not believe it, but all these things are a bore.

HAZEL *(goes to him)*. Talk of matrimonial misery—what is it compared to the awful doom of a bachelor devoted to sport?

GREEN. Oh, I say, don't make sport of a man in mortal agony. Be heroic, come to the rescue, take the umbrageous curio. *(Handing HAZEL his umbrella.)* The idea! Billing and cooing still—a year after marriage, too. It's an outrage on society!

ARTHUR *(having unloaded him)*. So it is, Green! Now, tell us, to what do we owe your sudden advent here?

GREEN *(circles and sits left)*. To the same old lady, Dame Rumor, the despot of my life.

HAZEL. Ah, what monstrous thing has she reported here?

GREEN. Monstrous bliss! The fame of your fishes, the taste of your game, the sound of your kisses is wafted on the breath of rumor to the uttermost end of an envious world. So here am I, with all my senses, wild to see, hear, smell, taste and touch. I'll begin with touch. Give me your fists, ye pair of blissful curiosities! *(Taking them by the hands, he points to her hand.)* Won't you share your monstrosities with me?

HAZEL *(with laughter)*. All we can.

GREEN. All but the kisses, I suppose.

HAZEL *(sitting)*. But what are you going to give us for letting you into our paradise?

GREEN. For you I have some news, and for that mortal I have a sermon.

ARTHUR. Well, let it be a galloping sermon, then. I'll go and order the horses at once. *(Strikes bell on table.)*

GREEN. Capital!

ARTHUR. I'm off. Beware, I have my eye upon you. *(Exit.)*

GREEN. Keep your ear off, that's all we ask.

*(Enter BARNEY, R.)*

HAZEL. Now for your news.

GREEN. I'm just from Blackburn Mill.

HAZEL. And you have letters for me?

GREEN. No—your father declares that the first who writes you shall leave his house.

HAZEL. Is he still so angry with me then?

GREEN. Angry with you? That's putting it mild. I call him the pig-headedest old heart I ever knew. He won't even let them breathe your name. In fact, there were some men from London at the old mill asking for you; he told them he never had a daughter!

HAZEL. Someone looking for me? Who could that have been—I know no one in London. But how did you learn all this?

GREEN. Dolly told me.

HAZEL. Dolly, is that what you call her?

GREEN. Oh, yes, if a person's name is Dolly, no harm to call her so. Oh, I forgot, you don't know, do you?

HAZEL. Know what?

GREEN. Why, about Dolly—she's going to make a fool of herself.

HAZEL. How?

GREEN. By becoming the better half of P. Green. Pity, isn't it?

HAZEL. Do you mean to say you're going to marry my cousin?

GREEN. Oh, no. She's going to marry me.

HAZEL. Oh, I'm so glad. *(Offers her hand in congratulation.)*

GREEN. You may not believe it, but so am I.

HAZEL *(sitting on couch)*. Tell me all about it.

GREEN. Oh, it was all just like Dolly herself, short and sweet. After you left Lancashire, the doors of the old mill were sternly closed, especially against me. But it didn't matter, you see. I always have an object in life, so suddenly I became interested in dams—mill dams. There was one near the mill; there always is a dam attached to a mill. I used to visit that dam and sketch the dam—the sight of any-thing dammed was a relief to me. Weeks passed, but the door of the old mill remained closed. Fever ensued; I got dam on the brain and went about muttering dam, dam, all day. However, nothing could dampen the ardor of my disease. At last the crisis approached, Dolly appeared, and took Pitty. Yes, she relieved my delirium and con-sented to become ma-dam.

HAZEL. You dear, silly old thing. So you're going to become my cousin.

GREEN. Bless me—so I am. I didn't think of that! Now, will you permit me? *(Kisses her hand.)*

*(ARTHUR enters.)*

ARTHUR. Hallo! I say!

GREEN. So do I—I say. I not only say, but I do, don't I? I say, cousinship is good. *(He kisses HAZEL's hand again.)* A duty I owe to society.

ARTHUR. What does the rascal mean?

HAZEL. Something wonderful.

GREEN. Hush! Quietly; his nerves are weak. Have you ordered the horses?

ARTHUR. Yes, but—

GREEN. But me no buts. Hazel, my dear, go and get ready to drive, and leave this reprobate to the tender mercies of the family high minister, your cousin, Pit.

HAZEL. Oh, very well. Don't forget the sermon. *(Exit.)*

ARTHUR. Now, sir, please explain? *(Slaps GREEN on back.)*

GREEN. I explain? Why, sir, I've traveled three hundred miles to make you explain.

ARTHUR. Explain what?

GREEN *(handing ARTHUR piece of newspaper).* That, sir.

ARTHUR *(reads).* "Another important engagement in high life announced—that of Lord Travers to Lady Maud Wetherby."

GREEN. Yes, sir; that, sir, is a cutting from the *Morning Post*—a most respectable paper—a very reliable authority.

ARTHUR. Evidently.

GREEN. I don't see anything to laugh at.

ARTHUR. Silly, how can I marry since I am already married?

GREEN. But confound it, sir, you're not married.

ARTHUR. Are you mad?

GREEN. Yes, sir, I am, blind mad—who wouldn't be under the circumstances?

ARTHUR. By Jove—you are insane!

GREEN. Insane? It is you who are insane. Is it nothing to deceive an honest girl into believing she's married when she isn't? Is it nothing to be a smooth, cool, calculating villain, and stand there and look as innocent and serene as an angel?

ARTHUR. My dear boy—of whom are you talking?

GREEN. Oh, this is wicked—wicked—Travers. That's pure malignant cruelty. Haven't I always been a loyal friend?

ARTHUR. Of course you have.

GREEN. Then why couldn't you have trusted me?

ARTHUR. I've never distrusted you.

GREEN. Oh, yes you have; you dealt with me in a beastly manner. You've made me an unconscious accomplice in a piece of business I despise.

ARTHUR. There you go again. Can't you just tell me plainly what in the world you mean?

GREEN. Travers, you're either the most accomplished hypocrite or the biggest fool in the world. If you really don't know—well, I don't know how to begin. You see, I've been sneaking about the old mill lately, and a rumor reached me there that just covered me with goose flesh. It seems old Squire Rodney has been looking into your affairs, and by Jove, he swears you've deceived Hazel!

ARTHUR. Deceived her? How?

GREEN. He said that your marriage to her was a pretence, a farce, a lie!

ARTHUR. And you, my friend, believed him?

GREEN. How could I help it? The whole thing is so circumstantial. He declares that he has positive proof that you went towards Scotland with the pretence of marrying Hazel by Scottish law, but that you cunningly stopped on the border and went through the flimsy Scottish ceremony on English ground.

ARTHUR. An infamous slander!

GREEN. Can you prove that?

ARTHUR. I'll soon convince you. *(He strikes the bell.)*

GREEN. How?

ARTHUR. By the testimony of a witness to my marriage—Barney.

GREEN. Barney! He's the very one Rodney named as your accomplice.

ARTHUR. Accomplice? We shall see—I'll call him.

GREEN. Wait—before you call him—I have more to tell you.

ARTHUR. What more?

GREEN. Dolly told me that there were two men from London calling at the mill to inquire for Hazel, but that Dunstan told them he had no daughter.

ARTHUR. Of course, he would—the ill-tempered old fool!

GREEN. But neither Dolly nor I could figure out who could be looking for Hazel, so when I was last in London, I took it upon myself to make some inquiries.

ARTHUR. And what did you discover?

GREEN. Very little—I was only able to find out that the gentlemen who called are representatives of the law firm of Bates & Bristol. I went to them to discover what I could, but they were very sparing with their information and would tell me nothing. I made up my mind to ask you when I came here, since I knew you would be familiar with her affairs. What do you know of it?

ARTHUR. Not a thing. I can't think why any law firm would be trying to communicate with Hazel.

GREEN. Unless old Rod is still trying to find her—and hopes to locate her through them. It seems they handle a good deal of estate work. Could it be that your wife is coming into a large inheritance?

ARTHUR. Nonsense, you know her family has nothing.

GREEN. Of course, but still—

ARTHUR. Forget it, Green—it is presently much more important that I settle with Barney! If he's been in league with old Rodney to disgrace my wife, he shall answer for it!

GREEN. Hold on! Let me question him. We want to get at the truth, you know, and these chaps easily slip into a lie.

ARTHUR. I don't understand.

GREEN. You will presently.

*(Enter* BARNEY.*)*

Barney, your master called you because the time has come for us to settle a certain matter, and we wish to be sure that everything is all right, you know.

BARNEY. Faith, sir, I'm at your service.

GREEN. Well, then, my good Barney, tell us frankly, are you quite sure that the town where Lord Travers went through the ceremony of marriage with Miss Kirke was not in Scotland? Well—answer my question.

BARNEY. I will, sir, when my master bids me.

GREEN. Shall he answer my question?

ARTHUR. Certainly, Barney, speak freely.

BARNEY. Well, then, sir, your question be a quare one.

GREEN. In what respect?

BARNEY. Do ye think I'd betray my master?

GREEN. Of course not.

BARNEY. I was brought up in the service of the gentry, sir, all my life. I know how to look after my master's interests, so of course I took good care to have such a marriage as he wanted come off in the wrong place.

GREEN. What place was that?

BARNEY. Faith! The wrong place for a Scottish marriage is the English side of the Scottish line.

ARTHUR. Do you mean to say that the inn you took us to was on the border, but not in Scotland? *(Goes to* BARNEY, *appalled.)*

BARNEY. Of course, I do, sir.

ARTHUR *(frenzied).* You miserable, dastardly villain, I could kill you! *(He grasps him by the throat.)*

BARNEY *(pleading).* But sir, I only followed your orders to the letter. Didn't you come to me all of a sudden one night at the old tavern at Blackburn, and didn't you say, "Barney, I want to get married to onst in Scotland"?

ARTHUR. I did, you rascal!

BARNEY. Didn't ye tell me to take ye to the borders?

ARTHUR. I did. Well?

BARNEY. Well, sir, so I did. To the borders of matrimony, as I thought ye intended.

ARTHUR *(shaking him).* Idiot! Scoundrel! Wretch! Hazel dishonored *(Steps back.)* —and by me—by me! Oh, this is horrible!

(GREEN *interferes, saying* "Travers, Travers." *In agony* ARTHUR *turns away.)*

GREEN. There's something better to be done now.

ARTHUR. Yes, you are right. We will go find a curate, and I will marry her at once. *(To* BARNEY.*)* Imbecile! I'm about to take measures partially to amend the outrage you have committed. Tell my wi— yes, before heaven, she is my wife—tell my wife that I have been called away, but will return soon. And understand, not a word of this to anyone.

BARNEY. Oh, master, I did not mean—I mean—no sir, not for the world!

ARTHUR. Come then, let us hurry! Every instant now is torture until Hazel is my wife.

*(Exit* ARTHUR *and* GREEN.*)*

BARNEY. Faith, thin, I can't make this out for the life o' me. He's lost his head as well as his heart, and to a peasant's child, too. *(Looks off.)* Eh—who's this coming up the walk? It's Squire Rodney. That bodes this house no good. Holy murther! Who's that behind him? If it isn't Lady Travers herself! The powers protect us—she's found us out! What shall we do—what shall we do?

*(Enter* RODNEY, *followed by Lady Travers, old, very ill, leaning on* RODNEY's *arms.)*

RODNEY. This is the place, my lady.

LADY TRAVERS. Barney, is that you?

BARNEY. Yes, your ladyship, I belave it is. I'm not quite sure.

LADY TRAVERS. I thought you were abroad with my son?

BARNEY. Yes, ma'am, I'm with your son, and sure I bane abroad too—leastways, I don't feel at home.

LADY TRAVERS. Is my son here?

BARNEY. No, my lady.

LADY TRAVERS *(aside)*. So much the better. Is the lady of the house in?

BARNEY. Is it Lady Carringford ye mane, my lady?

LADY TRAVERS. It is not Lady Carringford that I mean.

BARNEY. She knows all! She is in, my lady.

LADY TRAVERS. Inform her that a lady would speak with her on important business.

BARNEY. I will, my lady.

LADY TRAVERS. Stay—not a word of who it is.

BARNEY. Oh, not for the world, my lady.

LADY TRAVERS. You may go.

BARNEY. Thankee. Faith! I wish I were anywhere out o' this! *(Exit.)*

LADY TRAVERS. Mr. Rodney, I deem it best I should see this girl alone.

RODNEY. Yes, madam, you are right—I shall wait outside. Be kind to her, Lady Travers, for the wrong is not of her doing.

LADY TRAVERS. You're sure her marriage to my son—

RODNEY. Alas, my lady. It was none at all—none at all.

LADY TRAVERS. Thank heaven for that! You may go and wait for me at the hotel.

RODNEY. I will, my lady. Oh, madam, Heaven will bless you for this day's work. *(He exits.)*

LADY TRAVERS. His blessings are worse than any curse! I am helpless and must have his aid. Why is the girl so long in coming?

*(Enter* HAZEL.*)*

HAZEL. You wished to see me, Madam?

LADY TRAVERS. I did, please be seated near to me. *(Aside.)* The old story, the fatal power of a handsome face!

HAZEL *(aside as she gets chair).* What a strange commanding tone! I wonder who she is?

LADY TRAVERS. I am Lady Travers. *(*HAZEL *starts.)* You need not fear me; I have not come to curse, but to beg.

HAZEL. To beg of me? But why, madam?

LADY TRAVERS. Because in your hands lies the honor of an old and noble family. I see in your eyes the womanhood that has so be-witched my son. And to that womanhood, I beg, beseech, implore a fearful sacrifice from you.

HAZEL. Madam, ask any sacrifice I can make in honor, and I will gladly make it for your son.

LADY TRAVERS. Alas! You know not what you promise. Listen! My father had a ward whose fortune he wrongfully used and lost. Upon his dying bed he confessed this to me, and made me promise to hide his shame by marrying our only son to this ward. I promised, and have lived since but to keep my word and save our honor.

HAZEL. Oh, how terrible.

LADY TRAVERS. My son never knew why I was so determined to make this match, but he, to humor me, promised to marry Lady Maud. Suddenly I heard he was living here with you. With grief and shame I gathered strength enough to drag myself here, to implore you to save us all.

HAZEL. Oh, what can I do? What can I do?

LADY TRAVERS. Within a month Lady Maud will come of age and demand a settlement of her estate. Nothing but her marriage to my son can save him from ruin and shame.

HAZEL. Oh, how horrible!

LADY TRAVERS. Leave him—leave him at once.

HAZEL. And never see him again? No, no, you ask more than I have strength to do—besides, what use is it? I am his wife.

LADY TRAVERS. What if you were not his wife?

HAZEL. Ah, then, perhaps Heaven would give me the courage to fly for his sake.

LADY TRAVERS. It will *(Rises.)*, heroic girl, for he is free—you are not his wife!

HAZEL. Not his wife? Oh, how terrible!

LADY TRAVERS. As he has deceived me by loving you, so he has betrayed you by a pretended marriage.

HAZEL. 'Tis false! I'll not believe it! Give me the proof!

LADY TRAVERS. Ah! Have mercy or I shall die! Have courage, child! *(Sways —gasps.)*

HAZEL. Courage for what? No, never! He shall right my wrong. He shall make me his honorable wife or I will—

LADY TRAVERS. Stop, child, stop!

HAZEL. I see it all! It is my father's curse, my father's curse! You have asked me to go for his sake, the sake of the man who has so degraded me. Here is my answer. *(Takes off jewelry, puts it on table.)* I accepted these as token of love, given to an honored wife. I scorn them now. I scorn them all. *(About to take off wedding ring, stops.)* — No, not this. My marriage ring! *(Kisses it.)* This I have bought with a wife's love, a woman's perdition. This I will keep. *(Going.)* The rest I leave forever—I go to cover up his infamy with my shame—and may heaven forgive you all! *(She exits.)*

*(LADY TRAVERS collapses and falls back in her chair. ARTHUR enters and sees jewelry on table, LADY TRAVERS in chair, as the curtain falls.)*

CURTAIN

MUSIC NOTE. *During* HAZEL'*s final speech, music starts. At beginning, it is a slow soft funeral dirge. Then it leads into "Goodbye, the Golden Links of Love Are Broken".\* A barbershop quartet in formal evening dress can come on R. and sing:*

Goodbye, the golden links are broken,
Goodbye, the parting words are spoken,
Goodbye, you have back every token,
Goodbye, goodbye, I leave you now, sweetheart, goodbye!

*They hum during the rest of her speech, then at end of speech they sing:*

Goodbye, goodbye, I leave you now, sweetheart, goodbye!

If preferred, HAZEL *can sing "Goodbye" solo, at the end of her speech, before she says, "And may heaven forgive you all!"*

*\*Music on page 373.*

# ACT THREE

## SCENE ONE

SCENE: *Evening, kitchen at Blackburn Mill. The door is lit by glow of fire. A clothes-drying rack with towels on it sits before the fire. There is a clock and cupboard, in which are pipe, matches, tobacco, food, dishes; a lighted candle on table.* MERCY *is discovered at table U.C. Lights are half down; clock strikes eight.*

MERCY. Eight o'clock. Time for evenin' prayers—now to put awa' the linen. *(She puts away in drawers outside. Pipe is heard playing.)* What's that? Strange! Met used to play that tune, and it sounds like Met, too. What can it mean? Has she left Hazel? Aye, perhaps she's come with her. Met! Met! Is that you? Met! Met! It is you!

*(Enter* MET, *U.L., pale, ragged and haggard.)*
Come in, girl, and tell me the news! What's the word? Speak, girl, speak!

MET. I want her—where is she?

MERCY. Who?

MET. Hazel—I want her—I've tramped four hundred miles to find her.

MERCY. My heart, lass! What are ye sayin'?

MET. I must see Hazel—she's here.

MERCY. Hazel here? No, she's not here.

*(*MET *staggers to a chair.)*
Mercy on us, what's coom to thee?

MET. Not here? Where can she be, where can she be?

MERCY. Wi' her hoosband, I suppose.

MET. No, no, she left him a month ago.

MERCY. Left him! Why?

MET. I don't know—I don't know.

MERCY. Where did she go?

MET *(seated)*. Why, I thought she'd coom here, so I followed her on foot *(Rises.)*, but I'll go back again. I'll walk till I die, but I'll find her.

MERCY. Ah, what do you mean, Met, what do you mean?

MET. Mean? I mean there's something wrong. That man's mother came to the house—she was found dead there and Hazel gone.

MERCY. Great heavens, Met! You frighten me!

MET. Hazel is somewhere wandering now as I have been for a month—ill, cold, starving, perhaps, as I am! But I'll go to her; I must. I will find her.

MERCY. Stop—I'll go wi' thee, lass.

MET *(takes her hands)*. Oh, mistress, heaven will bless you for that word.

MERCY. But you must wait until after prayers; Dunstan would miss me if I went off now; he'd ask questions, and oh, Met, he must not know—he's been very ill—this news would kill him.

MET. Then, mistress, you go to the master. I'll run down to Squire Rodney's house. If I can find him he will help me.

MERCY *(picks up lantern and follows her to the door)*. Aye, so he will. Then go, go quickly; I will meet you at his house within an hour.

MET. Never fear, missus, we'll find her now for sure. *(Exit.)*

MERCY. So we will—so we will. *(Hangs up lantern and exits.)*

*(*PITTACUS *enters.* ARTHUR *follows.)*

ARTHUR. Well?

GREEN. Not a soul in sight. All is quiet as the grave.

ARTHUR. Look yonder, she may be inside. Well? *(*GREEN *opens door U.R., draws back and removes his hat.)*

ARTHUR *(removing his hat)*. And Hazel?

GREEN. Is not among them.

ARTHUR. Oh, shall I never find her? Never see her precious face again?

*(*DUNSTAN*'s voice is heard in closing verses of a psalm.)*

GREEN. Their prayers are over now; they'll soon be here, and when they come, we'll ask them if they have heard anything of your—of her.

ARTHUR. I have searched for her everywhere without discovering a trace. My last hope has been to find her here. If we fail now, I shall believe the worst.

GREEN. And what is that?

ARTHUR. That she has taken her own life—murdered by me! Oh, the thought will drive me mad!

*(*GREEN, *rising, follows him, pacifying, and pats him on the shoulder.)*

GREEN. Merciful powers!

ARTHUR. What is it?

GREEN. We forget—they'll recognize you!

ARTHUR. And if they do?

GREEN. The old miller hates you! If he knows where Hazel is, you are the one man in the world he'll keep her hidden from.

ARTHUR. What are we to do?

GREEN. Leave me till Dolly comes, and when once I set her tongue at work, we'll soon know. Go, wait outside until I have a chance to make her talk.

ARTHUR. You'll find me at the seat near the lock. The moment you get news.

GREEN. I'll fly like lightning to tell you all.

ARTHUR. If I find her not this time I shall despair, I shall despair. *(He exits.)*

GREEN. Poor fellow, he's broken-hearted, and yet it would do no good to tell him till we find Hazel, and I can prove what I suspect about old Rod.

DOLLY *(offstage)*. All right, aunt, I'm going.

GREEN. Dolly's voice! She's coming! She'll see me! The shock might shake her. *(He leaves gloves on table and hides behind clothes-drying rack.)* I'll retreat and spare her feelings for a while.

*(Enter* DOLLY.*)*

DOLLY. And don't forget to tell Squire Rodney that Uncle Kirke wants to see him here tonight. *(*DOLLY *goes to table, sees glove.)* Dear me! What's this?—a glove! Whose glove? *(Smells.)* Pittacus! *(Turns glove.)* As sure as I'm a woman! So he's been here and gone away without a word!

*(*GREEN *looks out, unseen by* DOLLY.*)*

Oh, that's just like the heartless brute—six weeks since he left me, promising to go and see Hazel and send me news of her; not a word since then. *(Tearfully.)* Oh, these men! these men! Why are they ever made? I can't see the use o' the faithless things.

*(*GREEN *comes up behind her. She continues crossly.)*

Oh, don't I wish I had him here now, how I'd make his ears burn and his head ache!

*(*GREEN *dodges behind clothes rack.)*

How I'd warm his cheeks for him!

*(She slaps glove across her hand, then puts it in her apron pocket. Takes clothes from the rack, slams them into basket. While she does so,* GREEN *dodges behind remaining clothes in an attempt to hide.)*

The base, deceitful hypocrite! Pretending he couldn't live a day without me! *(Slams towel in basket.)* And then leaving me here *(Slams another towel in basket.)* for weeks and weeks *(Same.)* with a breaking heart!

*(*GREEN *snatches the last towel.)*

Mercy! Who's that?

*(Recoiling to chair at right of table, she tips it over and falls. There, as she stares up at* GREEN, *he peers over at her.)*

What! So you're there, Mr. Green?

GREEN. No, Dolly, I'm not there, I'm here. And I'm not Green, I'm blue—truly blue, to see you so severe. *(Kneels to her.)*

DOLLY *(moves away, leaving him kneeling)*. Don't! Don't touch me, sir!

GREEN. Dolly, Dolly, I say! *(Rises and follows her.)*

DOLLY *(moves about the room paying no attention to him)*. Who cares what you say?

GREEN. But, Dolly, I want—

DOLLY. Who cares what you want?

GREEN. But really, my darling—

DOLLY. Don't dare to "darling" me—after—after what's happened!

GREEN. What's happened?

DOLLY. Oh, you know well enough. *(Slaps glove on table.)*

GREEN. Don't jag my glove in that manner! *(Aside.)* Ah, I see, Hazel's been here and told Dolly everything and she thinks I've been an accomplice in this infernal business. Don't, Dolly, don't.

*Pittacus pleads with Dolly to be more understanding, as he tries to unwind a snarl in the plot in this third act scene. Pittacus is Robert Montilla; Dolly is Gail Allen.*

DOLLY. Don't what, sir?

GREEN. Don't hold me to blame for what's happened—I swear I've spent every spare moment trying to straighten out all this mess and get back to you—and you'll soon find I'm not the man to blame.

DOLLY. Not the man who deserted me all these weeks? *(Aside.)* He is not the man, and he says this to my face. Oh, you brazen rogue!

GREEN. It wasn't me who did it—it was Barney—Barney O'Flynn and that villain, Aaron Rodney! And if Hazel's told you—

DOLLY. Hazel tell me? How could she tell me anything?

GREEN. Then she isn't here?

DOLLY. I haven't seen her blessed face for over a year—and never will see it again, I'm afraid.

GREEN. Hasn't Hazel been here? Has she been—

DOLLY. Here?

GREEN *(stammering)*. Don't you know?—No, she don't!     *

DOLLY. Know what?

GREEN *(stuttering)*. I—I mean that she must be—I that n-n-nothing!

DOLLY *(fiercely)*. Pittacus—you're deceiving me! Something's happened, don't deny it.

GREEN. I don't—yes—I don't—no—I do.

DOLLY. Where's Hazel?

GREEN. Bless me—that's—that's what I wanted you to tell me.

DOLLY. Then you don't know where she is?

GREEN. No, ding it! I wish I did.

DOLLY. Haven't you see her, then?

GREEN. Oh, yes, that is, no—not since—I say, I saw, I saw that I see, saw—Oh, what am I see-sawing about? I say that I see, that I saw that I see—

DOLLY. Not since when?

GREEN. Well, if you will have it—not since she ran away.

DOLLY. Ran away—from whom?

GREEN. From here—that is—

DOLLY. From her husband, you mean?

GREEN. Y-yes, I suppose I do.

DOLLY. Suppose you do? Don't you know he's her husband?

GREEN. I don't. I only know that life's a nuisance, and it's a swindle I was ever born. *(Sits.)*

DOLLY. Pittacus, Pittacus *(Kneeling to him.)*, what do you mean? What's come to Hazel? Why has she run away—and why do you talk to me so strangely?

GREEN. Dolly, my darling—don't look so miserable—and I'll try to tell you. You see—

DUNSTAN *(offstage, calling)*. Dolly, Dolly! child!

DOLLY. That's Dunstan! He's wanting me—hurry—tell me quick.

GREEN. No—not now—he'll come and hear me and he must never know. I must run, dear—meet me outside near the old tree, as soon as you have found out what he wants. *(Rises, starts to go.)*

DOLLY. All right, I'll come to you the moment I can get away from uncle.

DUNSTAN *(inside)*. Dolly, child, are you comin'?

DOLLY. Yes, uncle, I'm coming.

GREEN *(detains her)*. Why don't the old bear come to you?

DOLLY. Why, poor dear heart, he's blind.

GREEN. Blind!

DOLLY. Yes, just after you went away he got news of some kind that made him awfully ill. For days he was out of his mind raving about Hazel, and when the fever went away, it left him blind.

DUNSTAN *(appears in doorway, old and broken)*. Why, Dolly, child, what keeps ye so long when thee hears me call?

DOLLY *(runs to him)*. I had work to finish here, uncle.

DUNSTAN. Bring me my pipe, child, I have much thinkin' to do tonight, and nothin' helps me think like my pipe. *(He sits.)*

DOLLY. All right, Uncle dear, I'll bring it to ye.

*(DOLLY goes to GREEN, sees him out the door, where he points outside to indicate that she will meet him. She motions "yes." He kisses her loudly and goes out.)*

DUNSTAN. What be that?

DOLLY. What's that, Uncle?

DUNSTAN. Tha' noise.

DOLLY. What noise, uncle?

DUNSTAN. 'Twere a noise that sounded like a kiss, girl.

DOLLY *(filling his pipe)*. Oh, it must have been—the sputtering of the fire.

DUNSTAN. The only fire I ever heard spooter like that be the fire o' love, lass. Who's been here?

DOLLY. When, uncle?

DUNSTAN. Joost now.

DOLLY *(hands him his pipe)*. Here's your pipe, Uncle. *(Kneels.)* Will I light it for you? *(She strikes a match.)*

DUNSTAN. Aye, lass, do. I wish thou couldst only light my eyes as easy as thou lightest the pipe. *(She lights it for him.)*

DOLLY. Oh, Uncle, don't talk like that. I can't abide it. *(She puts her arm around his neck and places her cheek against his head.)*

DUNSTAN. There, there, child, I'm a weak old fool to bother you with my burdens. Go, find thy Aunt Mercy, she be above stairs. Tell her I must see her and then get thee to bed.

DOLLY. All right, Uncle. *(Aside.)* I'll not go to bed this night until I've got news of Hazel. *(She exits.)*

DUNSTAN. There's no use; even the pipe can't comfort me tonight.

*(HAZEL opens window and looks in. She is pale and ragged. She sees DUNSTAN and pauses.)*

I must tell my poor wife a' now. It's hard, bitter hard, to leave the mill—a pauper, too—but it moost be done. Better starvation—death—anything—than more debt to Squire Rodney! Oh, that child

of mine—my only bairn—why should she have been her feyther's
curse? Oh, my old heart is heavy tonight! Would that I were dead!

*(He sobs.* HAZEL *moans and drops her head on the sill.* DUNSTAN
*starts up.)*

Who's there? Someone at the window. Who is it? Is there any one
there? That's strange. *(He feels his way toward the window.)*

*(Enter* MERCY.*)*

MERCY. What art doin' there, Dunstan?

DUNSTAN. I could ha' sworn, wife, that I heard someone at the
window.

MERCY. Someone at the window?

DUNSTAN. Aye, I heard a noise like a moan, and then, when it died
out, it seemed as though the window was closed, quick and sharp
like.

MERCY. What if it were Hazel? Child, I know it is, child, I know it is.
Yes, it's my child, my darling, longin' to return! Come, Dunstan
*(*MERCY *takes* DUNSTAN *to his chair.),* sit down, and let me speak to
thee. Perhaps I can make thee understand the noise at the window.

DUNSTAN. What dost think it were wife? *(Sits.)*

MERCY. Dost' know what day this be, sweetheart?

DUNSTAN. Thursday, I believe.

MERCY. Yes, Thursday, the tenth day of October.

DUNSTAN. Ah! Ah—a—a!

MERCY. This day two and twenty year ago our Hazel were born.

DUNSTAN. Hist, wife, hist! Don't 'mind me o' that day now.

MERCY *(kneels to* DUNSTAN*).* Why not, oh, father dear, why not? That
were a sweet day to us then.

DUNSTAN. Aye, but it is a bitter day to us now.

MERCY *(rises).* Feyther, what if thy child were at thy door now,
longin' to come back to the old house?

DUNSTAN. I'd bid her begone.

MERCY *(backs away).* Oh, Dunstan.

DUNSTAN. I'd point at these sightless eyes and say, "This be thy
work." I'd point at thee and say—

*(Wind sounds outside.)*

"Look at thy mother, a beggar wi' thy feyther in the street, thy work,
too."

MERCY. What dost mean, Dunstan?

DUNSTAN. I mean, Mercy, wife, that the end be coom. I owe everything we gotten in the world to Squire Rodney—an' debt to him I
can bear no longer now. I've sent for him to coom this very night and
take possession o' the mill—and tomorrow thee and I an' Dolly
moost wander out beggars, but beggars no longer to the man our
own flesh and blood has wronged.

MERCY. Oh, Dunstan, can ye never forgive?

DUNSTAN. Never!

*(The wind sounds.)*

Strangers she chose; to strangers let her look, for she be dead to us forever.

(HAZEL *moans and drops her head.* DUNSTAN *starts.*)

Hark—that moan again!

MERCY (*going to the window*). Aye and see—the window's open! Oh, Dunstan, what if it be our child, our Hazel!

DUNSTAN. Hoot, woman, it were the wind!

(*The wind sounds again.*)

There's a storm comin' up. Maister Rodney 'ull not be here tonight. Better lock up the mill. Close the window, wife, and bolt the door, then get thee to bed.

(MERCY *goes to window and looks out.* DUNSTAN *feels his way to the door.*)

Mercy, I'll go once more over the old mill I've loved so long and these hands have tended so well. Goodnight, wife, goodnight.

MERCY. Good night, Dunstan, and may the angels be wi' you, this last night i' the old mill.

(DUNSTAN *exits.*)

An' my child may be out in the night—homeless and hungry! No, no, I'll go for Maister Rodney. He will save Hazel, an' he's able to break the iron o' her fayther's will. (*Exit, weeping.*)

(HAZEL *appears at window. Then slowly opening the door, she steals wearily in and shivers over the fire.*)

HAZEL. Oh, how cold I am. But no fire will ever warm me again. (*Looking about.*) And this is the home, the home that I have lost, the home that I have cursed. My father's chair! How often have I sat upon his lap, my arms around his neck and heard him sing his dear old songs! How often have I knelt here at my mother's feet and prayed as I can never pray again! (*She sinks on her knees by the chair.*) Oh, father, father, Heaven has heard your curse.

(*With a sob, she buries her face in chair.* DUNSTAN *appears, R. He gropes across the room, places his hand on the back of the chair where she kneels. She draws back; he starts.*)

DUNSTAN. What be that?

(*The wind sounds.*)

Nothing but the sobbing of the storm. Ah, it does me good to hear it. It sounds like the voice of my own heart. Dear old mill, my eyes will never—no, never more behold thee (*He goes from place to place touching.*) and my hands have felt thy timbers for the last, last time.

(HAZEL *follows him across the room, removes a chair from his path, kisses the lapel of his coat.*)

But God's will be done! God's will be done!

(*He gropes his way to the door L., lifts his hands in prayer, and exits D.R.* HAZEL *goes back and bows her head on the arm of the chair.* RODNEY *enters U.L. He is warmly dressed against the storm.*)

RODNEY. Ah, a fearful night! Is that you, Dolly? So—Hazel, you've come back! Can it be that you have seen the error of your ways?

HAZEL *(rising)*. Don't speak to me! Let me go—away from here, forever!

RODNEY *(stopping her)*. Let you go now? Never!

HAZEL *(turning to him)*. But you do not know!

RODNEY. Yes, Hazel, I know all. I know that when you broke your promise to me, you went to the arms of an unscrupulous villain, who deceived and dishonored you. But see, we are willing to forgive you. Your mother's arms, your father's home—yes, even I am willing to take you back.

HAZEL. Mr. Rodney, you know not what you say. My father but now, a moment ago, declared that he would never own me again in this world. Tomorrow he leaves this dear old mill, driven hence by my broken promise, by my own shame.

RODNEY. Dunstan quit the mill?

HAZEL. Alas, sir, who can prevent it now?

RODNEY. You, girl.

HAZEL. I? Impossible! He would never accept a service from such as I.

RODNEY. Yes, one service, that would pay his debt to me.

HAZEL. What is that?

RODNEY. Keep your promise and become my wife.

HAZEL. Sir, I am an outcast—dishonored—you would marry me?

RODNEY. Indeed, girl—I would—and soon! *(Aside.)* I must convince her or all will be lost! *(To* HAZEL.*)* I know you thought you loved that scoundrel, but now that you've found him out—reprent your folly and keep your promise to me!

HAZEL. Oh, what shall I do, what shall I do?

RODNEY. Marry me—save your father—promise you'll do this.

HAZEL. I will—on one condition.

RODNEY. And what is that?

HAZEL. Call my father—he is blind—he cannot see me. If he consents to let me pay his debt, you shall have my hand and I will be your wife.

RODNEY. I'll call him instantly. Wait here.

*(*RODNEY *goes toward the door.* DUNSTAN *enters.)*

DUNSTAN. Why, Mr. Rodney, is that you, sir? I did not think you'd coom in this fearful storm.

RODNEY. You sent for me—I was delayed, but here I am. Tell me— what is it, Dunstan?

DUNSTAN. Maister Rodney, for five long years I've been in debt to you *(He sits.)*, a debt I thought my child would pay, but—well—when she broke faith and left us, I strove hard to make the old mill earn enough to pay the money I owed ye. Fever laid hold on me and left me blind. All hope is over for me now—and so I've called ye to ask one more favor of ye—take the mill, but spare poor Mercy and me.

Let us live out our miserable years in peace in this old home—

RODNEY *(crossing to* DUNSTAN*).* But Dunstan, you needn't lose the mill.

DUNSTAN. Yes, I must, for I and mine have wronged ye in every way. I'll do penance for my child as a beggar in the street.

RODNEY. Let Hazel do penance for herself. Let her pay the debt by marrying me.

DUNSTAN. What do ye mean, man?

RODNEY. I mean, Hazel is free!

DUNSTAN. Free o' what? The stains o' shame? *(Rises and crosses to fireplace.)* No, she can never pay any debt o' mine.

RODNEY. Dunstan, it is the only way, hear me!

DUNSTAN. Never—not one word!

*(HAZEL kneels before him.)*

If she were here now, before my very face, kneeling at my feet, praying for my consent to marry ye,—I'd tell her nay, never! I'd tell her she had wronged ye bad enough without seeking to make ye hoosband to a dishonored creetur like herself!

*(The wind moans.* HAZEL *sinks to the floor.)*

RODNEY. So you'll not consent to have her marry me? *(He lifts her and places her in chair.)*

DUNSTAN. Never!

RODNEY. Then I'll marry her without your leave! I'll speak to Mercy and have her consent.

DUNSTAN. That ye'll not, sir, and mind this—Mercy has given her word not to set eyes upon her child without my consent. She'll not lie, not even to please you, Maister Rodney, and so good night, good night, Maister Rodney, good night. *(Exit.)*

RODNEY. Oh, hard-hearted man! May the devil curse your iron-will and break its strength forever! Hazel, don't mind that now. All the world knows that a mother's love—Hazel!

HAZEL. Mr. Rodney, do you want me still?

RODNEY. More than life—or all the world!

HAZEL. Then leave me for now. Leave me and let me be alone for tonight. Tomorrow will settle all for the best.

RODNEY. Must I leave you then?

HAZEL. If you care for my happiness.

RODNEY *(kisses her hand).* Then until tomorrow—tomorrow when we'll be together. Good night my darling; I hear your mother coming; you can rest on her heart tonight and be at peace. Good night, Hazel. *(Exit.)*

HAZEL. All is over. I know the worst now, and I know what I must do. I'll go, and there in the water that has brought so much misery to this home, I'll drown my sorrows and my sins. *(Going.)* Good-bye, old home—farewell, sweet memories, fond hopes—farewell, mother, father, life—life—life!

*(She goes out. The wind moans louder. After a pause,* DUNSTAN *speaks outside.)*

DUNSTAN. Mercy, Mercy, where be ye? *(Entering.)* Why don't ye answer me? Mercy has gone, where can she be? Oh, why don't ye answer? No one here, the house deserted! What can it mean?

MET *(outside).* Help! Help! She's drowning. *(*MET *enters.)* Drowning! Hazel's drowning! I saw her jump in—it's Hazel, Hazel! *(Rushing across at back.)* Hurry, help, help! *(Exit U.R.)*

DUNSTAN *(in horror).* Hazel, drowning! Dying! Here, before my face? No, no, I'll save her! Ah, heaven! I cannot! I am blind! *(Falling on his knees.)* Oh, God! This is thy punishment! I was blind when I drove her out—and now, when I could save her—I cannot see—I cannot see—I cannot see! *(He falls to the ground and kneels with clasped hands and face upturned in agony.)*

CURTAIN

## SCENE TWO

SCENE: *Same as Scene One. It is the following morning; the fire is out; the table is cleared; a jug of water and a mug are on the table.* DOLLY *is discovered asleep in a chair, head in arms. Enter* GREEN *with cigarette.)*

GREEN. Dolly! Dolly! How lovely she looks—yes, a veritable sleeping beauty; but her time has come—the prince is here, and will wake her with a kiss. Will you permit me? Of course she will.

*(He kisses her,* DOLLY *makes a motion as though brushing away a fly. He kisses her again.)*

She's the kind of a fish that won't rise at a fly. Fire in the shape of a kiss is a failure—we'll try smoke. *(He blows smoke in her face.)*

DOLLY. Pah! *(She awakes with a sneeze.)* Smoke—Where's the fire?

GREEN. Here—here—in my breast—consuming my heart for you.

DOLLY. Oh, Pittacus, I'm so glad you've come! I have so much to tell you! Such strange things have happened!

GREEN. I adore strange things—that's why I adore you *(He embraces her).*

DOLLY. Hush—my aunt—

*(*MERCY *enters.)*

MERCY. At last he seems to be asleep. What, you here, Mr. Green?

GREEN. Well, madam, you may not believe it, but I rather think I. am.

MERCY. And Hazel, my child, have you news of her?

GREEN. Well, you see—that is—does she know the truth?

DOLLY. Nothing from me.

MERCY. Well, sir, can't you answer me?

GREEN. Yes, of course—that is—I could if you—I—we—only knew what you meant.

MERCY. Something terrible has happened—I feel it in my heart—but I am so dazed with grief. I can't quite make it out. Last night Met appeared, told me Hazel had left her husband and could not be found. I promised to meet her at Aaron Rodney's house. I went there late last night. Neither Met nor Maister Rodney were there. I hurried home and found my husband dangerously ill. What happened while I was gone, I cannot say, but I think Hazel must have come and—

GREEN & DOLLY *(eagerly)*. Well, well?

MERCY. I fear he heard her—had a fit of rage, drove her out again, and was struck down by the power of his passion.

GREEN. Impossible! If Hazel had been here she would not have gone without a word to you.

MERCY. It's hard to think it, and yet, I cannot tell—I cannot tell.

*(RODNEY enters.)*

Ah, thank heaven! Maister Rodney, have you seen Hazel?

RODNEY. Certainly—here.

ALL. Here?

MERCY. Then she is coming!

RODNEY. Coming? Has she gone?

DOLLY. We do not know.

GREEN. Great heavens! I see it all—she's with Carringford!

MERCY. Her husband?

GREEN. Yes, he came down here with me last night to look for her. When I returned to our lodgings, he was not there. I didn't mind it, for ever since she left him, he's had a fashion of wandering out at night till very late.

DOLLY. Yes, go on.

GREEN. When I woke this morning, he was still not in his rooms.

DUNSTAN *(offstage)*. Water! Water!

MERCY. Hark! 'Tis Dunstan!

DUNSTAN *(appears in doorway)*. Water—Water—Water!

RODNEY. What does this mean?

MERCY. Ah—he's raving again!

*(DUNSTAN enters.)*

DUNSTAN. Quick—water, water—I'm burning up! This is the lake that burneth forever—remorse, remorse, remorse! Water—no, no—take it away—'twas water killed her.

RODNEY. What's that he says?

DUNSTAN. Hark—I hear that cry again! Oh, God—save her—save her—she's drowning, drowning!

ALL. Drowning!

DUNSTAN. Yes, she was drowned! I did it—I held her till she died—I couldn't help it. Something forced me on. What was it? What was it? This hard, hard, heart of mine. See, see? There she goes to the mill—

she beckons me! Quite right, lass, quite right. Yes, take me to the mill, take me to the mill! The noise will drown the awful voices here, here. Yes, child, I'm coming—coming—*(He exits D.R.)*

GREEN. And this is the bitter end of all! No, no—there's something still to do, a duty that must be done.

MERCY *(starting up)*. Where are ye going?

GREEN. To search for Hazel—'neath the mill stream.

MET *(rushes in)*. Mistress—oh, mistress!

*(MERCY embraces her.)*

MERCY. Hark! 'Tis Met! She must have news of her!

MERCY. Where is she, lass? Where is she?

MET. Coming here with her husband! God bless him! God bless him!

MERCY. Heaven be praised!

MET. Last night when she fell in the river—I called for help and jumped in. The river was running strong, and when I caught her in my arms, she was unconscious. I was growin' faint and beginnin' to despair—when I saw him standin' on the bank. I shouted; he heard and plunged in!

MERCY. My child drowning!

GREEN. Go on—go on!

MET. Ah, it's a stout heart and a strong arm he has—Hazel's hoosband! He landed us both near Deacon Woodford's house. There he took us, and brought us back to life.

MERCY. Thank heaven! Thank heaven! *(She weeps with joy.)*

*(HAZEL appears L., followed by ARTHUR. DOLLY crosses to HAZEL.)*

HAZEL *(holding out her arms)*. Mother! Mother!

MERCY *(embracing her)*. My child—my own precious child! *(To ARTHUR.)* You've earned the right to call my Hazel "wife," and I can't help knowing thee'll be good to her and honor her, sir. And surely now her father must forgive thee both!

*(All gather round MET, who is dancing with happiness.)*

ARTHUR. I pray he will, for she's never ceased to grieve—tho' I've done all I know to make her happy. Oh, Green, this is a happy day, but I thank heaven my mother never lived to see it.

GREEN. Why so, Arthur?

ARTHUR. I told you of the shame that was overhanging our house?

GREEN. You did.

ARTHUR. Well, I ordered my solicitors to settle my estate, and satisfy every claim of Lady Maud's against my grandfather, if it took every penny I had in the world. He observed my orders, and there remains to me now—

GREEN. Nothing?

ARTHUR. Nothing but my own hand, my own brains, and the endless wealth of my love for her—my beloved wife.

RODNEY. Wife! This farce has gone too far! Madam, I had tried to spare you this—knowing the burden you already bear—a faithless daughter, failing mill, and Dunstan gone blind, but it is time you knew the truth about this man whom you are about to take into the bosom of your home. Not only has he taken your innocent daughter from the protecting arms of her betrothed husband, but he has dishonored her with a false marriage—a base deceit practice with the connivance of his servant, Barney—whose false tongue can be purchased for a shilling!

MERCY. Can this be true?

GREEN *(steps out).* Squire, as a teller of tales myself, your story interests me, but I beg of you, before you go on, I have a tale of my own I'd like to tell. Will you permit me?

DOLLY. Yes, let him tell it.

GREEN. Well, as I once told Miss Dolly, I have great faith in the power of a yarn to undo a snarl, so, since our friend Mr. Rodney here, has put things in such a snarl—*(Crosses, sits on edge of table as storyteller.)* It all begins, as good tales should, with "once upon a time." Our villain, then a young man in his prime, journeyed to London where he proceeded to live in princely style, and nightly visited the gaming tables. But, Capricious Fortune smiled not upon him at the wheel. Instead, her smile came from a woman, not young, not beautiful, but possessed of charms far more appealing to our fair young man. For the spinster, though her locks were gray, had just come into a small fortune. He courted her, married her, and when her funds were nearly gone, bade her fond farewell!

RODNEY. Your tale is entertaining, sir, but hardly at this time.

ARTHUR. No, let him finish.

GREEN. Then, there were others, much the same, all of whom were happy to turn their securities to cash, and all for the honor of earning the prefix "Mrs." But ah, the fleeting days of love! Again he's called away. This time, you truly might not understand: the girl was but a child, untutored, innocent, hardly one to appeal to the jaded tastes of such a man as our hero had become. But wait! She had one virtue in common with all the previous loves—for her inheritance, which would not be hers until she came of age, could be reckoned in figures astronomical! While the other fortunes had been in stocks and bonds, this one was limitless—and this time in diamonds!

RODNEY. Rubbish! I'll hear no more of this.

*(He crosses as though to leave.* GREEN *and* ARTHUR *restrain him.)*

ARTHUR. You will listen.

GREEN. Yes, you will. You'll hear me out! I've spent months tracking down all the loose threads of the warp, and all the golden strings of Cupid's bow. Squire Rodney, there's a man from Scotland Yard waiting outside for you now!

RODNEY *(pulls gun, steps back).* Stand back! You'll never get me now. I've waited far too long that you should spoil my plans!

(INSPECTOR *enters.* GREEN *and* ARTHUR *struggle to take gun from* RODNEY. *They all push him out the door, still struggling for gun. As they exit, a shot is heard.)*

DOLLY *(rushing to door).* What is it? Are you hurt?

*(Re-enter* GREEN *and* ARTHUR.*)*

GREEN. 'Tis only justice, Dolly, he is dead!

ARTHUR. Yes, and by his own hand!

*(Enter* DUNSTAN *D.R.)*

DUNSTAN. What's that, Mercy? Mercy, wife, where are you?

HAZEL *(anxiously to* MERCY). He'll not drive me out again?

MERCY. No, child, no. Dunstan, thy child is home.

DUNSTAN. She's alive, saved?

*(*MERCY *goes to* DUNSTAN. ARTHUR *stands behind him.)*

MERCY. Aye, Dunstan, by her hoosband. The man who took her from thee has brought her back to thy arms.

DUNSTAN. Where is she? Where is she?

MERCY *(arm around* HAZEL *as they cross to* DUNSTAN). Stretch forth thy hands and feel her face.

*(*HAZEL *kneels,* MERCY *guides* DUNSTAN's *hands.)*

DUNSTAN. Oh, my child.

HAZEL. Yes, thy child, thine only child!

DUNSTAN *(raising her to her feet).* Hazel, Hazel, coom to my arms! Know thy feyther's heart!

TABLEAU, HAZEL, DUNSTAN *and* MERCY *in embrace C.* DOLLY *and* PITTACUS *U.R.* MET *joins* ARTHUR *U.L.* GREEN *steps C., bows.*

GREEN. Will you permit me?—Thank you. 'Twas our way from earliest time, of winding up a play. A kindly custom—actors know its worth. *(Stepping back and indicating scene.)* Peace after pain, and after sadness, mirth.

**CURTAIN**

# The Spoilers

OR

## There's Never a Law of God or Man Runs North of Fifty-Three

A Melodrama in Three Acts
as adapted from the 1906 script
by Rex Beach and James MacArthur

# CAST OF CHARACTERS

CAPTAIN STEPHENS, of the S.S. Yukon Queen
FIRST OFFICER, to the captain
SHIP'S DOCTOR
ROY GLENISTER, owner of the Midas mine
JOE DEXTRY, his partner
HELEN CHESTER, niece of Judge Stillman
ARTHUR STILLMAN, a federal judge
ALEXANDER MCNAMARA, receiver of the Midas mine
WILTON STRUVE, District Attorney
CHERRY MALOTTE, dance hall girl, who wants to be good
DRURY CHESTER, the "Bronco Kid" and Helen's brother
DUCHESS, proprietor of the Northern Lights Saloon
FLAPJACK SIMMS, foreman of the Midas mine
MRS. CHAMPAIN, in search of a shrewd investment
POLICE OFFICER
SECOND MAN
GAMBLER

# SYNOPSIS OF SCENES

Time: The year 1900

Place: Alaska, during the great gold rush

## ACT ONE

Midnight aboard the S.S Yukon Queen at dock in Unalaska, in the spring.
"The Door of the Golden North"

## ACT TWO

Law offices of Dunham & Struve, Nome, Alaska, midsummer.
"The Coming of the Law"

## ACT THREE

**Scene One:** The Northern Lights Saloon, Christmas Eve.
"A Northman's Love"

**Scene Two:** The Midas of Anvil Creek, Christmas morning.
"The Promise of Dreams"

# About the Play

*"Just as glad to see us as if he'd run a nail in his foot," exclaims Flapjack to Joe Dextry in McNamara's office. Johnny Horton as McNamara, Phil Webber as Dextry, and John Hazleton as Flapjack Simms.*

First produced on Broadway in 1906, *The Spoilers* is a story of the early days of the Yukon gold rush. It is reputed to have been based on an actual court case, with the names of the involved persons only thinly disguised in the 1901 Rex Beach novel and in the later dramatization in collaboration with James MacArthur.

Although it was not a great success on Broadway, *The Spoilers* soon became a favorite of audiences the country over with stock companies, which were still popular in the early part of the century. It was first filmed by Universal Pictures in 1914 with Tom Santschi and William Farnum. Four other movie versions followed in 1923, 1930, 1942 and 1955, each with its own set of current stars. Milton Sills, Noah Beery and Anna Q. Nilson appeared in the 1923 version; Gary Cooper, William Boyd and Betty Compson in 1930; but the classic appears to have been the one with Randolph Scott, John Wayne, Richard Barthelmess and the incomparable Marlene Dietrich in 1942. The final filming in 1955 featured Anne Baxter, Jeff Chandler and Rory Calhoun.

See page 316 for a fascinating footnote to this play.

This scene from the 1942 film of The Spoiler (Universal) illustrates how differently a script may be written for film than for stage. Many extras were used for this scene in the Northern Lights Saloon. On stage such a scene would be played with only the main characters. Here, Marlene Dietrich is Cherry Malotte; Randolph Scott is McNamara; John Wayne is Glenister; Harry Carey is Dextry; Richard Barthelmess is the Bronco Kid. A review states: "The big scene is the fight, originally made one of the classic brawls of filmdom by Tom Santschi and William Farnum. The slugging match in the final reel between Wayne and Scott is something that apparently could be staged profitably in Madison Square Garden. It is that spectacular, starting from Miss Dietrich's boudoir, cascading through a balcony to the floor of the ginnery, out to the street, and finally winding up in the wagon-churned mud of the road."

# PRELUDE

SCENE: *The house lights are lowered and the stage is in complete darkness, when the first bars of music of the miners' opening song are played. When the curtain ascends, a drop scene (as far back on stage as the set behind will allow) comes into view. As "the rays of the midnight sun" grow brighter and illuminate the scene, they disclose a mountainous coast rising into majestic, barren ranges still white on peaks and gullies with snow. They bring out the purple and white distances, shimmering in burnished copper ripples on an oily sea. The music reaches its culmination, then diminishes as the rays gradually die away, leaving the stage in complete darkness again.*

*The drop is now lifted, leaving the set of Act One in view. The music of "The Lousy Miner" is taken up with guitar and mandolin offstage, and the miners sing.*

MINERS. (SONG: *"The Lousy Miner"* \*)

It's four long years since I reached this land
In search of gold among the rocks and sand,
And yet I'm poor when the truth is told,
I'm a lousy miner,
I'm a lousy miner in search of shining gold.

My sweetheart vowed she'd wait for me,
Till I returned, but don't you see?
She's married now, so I am told,
Left her lousy miner,
Left her lousy miner in search of shining gold.

*\*Music on page 374.*

# ACT ONE

SCENE: *Midnight on board the S.S. Yukon Queen at dock in Unalaska. Main deck of ship, with cabins U.R., rail across U., showing sea and dock.* CAPTAIN *is discovered on deck. He is in his early forties, gruff, but kindly. He wears a uniform and cap. The ship's bell strikes the midnight hour, 8 bells. Enter* FIRST OFFICER, *also in uniform, but bareheaded. The* CAPTAIN *turns sharply and meets him C.*

CAPTAIN. Well, any sign of the doctor?

OFFICER. No, Captain. He's hardly had time yet.

CAPTAIN. Time? If he dallies much longer, he'll land us in quarantine.

OFFICER. The report may not be true, Captain.

CAPTAIN *(pacing and looking anxiously off)*. I hope to God it ain't. This gold stampede is the chance of a lifetime. The Company pays five thousand a day for this ship—a week from Unalaska to Nome—thirty-five—forty—aye, maybe fifty thousand we stand to lose!

OFFICER. Don't think of it, Captain. Even if the Ohio is quarantined with smallpox, we should be able to clear.

CAPTAIN *(more hopefully)*. Right! That's the talk, mate! Keep the steam up and be ready to go at a moment's notice.

OFFICER *(going)*. Aye, Captain. *(Exit.)*

*(Deck lights are switched on. As* FIRST OFFICER *goes, enter* MRS. CHAMPAIN, *a small prim woman of uncertain age, adventuring to Alaska to look for shrewd investments. She is very conservatively dressed.)*

CAPTAIN. Aye.

MRS. CHAMPAIN. Ah, there you are. I've been looking everywhere for you.

CAPTAIN. Well, here I am. What is it now?

*(Enter* CHERRY MALOTTE, *a dance hall girl who has followed the gold rush to Alaska. She is very pretty and vivacious and a bit over-dressed.)*

CHERRY. Oh, Captain.

CAPTAIN. Well, Cherry, did you find your friends?

CHERRY. Not a sign. They must have gone ashore.

MRS. CHAMPAIN. If you don't mind, I was speaking to the Captain.

CHERRY. That's nothing new, you're always speaking.

MRS. CHAMPAIN. As I was saying, Captain, dear, what time do we sail?

CAPTAIN. Any minute now. *(Pushes her toward door.)* You might as well go back to your cabin.

MRS. CHAMPAIN. Well, if that's the way you feel.

CHERRY. Buy an organ for it, Mrs. Champain.

*Cherry: "Buy an organ for it, Mrs. Champain." (Marilyn Sue Garrett is Cherry; Arlen Dean Snyder is the Captain; Mina Zenor doubled as Mrs. Champain and Duchess in the Imperial's 1959 production.)*

MRS. CHAMPAIN. Well, I'll not stay for more of your insults, brazen creature. *(Exit.)*

CHERRY. Captain.

CAPTAIN *(familiarly)*. Well, Cherry?

CHERRY. You are not sailing before daylight, are you? I heard you say just now—

CAPTAIN. That we sail any minute. That's so. Well? Got a sweetheart coming on board?

CHERRY. No—no, but Mr. Glenister hasn't come back yet, has he?

CAPTAIN *(laughing at her)*. So that's your game. Why, you've chased that young fellow from Dawson to Denver and back again, and I'll wager if he knew you were here, he'd stay on shore just to avoid you.

CHERRY *(shamelessly)*. Never mind your taunts! My love for Roy Glenister is no secret. But you must give him a chance to get aboard before you sail. You don't understand—

CAPTAIN *(impatiently, looking off)*. I'm sorry, but I can't wait. You don't know what's in the wind.

CHERRY *(with determination)*. You can't sail without him. He owns the richest mine in Alaska, and they'll jump his claim if he doesn't reach Nome on the first boat.

CAPTAIN (*turning from back rail, and crossing as if to go up steps*). Well, that's his lookout, ain't it? I told him and Dextry not to go ashore, but they would do it. (*Ascends steps to bridge.*)

CHERRY. There's a chance he may be back in second cabin. There's a faro game going on there and if he's come aboard that's where he'll be.

(*Enter* SHIP'S DOCTOR *hurriedly. He is middle-aged, and he carries a doctor's valise.* CHERRY *stays to listen. Ship's bell strikes half after twelve — one bell.*)

DOCTOR (*seeing* CAPTAIN *on bridge*). Captain—

CAPTAIN (*coming down quickly*). Well, well—what news, Doctor?

DOCTOR. The report is true. Smallpox has broken out on board the Ohio, and she's in quarantine for thirty days.

CAPTAIN. Good Heavens! Did you see the health inspector?

DOCTOR. Yes. He says if we're not out of port by daylight, he'll tie us up, too.

CAPTAIN. Then there's no time to lose. We must clear while we have a chance! (*Ascends steps rapidly.*) Great heavens, smallpox! (*On bridge, he blows a whistle.*)

CHERRY (*coming to* DOCTOR). Captain, Doctor! You're not really getting under way?

DOCTOR. Yes, we'll be free in five minutes. (*Exit.*)

CAPTAIN (*shouting*). Stand by to let go the head line.

CHERRY (*shouting up to* CAPTAIN.) Captain Stephens—

CAPT. I'm sorry, but I can't listen now—

CHERRY. Oh, it's a shame, a perfect shame—where can Glenister and Dextry be?

(*Commotion heard off R.*)

CAPTAIN. Hello, what's this?

(CHERRY *rushes to rail.*)

CHERRY. There they are now.—It's a fight! Oh, wait—wait—

CAPTAIN. By Jove, they're pursued. Look, Glenister's knocked one of them down. Ah! Dextry's got the other—they're coming—(*Puts hand to mouth, shouts.*) Hurry up! We're casting off!

(*Steamer whistle sounds.*)

That young Glenister is always in trouble.

CHERRY (*elated*). They're coming—They're going to make it—

CAPTAIN. (shouting). Let go that aft line! Stand by to take on those passengers! (*Exit into pilot house.*)

(*Backdrop is rolled to indicate ship is free from her moorings, but not started yet.*)

CHERRY (*at back*). There's someone with them. It's a woman. I wonder who she is.

(*Enter* ROY GLENISTER, JOE DEXTRY *and* HELEN CHESTER, *after a snatch of chorus from miners offstage, as backdrop is rolled to indicate ship is sailing.* ROY GLENISTER *is a handsome young man in his mid-twenties.* JOE DEXTRY *is a stocky man in his forties,* GLENISTER's *partner in the Midas mine. He shows the results of long days and nights spent in the out-of-doors. His face is lined, his hair graying. Both men wear warm miners' clothing, work boots.* HELEN CHESTER, *niece of* JUDGE STILLMAN, *is a young woman of fragile beauty. She is well but conservatively dressed.* CHERRY *puts clenched hand to her lips and then exits, unobserved.)*

GLENISTER *(to* DEXTRY*).* Close shave that, Dex! *(Feels his neck gingerly.)*

DEX. Boy! I don't know of a more divertin' five minutes than the one we're just closin'.

GLEN *(laughing).* I wouldn't have missed it for a forty dollar dog! *(Rubbering in* HELEN's *direction.)* Well, Miss, let's have a look at you in the light.

*(She breaks and comes down a step or two. Both men, it is plain, are amazed to find a girl like her here.)*

HELEN. What kind of men are you to fight in the dark for a strange woman? *(There is a moment's pause.)* Well—will you let me—shake your hands?

DEX *(they both make for her hand at once).* I make oration Miss, you're the gamest little chap ever I fought over, Mexicun, Injun or white.

GLEN. Why—er—excuse me, Miss—but you—you aren't quite the kind of girl I expected to see.

HELEN *(shrinking from* GLEN's *admiration and addressing* DEXTRY*).* I suppose you think I've done something dreadful, don't you? But I haven't. *(Shaken and nervous, but trying to make light of it and regain her composure.)* I had to get away from the Ohio tonight because— well—for certain reasons. It was so good of you to fight them back.

DEX. We got you aboard after a tussle, all right, but I don't know what we'll do with you now you're here.

GLEN. It's awfully crowded, but I'll wake up the steward and have him find a place for you.

HELEN *(lays hand on* GLEN's *arm, anxiously.)* No, no! Don't do that. I mustn't be seen tonight or they'll send me back.

DEX. Send you back! Why, this here is a gold stampede. There ain't no turnin' back.

HELEN. I daren't risk it. Please hide me for tonight—till we're well at sea—then I'll tell you everything. Won't you help me?

GLEN *(impulsively).* Help you? Why—I'd string money on it.

DEX. Sure, Mike, and see here, Miss—you just take your time on explanations. Morals ain't our long suit. Everybody is privileged to look out for his own game up here. A square deal and no questions asked.

HELEN. But you don't know what I've done.

DEX. We don't give a damn what you done. *(Embarassed and apologetic.)* 'Scuse me, Miss, them little cuss words hang around the back of mouth amongst the holler teeth just waitin' to hop out that-a-way.

(HELEN *laughs, tolerant and amused.*)

GLEN. So you want to stowaway? Very well. Take our cabin and we'll go below. Eh, Dex?

DEX. Suits me—

HELEN. Oh, I can't do that. Isn't there some place you can hide me for tonight?

GLEN. Nobody will see you in there, Miss. *(Opening cabin door.)* Here's our stateroom. Just make yourself at home.

HELEN. You've been so kind already. I feel like a thief to take your room this way.

DEX *(holding door open for* HELEN *to enter).* That's all right, Miss. We don't mind so long as you don't get to likin' our room better than our company.

(HELEN *enters and shuts cabin door.*)

DEX *(winking).* How's that?

GLEN. Seems to me I've heard it before.

DEX *(serious now, as he fills pipe and lights it).* What gets me is— what brings her here? She's a fine girl, pretty too.

GLEN *(cynically).* Yes, too pretty to be alone—or anything but what they are.

DEX *(growling sourly).* This north country has plumb ruined you, boy. You think they're all alike—an' I don't know but what they are—'cept this one.

GLEN *(musingly).* I had an ancestor long ago who buccaneered among the Indies. Sometimes I think I have his blood in me. Oh, he was a devil! *(Laughs low and fearsomely.)* I can hear him now whispering to me—something about the spoils of war.—Why not? I fought for her tonight, Dex, and I'm strong enough to take what I want. *(Flexes his arms feeling his strength.)*

DEX. Careful you don't bust. I've seen men drunk on mountain air before.

GLEN *(laughing and making a face at* DEXTRY's *tobacco smoke).* Gad! What a smudge! You ought to be in quarantine.

DEX. I'd rather smell like a man than talk like a kid—

GLEN *(laughing, then musing again).* Who can she be? She's too beautiful to be good.

DEX. Well, she ain't too beautiful to be hungry; I'm going to get her some grub. I hope the cook's still around. *(Exits.)*

(CHERRY *enters.*)

CHERRY. Well, boy!

GLEN *(surprised and glad).* Why, Cherry! Where on earth did you come from?

CHERRY. I came aboard tonight at Unalaska. I heard you were here.

GLEN. I'm glad to see you again, little girl.

CHERRY *(jealous).* Who is this woman you were fighting over?

GLEN. What woman?

CHERRY *(hotly).* Oh, don't try that. I saw it all. Who is she?

GLEN *(laughing at her).* Jealous again. *(Slaps* CHERRY *on rear.)* Well, there's nothing to it. Dex and I happened to be coming down the wharf when she came running out of the darkness pursued by sailors. She called for help, and naturally, we gave it to her.

CHERRY. I wonder if you are lying.

*(GLENISTER shrugs shoulders, lights a cigarette.)*
Well, I have news for you—news about the mine.

GLEN. About the Midas? What is it?

CHERRY. There's some kind of plot on foot to take it away from you.

GLEN. Why, that's ridiculous! We discovered it. We own it—and we'll keep it.

CHERRY. Listen, Roy. I got this tip straight. Watch out for a man named McNamara. Don't let him lay hands on the Midas, that's all.

GLEN. But, Cherry, Congress has given us a code of laws and is sending courts to administer them. There will be judges and marshalls and—

CHERRY. That's just it. Those are the best cards in the deck.

GLEN. Your news doesn't worry me. In fact, I almost wish somebody would jump the Midas—I'd enjoy the exercise.

CHERRY. Well, maybe you'll have the chance. Anyway, I've warned you. Tell me—you don't really care for this other woman?

GLEN. Why, I never saw her till tonight.

CHERRY. Then kiss me, boy.

GLEN. No, that is all over. I told you so when I left Dawson.

CHERRY. No, it isn't! You think it is, but it isn't. I love you too much to let you go.

GLEN. Not so loud.

CHERRY. Oh, let them hear. I'm not ashamed. Don't you understand? You're everything clean and fine and good I've always wanted. I'll make you love me—I will—I will. Oh, what must you think of a woman who will beg?

GLEN. I'm sorry you feel this way—it isn't my fault—

CHERRY. Yes—yes—

GLEN.— and I'm honest with you now. I thought I loved you once, but it wasn't love. Love must be something different—but I've never known it. I've sometimes thought that to live through a great love would be worth any cost—even though I lost.

CHERRY *(gently).* I hope you never have your wish, boy. There's more pain than pleasure in that kind of love.

*(Ship's bell strikes one A.M., two bells. Voice of lookout calls "All's well." GLEN and CHERRY, standing silent and serious, start.)*

GLEN. One o'clock already!

CHERRY. Well, boy, I wish you luck. As soon as I'm settled, I'll see you again. Goodnight. *(She moves off.)*

GLEN *(gazing at cabin door).* Who can she be and—why is she alone

in this land? Why did she come to me out of the dark, if I'm not to
have her?

(HELEN *enters from cabin, looking about furtively.*)

HELEN (*relieved at seeing* GLEN). I'm too nervous to stay inside. No
one will see me here, will they?

GLEN (*advancing gladly*). If we hear anyone coming, we can go in.
The old man is down below making signs to the cook.

HELEN. I've been thinking that I ought to explain my actions to
you.

GLEN. We don't need explanations. You were in trouble, that was
unfortunate; we helped you, that was natural; no questions asked—
that's Alaska.

CAPTAIN (*offstage*). I'll have the quartermaster see to it.

GLEN. Look out, here comes the Captain.

(*Both enter stateroom hurriedly.* MRS. CHAMPAIN *crosses, stops
and gazes after them.*)

MRS. CHAMPAIN. Well—nice doings, I must say. I wonder who she is!
(*Exit.*)

(CAPTAIN *has appeared on bridge and is descending when* DEXTRY
*appears with tray of dishes. As he goes toward stateroom, the*
CAPTAIN *comes down, and* DEXTRY *sees him too late to retreat.*)

CAPTAIN. What have you there, Dextry?

DEX (*coaxingly*). Just a little lunch for the boy. (*He twirls food tray
under* CAPTAIN's *nose.*)

CAPTAIN. Lunch! At this time of night!

DEX. Well, a fightin' man's stomach don't know what time of night
it is!

CAPTAIN. Oh, I see. Well, all right then.—Say, you nearly got left
tonight, didn't you? Served you right if you had. (*Confidentially.*)
Why don't you make Glenister cut these Alaskan women? I see
Cherry Malotte is after him again. Take my advice; there's nothing in
it. Well, don't let the grub get cold. I believe I'll go inside with you
and have a bit myself.

(DEXTRY *gets between* CAPTAIN *and cabin door.*)

DEX (*embarrassed*). Well—er—the boy ain't feelin' too good after
the scrap—

CAPTAIN. So much the better—there'll be more for me. (*Rattles door
knob.*) Open up, Glenister, open for inspection!

(*Door opens;* GLENISTER *comes out, makes to close the door after
him, but* CAPTAIN *has spied* HELEN.)

Hold on! Who's your friend?

(HELEN *comes out.*)

Ah, not feeling well, eh? I thought I knew all our lady passengers.
Well—introduce me.

GLEN. I—ah—I didn't catch the name myself.

CAPTAIN. What?

GLEN. Oh, there's not much to say. This is the young lady we
brought aboard tonight.

CAPTAIN. So, stowing away ladies in your cabin, eh? Novel and highly moral scheme that. Well—whose is she? Quick!

HELEN *(distressed and trembling)*. Oh, please!

CAPTAIN *(to* GLENISTER*)*. Yours, of course, I suppose?

GLEN *(quietly)*. No.

DEX. Hold on, Cap. This girl had to make a quick get-a-way—

CAPTAIN. That story won't do! What was she running away from?

HELEN. I can answer your questions. It's true—I ran away. *(Moves to C.)* I had to. Then when the sailors followed me, these men beat them off. I can't explain how important it is for me to reach Nome at once, for it is not my secret. But it was enough to take me away from my uncle in Seattle at an hour's notice when no one else could go. I must get to Nome. It's life or death.

CAPTAIN *(eyeing her sharply, then softening a bit)*. But, my dear miss, the other ships will get you there just as soon as this one.

HELEN. The ship I left will not.

CAPTAIN *(starts, points at her fiercely)*. What's that? What ship do you mean?

HELEN. The Ohio!

CAPTAIN. The Ohio. Good God! You dare to stand there and tell me that! *(Turns on* DEXTRY *and* GLENISTER*.)* D'ye hear that? You've ruined me. I'll put you all in irons. My God! The Ohio!

GLEN. What do you mean?

DEX. Calm down. What's up?

CAPT. What's up? There's smallpox aboard the Ohio, and this hussy has broken quarantine. Now we'll be held up at Nome. They'll put us in quarantine for thirty days.

GLEN. Great Heavens. We'll lose the Midas.

DEX. They'll jump our claim.

HELEN. Don't blame these men, sir; they didn't know. I am the one at fault. I had to get away.

CAPTAIN. How do I know that? What's that got to do with me and my ship?

*(*HELEN *looks at* DEXTRY *and* GLENISTER *who have gone up L.,* GLENISTER *pacing,* DEXTRY *relighting his pipe. She resolves to take the* CAPTAIN *into her confidence.)*

HELEN. I have papers here that must be delivered. *(Pulls large envelope halfway from bosom of dress.)* My name is Helen Chester. I'm the niece of the new Federal Judge who is coming to Nome to open court, and I carry important documents that could not be entrusted to the mails. If these papers are not delivered, it will mean riot and bloodshed. I can tell you this much: it concerns the richest mine in all the north, held by desperate men who don't own it. I must get through.

CAPTAIN *(eyeing her sharply and suspiciously)*. I'm sorry, but I must do my duty.

GLEN. Captain, if this ship is delayed, we will lose the Midas.

CAPTAIN. And what d'ye think I stand to lose? I'll tell you what: I'll isolate this young lady in one of the staterooms, and turn her over to the health inspector at Nome.

HELEN. Oh, you wouldn't do that.

GLEN. You'll have mutiny in an hour, if you do. Your passengers are all mad with the gold fever, and they won't put up with any delay.

DEX. Sure! And your firm will be liable for damages for your carelessness.

CAPTAIN *(enraged)*. My carelessness!

DEX. Sure, that's a statuary offense.

CAPTAIN. Curse your insolence! My carelessness! I'll hand her over to the ship's doctor! I'll wash my hands of her!

GLEN. See here, now. Go easy. This will mean your ruin just as sure as it will mean ours. You'll lose your job, and that's a cinch. On the other hand, we'll be in Nome before this girl could show symptoms of the disease, even if she had it. If you say nothing, nobody will know. We'll keep her hidden. Go up forward to your bridge, sir, and forget you stepped in to see yours truly. Think—think what it means to us all!

*(CAPTAIN hesitates, looks at HELEN kindly, and relents.)*

CAPTAIN *(brusquely)*. You'll have to take care of the steward, then. *(To HELEN.)* Don't feel hurt over what I said, Miss—I made a mistake. And when you get to Nome, make your sweetheart marry you the day you land. You are too far north to be alone. *(He exits into pilot house.)*

DEX *(fanning himself)*. Thank you for them kind words.

HELEN *(sinks into seat)*. Oh, I'm glad. You have saved me twice tonight. How can I ever thank you?

DEX. Don't try. Just dig into this grub. It ain't hot, but it's healthy.

HELEN. No—please, I'm not hungry.

DEX. Yes, you be.

HELEN. No—you're very kind, but please—I can't just yet.

DEX. Try a bite—it's right good.

GLEN. Let her alone, Dex. She didn't ask for it to begin with, and she's said she's not hungry.

DEX. I know—but all these good vittles—

GLEN. Well, if they're so good, eat 'em yourself. But get them out of here.

HELEN. Please—he was only being kind—

DEX. That's all right, Miss. I'll jest have the cook warm 'em up a bit.

HELEN. And thanks again. I hope I haven't hurt your feelings.

DEX. Don't think nothin' of it, Miss.

HELEN *(calling to GLENISTER)*. Mr. Glenister, what portent do you see that makes you stare into the night so anxiously?

*(DEXTRY gets up and saunters about, finally exits.)*

GLEN *(coming to HELEN)*. I'm trying to read the message of the North.

HELEN. And what does it say to you?

GLEN. It says: "This is God's free country where a man is a man, nothing more. If you've been square, so much the better; if not, leave it all behind and start again on the level."

HELEN (*stirred by his seriousness*). I feel I am going to like the North.

GLEN. Perhaps you will, though it's not a woman's land—yet.

HELEN. What led you here? You must love the North.

GLEN. Yes, I do. When you've lived the long June days and heard geese honking under a sunlit midnight, or when once you've hit the trail on a winter morning so sharp the air stings your lungs—well, it gets in your blood, that's all.

HELEN (*with a laugh to relax the tension*). You are quite poetical for a savage.

GLEN (*changing subject*). Tell me—what brings you up here? Vaudeville? (HELEN *shakes her head.*) Dance hall?

HELEN (*amused*). No—I toil not—neither do I spin—in the dance halls.—I herald the coming of the Law!

GLEN. Bah! I'm afraid of it in this country. We've relied on our courage and our Colts. (*Touches hip pocket.*) But we'll have to unbuckle them both when the law comes.

HELEN. The Colts may go; but the courage never. But, there is something else that brings me north. I have a brother wandering somewhere in this country. He left home when mother died, and I've never seen him since. I got news of him indirectly once at Dawson. Bad news. I heard that he—drank.

GLEN. He probably ate too, most men do. (*Seriously.*) No, I don't like to think of the law. So far we have had peace up here, and justice, but a warning has come to me already that there is a plot on foot to rob Dex and me of the Midas—that underneath this cloak of justice you call the law, there is a dagger whetted for us fellows who own the right diggings.

HELEN. You're wrong. Law is the foundation. If you own the Midas, the law will protect you.

GLEN. I don't care—I like the old way best. I want to stay where life is what it was intended to be—survival of the fittest. I'm a primitive man. My pleasures are violent and my hate is bitter in my mouth. What I want, I take—whether wine or women—or spoils of war.

(*He takes her hand and looks into her eyes. She lets him hold it a moment, then quickly draws away.*)

HELEN. Spoils of war? I don't understand. Why shouldn't you? To the victor—well—you know the rest.

GLEN (*following her*). You're right. I shall not fail to take them. (*He seizes her violently and kisses her on the mouth. She seems paralyzed with surprise.*)

HELEN (*struggling violently*). Oh!

(*She strikes him with her fist, but he pays no heed, kissing her again and again.*)

GLEN (*laughing*). There's never a law of God or man runs north of

53. What I want—I take. *(Releases her. Then, quietly.)* I am going to love you, girl.

HELEN *(breathless and outraged).* And may God strike me dead if I ever stop hating you!

> *(She turns to get away from him, when there is a shot off and sounds of rising turmoil. They pause, alarmed.)*

GLEN *(sharply).* Go into the cabin—quick! There's trouble here.

> *(HELEN gazes off, GLENISTER goes to her, also looking off toward fight.)*

Quick! I say, it's a fight!

> *(GAMBLER rushes across, followed by SECOND MAN, revolver in hand; GAMBLER turns and faces SECOND MAN.)*

GAMBLER. Don't follow me, you damned crook!

SECOND MAN. Will you pay that bet?

> *(He covers GAMBLER with gun, and crosses opposite where HELEN is cowering. GLENISTER sees her peril and goes to her. They are directly behind GAMBLER.)*

GAMBLER. No, it's a crooked game!

GLEN. My God! We're in line!

> *(He seizes HELEN, forces her down to her knees against the wall, then crouches over her with his arms about her, shielding her with his body. SECOND MAN fires, GAMBLER runs off, SECOND MAN in pursuit. DEXTRY rushes on, GLENISTER is supporting HELEN.)*

DEX. Be you hurt?

GLEN. No, thank Heaven! But we were close to Kingdom Come— Look at this!

> *(He indicates bullet hole in wall, right over where they were crouched. HELEN looks and covers her eyes, staggers away.)*

DEX. Holy Mackerel! When they started shootin', I thought sure it was sweet music for you!

HELEN. Oh, it was awful! *(She shudders.)*

DEX. Yep! All over a twenty-dollar faro bet. I'm goin' to see if they caught him yet. *(Exit)*

GLEN. Your introduction to the North is tragic, Miss. It's not all like this.

HELEN. And so I am indebted to you again! *(Angry and impetuous.)* Am I never to be done with your services? You take advantage of my loneliness to insult me, and the next moment risk your life for me. What manner of man are you?

GLEN. I don't know—I never thought—Now that the madness has died in me I—I'm sorry for what I did—just now—I've known the other kind of women so long that I—blundered. *(Gazing at her.)* Yes—you are different—forgive me.

HELEN *(shudders and shrinks away).* I can never do that. You have saved my life and I am grateful—but, how I loathe you for that other—*(Puts hands to her face.)*

GLEN. I have no excuse save that I am a man of the woods and the mountains. My blood is red.

HELEN. There's something way back in you that I fear—something ferocious, wild and crouching.

GLEN. Perhaps you're right. But I can end all that. I'll put by the old things and I'll let them rope and throw and brand me. *(With a winning smile.)* I'll sit on a tabourette and drink weak tea. I'll put away revenge and ambition even, if it will make you like me a little bit.

*(Enter* CHERRY. *She watches them jealously.)*

HELEN *(at cabin door, opening it).* I think I might learn to forget my hate if you did; that is, if you really mean what you said. But you can't—you're a savage. *(She exits into stateroom.* CHERRY *starts forward eagerly, pauses.)*

GLEN. A savage! *(With a bitter laugh.)* She's right. I am a savage. Yet I'd give all the riches of the Midas to undo what I did tonight. *(Looking at her door.)* I wonder what her name is!

*(Ship's bell of two* A.M.—*four bells. Sailor's voice sings out: "All's well.")*

**CURTAIN**

# ACT TWO

SCENE: *Law offices of Struve, Nome, Alaska. Stage shows outer office, door to Struve's private office. When curtain rises, the* BRONCO KID *is discovered seated near stove. He is* DRURY CHESTER, HELEN CHESTER'S *brother, who has become a professional gambler. He deals at the Northern Lights Saloon. About thirty years old, languid in movement, yet alert, he is dressed in a neat business suit. He rolls and smokes cigarettes interminably. Enter* WILTON STRUVE, *the District Attorney, good-looking, clean shaven, and in his early forties. He considers himself quite the ladies' man. His dress is fastidious and a bit flashy. He goes to the sideboard and pours a drink.*

STRUVE. A little "hootch," Bronco?

KID. Nope, I'm hitched to the hydrant.

STRUVE. Well—happy days! I've finished my case for the day, and now my client can rest easy. *(Puts bottle back in cabinet.)*

KID. Just as easy as if he was asleep with a ten-year-old timber wolf.

STRUVE. I'd like you to know I'm an honest man.

KID *(laughing quietly)*. You mean you'd like me to think so. You belong to the Nearly Club—you're nearly honest.

STRUVE. I tell you—

KID *(turns round and straddles chair leaning arms on chair back. He faces* STRUVE *and stares him down)*. Struve—I'm wise to you and your receiver McNamara and old Judge Stillman, and all the rest. I know your game.

STRUVE. Tch! You've heard this talk around town, but there's nothing to it. *(*KID *stares at him with a knowing smile and a wink and smokes silently.)* You can't name one illegal thing that has been done.

KID. Cut it, pal. It's none of my business. My graft is gambling, and I'm always glad to see another crook get ahead in his own line.

STRUVE. Just because the miners are against us, it doesn't mean we're crooked. The Midas was jumped. I bring suit to enjoin Glenister and Dextry from working the property; the court ejects them from the premises and appoints McNamara as receiver to work the claim. Now, isn't that logical? Isn't that legal?

KID. You read your lines like a "legit," but they make me laugh. I know the man McNamara hired to jump the Midas—and I know what he paid for the man's quit claim deed.

STRUVE. I tell you, Kid—

KID. Nix, Bo! Don't hand me that stuff. But let me put you wise to something for your own good, Struve. Now this is down low—as between two crooks.

STRUVE. I tell you I'm no crook.

KID. As you were—as you were! *(Laughs quietly.)* There's three things don't want to get next to you for their own good, Struve—

gold, whiskey and women. 'Specially women! Well, let me tell you—I know Glenister and I know Dextry, and they're getting desperate.

STRUVE. I tell you I've done nothing to answer for.

KID. All right! A word to the wise beats the bookmakers. I want to write some letters. Mind if I use your room?

STRUVE. Go ahead. You'll find stationery in my desk.

KID. Thanks. *(Goes into* STRUVE's *private office.)*

STRUVE. I wonder if the Bronco Kid's on. I've been afraid of that. The game is too bold. *(Takes another drink.)* Well, damn it, it's worth the risk. Nobody can prove anything—unless—they were to get onto the papers the Chester girl brought in. *(Goes to safe.)* It makes me nervous having them around here. *(Opens safe and extracts papers.)* Ah!

*(Voice heard outside.* STRUVE *turns and looks toward outer door.)* Um—McNamara and the Judge.

*(Enter* JUDGE ARTHUR STILLMAN, *a federal judge, a bumbling ineffectual person whose once sharp faculties are fading. As he enters, he holds door open to let in* ALEXANDER MCNAMARA, *and closes it after him.* MCNAMARA *is a successful and scheming lawyer, confident but always wary. He is about forty and well-dressed in a professional, business manner.)*

JUDGE. Public opinion is against us—it's becoming a menace—

MCNAMARA. I don't care. We are within the law. *(As he crosses, he sees* STRUVE *at safe; goes quickly to him, snatches papers from his hands, replaces them in safe, and closes the safe door.)* What are you doing with those papers? Lock 'em up, and let 'em alone.

STRUVE *(sullenly)*. I was just running them over to see if they were all right.

MCNAMARA *(sitting, looking at letters and papers)*. You've been drinking. Heavens, man! Won't you quit that?

STRUVE. No, I won't; and I won't be preached to, either. Understand? You run your business and I'll run mine.

JUDGE *(anxious to placate)*. Come, come, gentlemen—we're all right from a legal standpoint.

MCNAMARA. No doubt of it.

JUDGE. The injunctions were issued properly and McNamara appointed receiver in due form.

MCNAMARA. Yes, and who was better fitted for the position than I—an old and trusted friend of Judge Stillman's. *(With an easy laugh.)* They can't pick a flaw. The mines are working every day and there's half a million in bullion at the bank—in my name. Why, the Midas alone yields five thousand a day.

STRUVE. Oh, it's big all right—almost too big!

MCNAMARA. Yes, it's the biggest scheme that ever came North, backed by the biggest men in Washington. You ought to be satisfied.

STRUVE. Lord, I'm satisfied. But suppose anything went wrong—

suppose the names and addresses and figures in those papers *(Indicates safe.)* leaked out.

MCNAMARA. No danger, I'd burn them at the first sign.

STRUVE. Well, it's dangerous—

MCNAMARA. Dangerous? Bah! Where's the danger? We've got the law—or rather we are the law. Now let's get to work. *(He rises with papers in hand, and comes down.)*

STRUVE. Have you heard from Bill Wheaton? Glenister's lawyer?

MCNAMARA *(With his hand on door knob)*. No—and I'm not afraid of interference from him or from the Frisco courts—

STRUVE. He's been gone thirty days—he's about due.

MCNAMARA. That's another reason to keep those papers locked up. We're safe as long as we have them. *(He exits into private office.)*

*(JUDGE seats himself at left of table wearily. BRONCO KID coughs loudly in STRUVE's room.)*

JUDGE *(rising, nervously)*. Who's in there?

STRUVE. Don't be nervous. It's nobody but the Bronco Kid. He's writing some letters.

JUDGE. Oh, he's all right.

STRUVE. Say, I've never thought to ask you how Miss Chester came to bring in those instructions. She took a long chance.

JUDGE. We had nobody else to send. She had no idea of the content of the documents—I only told her they must be served before I arrived or there would be litigation, riot—bloodshed!

STRUVE *(laughs, slaps JUDGE on shoulder)*. Well, you certainly frightened her nearly to death. You'd have thought the safety of the whole country depended on her.

JUDGE. Yes—I lied to her—my own niece. It seems I do nothing but lie nowadays. I don't like it.

STRUVE. Nonsense!

JUDGE. These last few weeks have been too much for me. This is a country for young men—I'm too old—too old.

*(Enter MCNAMARA with papers; he goes briskly to table as before.)*
Alec—I'm going to lie down a bit.

MCNAMARA *(without looking up)*. All right, Judge.

*(Exit JUDGE.)*

STRUVE. The old man has lost his nerve.

MCNAMARA. Yes, I'm sorry I brought him.

STRUVE. I've been warned again to watch Glenister and Dextry.

MCNAMARA. Bah! When we put them off the Midas six weeks ago, you said that young fellow was dangerous, but he obeyed orders like a sheep.

STRUVE. That puzzled me, I'll admit. I know he's a fighter—besides—*(Watches MCNAMARA.)* he's in love with Helen Chester.

MCNAMARA *(looks up, sternly)*. You told me that once before. If I really thought so, I'd—

*(Outer door opens, Enter MRS. CHAMPAIN, in afternoon dress.)*

STRUVE *(makes a face)*. Excuse me. *(Goes to cabinet, takes bottle and glass with him, and exits into his room.)*

*(MCNAMARA rises, offers chair to MRS. CHAMPAIN.)*

MRS. CHAMPAIN. I'm so glad to find you in, Mr. McNamara. You know the Humming Bird mine? My husband told me how you got the Midas, and I said to myself, "How nice if I could get the Humming Bird. It would be such a surprise for Mr. Champain." You know he always says I'm not practical. But I am. So I sent our hired man out last night to jump the Humming Bird and now I want to know if you won't be my receiver.

MCNAMARA *(sarcastically)*. And your husband thinks you're not practical?

MRS. CHAMPAIN. Indeed he does. Why, it's perfectly simple, isn't it? All you do is pick out the richest mine you see, hire somebody to jump it, then you be the receiver and keep the gold. Of course you have injuncted all the best mines yourself, but I thought the Humming Bird was the next best, and I'd like to have it.

*(The effect of this scene should be comic satire, almost a burlesque of MCNAMARA's high-handed game.)*

MCNAMARA. Hold on—hold on. I think your husband failed to explain a few points.

MRS. CHAMPAIN. Oh, pshaw! I didn't anticipate the least trouble. He said you could do whatever you liked with the court.

MCNAMARA. He did, eh?

MRS. CHAMPAIN. Of course, I know very little about these things—

MCNAMARA. Madam—a little knowledge is a dangerous thing—more is worse.

MRS. CHAMPAIN. Then you can't do it? Not even if you took half the gold?

MCNAMARA. Half?—I'm afraid not.

MRS. CHAMPAIN *(huffily)*. Oh, I see. You wouldn't act as receiver on my claim for half, when you could be your own receiver and get it all. *(Rising.)* I'm afraid I don't know much.

MCNAMARA *(rising too, elaborately)*. You wrong yourself. I have never heard the proposition put more clearly. *(MRS. CHAMPAIN glares at him. He goes on with explanatory air.)* I refer, of course, to the mining matter.

MRS. CHAMPAIN. Of course, of course.

MCNAMARA. Now, if you would care to make another appointment, we can talk about it. *(Looks at watch.)* Right now, I'm expecting Miss Chester and I am sure—

MRS. CHAMPAIN *(stiffening)*. No, thank you, I don't want to meet the young person. *(Draws in her skirts.)* One can't be too particular in a place like this.

MCNAMARA. Why—! I don't understand.

MRS. CHAMPAIN. Probably not, Mr. McNamara, but all the women in the camp do, and all the married men. We women must protect ourselves in a lawless land. I've taken pains to let them all know what I saw on board the Yukon Queen. Scandalous! Why, I wouldn't speak to her, nor to Roy Glenister either—and the Judge such a nice old man—ah, such a pity—

(*Outer door opens and* HELEN *enters in street dress.* MRS. CHAMPAIN *sees her, elevates her head, sniffs virtuously.*)

Good day, Mr. McNamara, I must be going. (*She ignores* HELEN *with disdain and exits.*)

HELEN (*looking after her*). Oh—I can't stand this. Last night at the dance the women cut me—and when I demanded an explanation, they sneered at me. (*Hides her face in her hands.*)

MCNAMARA (*approaching her gently*). I'm sorry Helen. I never knew the scandal would reach your ears. I shall have to kill that man some day.

HELEN. What man?

MCNAMARA. Glenister, of course. The scandal couldn't have come from any other source. He boasts that you were his—well, his guest on the Yukon Queen—

HELEN. Glenister—why he wouldn't talk of me that way—he's an honest man.

MCNAMARA. You may think so, but it's the talk of the camp. See here, Helen, what is the use of waiting until we return to Washington? Why not marry me now?

HELEN. No—not yet. You promised not to urge me.

MCNAMARA. But now I must—think what your existence will be in this half-born mining camp, now that decent women have turned against you. Be my wife, and I'll end it all. The judge is a weak old woman, and can't help you—

HELEN. Oh, if I could only find my brother!

MCNAMARA. Helen—it's hopeless. You'll never find your brother. Let me—(*Takes her hand and draws near to her.*)—let me be your protector.

HELEN. Don't think me ungrateful, Alec. Oh, I don't know what to do.

MCNAMARA. Then let me decide for you.

(*He is about to take her in his arms, when* STRUVE *is heard whistling.* MCNAMARA *recovers.* STRUVE *enters.*)

STRUVE. How d'ye do, Miss Helen? Anything I can do for you? (MCNAMARA *glares at him.*)

HELEN. No, thanks. I just came to see if Uncle Arthur has found any trace of my brother Drury.

(STRUVE *sits with his back to them.*)

MCNAMARA (*in a low voice*). Will you be my wife, Helen?

HELEN (*leaving*). Please give me a little more time. I must think.

(MCNAMARA *turns, takes his hat, and exits through outer door.* HELEN *pauses until he goes, then takes a step toward* STRUVE, *hesitating, then finally blurting out.*)

Mr. Struve—I wonder if you would answer a question truthfully.

STRUVE *(turns quickly, surprised)*. A lawyer's business consists of answering questions truly.

HELEN. I said truthfully, not truly. What is this rumor of a gigantic plot to rob the miners?

STRUVE *(eyeing her with open admiration; cynically)*. Give, give, give! A women's cry! Give me this, give me that! Why don't you ever offer something?—Look, I can help you *(Rises suddenly and puts chair behind him.)*, but not gratis!

*(Pause, as they face each other.)*

HELEN. Please—it's not curiosity—can't you see I must know?

STRUVE *(taking a step toward her)*. You say it's not curiosity. Well, whatever it is, I'll place a bet you'll never rest till you know the contents of those papers you brought. That was a trick to make Paul Revere's ride slow to a standstill!

HELEN. What do you mean? Tell me!

STRUVE. Suppose I told you those documents told the truth—whether your uncle and the rest of us are in the right, or whether we deserve lynching.

HELEN. I'd give my life to see them.

STRUVE. Well—you may see them. They're in that safe. *(Indicates safe.)* Will you trade?

HELEN *(excited)*. Yes—yes. Give them to me.

STRUVE *(making as though to embrace her)*. Then a kiss to bind the bargain—to apply on account—

HELEN *(retreating)*. No, no—not that—not that!

STRUVE *(pauses craftily)*. Suit yourself, but you'll change your mind. *(He crosses to chair.)*

*(Enter* BRONCO KID. *He sees* HELEN, *starts, stares at her, pauses a moment while* STRUVE *goes on.)*

When you do, I'll give you proof—if you pay the price. I'm no extortioner, just a bargainer of no mean ability.

*(The* KID *tiptoes back into room.)*

HELEN. Oh, I don't know why I've listened so long! *(Goes quickly to door.)* You're a panther! *(Exit.)*

STRUVE *(lighting fresh cigar)*. Graceful and elegant brute that—but with sharp teeth and sharper claws.

*(Enter* BRONCO KID, *cautiously. Seeing* STRUVE *alone, he comes down and seizes him by the shoulder roughly.)*

KID. Who was that? That girl?

STRUVE. Judge Stillman's niece.

KID. Her name?

STRUVE. Helen Chester.

KID. Helen—

STRUVE. Why? Look good to you, Kid? Well, same here, so hands off, see?

KID *(seizing* STRUVE *fiercely)*. You—*(Then, in contempt.)* Bah! I'm a fool.

STRUVE. Why, Kid, what's the matter?

KID. Don't you try it. See? *(Exit, banging outer door after him.)*

STRUVE. Gee! Bronco's got the worst eye in the camp! Ugh! Think I'll have a drink. *(Exits into his office.)*

*(Enter DEXTRY and FLAPJACK SIMMS through outer door. SIMMS is an uneducated hillbilly miner with a lot of natural savvy and a sense of humor. He is between 40 and 50 years old, very tall and thin, and entirely bald, with only one or two front teeth. His clothes are extremely loose, much too large for him. Both men observe surroundings curiously on entering.)*

DEX. I reckon this is the joint, Flapjack.

SIMMS. Which this yere is the first law shack I ever see. *(He looks about.)* This yere fuss is all Glenister's fault. If he'd a put up a fight in the first place, we'd a been working the Midas today 'stead of loafin' aroun' a disrepptiable dive like this un.

DEX. He's lost all his sperrit. I don't believe in givin' up nothin' that you have in your mitt. A bird in the hand is the noblest work of God. *(Walking about.)* I wonder where the big smoke is. *(Knocks on door.)*

*(Enter HELEN.)*

HELEN. Why, it's my friend.

DEX *(highly pleased)*. It ain't nobody else—and this here is Flapjack Simms, our foreman. Leastways, he was, when we had a mine.

*(SIMMS removes hat, wriggles with embarrassment.)*

Now he ain't nothin' but a kind of human bein'.

HELEN. I am glad to know you, Mr. Simms.

*(SIMMS, greatly abashed, tries to speak, but only moves his lips.)*

What was that you said?

SIMMS *(tries again, fails, fills up his chest and this time, shouts loudly, his voice seeming to burst forth beyond control)*. Glad to see you!

DEX. Easy over the rough spots.

HELEN *(amiably)*. If you're Mr. Dextry's friend, I know I shall like you.

*(SIMMS grins and giggles.)*

DEX. Have ya had any news of that long lost brother o' yourn?

HELEN. No, not a sign. *(Turning half away.)* Oh, if only he knew how much I need him now.

DEX. You ain't in trouble, Miss—?

HELEN. Oh no—and how have you been getting on?

DEX. Fierce! I'm broke.

HELEN. That's a shame.

DEX. No, Miss, it's a coincidence. All of us is broke—Glenister, Flapjack and little me. We've even taken to sleepin' in three-quarter beds to save money.

HELEN. Three-quarter beds?

DEX. Uh-huh! Three beds at a quarter a piece.

HELEN. Oh, I'm sorry. How does—Mr. Glenister feel?

DEX. I don't know how he feels, but he acts like a beast of burden. Just stands around, and flaps his ears at the insecks. When he gets tired experimentin' with this new law game, I'm gonna step in and do some business on a common-sense basis.

HELEN. You talk as if you wouldn't get fair play.

DEX. We won't. I look on all lawyers with suspicion.

HELEN *(as if it suddenly struck her to ask)*. Tell me—who is Cherry Malotte?

DEX. Cherry? Well, now you ask—I don't hardly know. She came to Dawson the winter of '97 and in two days she had the brotherly love of the camp turning back handsprings. Glenister saved her life once and—well—she sort of likes him for it.

SIMMS. That gal is all the money, forty ways from the ace. She's the friend of every poor man from Dawson to the Yukon. Why, she's grubstaked 'em when they was busted and nursed 'em when they was sick. She's fed half the stew-bums in camp. Why, she's fed me lots of times.

DEX. Steady, boy.

SIMMS. I'd go to hell for her! *(Realizes what he has said, and claps his hand to his mouth, rapidly retreats up to window.)*

DEX. Don't mind the cuss words, Miss. In this country we figure profane langwidge is like steam to a locomotive, requirin' more to run up hill than on the level, and inasmuch as there ain't but few men on the level, everybody swears.

SIMMS *(hanging out of window)*. Yere 'e comes. Yere's the boy.

*Helen Chester, new to the rough mining scene, inquires about her brother. None of them know that she is asking about "The Bronco Kid," a gambling house dealer. Joe Dextry (Jerry Hayes); Flapjack Simms (Steven Hornibrook); Helen Chester (Kate Kelly); Roy Glenister (Herbert Kouba) in the 1970 production.*

DEX (*sighs with relief*). A-ah! We're goin' to end our troubles today, Miss, I ain't follered the totterin' footsteps of the law none to clost, but I reckon when the boy take a hand in the game, it'll be a show-down.

(*Enter* GLENISTER. DEXTRY *crosses to him.*)

GLEN. Hello, Dex.

DEX. Hello boy, any news?

GLEN. Another pack of papers from Wheaton in San Francisco—his way may be legal, but it sure is slow.

DEX (*as* HELEN *comes toward* GLENISTER). Well—we've waited this long—guess it won't hurt me none to keep it till you've talked to the lady—(*Joins* SIMMS *at window.*)

GLEN. I'm mightly glad to see you. I've come down from the hills a dozen times on the chance of a glimpse of you. It has been a long time—

HELEN. Please—don't talk like that.

GLEN (*rebuffed*). I've wrung my soul for what I did that night—

HELEN. It isn't that—I have been thinking it over since I came North, and I see that it wasn't an unnatural thing for you to do. I don't mean that it was pardonable, for it wasn't, but I'm sufficiently broad-minded not to blame you unreasonably—I mean that I—I think I could like you in spite of it—

GLEN. I've been trying to harness myself, but it's a hard job. If you'll be patient, I'll prove I can come to you with my soul in leash. You'll see—let me try—

HELEN. Oh, please don't. You must not. Why do you insist?

GLEN (*calmly*). Because I never give up anything I want.

HELEN (*hotly*). Then it is because you are a savage—I was right.

GLEN (*smiling*). I remember someone who went through perils on land and water and never gave up until she got what she wanted. (*Tenderly.*) And she was no savage.

HELEN. That was different. (*Changing subject.*) By the way, did you hear what happened to the good ship Ohio?

GLEN. No, I've been too busy to inquire.

HELEN. She was sent to Egg Island with every one on board. She has been quarantined there and may not get away this summer.

GLEN. What a disappointment to the poor devils on board.

HELEN. Yes, and—only for what you did, I should be one of them. Believe me, I am grateful—

GLEN. I didn't do much. The fighting part is easy. It's not half so hard as to give up your property and lie still while—

HELEN (*a new light dawning in her eyes*). Then you—you took my words—seriously?

GLEN. So seriously that I wouldn't fight when they put me off the Midas, although I knew I was right.

HELEN (*eager, in spite of herself*). You did that because I said—because I called you a savage?

GLEN. You were right—I've been a savage—oh, girl, girl *(He seizes her hand in both of his. She is drawn to him, and looks up into his face.)*—don't you know how it is with a man when he loves a good woman?

HELEN. I know. I feel the change in you. *(Suddenly recalling herself and withdrawing.)* No, no, not yet, I'll tell my uncle you are here. *(Exits into office.)*

> (DEXTRY *turns from window as door closes and comes to* GLENIS-
> TER, *who is staring rapturously after* HELEN.)

GLEN *(without turning)*. Dex, I am going to marry that girl.

DEX. I dunno if you be or not. Better watch McNamara.

GLEN *(turning on him)*. What?

DEX. I ain't blind. I kin put two and two together.

GLEN. You'll never put those two together. That man's a rascal. Besides, it can't be. *(Puts his hands roughly on* DEXTRY's *shoulders.)* Oh, Dex, I love her so much that—*(He thrusts* DEXTRY *off, playfully.)* You can't understand.

DEX. Um-m! I suppose not. *(Rubbing his chin sagely.)* I'll allow that McNamara may be a rascal, but he's a good-lookin' rascal, and as for manners, well, his makes yours look like a logger. *(GLEN turns and listens with a frown.)* And he's a brave man, too. Them three qualities are trumps and warranted to take any queen in the deck—red, white, or yellow.

GLEN. If he dared!

DEX. I've been sizin' up this here situation keerfully, and I've just about decided you've finally met your match.

> (GLEN *and* DEXTRY *face each other with level gaze.* SIMMS *comes from window and breaks in.)*

SIMMS. Well, where's them papers you had from the law sharp?

GLEN. Here. *(He takes papers from his pocket.)* They've just arrived and I haven't looked them over yet—probably just more of the same. Law must be a mighty long process.

> (Outer door opens, and MCNAMARA enters briskly. He scarcely glances at GLENISTER, but crosses straight to table, removes his hat, and takes a cigar. Not until he has lighted it does he speak.)

MCNAMARA *(brusque and demanding)*. Well, what do you want?

DEX. Just as glad to see us as if he'd run a nail in his foot.

> (GLENISTER *is absorbed in reading papers. He becomes excited as he reads.)*

MCNAMARA. Well, come to the point!

GLEN. It's here, boys, it's here! We've won! Mr. McNamara—our lawyer, Bill Wheaton, in San Francisco has just filed certified copies of these with the clerk of the court. You're to turn the Midas back to its rightful owners, together with all the gold you have removed and have in your custody. And you're to produce your books of account, safe deposit keys, and about five hundred thousand dollars in gold! Say, Dex, we finally found us an honest lawyer!

*(He hands papers to* MCNAMARA, *who pockets them without looking at them.)*

MCNAMARA *(quietly).* Well, I won't do it.

*(All gasp in astonishment.)*

GLEN. What! You can't help yourself—it's all in those papers—

MCNAMARA *(rising to full height).* Can't help myself, eh? Watch me. Don't think for a moment that I went into this fight unarmed. Writs of supersedas! Bah! *(Snaps fingers.)*

GLEN. We'll see whether you obey or not. Where is the Judge?

MCNAMARA. Never mind the Judge. I'll see him myself. *(Exit quickly.)*

DEX. Well, what d'ye think of that?

GLEN. Judge Stillman will have to obey the orders of his superior court. There's no way out. McNamara has made a fool of me for the last time. We've fought him fair, and if he doesn't yield, by Heaven, there'll be murder!

DEX *(slaps* GLENISTER *on back, heartily).* Them's the first decent words you've said in a month. They're man's size, them words are. They're growed up, and got hair on their chests. Boy, I'm with you.

SIMMS *(loudly).* Let's us hop in and clean up the whole damn mess like we was killin' snakes.

*(Enter* MCNAMARA *followed by* HELEN. MCNAMARA *comes out, but* HELEN *stays at doorway, looking apprehensive.)*

MCNAMARA. Haven't you gone yet? I told you it was no use.

GLEN *(advancing on him).* We've had enough of your crooked work, you infernal scoundrel. Give me back the Midas, or I'll make it man-to-man and fight you like a dog.

MCNAMARA. Ha. Threats at last, eh? I thought that was your work. You don't know anything but fighting. You can't threaten me, understand? *(To* HELEN, *mockingly.)* Behold your knight of the six-shooter, who's afraid to meet me alone, but brave enough when I'm with a woman.

GLEN *(furiously).* I hide behind no woman's skirts and I'll choke those words down your throat.

HELEN *(goes to* GLENISTER *and talks to him apart, beseechingly).* Can't you be a man and let the law take its course? You must win if your cause is just.

*(Chorus of "The Lousy Miner" is heard outside, as sung by passing miners on street below.* MCNAMARA *has resumed work at table, unheeding save for an occasional glance at* HELEN *and* GLENISTER. SIMMS *and* DEXTRY *are waiting and talking in dumb show.)*

GLENISTER. I hate the sight of his sneering eyes.

HELEN *(as the song is loudest, laying her hand on his arm).* Listen, that's the song they sang on the Yukon Queen—the song we heard together—remember?

GLENISTER. Yes, yes. You called me a savage that night, and I vowed I'd change. Well, I will. Don't be afraid—there'll be no trouble here.

(HELEN *smiles her thanks.* GLENISTER *addresses* DEXTRY *and*
SIMMS.)

Men, this is no time for fighting. We'll abide by the law. *(To* HELEN.*)*
Please bring in the Judge.

(*She is about to go into room when* SIMMS *comes down suddenly*
*and draws his six-shooter on* MCNAMARA.*)*

SIMMS. I'm goin' to cop him—just for luck. *(As he raises weapon,*
GLENISTER *takes it from his hand.)*

GLEN. None of that. I'll have no violence here.

SIMMS (*disgusted*). Well, of all the eighteen kinds of damn fools,
you're the kindest. I could of got him easy. (*Stamps up angrily.*)

(GLENISTER *places the revolver in his hip pocket.*)

MCNAMARA *(to* HELEN*)*. You'd better retire. Allow me.

*(He opens door.* HELEN *exits.)*

Now, I'll bring in the Judge. *(Exit, closing door after him.)*

DEX *(disgusted)*. Boy, when it comes to soft talk, you are sure the
Custard Kid. What have you got in your veins anyhow—it sure ain't
blood!

GLEN. Don't worry about my blood. It's all right and you can mark
a ticket on it.

DEX *(looking him over)*. Well, you're sure far from a well woman.
*(Paces about anxiously; goes up as* GLENISTER *talks.* SIMMS *has returned*
*to window.)*

GLEN. I'm sick of the fighting game, that's all. We'll abide by the
law. If only we knew what these people are up to, if we had a chance
to spy on them.

DEX. We've hired detectives but all they detected was that we're
broke—then they quit. *(He pulls back portiers of cubbyhole.)* There
don't seem to be any way of spying on this outfit. *(Goes into little*
*room.)* I wonder what they keep here. *(Turns and looks out; starts as*
*though an idea had struck him.)* Say, what's the matter with this?
*(Indicates by backward shake of head.)*

GLEN *(lays finger on lip, nods head affirmatively.* Sh-h-!

(MCNAMARA *and the* JUDGE *enter as he does so.* JUDGE *has papers*
*in his hand.* MCNAMARA *takes a seat at table.)*

JUDGE. I have looked over these papers, Mr. Glenister, and I can't
enforce them.

GLEN. Why not?

JUDGE. I do not believe they are genuine.

GLEN. Not genuine? They are certified copies of orders from your
superior court in San Francisco.

JUDGE *(slaps papers)*. These signatures may all be false. You may
have signed them yourself—

GLEN. What? You accuse me of forgery? Listen, we're all poor fellows, thanks to your robberies, but we're not quitters, and we'll not
give up!

DEX *(wound up and ready to unbosom his mind)*. Let me talk, boy!
There's been a whole lot of time wasted and a lot said, but I've got a

word for you and your French poodle. *(Indicates JUDGE.)* Glenister may be willin' to let you run his business, and being his pardner, I accedes graceful. But, brother, don't go pressin' yer luck, for some day I'll drop in here and bust you where you look the biggest—with this—*(Suddenly jerks out a huge Colt revolver.)*

(JUDGE *draws away frightened.* MCNAMARA *retains his position, nonchalant and smiling coolly.)*

MCNAMARA. Any time you feel like it.

(JUDGE *retreats cautiously and exits into his room.)*

DEX *(putting weapon back in its place)*. All right, son. You go ahead and wear this court in your pocket like a Waterbury watch, but if it don't keep correct time, I'm goin' to come in here and uncoil its mainspring. That's all. *(Starts to go.)*

(GLENISTER *is waiting. He has been seen peering into cubbyhole as if planning to risk hiding there).*

Come along, boy.

(GLENISTER *lays his finger on lip, reminds him of hiding place.)*

MCNAMARA *(rises, turns his back)*. I've enjoyed your call, gentlemen. *(Takes up newspaper.)* Drop in any time. It breaks the monotony.

(GLENISTER *steps into cubbyhole, unseen.* DEXTRY *exits banging door noisily. Enter* STRUVE, *whiskey glass in hand. He looks about cautiously.* MCNAMARA *is still reading newspaper.)*

STRUVE. Have they gone?

MCNAMARA *(puts down paper)*. Yes. Drunk again, eh? *(Paces back and forth.)* You're drinking too much of late—even for you—

STRUVE *(falls into chair)*. You're wrong. 'Tain't too much.

MCNAMARA. You can see, by what has just happened that we'll need every one of our faculties, mental and physical. You can't fight booze and keep in condition—nobody can.

STRUVE. Objection overruled. I'm like the motion to adjourn— always in order.

MCNAMARA *(throwing up hands in disgust)*. A drunkard for a District Attorney. An old woman on the bench—you're quitters, both of you.

STRUVE. The Judge is a quitter—sure thing. Why, he ain't half the man his niece is. There's a girl for you. Say, what'd we do without her, eh?

MCNAMARA *(pacing)*. Umph.

(GLENISTER's *face is seen at the cubbyhole's open window from time to time, taking in the scene.)*

STRUVE. Wasn't it funny how she worked that fool Glenister? Jove, it took nerve to bring in your instructions the way she did. *(He chuckles tipsily.)* Say, she looked good to me the first time I saw her. On the level, Mac, I'm crazy about that girl—and I'll have her too. *(Pounds table.* MCNAMARA *stops abruptly.)*

MCNAMARA *(looking dangerous, but cool)*. So—you mean to marry our clever young friend?

STRUVE *(chuckles)*. Marry—ha, ha. That's a good one. Look at that hair. *(Bows head forward.)* It's gray—not red. Do I look like the marrying kind? *(Lies back in chair, stretching his legs.)* Mac, I've got her where she'll have to come to me. I've made the proposition—she can't refuse.

> *(MCNAMARA, without a word, leaps at him, seizes him by the throat and forces his head and shoulders back upon table so that STRUVE's face is turned upward. They struggle. MCNAMARA places his knee against STRUVE's body and holds him down. STRUVE's hands flop, then he collapses. MCNAMARA throws him out on the floor, where he falls limp. GLENISTER's head is almost through the window in the excitement of watching. MCNAMARA sits, lights a cigar, then takes a glass of water from the table and dashes it over STRUVE's face. STRUVE stirs, groans, tries to rise, feels the back of his neck, stares up at MCNAMARA in terror.)*

MCNAMARA *(without removing cigar from his teeth)*. Get up!

STRUVE *(obeying)*. Why—did—you—do that?

MCNAMARA. Because I'm engaged to marry that girl. Now get out before I kill you.

> *(STRUVE gets his hat, shambles across and, with look of hatred, exits outer door.)*

Another enemy. I'll have to look after those papers—the damned fool.

> *(Goes to safe, opens it, kneels before it and searches among the contents. The sound of a book falling is heard in the cubbyhole. MCNAMARA whirls and draws his gun, listens an instant, then shakes his head.)*

Hold on, Alec, you're getting nervous, and that won't do.

> *(Instead of replacing the weapon, he naturally lays it on the bottom of the safe, just inside the safe door, and resumes his search. GLENISTER emerges from cubbyhole, reaching out his hand blindly. He is like a drunken man as he crosses, cat-like, without disturbing MCNAMARA.)*

GLEN *(after a pause; hoarsely)*. It's a lie.

> *(MCNAMARA whirls, leaps to his feet, and instinctively slams the safe door as though to guard the contents.)*

MCNAMARA. You.

GLEN. Tell me you said it to close that knave's mouth. *(Piteously.)* It's a lie, isn't it?

MCNAMARA. What are you talking about?

GLEN. I heard it all—I was hiding there—

MCNAMARA *(hisses)*. So you overheard. No, it's not a lie. She will be my wife.

GLEN. No—not that. I mean about the papers. She didn't know what message she carried. Tell me she's innocent. Tell me she didn't know and I'll forgive everything. Take her—and the Midas too—but don't kill my faith in her, for God's sake.

MCNAMARA *(deliberately)*. It is all true.

GLEN. No, no. She's not like the others. Why, her smile makes you glad and her eyes are as clear as a mountain pool. (MCNAMARA *stands unmoving.*) Don't say she knew—all the time?

MCNAMARA (*slowly*). She knew it all. And she will be Mrs. Mc-Namara.

GLEN. You're a liar. The scheme was yours, and you made her do your dirty work. Say it—say it quick.

(MCNAMARA *stands unflinching, letting the ugly facts sink in.*
GLENISTER *begins to doubt, staggers, then pulls himself together, and bursts into fit of laughter.*)

So, they're all alike, are they? Damn you. She's crooked like the rest? She fooled me with her pretty innocence. She played with me, and took the Midas for her lover? (*He covers his eyes for a moment.*) Oh God, no—not that. (*Then resolutely drawing himself up, he faces it.*) Well, she did it; you've got me where you wanted me, but I'm absolved from my promises—I'll be a fool no longer. (*Draws his weapon.*)

MCNAMARA (*retreating*). Hold on—you can't do that—I'm unarmed.

GLEN. You lie again. Take off your coat. (*He obeys.*) Turn around (*He does so.* GLEN *lowers his weapon.*) You can't escape me this way. I'll fight you fair. (GLENISTER *goes to safe, lays his gun on top of it, strips off his own coat.*)

MCNAMARA. What are you going to do?

GLEN. I'm going to choke those lies down your throat. Can you fight?

MCNAMARA (*stiffens*). I was never beaten.

GLEN. I'll break you with my naked hands.

(*They crouch and rush together, and wrestle about, overturning furniture. Quietly and stealthily they struggle, seeking an advantage.* MCNAMARA *reaches up and grasps* GLENISTER's *face with his right hand.* GLENISTER *releases his hold and leaps back, freeing himself.* MCNAMARA *rushes to safe and reaches for* GLENISTER's *gun which is in plain sight on top of safe.* GLENISTER *pursues him.* MCNAMARA *places right hand on gun. He is facing sofa, his body against it as* GLENISTER *seizes him about the waist, grasps* MCNAMARA's *right wrist in his right hand, thus pressing his breast to* MCNAMARA's *back.*)

Traitor!

(GLENISTER *slips his left hand up and over back of* MCNAMARA's *neck, thus securing the hammerlock hold.* MCNAMARA's *head is bowed forward. They struggle.* GLENISTER *gradually forces* MCNAMARA's *right arm back, down past his side, and across his back as in wrestling. At the word "Traitor," enter* HELEN *and* JUDGE. *They pause aghast.*)

HELEN (*to* JUDGE). Oh, stop them—stop them!

(JUDGE *hangs back, helpless.* HELEN *runs to open window and calls outside.*)

Help—help—quick!

*(She turns and watches. Sound of footsteps and enter* STRUVE, CHERRY, DEXTRY *and* SIMMS. *All except* STRUVE *stand and watch.* STRUVE *crosses to interfere.)*

STRUVE. What's the trouble?

JUDGE. It's murder.

*(*STRUVE *rushes forward towards the wrestlers, but* DEXTRY *steps out and seizes him and whirls him aside, so that* STRUVE *reels backwards, across table.)*

DEX. This is a fair fight, and you stay out of it.

CHERRY. It's the hammerlock—he'll break his arm.

*(*GLENISTER *forces* MCNAMARA's *arm upward, pauses, heaves his shoulder as though in a final burst of strength.* MCNAMARA *cries out loudly. Gun falls from his grasp. He sinks forward to his knees, then on his face.* GLENISTER *reels back, staggering.* CHERRY *runs forward, supporting him on left side. He throws arm about her, grabs her shoulder for support. He is exhausted, panting— stands gazing at* MCNAMARA. DEXTRY *is on his other side.)*

HELEN. He's killed him. *(She runs to* MCNAMARA, *kneels, lifts up his head.)*

GLEN *(hoarsely, as if to himself).* It's true—she loves him.

*(*STRUVE *is seen gloating over downfall of his rival.)*

JUDGE *(shaking his fist).* You've murdered him. You'll hang for this young man. *(He joins* HELEN *by* MCNAMARA's *side.)*

GLEN *(with a weary smile).* Oh, no, he's alive. But I beat the traitor. And I broke him with my naked hands!

HELEN *(to* GLENISTER *with loathing and reproach).* You did this—you monster—and after all your fair words and promises. You swore you would not fight again—you—you—savage!

GLEN *(swaying toward her—in despair).* You don't understand—girl. You don't understand.

HELEN. You tricked me! Oh, you wild beast!

GLEN. She says I tricked her—I. *(Laughs wildly.)* God! It's true—it's true—*(He catches at* DEXTRY's *shoulder with his right hand to steady himself.)* What did I tell you, Dex? They're all bad—all bad!

QUICK CURTAIN

# ACT THREE

## SCENE ONE

SCENE: *The Northern Lights Saloon, Christmas Eve. There is a bar, with bottles, glasses, etc. D.L. is a door to a private room. The outside door is fitted with heavy bar. Swinging doors lead to gambling room. A faro table with stools stands in the room, which is decorated with fir boughs in honor of the Christmas season.* DUCHESS, *dance hall hostess and proprietor of the Northern Lights Saloon, a most attractive woman of about forty, with dyed auburn hair and heavy makeup, is discovered behind bar, arranging it. Door is flung open; snow blows in. Enter* DEXTRY, *followed by* FLAPJACK SIMMS. *Both are clothed in fur parkas, fur caps, reindeer boots. They stamp snow from boots.*

DEX. Hi, Duchess—Merry Christmas!

SIMMS. Didn't think we'd make it.

DUCHESS. Welcome home! It's good to have you back.

DEX. Sixty miles since daylight. The dogs are dead.

*(They remove their mittens and caps, then pull off parkas, showing flannel shirts and belts underneath. Each wears a sheath knife.)*

SIMMS. Ought to be entitled to a drink fer Christmas, eh, Duchess?

DEX. I'm goin' to squander a lot of money on booze—I want it so bad, I'm gonna gargle it and snuff it up my nose.

DUCHESS. You sound like you hadn't had a drink for months—where've you been?

DEX. Up north to the new strike. Four hundred miles in ten days over heavy trails.

DUCHESS. Is it a good camp?

DEX. Well, I wouldn't say they could afford you yet, but you kin get two drinks for a dollar up there, tailor-made, too.

DUCHESS. Go on—what's a tailor-made drink?

DEX. Ha! Ha! A fit guaranteed with every drink.

DUCHESS. And how's the food?

DEX. Lots of it. Grub can be had for the asking. But they ask too much for it, so we came away. On the level, we ain't had a decent meal since we left this place. *(Turning and looking about.)* Show me the lunch counter and let my face bite it.

*(Enter* BRONCO KID *through swinging doors.)*

Hello, Kid.

KID *(shaking hands).* Glad to see you back, Dex. Hello, Flap.

DEX. What's new, Kid?

KID. Not much. McNamara still holds the Midas. And he's got the military to back him up and protect the gold.

DEX. Soldiers, eh? That sounds bad. What-a-ya hear from the boy?

KID. Glenister? I haven't seen him for weeks. They say he's up in the hills eating his heart out.

DEX. He'd be a durn sight better occupied operatin' on that human vermiform appendix McNamara.

KID. The miners have formed Vigilantes, I hear, and want to hang his whole outfit.

DEX. I'm with them. What-a-ya hear from Wheaton?

KID. Nothin', they say he's having trouble with the Frisco courts.

DEX. Rot this law talk. That's what sent me up the Artics. I couldn't stand to see the lawyers makin' a fool of Glenister.

DUCHESS. Here you go, boys, and Merry Christmas!

DEX *(raising his glass)*. The same to you, Duchess, and to you, Kid. Here's health to honest men—

*(He stops as he sees* MCNAMARA *and* STRUVE *enter in fur overcoats. They throw open their coats and seat themselves at table.)*

and damnation to lawyers.

*(STRUVE turns angrily.)*

MCNAMARA. Don't mind these fools.

DEX *(again)*. I say—damnation to lawyers.

*(They drink, glaring at* STRUVE *and* MCNAMARA.*)*

STRUVE. Bring us a drink, Duchess, whiskey.

*(DUCHESS starts toward them with bottle and glasses.* DEXTRY *strides after her, snatches bottle and throws it across room towards bar.* MCNAMARA *and* STRUVE *rise and confront* DEXTRY.*)*

DEX. I'm buyin' what booze is bein' bought in this place, and I don't recollect askin' you to join me.

STRUVE. This is a public place.

DEX. Well, I'm runnin' it private like tonight, see? And you can't drink here till I go.

MCNAMARA *(taking* STRUVE's *arm)*. Don't let's let him pick a fight. We'll go into the card room for our drink. *(To* DEXTRY.*)* Have your way, old man, I don't care to drink in your company. I'm particular myself.

*(Exit* MCNAMARA *and* STRUVE. DEXTRY *strides after them.)*

DEX *(as they go)*. Our day is comin' fast. *(Comes back to bar.)* Never you mind, men. It's mighty quiet around here for Christmas Eve. Wonder where everybody is?

DUCHESS *(looking about cautiously)*. Well, it's my idea the Vigilantes have decided to move tonight. Things have gotten worse and worse since you left, and the miners are getting desperate. They tell me there's not much hope from the Frisco courts, so they decided to take it in their own hands and clean out the whole lawyer crowd.

DEX. Well, they're finally gettin' some sense in their heads.

DUCHESS. Glenister's to lead them. Now don't say I said a word.

DEX. That's the best news I've heard since I came north last spring. The camp is cuttin' its wisdom teeth at last. Hey, Flap, do you believe in lynch law?

SIMMS. It's the king of outdoor sports.

DEX. Can you pull a rope?

SIMMS. Depends on who, where and what is attached tharto.

DEX. S'pose it's a lawyer.

SIMMS. Dex, we're wastin' time. Lead me to it.

DUCHESS. Sh-h-h. Take it easy. They've got spies out.

DEX. That's all right, I'm tongue-tied by nature, and as for my buddy here, well, he's the human hunting-case watch—never opens his face unless he's pressed. Come on, Flapjack.

*(They gather up their belongings.)*

So long, Duchess, keep your fingers crossed.

*(They exit. While they were talking, the* KID *seated himself at the faro table, shuffling cards idly.* DUCHESS *goes to him.)*

DUCHESS. Well, boss, It doesn't look like we're going to do much business tonight.

KID. It's early yet—maybe they'll be along later.

DUCHESS. Maybe so, but for all the good I'll do, I might as well be Helen Chester.

KID. Helen Chester? What do you mean?

DUCHESS. Aw, nothing much—just making a joke, I guess.

KID. Well, don't be making jokes about Helen Chester.

DUCHESS. And why not? She may kid some people, but take it from me, she's no better than the rest of us girls. *She's* out for the coin, too. She's out to marry McNamara—

KID. Stop it—what do you know about her?

DUCHESS. I know plenty. I'm tired of these hussies that masquerade as ladies. The whole town is on to her.

KID. On to her—what do you mean?

DUCHESS. Oh, can it, Kid. Didn't I come up on the Yukon Queen with her? Didn't I see them with my own eyes? She calls herself the Judge's niece, but she lived in Glenister's stateroom—

KID. Shut up, damn you—I say she's all right. She's a lady.

DUCHESS. What's the matter with you, Kid? She ain't no better than me. Ask Glenister. Everybody knows the story.

KID. It's a lie! If you mention her name again, I'll—

DUCHESS *(going to swinging doors)*. All right—all right—it's nothing to me. I didn't mean any harm, Kid.

*(She exits through swinging doors as* STRUVE *and* MCNAMARA *enter from gambling room.)*

STRUVE *(doggedly)*. I've got to have a drink, so you needn't preach, Mac. *(to* KID.) Here—give me some whiskey.

KID *(going behind bar. To* MCNAMARA). And yours?

MCNAMARA. Nothing for me.

*(KID serves whiskey to* STRUVE. *He returns to faro table while* STRUVE *and* MCNAMARA *converse.)*

STRUVE. Honest, Mac, I've got to steady my nerves a bit for this night's work.

MCNAMARA. Be careful.

STRUVE. The devil is in the young fellow lately. We'll have trouble arresting him.

MCNAMARA. Don't be alarmed. The deputies will shoot if he puts up a fight.

STRUVE. Well, they'll shoot all right. He's been a different man since he broke your arm.

MCNAMARA. I'll have his life for that. He has fought us at every turn. We've got to put him away.

STRUVE. I tell you there's no jail in the camp strong enough to hold him. The miners idolize him—they'd rise in a body—

MCNAMARA. Let them try. I'll hold him once I get him. I've got soldiers to fall back on now—if only he would resist. You understand?

STRUVE *(nodding).* Your scheme's all right. But you've got to get them first.

MCNAMARA. Oh, we'll get them. The warrants are out, the deputies are waiting. When I say the word, the net will close, and by daylight there won't be a Vigilante at large. *(Looks at watch.)* Come—it's getting late.

> (STRUVE *rises and goes to swinging doors, exits first.* KID *rises and comes to* MCNAMARA *about to follow* STRUVE.*)*

KID. Mr. McNamara—just a minute.

MCNAMARA. Well?

KID. I hear you are going to marry Miss Chester—the Judge's niece.

MCNAMARA *(curtly).* Well?

KID. Is it true? I want to know.

MCNAMARA. I don't see that it's any business of yours.

KID. No, I don't suppose you do. But I'm going to make it my business. Look here—(MCNAMARA *shows impatience.)* I'm going to trust you with a secret, because I know you're square with—my—sister.

MCNAMARA. You? You are her brother?

KID. Yes. I'm Drury Chester, but nobody up here knows me by that name. (MCNAMARA *frowns.)* Oh, you needn't look so disgusted. I know what I am, and I don't want her to know any more than you do that her brother is the Bronco Kid—

MCNAMARA. Well, what do you want?

KID. I want you to protect her. Take her away from here. I won't stand to hear her name dragged in the dirt—

MCNAMARA *(more interested).* So—you've heard the story, too?

KID. You mean—Glenister? It isn't true—say it isn't true.

MCNAMARA. She is your sister, and will be my wife. How could you believe it?

KID *(joyously).* It's a lie. I knew it couldn't be true. *(Shakes* MCNAMARA*'s hand.)*

MCNAMARA *(with cunning).* Yes, and I'll choke the lie down his throat some day. The brute is in love with your sister, and he knows I will make her my wife.

KID *(fiercely, under his breath, clenching his fists).* Glenister!

> *(At that moment, outer door opens and* GLENISTER *enters. He is*

*disheveled and desperate-looking. He strides in, sees* McNAMARA
*and halts.* McNAMARA *turns to* KID *and laughs knowingly, exits
quickly.* GLENISTER *goes to table and throws himself heavily into
chair.* KID *glares at him, moves to him, slips his right hand into
his coat pocket in which he has revolver.)*
Turn around!

GLEN *(turning slowly and looking at him in wonder).* What's the
matter with you, Bronco? What do you want?

KID. That's a hell of a question. I want you—and I've got you. *(Lifts
revolver in his pocket, as though to fire. Revolver is not drawn from
pocket and action is slight, but plain.)*

GLEN. Hold on. I'm not armed. You're no assassin, Bronco. You
might shoot a crook, but I've not harmed you.

　　*(*GLENISTER *remains rigid in his chair, looking at* KID *unflinch-
　　ingly.* KID *lowers his hand a bit, still in his pocket.)*

KID *(removing hand from pocket).* No—I guess not. But you'll have
to fight, you dog.

*Glenister: "Hold on. I'm not armed. You're no assassin, Bronco. You might
shoot a crook, but I've not harmed you." The Bronco Kid's gun found its way out
of his pocket in the 1959 production.* Left to right: *Cherry (Marilyn Sue Garrett);
the Bronco Kid (Steve Callahan); Duchess (Mina Zenor); Roy Glenister (Tom
Paxton).*

GLEN. All right—I don't know what this is all about, but I'll fight whenever I'm heeled right.

KID. I used to be a gentleman, and I haven't lost it all, I guess. Next time I won't wait.

(*He strides up and out swinging doors as* DUCHESS *enters and goes behind bar.*)

GLEN (*pounding table with glass left by* STRUVE *and calling loudly*). Hey—bring me whiskey—bring it quick and fast and often. I'm as dry as Death Valley in August.

(*Enter* CHERRY *through swinging doors. She looks about quickly, then, seeing* GLENISTER, *hurries to him.*)

CHERRY. Oh Roy, I've been hunting everywhere for you! (*Putting her hand on his.*) Boy, you must get out of here.

GLEN. Get out? What for?

CHERRY. There's a scheme of some kind to arrest you. I overheard—

GLEN (*to* DUCHESS). Where's my drink?

DUCHESS. Right here, Mister.

GLEN. Well, let them try to take me. They'll have a job for grown men.

(*Raises glass to his lips.* CHERRY *seizes it, and spills it on the floor.*

GLENISTER *half rises, grasps her wrist.*)

What the devil! That's my drink!

CHERRY. It's whiskey, boy, and you don't drink the stuff.

GLEN. Of course, it's whiskey. (*To* DUCHESS.) Bring me another, quick. I'm burning inside like a sawdust pile.

CHERRY. What ails, you, Roy? Booze is only fit for fools and brawlers. You've been thinking about that girl again.

GLEN. What of it? (DUCHESS *brings another drink.*) I'm thirsty—that's all.

CHERRY. McNamara never drank a drop in his life.

GLEN (*checking glass half-way to his lips*). Do you want me to copy from him?

CHERRY. Not copy, but profit. If you're not strong enough to master your own throat, you're not strong enough to beat a man who has mastered his.

(*Pianist begins to play "The Lousy Miner."* GLENISTER *puts down glass, but holds onto it. Springs to his feet, dashes glass to floor.*)

GLEN (*shouting*). Stop that damned music! I can't go anywhere, but I hear that song. It drives me mad!

(*Music stops.* GLENISTER *sits again, burying his head in his hands.*)

CHERRY. Why don't you forget that woman? Can't you see she's hand-in-glove with the gang? Oh, she's smooth, all right, with all her innocence, but she's wrong, wrong!

GLEN. Drop it, I tell you. And let me alone.

CHERRY (*rising, with fury of woman scorned*). Very well—I've needed this to show me where I stand. (*She goes to swinging doors, halts, looks back a moment, then exits furiously.*)

DUCHESS (*cautiously*). Well—I hear it's going to be a big night—

GLEN. What do you mean?

DUCHESS. The news is that McNamara plans to break the Vigilantes tonight. Fifty deputies, and the boys are looking for a fight.

GLEN. Where did you hear that?

DUCHESS. Seems a strange girl came to Dextry and warned him.

GLEN. A girl—who?

DUCHESS. They don't know—it was dark and she wouldn't give her name. They're to meet on the sand spit in half an hour, and every man's to arm himself. The boys asked me to pass the word along to you.

GLEN. I'll be there. So, it's a fight at last. I'll lead the Vigilantes to the Midas and take what belongs to us. (*Looks at his watch.*) Half an hour, did you say? I've a notion to try the cards to pass the time. (*Rises.*)

DUCHESS. Good luck to you, Mr. Glenister. But don't fail them. They're counting on you.

GLEN. Never fear. If luck is with me tonight, I'll win back the Midas. I'll be there.

(*As* GLENISTER *goes, enter* CHERRY *and* BRONCO KID *through swinging doors.* KID *looks at* GLENISTER *with hatred.* GLENISTER *laughs unconcernedly.*)

You'll have your chance, Bronco, don't be impatient.

(*Exit through swinging doors.* KID *drops cigar, stamps heel on it. He sits at faro table, takes out tobacco pouch and cigarette papers.* DUCHESS *is watching over swinging doors, absorbed in game inside.*)

KID. I'll down him yet, the hound.

CHERRY. Give me the "makings".

KID. I didn't know you smoked. (*Hands her pouch and papers.*)

CHERRY. I don't, but tonight I'm in for anything. I'm a fool—a fool! (*Lights cigarette, hands pouch and papers back to* KID.) I'll brand that chalk-faced hussy for what she is—a lady!

KID (*grimly*). She is a lady.

CHERRY. Don't tell me you love the girl, too? (*Laughs harshly.*) So—Glenister and McNamara have another rival. The woman's a wizard!

(KID *paces away from her; she crushes cigarette viciously and throws it away.*)

I could—I could kill him for what he said.

(KID *starts at her words and eyes her cunningly, unobserved by her.*)

DUCHESS (*turning from swinging doors excitedly*). Say, Bronco, you'd better look out your games, or Roy Glenister's gonna own your dump.

KID. What's the matter? Is he gambling?

DUCHESS (*as shouts are heard from gambling room*). He broke the crap game—now he's playing blackjack.

(*More shouts are heard.*)

Listen to that!

(CHERRY *runs up and looks through swinging doors.* KID *looks over her shoulder,* DUCHESS *behind them.*)

He broke the blackjack. What did I tell you? (*She exits through swinging doors.*)

CHERRY. There he goes. He's lost that one—his luck has changed.

KID (*takes her shoulder, turns her toward him*). Cherry—did you mean what you said about Glenister?

CHERRY. What?

KID. That you could—kill him? (CHERRY *flinches;* KID *sneers.*) Pah, I thought so. You love that man even after he's treated you like a dog.

CHERRY. I do not—I hate him. I'd ruin him if I could.

KID. Then listen to me. There's no time to lose. I'll get him into a faro game, open a flyer—lift the limit—you've got to help me.

CHERRY. You mean—deal a crooked bank?

KID. Yes, and you must keep cases. Do you know my signals?

CHERRY (*wavering*). Yes, yes, but it's dangerous, Kid. I've seen him mad and—

KID. Come. Don't be a fool. He won't see anything. (*Busy at faro table,* KID *takes revolver from gun drawer, cocks it, spins the cylinder, and places it in drawer of table.*) It's more than money I'm playing for tonight. This will be a cinch. Come, Cherry, give me the phony box.

(CHERRY *goes behind bar, comes back with faro box, takes box from* KID *and replaces it behind bar.*)

Don't lose your nerve, girl. Give me five minutes and I'll bring him in.

(*Exits through swinging doors.* CHERRY *looks after him. More shouts are heard from gambling room. Outer door opens, enter* HELEN. *She looks frightened, yet determined.* CHERRY *feels the cold air, turns to see who has entered. She stares as though she cannot believe her eyes.*)

CHERRY. What do you want?

HELEN. I—I want to see Mr. Glenister. You know him.

CHERRY (*harshly*). Oh, yes, I know him, and I know you, too. He's in good company right at present and I want to talk to you. (HELEN *turns away from her.*) Oh, don't be afraid. I know you are committing an unpardonable sin by talking to me—but I'll warn you, that bad as I am, I'm better than you, for I'm loyal to those that like me, and I don't betray my friends.

HELEN. I don't pretend to understand you.

CHERRY. Oh, yes, you do. I admire the way you've done your dirty work, but when you assume these scandalized, super-virtuous airs it offends me.

HELEN (*turning to* CHERRY). Why do you talk to me like this? I haven't done anything to you.

CHERRY. Oh, haven't you? I've done bad things; I've been forced into them—but I never deliberately wrecked a man's life just for his money.

HELEN. What do you mean by saying that I have betrayed my friends and wrecked anybody's life?

CHERRY. Well, Miss Helen Chester. I don't believe a word you've said, and I'll tell you nothing. So—your gang wants you to spy, do they?

HELEN. No, no, no. Can't you see? All I want is the truth of this thing.

CHERRY. Then go to Struve and get it. Get him to tell you. I won't. You've fooled better men—now see what you can do with him.

*(She exits through swinging doors.* HELEN *stands a moment, dazed; shouts are heard. Enter* STRUVE, *who tipsily sits at table. He sees* HELEN, *blinks and rubs his eyes. He stares at her; she stares back at him like a bird caught in a snare.)*

STRUVE *(bending forward and peering at her)*. Ha-ha, my pretty one. Caught, eh? The immaculate niece of Judge Stillman in a gambling den. Come—what's your game?

HELEN. I want those papers.

STRUVE. I know you do. Well?

HELEN. I want them at once—yes, at once.

STRUVE *(laughing unpleasantly)*. This is not the time for that kind of talk. There's a riot in the air tonight, and I'm busy. Come to my office tomorrow.

HELEN. Tomorrow may be too late. I want them now—tonight.

STRUVE *(meditating a moment)*. Then tonight it shall be. I'll shirk the fight. I'm in no humor for it, now that I've seen you. Let's see. You know the Sign of the Sled. It's a romantic little roadhouse on the Snake River trail. I'll meet you there in an hour.

HELEN. But the papers?

STRUVE. I'll have them with me. *(Rising and going.)*

HELEN. Very well—in an hour. I won't fail you.

STRUVE. You'd better not—my beauty. *(Exit.)*

HELEN. I must risk it. The blood of those men will be on me, if I don't stop this tragedy. I must have the proof. *(Pacing.)* Oh, he's there, but I can't be seen by all those people. They're coming this way. Where can I hide?

*(She exits.* CHERRY, KID, GLENISTER *enter.)*

GLEN. Hurry up. I want quick action for I've got only ten minutes to play.

KID. Close the door, Duchess. Mr. Glenister, this game is for blood. One of us is going broke.

GLEN. Go ahead, turn the cards. My luck has changed. Two hundred on the "little figure." Again, all right, now you have it all. Ten thousand on the Ace, coppered.

KID. Are you all set?

GLEN. Turn the cards. Broke.

KID. Now, are you satisfied?

GLEN. No, I'm not. Let me see that box.

KID. Let go; you've lost.

GLEN. Let me see it. I thought as much. This is a crooked box.

KID. You lie.

GLEN. You crooked polecat, give me back my money.

DUCHESS. Stop! Both of you! You've got to join the Vigilantes; you've promised.

GLEN. All right, but I'll be back, Bronco, and you'd better be prepared! *(Exit.)*

CHERRY. You gone crazy?

*(Enter HELEN, quietly.)*

KID. I knew you'd never do it; now get out! Follow him, your hero may need your skirts again tonight to save his yellow skin!

HELEN. Drury!

KID. My God! Helen! My little sister! Here!

HELEN. Oh, how could you hide away from me so long? I've hunted everywhere.

KID. I couldn't let you know. *(Hangs his head.)* Don't you see what I am? I'm not fit to speak to you.

HELEN. You are my brother—that is enough.

KID *(rising, suddenly recollécting)*. But what brings you to this dive—you?

HELEN. Drury—I must talk to Roy Glenister—you must take me to him.

KID. I'd sooner take you to hell.

*(Door opens suddenly and enter hurriedly MCNAMARA and the JUDGE. MCNAMARA bars the door after him.)*

MCNAMARA *(seeing HELEN)*, You here? *(Then to KID.)* The Vigilantes are after us. We've been betrayed.

JUDGE. They're on our heels. They saw us come in; I know they did.

*(HELEN stands by and tries to comfort him. MCNAMARA paces and glares at HELEN.)*

KID. What's happened?

MCNAMARA. Treachery—that's what! We raided the Vigilantes, but they were armed and waiting. They routed our men. Now some of them are in pursuit, and it means lynching, if we're caught. *(Stops pacing, pointedly.)* Somebody warned those men—

HELEN. I did.

*(JUDGE pushes her from him. MCNAMARA points at her.)*

MCNAMARA. You warned them.

*(The JUDGE falls into a chair, speechless and helpless.)*

HELEN. Yes, I warned them.

MCNAMARA. You did this for the man who has robbed you of your good name. You love him.

HELEN. No—I love no man. He trusted me and would have been my friend, but for you and your treachery. God knows what terrible wrong you have done him and his people. *(Back to table.)* I—I couldn't think that my own kin would deceive me and use me to

spoil and ruin honest men. Oh, I did your dastardly work well—you
(*To* JUDGE.) who were as a father to me—you (*To* MCNAMARA.) who
would have made me your wife. But I see the truth at last, and I shall
have proof before long. (*A sob catches her throat.*) I overheard your
intrigues tonight with Struve at the house—you didn't know I was
listening. It was torture, but it made a woman out of me. (*Sits on
stool.*) God help any girl who has to make the fight I made this night.
(*She covers her face with her hands.*)

 (*There is a pause, while* KID *comes to her and stands protectingly.
A loud knock on door.*)

MCNAMARA. There they are! You have won. There's no escape.

JUDGE (*in terror*). They will kill us. Oh, why did I come to this land?

HELEN (*moved by her uncle's plight*). Oh, Drury.

 (*Another double knock, someone tries door, shaking it.*)

—Do something. I never thought this would happen.

KID. There's one chance. They must not find you here—they'd
snatch you like wolves. (*Going to door.*) Get in here, quick.

 (*Another knock and voice.*)

VOICE. Open up, or we'll break in.

KID. Who's there? (*To* HELEN *and the others.*) Quick—quick.

 (HELEN *and* MCNAMARA *help* JUDGE *into room, close the door.* KID
*unbars door. It is flung open and* DEXTRY, GLENISTER *and* SIMMS
*enter.* SIMMS *goes to swinging doors and looks over.* GLENISTER
*carries a large Colt revolver.* KID *falls back.*)

KID. What do you want?

GLEN. We want McNamara and the Judge. Where are they?

KID (*carelessly*). I don't know. I haven't seen them.

GLEN. I've had enough trouble with you for tonight. Don't lie to me
again. We know they are here.

 (CHERRY *enters unobserved and stands observing scene.*)
Where does that door lead?

KID. It's only a card room—there's nobody there.

GLEN. I'll see for myself—out of my way.

 (KID *stands barring door.*)

KID. You can't go in there.

GLEN. And why not?

KID. Well—there's a woman there—she's hiding.

GLEN. We'll see about that.

KID. Stand back, I say. You're a hell of an outfit to make war on
women. I tell you, you can't see her, she's a decent girl.

GLEN. A decent girl in this dive—bah! That won't go. Tell her to
come out.

 (KID *makes grab for his gun.* GLENISTER *raises revolver and covers
him.*)

KID. You've got to listen to me—the girl is my sister—she came
here to see me tonight.

 (GLENISTER *hesitates.*)

DEX *(stepping in)*. She may be your sister, kid, but she ain't workin' at it.

GLEN. Come on, he's lying. We've run them down.

*(DEXTRY and SIMMS pull KID aside, holding him at gunpoint. GLENISTER covers door.)*

Come out with your hands up, McNamara—come out—quick!

*(Door opens slowly and HELEN enters. She closes door behind her. GLENISTER lowers his gun, dumbfounded.)*

GLEN. You!

HELEN. I heard all you said. You asked to see me—well, here I am.

GLEN. He called you his sister—this gambler. Is this a trick?

HELEN. No, it is the truth. That man is my brother—the brother I told you I was searching for.

GLEN *(looking from HELEN to KID)*. Forgive me. I didn't know. I thought he lied.

HELEN. I overheard a plot to arrest you all. I wanted to warn you; I searched everywhere and that's how I came to be here.

DEX. I might have known. It was you that came to me in the dark last night?

HELEN. Yes, and then I learned that Mr. Glenister was here, and that's how I found the brother I haven't seen since I was a little girl.

GLEN. Boys, you have heard what Miss Chester says. Do you doubt her?

DEX and SIMMS. No—no—

SIMMS. But they're here somewhere—we saw them come into this building—

DEX *(turning on him)*. We ain't here to make a gal betray her own blood. Now is that any way to talk? If we can't find them man's style, we won't be beholden to a woman. Besides, it's my idee they come through here and was on their way out to the Midas with their soldiers.

GLEN. Dextry's right, Flap. Come—let's go to the Midas.

*(CHERRY steps out.)*

CHERRY. Oh, you blind fools—you saw those men come in with your own eyes, and yet you let some sweet talk from a pretty, innocent face turn you back. She's protecting them. *(Points to door.)* The hussy lies to save her lover!

KID *(whispers hoarsely)*. That ends it.

CHERRY. Don't stand there! Go in and drag them out.

SIMMS. Cherry wouldn't fool us, Roy. *(Flinging the rope with hangman's noose from his shoulder.)* Here's their medicine. Let's bring 'em to it.

GLEN *(to HELEN)*. Is this true? Are they in there? My God, have you lied to me again?

HELEN *(staring at rope with horror)*. No—they are not—there.

*(DEXTRY and SIMMS move toward door.)*

GLEN. Wait—I'm leader here.

*(They fall back.* HELEN *looks at him piteously, sways toward him. He catches and supports her.)*

HELEN *(whispering desperately).* Yes, yes, they're in there. I lied—I had to. But you musn't—no—no—not if you love me.

GLEN. Fooled again.

*(*HELEN *half straightens up. He releases her. She leans against table, her face full of terror, her lips making signs of muttering, "No-no-no." This scene takes but a moment while* GLENISTER *is supporting* HELEN *until she recovers, and does not arouse suspicion.)*

GLEN. I'm this man's enemy. I'll bring him out.

*(He pauses an instant with hand on door and looks at* HELEN. *He squares his shoulders, opens door, steps within. The men half raise their rifles.* GLEN *reappears, slams the door, gives* HELEN *a swift look. He raises his arm and points at* CHERRY.)

GLEN. Boys, I believe that woman is in on the game. She's playing for time to let them escape. The room is empty.

*(Men turn on* CHERRY.)

Go—and be glad you're a woman, for if you were a man, you would answer to me for that lie!

*(*CHERRY *is stunned, gives* GLENISTER *unbelieving look, exits.)*

DEX. Hell, we're wastin' time. They'll get away from us yet. Pick up your death rattle, Flapjack. I'm bound for the Midas.

*(*SIMMS *takes up rope. They exit.)*

HELEN. I—I don't know what to say. I can never make amends for all you have done for us.

GLEN. For us. Do you think I sacrificed my honor—betrayed my friends—killed my last hope—for us? *(Flinging door wide open.)* Come out—don't be afraid.

*(*MCNAMARA *comes out holding up the tottering* JUDGE.)

*(To* HELEN, *roughly.)* No. You are not of my people, and don't understand. You called me a savage and you were right, but I would not change places with that man *(Pointing to* MCNAMARA.) for all the wealth of the Midas. You've taken my gold, you've robbed me of the love and respect of my comrades, you've cheated me out of all that makes life sweet; but there's one thing you gave me and you can't take away. I've found myself. I am no longer a savage. I am a man. *(He flings out door.)*

*(*HELEN *stretches her arms after him,* BRONCO *catches her.)*

**CURTAIN**

## SCENE TWO

SCENE: *The Midas, Christmas morning at daybreak. The Midas lies in a gap, with mountains rising on each side. When curtain rises, the stage is dark except for the glow of campfire by which* DEXTRY *is keeping watch. The curtain rises to music of "The Lousy Miner." Music ceases and* DEXTRY *is heard singing or whistling a snatch of the song. While he is doing so, enter* CHERRY, *panting and agitated.)*

DEX *(stopping suddenly, rising and pointing gun at* CHERRY*).* Hold on, there.

CHERRY. Is that you, Dex? It's Cherry.

DEX. Well, of all the—what do you want now?

CHERRY. Oh, it's been such a terrible night. McNamara's men came down from the mine last night, and the whole town is awake over the riot. They say you killed ten men in the fight? Is that true?

DEX. I don't know how many they lost, but as for us, well, we ain't got so much as a cold sore amongst us.

CHERRY. Didn't they make any resistance?

DEX. Naw! Have you seen McNamara—we ain't found him yet.

CHERRY. Yes, he's in town and has called out the troops and you'll all be shot.

DEX. Won't that be handy?

CHERRY. But Roy—has he come back? Where is he?

DEX. Somebody called him out o' here about midnight; said he was goin' to the Sign of the Sled. Some of the boys thought he'd got cold feet, but he said there was a woman in danger.

CHERRY. Oh, Dex, it was I who called him out last night.

DEX. Eh? How's that?

CHERRY. Helen Chester—

DEX. What? I thought you was—

CHERRY. Listen, Dex. She came to me last night and told me she was going to meet Struve at the Sign of the Sled. She begged me to help her.

DEX. The Sign of the Sled? Why, it belongs to Struve—surely she hasn't—

CHERRY. Yes. She went to save Roy and the rest of you. To get some papers that incriminate the whole gang.

DEX. Struve—alone with Struve—out there.

CHERRY. She doesn't know the game she's up against with Struve. I tried to warn her, but she wouldn't listen. Look, Dex, I lied and schemed against that girl, but that's all over now. I'm sick of deceit. *(Smiles piteously.)* I guess there's some little streak of good in me somewhere—

DEX. It's more than a streak, Cherry—you're my kind of people.

CHERRY. I don't want to—that is—I want to be her kind—his kind.

DEX. So you told the boy, and he rode off to find her?

CHERRY. And I told the Bronco Kid, too—he's her brother—
DEX. Yes, I know.
CHERRY. I wish to God I knew she was safe—and Glenister—
DEX (*listening*). Sh—somebody comin' up the gulch. Get out of sight, quick.
(*She disappears up over the bluff. Enter* GLENISTER, *listless and tired out.*)
GLEN. That you, Dex?
DEX. Yes, boy.
GLEN. What news?
DEX. McNamara's called out the soldiers.
(GLEN *starts, shakes head.*)
Ain't that hell?
GLEN. Dex, this is no victory. We're worse off now than we were before.
DEX. We've made a good fight, anyhow, whether we win or lose.
GLEN (*moodily*). My fight is made and won.
DEX. Speak out, Roy. What do you mean?
GLEN. My hardest battle has nothing to do with the Midas. I fought and conquered myself.
DEX. Awful cold marnin' for philosophy.
GLEN (*earnestly*). I mean I was a savage, Dex, just like you, till I met Helen Chester.
DEX. A savage, eh? Why, I ain't no savage. I'm gentle and forgivin' as a sheep.
GLEN. I've learned that the right thing is usually the hardest to do.
DEX. What good does it do you? She'll marry that big moose, McNamara.
GLEN. I know. That's what rankles me, for he's no more worthy of her than I am. But she'll do the right thing, depend on it. Why, do you know what she did this very night?
DEX. Gimme three guesses?
GLEN. She went with Struve, to the Sign of the Sled, to get proof that would save the day for us. That's why I left—and got there in time to find Struve whimpering that the Kid had shot him and carried off Helen.
DEX. Yeah—Cherry was here and told me.
GLEN. Poor Cherry.
DEX (*impatient*). Well, all this is gettin' us nowhere. I wish Bill Wheaton was here, but there's not much hope now that navigation is closed. Still—he swore he'd return with the backing of Federal Courts, if he had to crawl on his hands and knees. He may come in over the ice with a dog team.
GLEN. I've little hope of that, even if the Federal Court should support us.
(*Enter quietly behind them,* OFFICER, MCNAMARA *and* STILLMAN.)
OFFICER. Halt—hands up!
(*Both men obey.*)

JUDGE *(pointing to* GLENISTER*)*. Arrest that man, quick. Don't let him go.

DEX *(to* GLENISTER*)*. It's no use, boy. They've got us.

MCNAMARA *(laughing disagreeably)*. Yes, we've got you, and you'll pay the price this time.

GLEN. All right—I'm the one he's after. *(Glares at* MCNAMARA.*)* But I don't care. I broke him—I broke him with my naked hands.

MCNAMARA *(in frenzy of rage)*. Take that man away. Quick, I tell you, before I injure him. The law is in our hands and I'll make him answer.

*(Enter* FLAPJACK SIMMS *with shotgun in one hand, sheaf of papers in the other, which he waves aloft.)*

SIMMS. Guess that's where you got another think comin'—it ain't in your hands, it's in mine! See here, Roy, Wheaton just come in to town with these!

DEX. Well, spill it—what do they say?

SIMMS. How would I know—I ain't never had no use for readin', but Bill Wheaton says this is it.

*(*GLENISTER *looks them over.)*

Anyway, Wheaton says we kin give them their walkin' papers, so let's start 'em walkin'. *(He raises shotgun toward* MCNAMARA.*)*

DEX. Hold on, we got to be sure—

GLEN. God bless Wheaton! He's done it—removed Stillman and McNamara from office and the Midas is ours! There's no more court in Alaska till Washington sends men to set it up! *(Hands papers to* OFFICER.*)* You've played a shrewd game, with your senators, your politics and your pulls, but they're not all crooked, and you've played yourself out now. We'll make you dance for the mines you've gutted and the men you've robbed! *(To* OFFICER.*)* Serve those warrants!

OFFICER. They're all in order. Instructions from Washington court of appeals giving back the mines to these men. The case has been taken from your jurisdiction, Judge Stillman.

*(The* JUDGE *staggers and sinks to a seat.* MCNAMARA *stands upright and defiant.)*

MCNAMARA. You think I'll go to prison, do you? Well, I won't. I've nothing to answer for and no one can prove a thing. The Judge has been responsible for it all.

*(He exits, unbeaten and defiant; the* JUDGE *shambles after him, followed by* OFFICER.*)*

DEX *(shaking hands with* GLENISTER*)*. Well, boy, I never would'a believed it.

GLEN. It was a close shave, old man. They had us over the ropes.

DEX *(to* SIMMS*)*. Well, Flap, looks like we wuz wrong—Wheaton's one law sharp that's on the level—

SIMMS. Blamed, if he ain't. He says they'll go to jail for a little while—I say it's too good for 'em—we should'a had a lynchin'—

DEX. Lay off—we got our mine back—

FLAP. Well—guess I'll get back to town, just in case them miners feels different than you. I'd hate to miss the party *(Exit.)*

(GLENISTER *and* DEXTRY *are left alone.* CHERRY *has been silent and an unobserved spectator back on the bluff.* GLENISTER *sits and leans his head on hands, disconsolate.)*

DEX. Cheer up, boy, you'd think you were the loser. Don't you realize we got the old mine back? Buck up, pal, spring has come.

GLEN. Won? What do you know about it, Dex? The Midas—the world—I've lost—I've lost everything—with her. Now go away, old man, I want to be alone a bit.

(DEXTRY *looks at him with pity, shakes his head and mounts bluff and disappears.* CHERRY *comes down and stands before* GLENIS-TER.)

CHERRY *(gently)*. Well, boy, so it's over at last.

GLEN *(looking up wearily)*. Yes, it's all over, little girl.

CHERRY. Well—you don't need my congratulations—you know all I'd like to say. How does it feel to be a winner?

GLEN. I don't know. I've lost.

CHERRY. Lost what?

GLEN. Everything—except the gold mine.

CHERRY. Everything except?—You mean Helen—you mean you have asked her and she won't have you?—I'm sorry. *(She is struggling hard to keep her voice steady and looking away.* GLENISTER *looks up quickly, grasps her hand, in gratitude.)* I've suffered for the part I played, boy. It came to me all at once—what I was—and I—tried to make reparation. Oh, I want to be good—good all through. You believe me, don't you?

GLEN. Yes, yes, Cherry, of course I do.

CHERRY. I wish I had the power to make her love you—

GLEN. She's not for me, though I'll always love her. I've got my wish though. I know what love is—now that it's too late.

CHERRY *(with a half sob)*. Boy—don't—

GLEN *(rising and throwing off his mood)*. Oh, but I am selfish. What about you? Where will you go?

CHERRY. I don't know. It doesn't really matter now—the world is a large place *(Shudders.)* and very cold, for a woman.

GLEN. I'll see you sometimes, won't I?

CHERRY *(very gently)*. No, boy— I don't think so.

GLEN *(taking her two hands in his and kissing them)*. God bless you, Cherry, and keep you safe.

(CHERRY *exits. Enter* HELEN *and the* KID. GLENISTER *whirls sharply as if on the defensive.)*

KID *(throwing up arms in gesture of restraint)*. Glenister! Wait, wait, old man. I'm here as a friend.

GLEN. I know—you're her brother. We have no further quarrel.

HELEN. He wouldn't let me come alone and I had to see you at once.

GLEN. Had to see me—?

KID. I tried to keep her from coming, but she said it was the square thing to do. She learned that those documents told the whole story. That's why she went with him last night.

GLEN. Oh, it wasn't worth it. How could you?

KID. It seems Wheaton has done the work. The Judge and McNamara have been arrested. They will go to jail—

GLEN *(bitterly)*. Yes, for six months, perhaps, but what does that amount to? There never was a bolder crime consummated nor one more unjust. They robbed a realm and pillaged its people. They defiled a court and made Justice a wanton. They jailed good men and sent others to ruin. And for this they are to suffer—what? Six months? *(Laughs bitterly.)*

HELEN *(taking packet of papers from her bosom)*. This will tell the whole wretched story. *(Hands him packet.)* I find it hard to betray my uncle, but this proof is yours by right.

GLEN *(seizing packet eagerly and gazing at it triumphantly)*. Do you mean that? Do you mean the proof is here to convict them? *(HELEN nods silently; GLENISTER pauses.)* And you are giving it to me because you think it is your duty?

HELEN. I have no choice. But I also must beg a little mercy for my uncle who is an old man. This will kill him.

*(GLENISTER walks away a few paces, in deep agitation, then returns.)*

GLEN. You ask this for your uncle, but what of—what of the other? You must know that if one goes free, so will they both; they can't be separated. You ask this of me—a man of the mountains—a North man? To put aside my vengeance?

*(HELEN turns her face, hangs her head, traces pattern in the snow with her boot, refusing to look at GLEN who is gazing at her.)*

KID. It's almost too much to ask. But don't you think the work is done?

GLEN. I know—I know.

HELEN *(turns to GLEN protestingly)*. It is only fair that you should know—

GLEN *(stopping her)*. Please don't—you've said enough. *(Pause as he tries to master himself.)* I understand. *(He slips rubber band from the packet, tears the papers across and across into small bits, tosses them away.)* You're right. The work is done—and now—goodbye.

*(He passes his hand across his eyes, turns without looking at them and mounts the bluff in great dejection, stands with his back to them, as KID leads HELEN off sobbing, her face in her hands. Then GLENISTER half turns, stretches out his arms.)*

So, this is the end, and I gave him to her with these hands. *(He holds out hands and looks at them dazedly.)*

*(Enter DEXTRY and SIMMS from bluff.)*

DEX. Say, but you're the talk of the town. The boys want you to run for Congress if we ever get admitted as a state.

SIMMS. Speakin' of laws, goes to show me that this yere country is too blamed civilized for a white man. It don't look like there would be anything doin' fit to interest a growed-up person, for a long while. I'm goin' west.

GLEN. West? Why, you can throw a stone into the Bering Strait from here. You're so far west now you're going east.

SIMMS. The world's round. There's a schooner outfittin' for Sibeery in the spring—two years cruise. Me and Dex is figgerin' on gettin' out towards the frontier for a spell.

GLEN. Dex?

DEX. Sure. I'm gettin' all cramped up hereabouts. They're goin' to pave Front Street this summer, and there's a shoe-shinin' parlor opened up. Better come along, Roy. (*He watches the effect of his words on* GLENISTER, *fondly.*)

GLEN (*considers and seems half-inclined to yield*). That's true—I'll think it over.

DEX. Goodbye, boy. (*Shakes hands with* GLENISTER.)

SIMMS (*crossing to* GLENISTER). Goodbye, Roy. (*Shakes hands.*)

GLEN. Goodbye, Flap.

(DEXTRY *and* SIMMS *go to exit D.R. Both turn and "sniff." Exit.*

*Enter* HELEN. *She hesitates, then goes toward* GLENISTER.)

HELEN. I—I couldn't leave without thanking you—I had to come back—(*She is much confused.*) It was a noble thing you did just now. I am glad and proud.

GLEN. You've seen me at my worst, when I'd fought and lost, when I'd grown desperate with defeat!

HELEN. I think I know—and that's why I've come.

GLEN. Stop! Helen, since knowing you I have prayed to be worthy of the good in you, and that you might have patience to reach the good in me—but it's no use and when you go—

HELEN. But—I'm not going—unless—

GLEN. Oh God! Don't play with me—I can't stand that!

HELEN. Don't you see—I had to come back to you; you have made it so very hard for me—My savage!

(*They embrace.*)

CURTAIN

*Note:* During the 1970 run of *The Spoilers*, the granddaughter of Ida Malotte (Cherry Malotte in the play) was in the audience and made herself known to the people in the cast. When she saw that two of them, Steve Hornibrook and Steve Boggess, were from Yakima, Washington, she told them that her grandmother, then 92 years old, still lived in Wenatchee, and invited them to visit in the fall. This they did, and met a very charming and alert lady, the "Cherry" Malotte who had known all the real people involved in the claim-jumping affair (Flapjack, Helen and the Bronco Kid were Rex Beach's inventions). She reported that McNamara escaped the law by fleeing to San Francisco, where, for many years, he habitually wore a long full black overcoat, hiding two full-size shotguns strapped under his arms. However, in spite of such precautions, he met his fate when he became involved in another shady deal and was gunned down on the streets of San Francisco.

# 4 Directing for Melodrama

Directing classic Victorian melodrama, the style set forth in this book, requires that the director have a knowledge of and respect for the material, as well as a dedication to preserving the intent of the playwright at the time the plays were first written and produced. It is possible to gain insights by reviewing accounts of original casts and theatres where the plays were first performed. But don't stop there. You need to review the particular period in history and the arts of the place and time in which the play is set. Only the director can keep that awareness alive in the cast.

When beginning rehearsals, it is a good idea to describe briefly the background against which the play was set. Explain to the cast the important historical events that may have influenced the playwright and the social and political attitudes that prevailed. For example, a strong sense of social class is apparent in all the melodramas in this collection. In *The Two Orphans, Hazel Kirke, After Dark* and *Under Two Flags*, it is between nobility and commoners. In *The Ticket-of-Leave Man* it is between working people and street criminals. In *The Spoilers*, it is between the formally educated and the roustabout workmen. It is valuable to discuss social class and background with cast members individually to help them discover the essence of the characters they will portray. Allegiance to the intent of the author and complete sincerity in creating a role is of the utmost importance. Any tendency on the part of actors and actresses to burlesque situations and emotions will only detract from the quality of the play.

The style of melodrama is only slightly "larger than life," as is that of Shakespeare or Molière. Period costume, with flowing lines and more elaborate decoration than in modern plays, easily lends itself to larger and more fluid movement and gestures. Action and vocal styling may benefit from being somewhat enhanced and emphasized, but it must never be exaggerated in the style of Delsarte.

*Lady Travers typifies the attitudes and expectations of nobility as she advises Hazel of the marriage she has arranged for her only son. It was commonly accepted that children would honor promises, made when they were very young, out of a sense of filial devotion and duty.* (Hazel Kirke)

*Cigarette, madcap, volatile "child of the army," encounters her rival, the Lady Venetia, nobly born and educated, whom she has dubbed "The Silver Pheasant." Cigarette realizes that she can never compare to Venetia in birth or manners, but she vows to fight for the man she loves, nonetheless.* (Under Two Flags)

*La Frochard, street criminal of Paris, confronts the proud Countess Levant in front of St. Sulpice, as she forces the blind Louise to sing for gold pieces. A street-hardened thief, Frochard takes pride in her ability to provoke pity and money from the envied upper classes.*

*(The Two Orphans)*

*"Blood will tell!" By the final scene of **After Dark**, it has been revealed that Eliza is the daughter of the well-born but downfallen Old Tom, and she is reunited with George Medhurst, heir to a fortune and a baronetcy. Dicey and her accomplice in attempted extortion are defeated, as their evil deeds are discovered and punished.*

Either the "interior" or "exterior" method of direction is appropriate, depending upon the attitudes and experience of director and cast. The "interior" method requires in-depth discussions of characters, their motivations, attitudes and purposes, while the "exterior" method depends more upon dress, makeup, mannerisms and movement. A blend of both styles is the ideal. It is, of course, easier to achieve if a play is to have a long run than if it will be seen for only a few performances.

"Tableau" is a device much used in 19th-century plays, one

that is especially effective at the end of a scene or act. In a tableau, the scene is made into a stunning stage picture: the action is frozen and held, as lights come down, and the music swells to increase the impact of the dramatic situation.

It is important to understand what the accepted standards of manners are for any given period. For instance, in *The Ticket-of-Leave Man*, Robert, a wellbred young man from the country, would not think of making an intimate gesture toward May in the first act, since he perceives that she is a "respectable" young lady. Not until they have formalized

*Country-bred, simple-hearted Dolly Dutton is bewildered, and at the same time, captivated, by the charming Pittacus Green. Pittacus, a rare character, well-versed in literature, spouts classical references as he plots to break the iron will of Dunstan Kirke, father of Hazel.*

their intent to marry does he embrace and kiss her. The same distinction prevails in *The Spoilers*, with the clear difference verbalized by Dextry and Glenister on the probable characters of Helen Chester and Cherry Malotte.

The best of the melodrama scripts of the 1850-1900 period depict memorable, well-written comedy characters. Played as the scripts indicate, they provide ample diversion from the often tragic and extreme problems of the principal characters. Typical of the well-developed comedy figures are Pittacus Green in *Hazel Kirke*, Sam and Mrs. Willoughby in *The Ticket-of-Leave Man* and Flapjack Simms in *The Spoilers*. Auguste Picard in *The Two Orphans* is quite a different type, consciously witty and more sophisticated.

Dialects are important to several of the plays included here. The Scottish brogue of Dunstan and Mercy Kirke, the Irish of Barney O'Flynn and the proper British speech of the upper-

*Left: In* The Ticket-of-Leave Man, *Sam Willoughby is a boisterous teenager in the care of his poor grandmother, who finds raising him too much of a challenge. Their affectionate bickering adds a unique comic touch. Right: In* The Spoilers *Flapjack Simms and Joe Dextry have been educated by life rather than books. Simms' shyness in the presence of a "lady" and his dogged eagerness to take the law into his own hands help to make him a memorable comic character.*

class characters all add flavor to the presentation of *Hazel Kirke*. Cigarette's North African French accent spices *Under Two Flags*, and Sam and Mrs. Willoughby's Cockney offers contrast to the cultivated speech of Mr. Gibson in *The Ticket-of-Leave Man*. When you pay attention to this detail, you add richness and authenticity to the production.

It's always better to use a light dialect rather than a heavy one, for several reasons. First, the dialect must not be so heavy as to interfere with the audience understanding the dialogue. Second, concentration on the correctness of the dialect may, in some instances, interfere with the development of the player's character. The director may need to offer basic dialect assistance, and, with the help of one of the excellent dialect books available, it is possible to achieve amazing results in a short period of time.

Melodrama is strongly concerned with basic human emotions: love, laughter, grief, pain, the struggle between good and evil, happiness and misery. Everyone who will be conveying these feelings across the footlights should approach the effort with "heroic seriousness." Melodrama traditionally evokes enthusiastic audience response, as is intended, but this should not be allowed to become audience participation or interference. To preserve style and flavor in any of these plays, actors and actresses must strive constantly to maintain the "fourth wall" that separates them from the audience. They must sustain pace and style, undisturbed by audience comment or reaction. Unless audience response is kept within definite bounds, a well-knit production can rapidly deteriorate into a travesty of the original, entirely destroying the integrity of the piece.

# 5 Scene Design for Melodrama

Scene design during the late 1800's, along with other art forms, leaned toward the overblown and ornate. The Victorian period produced extravagant styles in clothing, furniture, fabrics, and this, of course, was reflected on the stage. Scene designers and painters vied with one another to produce the most elaborate stage paintings, and technicians added spectacular special effects. Competition among theatres was lively, with managers trying to outdo one another in engaging stars, discovering new play scripts, or pirating successful plays from other countries.

Crowds rushed to see the newest and most spectacular of stage settings and special effects. Charging horses appeared in smoke-filled battle scenes; fire engines raced across the stage; and houses and ships crackled and burned. In 1887, Joseph Arthur's *The Still Alarm* created great excitement both in the United States and in England when the author and producer collaborated to create on stage the sensational spectacle of a fire house when an alarm comes in. A later play, *Sea of Ice*, Edward Stirling's translation from the French, featured an ice floe breaking apart in the Atlantic. On one section was a babe in a basket, on the other the bereft and grieving mother floating helplessly away. A Denver newspaper, covering a performance in 1862, gave this account:

> The stage showed a truly arctic character—tall blocks of ice around, the floor white or gray. Presently there are symptoms of the ice "breaking up"; the sea begins to gain on the ice, and finally only one small fragment is left. The effect was admirable and complete.

How was this spectacular effect accomplished? By simple means. Strips of whitened canvas, representing the ice, were slowly drawn away both right and left, revealing what seemed to be water underneath. The water was made of black fabric, rather than of blue or green, as might have been expected. The effect was startling, contrasting as it did the stark white against what appeared to be the inky depths of Arctic waters. The artist had achieved the desired effect.

Modern adaptations of melodrama sets might begin with a search for scene plots and pictures of earlier productions. These examples are an excellent guide, and the ideas you get from them can lend authenticity and flavor to the new production. Some backdrops—such as Notre Dame Cathedral

*This illustration of the boathouse scene (Act Three, Scene Two) the abode of the Frochard family, appeared in the* Penny Illustrated *in the 1880's. The design is much like the one used by the Imperial Players in the 1957 production (see page 340). In the New York production (page 327), with large spaces to dress, the scale has been considerably expanded, lending a different mood.* (The Two Orphans)

FROM THE ORIGINAL NEW YORK PRODUCTION
UNION SQUARE THEATRE DECEMBER 1874

*Jacques and Pierre fight to the death in the Frochard hideout.*
(The Two Orphans)

and the Pont Neuf — vary only with the talents and interpretations of the designers and artists. Others, such as the underground railway in *After Dark*, require more ingenuity. While earlier versions incorporated a telescoped train that could be expanded to rush across the stage, more simple improvisation might create a track that runs across the stage, with a strong offstage headlight and sound effects increasing in intensity as the train seems to speed toward the victim. A frantic, last-minute switching of track might deflect the light, and the train might be heard trailing off in another direction.

In an 1869 Denver showing of *Under the Gaslight*, a similar railroad scene suffered technical problems. Frank Zern, writing in *Early Day Show Houses and Actors* in 1910, described the event:

When, after some considerable delay the train did not appear (on the stage), Langrish came before the footlights and announced that owing to a smash-up the train was delayed. But Spencer, who was taking tickets at the door, had come inside to see the fun and said, in a tone of voice so that nearly everybody in the house could hear, that was not the matter, but that the cow-catcher had dropped a calf.

It is urgent that producer, director, scene designer, costumer, music director and choreographer all collaborate in designing the entire production. None of these people should be deprived of their individual creative function, but each can contribute to the work of the others to produce the desired effect. First, the scene designer must take into consideration the ground plot of the stage and work within its dimensions. Next, it is essential to understand thoroughly the place, time and mood of each scene and its sequence in the play. A ground plan for each scene is drawn and reviewed for any special considerations by director, scene designer and costumer. The illustrations here and on the next pages pertain to *The Two Orphans*.

## -Act 1-

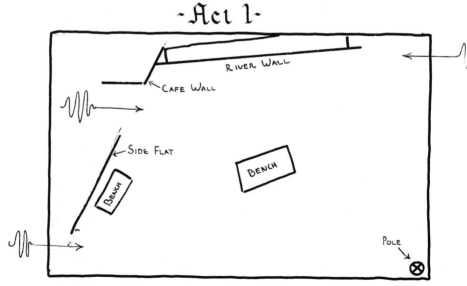

Sc 1 -An open square near the Pont Neuf-

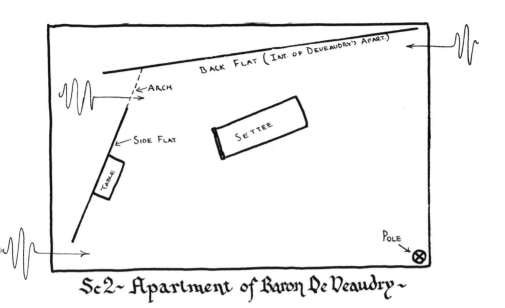

Sc 2 - Apartment of Baron De Veaudry -

Act 2 -

Sc 1 - Office of the Minister of Police -

# Act 2~cont.

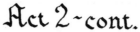

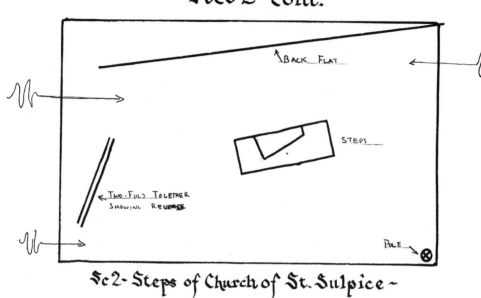

↑ BACK FLAT

STEPS

← TWO-FOLD TOGETHER
SHOWING REVERSE

POLE

## Sc 2~ Steps of Church of St. Sulpice ~

↑ BACK FLAT

↑ PRACTICAL WINDOW

← SAME TWO-FOLD AS
IN Sc. I ~BUT NOW
BLOCKS DR ENTRANCE

CHAIR

TABLE

← CHEST

POLE →

## Sc 3~ Henriette's Rooms ~

# Act 3~

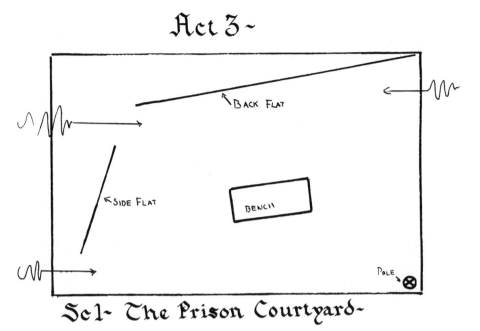

## Sc 1~ The Prison Courtyard~

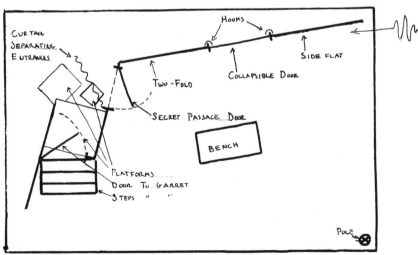

## Sc 2~ The hut of La Frochard~

In a multi-set show, it is often possible to divide the stage into two areas: then the action in one may shift to action in the other, or move from one to another during a scene. In other instances, darkening the upstage area while shifting characters downstage and changing lighting may help to cut down on the number of scene changes. You can sometimes accomplish the same thing with double-sided flats that can be turned and re-positioned to provide another set. In any case, the designer must see to it that changes can be made rapidly, with a maximum scene shift of three minutes.

*A color wash of the set for Act One of* The Spoilers. *Note the ship's ladder D.L. By establishing that area downstage, the designer gave the director two playing areas in one: the downstage area of the ladder (beyond it is the stateroom in which Helen is stowed away) and the main deck. Both are shown on page 333.*

Where overhead space is ample, roll drops can be invaluable for fast scene changes. Then only stage pieces — furniture and props — need to be changed to proceed with the next scene.

In *The Spoilers*, the effect of the ship pulling away from shore was done with a painted backdrop on a roller from stage left to stage right. It was slowly rolled at the appropriate time to give the illusion of movement.

Above: *Helen Chester and Roy Glenister make use of that downstage corner, talking about survival.* Below: *The ship's rail is practical, backed with a canvas roll drop. Bales of cargo provide seating as well as establishing the* S.S. Yukon Queen *as a combination passenger and cargo ship.*

In *The Ticket-of-Leave Man*, an 18-inch-high stairwell entrance accommodated Maltby's descent into a non-existent cellar. The actor also received careful direction to make it appear that he was going down the stairs.

Eliza's desperate jump from Blackfriar's Bridge in *After Dark* was amply cushioned with pillows as she fell prone on the stage behind a set-piece bridge.

*"Which is the way, please, to Blackfriar's Bridge?"* the desperate Eliza asks in After Dark. *The backdrop, painted in dramatic blues, purples and blacks, sets the mood for this scene.*

The addition of one or more unusual or authentic features on any set adds to the audience's enjoyment. A working millwheel, rigged to turn slowly in Act One of *Hazel Kirke*, adds dimension to the scene.

A backdrop of carefully painted tombstones in a dark London churchyard provides an eerie setting for the final scene of *The Ticket-of-Leave Man*.

If it can be found, an old Persian rug can be hung on the wall at the Ace of Spades Wine Shop in *Under Two Flags*. If it is too worn and faded to decorate well, you can touch it up with bright marking pens.

Above: *This color wash for* The Ticket-of-Leave Man *uses perspective to great advantage to achieve a feeling of depth. The set-piece tombstones are made of light plywood, hollow, but built to appear solid. The real ones fade into the painted ones on the backdrop.* Below: *The Ace of Spades Wine Shop in* Under Two Flags, *complete with Persian rug and latticework.*

To create latticed windows, use panels of tinted plastic, placed where they are to be used and latticed with half-inch elastic, sprayed the desired color. These can be crossed in pattern and stapled or tacked to the frame for a durable, believable window or door panel.

For wallpapers, you can use actual wallpaper, if you want, but you can usually achieve a better effect with the use of cutout stencils.

*Prologue sets from two different productions of* The Ticket-of-Leave Man. Above: *Only a small amount of the set has been painted on the flats: the wallpaper has been stenciled, but a practical window and awning decorate the set.* Below: *The entire wall, including the window, has been painted onto the flats, even the awning at the rear.*

*May Edwards' apartment in* The Ticket-of-Leave Man, *as it appeared in two different productions.* **Above:** *Stencils have created the wallpaper.* **Below:** *Only the furnishings are actual; the rest of the set has been painted on the flats. The same antique brass bird cage was used in both productions.*

*The Ace of Spades Wine Shop, as designed in two different productions of* Under Two Flags. *Above: Most of the effect is achieved by dimensional painting on flats. Below: The latticework and arches are both practical. Low set pieces with brass tray and cushions give the effect of an Algerian wineship. Note the footlights: made from breadpans painted black. These were used at the Imperial for many years. We still use footlights extensively, but now we have new ones made to look like the old gaslights with chimneys.*

Above: *In* The Two Orphans, *Henriette pleads with the Count Levant as the Officer arrests her. The fireplace and drapes in her room are painted on the set. Only the chair and bench are set pieces.* Below: *In the prison scene of* The Two Orphans, *a low wall encloses the courtyard of the prison. The church and churchyard are painted on the backdrop. A gate U.R. leads into the prison.*

*The Frochard hideout in* **The Two Orphans,** *an abandoned boathouse, is cluttered and untidy, with a boarded-off passageway. This set has been created with paint and fishnet. Take a look at pages 326-327 for the same scene as it was designed in the 1800's.*

*The Bridgewater Arms set in* **The Ticket-of-Leave Man** *has been created with a painted backdrop and a few tables and chairs. Here Bob Brierly lectures Sam Willoughby on the wages of sin.*

*Color wash illustration of the backdrop for the Silver Bell, Dicey Morris's gambling hall in After Dark. The card table and bar were actual pieces of furniture. The painted backdrop was the rest of the set —impressionistic —with the suggestion of elaborate architecture and glittering lights. As a general rule, scene designers with formal art training, and who are also painters, design sets with a great deal of painted-in detail, while those with less formal art experience lean toward more realistic construction and decorating of sets.*

*Arthur asks Hazel: "You're not yet tired of these iron bonds of matrimony?" (Act Two, Scene One of* Hazel Kirke.*) At home with Arthur and Hazel, it's difficult to make out the French doors U.C. that look out into a country garden. But it's possible to see the family portraits that make up the rest of the room. They indicate Arthur's affluence, and are a simple way to create an elegant setting.*

*Dunstan tells Squire Rodney: "If she were here now, before my very face, kneeling at my feet, I'd tell her nay, never!" (Act Three, Scene One, of* Hazel Kirke.*) Dunstan Kirke's home at Blackburn Mill has a rough stone interior (painted flats). It is sparsely furnished, but immaculately clean. The window at the back is practical; that is where Hazel is seen when she tries to plead with her father.*

*The sketches here are Walter Wilson's color washes for two of the sets in* The Spoilers. *Color washes such as these are prepared as roughs and altered or embellished as the production takes shape. Above:* McNamara's *office requires a practical stove and safe, items that need to be built of light materials for easy scene changes; but they must be sturdy enough to sustain the violent action of the fight that takes place in the room. Below:* The Midas, Act Three, Scene One.

Designing for a small stage offers special challenges and rewards. The ground plan must take into account the length of each scene and the type of action involved, especially specific business and the effects called for in the script. A confined space, with severe limitations, such as the Gold Bar Room stage at the Imperial, with no fly space and no wings, limits the designer's choices; however, careful research done early in the design process will aid in fitting the pieces together in a visually exciting way.

Attention to detail is essential when space is so limited that "panoramic vistas" can be no larger than eight feet high and 15 feet wide. But this brings us to one of the surprising advantages of the small stage; there is no need to fill vast expanses of empty space with scenery and furnishings. Budget turns out to be less of a problem, since set "walls," furniture, dressings and props can all be created with less expenditure for raw materials and labor. Materials and techniques which would be financially impractical on a larger stage become eminently workable in a confined area. More expensive fabrics and furnishings may be used, rendering the sets more durable for a long run.

*Often a single item can set the tone for an entire scene. In* The Spoilers, *the nude painting behind the bar establishes the mining camp saloon atmosphere. Though not visible here, Christmas decorations were hung on this set, adding a festive touch and indicating the winter season.*

As plans for a play progress, frequent conferences need to be held to ensure that the colors used on the set suit the mood the director is trying to create and complement the shapes and colors planned by the costumer. The scene designer needs an explicit understanding of the director's placement of characters and their movements on the set in order to provide enough room for the action and leave planned areas open for movement. Always keep in mind the "fourth wall," and eventually you'll create the stage pictures you want.

# 6 Properties

Soon after a show is cast, the director will assign someone to go through the script carefully to prepare a detailed prop list. It needs to be done about as illustrated on the next page, with each item carefully noted scene by scene and character by character. Most of the items will be easy to find, but some will present problems and lead to quite a search.

The well-stocked melodrama prop room is an adventure in itself. It boasts duelling swords, duelling pistols, doctors' bags, travellers' trunks, a fireplace or two that can be made smaller or larger and can be adapted for a miner's cabin, as in *The Spoilers*, a country house for *Hazel Kirke* or a formal drawing-room in *Under Two Flags*. An office safe is a must (*The Ticket-of-Leave Man* and *The Spoilers*), as are handcuffs (*The Ticket-of-Leave Man*), a policeman's nightstick (*After Dark*), various musical instruments, such as Met's pipe (a flute or recorder) in *Hazel Kirke*, and a guitar for May Edwards in *The Ticket-of-Leave Man*. There is always a need for wire-rimmed eyeglasses, beaded purses, hand-painted fans for ladies, canes and walking sticks, parasols and fancy hatboxes.

Cards, dice and gambling equipment need to be at hand. You need a buggy whip, a riding crop, a stock of men's pipes for every type of character from Hawkshaw to Sam Willoughby to the insouciant Cigarette. A faro board adds an authentic touch to the gambling scenes in *The Spoilers* and a knife grinder's wheel and cart must be provided for Pierre in *The Two Orphans*.

Choose the person you'd most like to have on your team for a scavenger hunt to be your prop master or mistress, for it takes the exercise of a lively imagination to know where to begin to look for unusual items. Second-hand, antique and *junque* shops are fun to browse, even if you don't find the thing you're looking for, and you can make notes on what is available in case you need it for other productions. If you spot an old railroad lantern, a brass-headed cane, a worn leather valise, or other interesting articles at a reasonable cost, add them to your proproom, if at all possible. So many once-worthless items have been picked up as antiques in recent years that once-common articles are almost impossible to find.

It becomes a housekeeping nightmare to catalog and store all the goodies that might be just the thing for the next play, but that catalog can also provide many happy memories as each piece is reviewed for the next production.

## PROPERTIES

### ACT I

| HAND | | SET |
|---|---|---|
| 2 SACKS OF GRAIN | — JOE | |
| CRAYON | — JOE | BENCH |
| PIPE | — MET | TABLE |
| 2 BUNDLES | — MERCY | BARREL |
| PENCIL & PAD | — MERCY | |
| BUNDLE | — DOLLY | |
| LETTER | — RODNEY | |
| LETTER | — BARNEY | |
| BROOM | — DOLLY | |
| BASKET & FLOWERS | — HAZEL | |
| VEGETABLES | — DOLLY | |
| LETTER | — DUNSTAN | |
| LETTERS (2) | — HAZEL | |
| 2 PACKAGES | — DUNSTAN | |

### ACT II

| | | |
|---|---|---|
| BASKET & FLOWERS | — MET | FLOWERS |
| MONEY | — RODNEY | CIGARETTE BOX / MATCHES |
| FISHING GEAR | — PITTACUS | TABLE |
| LETTER | — ARTHUR | SETTEE |
| NEWS CLIPPING | — PITTACUS | |
| EARRINGS | — HAZEL | |

### ACT III

| | | |
|---|---|---|
| LANTERN | — MERCY | TABLE |
| LINEN | — MERCY | 2 CHAIRS |
| GLOVE | — PITTACUS | PIPE RACK |
| CIGARETTE | — PITTACUS | ASH TRAY |
| PIPE / MATCHES | — DUNSTAN | TABLECLOTH |
| GUN | — RODNEY | |
| PITCHER / CUP | — DOLLY | |

# 7 Costuming

Costuming for 19th-century melodrama presents a challenge, since melodrama ranges in time across many periods of history, to different countries, and portrays the life-styles of noblemen, peasants, servants, businessmen, soldiers and scullery maids. Within the scope of this book of six scripts, the simplest to costume is probably *The Spoilers*, but still it presents the problem of providing furs or a reasonable facsimile for the Alaskan winter scene.

*A fur-lined cap was provided for Flapjack, a heavy woolen coat and flannel shirt for Glenister, and fur hat and fur-collared coat for Dextry. A good assortment of furs, collars, coats and caps can be very helpful in styling a show such as* The Spoilers.

Even though the dates of *The Ticket-of-Leave Man* (1863), *The Two Orphans* (1865) and *After Dark* (1868) are all within the same period, the differences in costume are marked. Fashions differed radically from the streets to the salons of Paris in *The Two Orphans* and the teeming streets of London with its lower classes as depicted in *After Dark* and *The Ticket-of-Leave Man*. The upper classes of England frequently and freely adapted from French fashions. In many cases, the clothes

*Costume sketches by William Damron, Jr., for* After Dark, *with swatches of material. While Dicey Morris' costumes lean toward the over-decorated and flashy, they still indicate her vanity and longing to dress as well as the upper classes. Rose Edgerton, who can easily afford to have her trousseau made of the finest fabrics by the most prestigious dressmakers, chooses fabrics and patterns in a more quiet and refined style.*

worn by the working classes were the outmoded and discarded clothing of the well-to-do, passed on as hand-me-downs. As a result, they were ill-fitting and shabby. The poor kept what dignity they could muster by preserving "best" clothing for special occasions. "Best" clothing, usually cheap imitations of upper class garments, were made in the workshops of underpaid seamstresses, many of whom "took in sewing" for a livelihood. This was considered a respectable occupation, as evidenced by May in *The Ticket-of-Leave Man* and Henriette in *The Two Orphans*.

*When Green Jones and Emily arrive dressed for Bob and May's wedding, Emily's dress is elaborate, in showgirl high style; Green is in full dress. May's gown, simply and lovingly made by her own hands from material given her by Mrs. Gibson, is conservative. Mrs. Willoughby has taken her "best" black suit, reserved for weddings and funerals, out of the trunk especially for this great occasion.* (The Ticket-of-Leave Man)

While Grandma's attic may yield an occasional costume or accessory for some of the early melodramas, they would prove valuable for only a few performances, since most of the materials, after being stored for long periods, fray and are ruined in a short while. And unless Grandma has joined the recent craze for exotic dancing, her treasures would offer little of value for *Under Two Flags*, with its belly dancers and the

French Foreign Legion, or for *The Two Orphans*, with its Normandy peasant dresses for Henriette and Louise.

Left: *Belly dancers in* Under Two Flags *wear satin bra tops and sheer harem pants with satin girdle falling below the navel. Tops and girdle are decorated with metallic braid and "jeweled" with large colored stones. A veiled headdress is also decorated with braid and stones. They wear ankle chains and are barefooted.*
Right: *The two orphans are costumed in Normandy peasant dress. Their skirts are of a rough homespun kind of fabric. Their laced vests are of corduroy, hand-embroidered in bright colors, into which shiny decorative buttons have been worked. Blouses are made of a sheer white fabric, with wide, starched bertha collars.*

Thus it becomes necessary to research the times, places and life-styles of the characters portrayed. Often this involves a fascinating dip into classic or contemporary novels as well as history books and costume texts. The drawings and descriptions which appear in accounts of original productions are invaluable.

Among the many excellent costume books available, one of the most valuable and detailed is Fairfax Proudfit Walkup's *Dressing the Part.* Another very helpful text for the period of melodrama is *Victorian Costume and Costume Accessories* by Anne M. Buck, B.A., F.M.A., Keeper of the Gallery of English Costume at Platt Hall in Manchester since 1947.

When making costume notes and sketches for any particular production, make special note of the basic silhouettes for both men and women. Pay particular attention to shoulder widths, location of waistlines, length of skirts and trousers, prominence of bustlines for women, fitted or loose coats for men. Also observe the differences in dress between the upper and working classes.

*In the first scene of* Under Two Flags, *Venetia wears a light summer gown, with matching hat, cummerbund, gloves and drawstring bag. Bert Cecil wears light daytime trousers, tweed coat, velvet vest, and white shirt with paisley foulard tie. The Countess wears a dressy black suit, also with matching accessories. She carries a rolled umbrella.*

Once research has been completed, sketches· and color washes must be coordinated with colors to be used in scene design. Then fabric selection can begin. The costumer needs to find styles of prints and fabric textures that resemble those used in the period in which the play is set. It's important to test to make sure they won't change color under stage lighting and that they will drape properly and hold their shape after laundering or cleaning (you can check this by washing or cleaning a small swatch of the fabric).

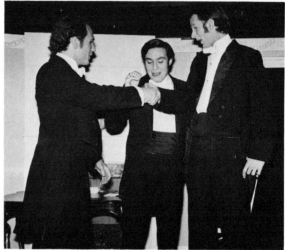

*Rockingham, Bert and Rake celebrate their decision to join the Foreign Legion, after Bert has been spurned by Venetia.*

*Full formal dress is required for these men and for the Marquis de Chateauroy in Act One, Scene Two of* Under Two Flags, *at the Countess' party.*

Second-hand clothing stores often yield a bonanza for men's costuming. With the alteration of the width of a lapel, the addition of satin or velvet piping, and by shortening or lengthening and fitting, many modern items of male apparel can be adapted to period dress. Suits from the 1950's or 1960's can be changed into 1800's styles with the addition of a buttonhole or two. Patch pockets can be added, and loose jackets made into fitted ones with the addition of darts.

Items such as men's frockcoats, morning coats and leisure jackets are seldom available except through professional costume houses, and even when available, they are often of poor quality. It's best to construct these items in the costume shop, if you're lucky enough to have one, when costumers have time to do the extra work.

Boots and shoes present special problems, some of which can be solved again with a visit to used clothing stores. You can adapt modern boots by adding imitation leather cuffs; you can disguise dress shoes by adding spats and leggings constructed of imitation leather fabrics. Generally, because of dress lengths, women can wear character shoes available in dance outfitting shops.

The formal white wig sometimes worn by the men in *The Two Orphans* may be made by modifying and re-styling modern platinum blond wigs, powdering them, and adding ribbons at the back. Uniforms of the French Foreign Legion can be constructed by using basic men's blue work clothing, with the addition of a diagonal white twill stripe across the chest and wide, bright red cloth sashes.

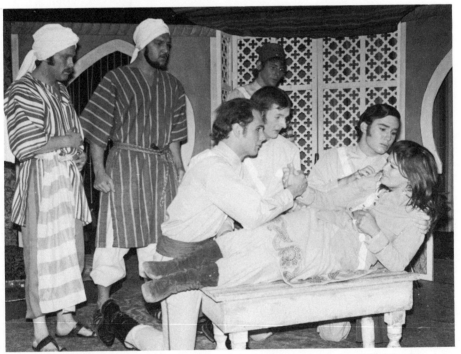

*Cigarette's death scene in* Under Two Flags: *"Tell them in France I died for the flag." The Arab soldiers are dressed partly in their own colorful striped robes with sashes, partly in bits and pieces of Foreign Legion uniforms. They wear turbans and sandals. Entamaboull (rear) wears the Turkish fez, as does Cigarette in earlier scenes. In this photograph you can also make out the Moorish-style draped ceiling, created with pieces of cloth hung from long poles suspended on hooks overhead.*

Particularly unusual items, though, such as authentic Scottish kilts and sporran for Dunstan Kirke in *Hazel Kirke* are better rented from a costume house. Construction of this costume would require special knowledge and skills as well as a

*"I'd tell her she had wronged ye bad enough, without seeking to make ye hoosband to a dishonored creature like herself," Dunstan tells Squire Rodney in Hazel Kirke. For the 1967 Imperial production, by good fortune, durable, polyester authentic pattern Scottish plaids were available in the fabric stores. The costumes worn in this photo were constructed in the Imperial costume department, as was the one on the cover of this book.*

considerable expenditure for yards of expensive wool tartan.

Costume construction little resembles the "stretch and sew" procedures of the present day. Except when working with experienced professional costumers who can confidently cut into an expensive bolt of fabric without first constructing a pattern, it is wise to begin with muslin mock-ups. These inexpensive models can be pinned, fitted piece by piece and re-cut, and then used for a pattern for the actual costume.

Many special features can be built in and reinforced to make certain the costume changes can be made rapidly. The

*"I have found strength to resist you," Jeanette tells the wicked Jacques. "I am ashamed of the life I lead and of the infamy into which you have plunged me." During rehearsals of* The Two Orphans, *both Jeannette and Jacques insisted that their stage training in controlled but convincing violence would prevent bruises when he grabbed her arm. However, a few days into the run, with a sore shoulder and a black-and-blue upper arm, the actress readily agreed to sacrifice a slender silhouette for a padded arm guard added to her costume.*

director should be consulted to determine whether or not a special strain will be placed on a certain costume—or part of it—by the action of the play. If a character is to be grabbed or suffer a fall in performance after performance, padding should be provided and concealed within the costume to avoid injury to the person.

When you use fragile fabrics for women's costumes, it is better to construct a dress in two pieces rather than one, so that if replacement becomes necessary, only one portion needs to be replaced. If you're planning to use elaborate and expensive trims, design them to snap in place or attach with Velcro®, so they can be removed while the garment is being cleaned.

During the run of the show, a wardrobe person will need to check and maintain costumes before and after each performance, to mend rips, sew on buttons or tidy a wig. With this assistance, players can be more confident when they step out on stage, and the audience can appreciate their characterizations without being distracted by costume flaws.

But in spite of careful attention to detail, on every stage, at one time or another, fatal flaws appear: the Can-Can dancer forgets to wear underpanties over her opera hose, the overstuffed zipper gives it up in the middle of a tender love scene, or a lace cuff get entangled with a set piece and pulls it center stage.

In costuming, as in other areas of production, melodrama presents challenges and opportunities. While it is possible to rent full wardrobe from costume houses for many often-produced popular plays, there is no such easy source for melodrama. The time and effort you spend on costume research, design and execution, however, offer rich rewards.

# 8 Music for Melodrama

Music of many countries and composers was used in the presentation of early melodramas. In many instances, a musical score was written especially for the play; in others, musicians improvised to provide mood and specialty material for the characters. It was quite common for each of the principal characters to be identified by an assigned theme, played under portions of each of their scenes. Tender, haunting melodies were chosen for the young heroine; strong, straightforward tunes for the male lead; dark, threatening themes for the heavy. Variations on these themes, in tempo and key, added to mood and interpretation.

Often musical numbers were included for a single character or a duo, and all action on stage was frozen while the songs were sung, much as in later musical comedies. In some cases, trios or quartets—entirely unrelated to the action—appeared to render melodic comment on the scene, only to disappear again into the wings when the number was finished, while action and dialogue resumed on stage. This device is used in *Hazel Kirke* at the end of Act Two, when Hazel resolves to leave her husband.

*It's all very well in the planning stage to sit around and believe that a four-part harmony barbershop quartet will be used at a particular point in the play, such as this one in* Hazel Kirke. *But it's a very different matter when you're auditioning and suddenly make the discovery that there isn't a bass in the house! Or a high tenor! This was one of those fortunate things—lots of luck!*

In present-day production of melodrama, research often turns up specialty material that seems especially well suited to the drama. You can make musical numbers longer or shorter, and add or rewrite lyrics to adapt to any scene. With a few brainstorming sessions, you may create all new lyrics for an existing tune, especially selected to fit the spot in a script where you'd like to have a musical number.

It is always valuable to look into and listen to country music of the nation in which the play is set, and to choose ethnic tunes where French, Scottish, Irish, or other such characters are to be identified. For *Under Two Flags*, "Marche de la Légion Etrangère" (Angel Records' French Military Music Album), will provide the musician with suitable music to play under the soldiers' scene in Acts Two and Three. "Music for an Arabian Night" (Capitol Records) offers material to use as a basis for the belly dancers' scene. A simple

*May tries to give encouragement to Bob in Act Three of* The Ticket-of-Leave Man, *after he has been branded as an ex-convict every place he has sought employment. May tells him, "When better times come, as come they will, we will thank God for them together," and she cheers him with her song. "Keep on the Sunny Side."*

song is included for May to sing in *The Ticket-of-Leave Man*, and "Lousy Miner" conveys the feeling of men returning to their claims in Alaska. In some instances, as in the final scene of *After Dark*, the sound of a train is played offstage on a tape recorder. Sound effects records are available and are listed in the catalogues of most drama publishing houses.

Since melodrama usually deals with strong emotional situations, the action and dialogue often bring audiences to the brink of tears. When songs are introduced, they relieve the tension and allow the audience the relief of laughter. Eliza's "After the Darkness" at the end of Act Two, Scene One in *After Dark* is an example of this release.

Unless a musical score is available for a play, music to accent the action on stage must be improvised by the musician who accompanies it. This involves the use of phrases and snatches of music from the pianist's own repertoire together with a variety of tempos and chords. Take care that the music is played softly enough that it does not overwhelm the voices of the people in a scene. It should never intrude, but it can be used with great effect to enrich the spoken lines and increase

The garb of the piano player-accompanist varied according to the location and style of theatre in which a play was presented. In formal theatres, pianists wore tuxedos with tailored starched-front white shirts. In others, they dressed in more comfortable lightweight shirts with black bow tie, arm garter and flashy silk brocade or bright-colored striped silk vests to add that show biz touch. Pianist Danny Griffith (left) maintains an extensive wardrobe of specially tailored exotic fabric vests. Max Morath (right) adds a derby hat and a cigar. Bob Goodnow (page 360) likes colorful striped shirts and a straw hat.

*Pianist
Bob
Goodnow*

*Note the beautiful piano with the stained glass front. This is the original Gold Bar Room piano that we discovered in a building down the alley and moved into the hotel for our first performance in a corner of the dining room in late 1947. The action is worn out, but we still have the piano, and our musicians use it for practice.*

the emotional impact of a scene. It's best to play original or little known material, since familiar tunes may distract from the play.

Valuable sources of melodrama accent music are the public library collections of themes played by pianists who accompanied silent films. Early silent films depend heavily on melodrama scripts for their material, and, quite naturally, melodrama music was transferred to the theatres to accompany the films. With only printed dialogue at the bottom of the screen, the pianist in the pit supplied the all-important accent that augments the action. "Hearts and Flowers," "Entrance of the Gladiators," and "Springtime" were standard in the repertoire of movie pianists, along with favorite passages to underscore chase scenes, fights, or scenes of strong suspense.

A great deal of the excitement of putting together a melodrama derives from the unique blend of dialogue, action and musical enrichment that are the original creations of each individual set of producer, director, musicians and players. The musical background is a sensitive composition added by the musician once the play begins to take shape and form. It will not be alike in any two productions of the same play.

# 9 Olio

No book about melodrama would be complete without mentioning "olio," that traditional collection of readings, song-and-dance routines, songs and variety pieces that decorate the playbills of melodrama. The French called them *entr'acts*, the British "entertainments." The word "olio" apparently originated in Southern Europe and was used to describe a wide variety of entertainments. Some sources believe the word was a corruption of the Latin word *olla* (pot).

Originally, the acts were performed in front of the curtain on the apron of the stage. Their purpose was to divert the audience during scene changes and disguise the noise of the scene shift behind the curtain. Theatre programs of the 1800's offer a fascinating glimpse of the type of material used. An 1882 program from Wallack's Theatre in New York lists the selections to be interspersed throughout the evening by "The Band under the Direction of Mr. Henry Widmer." Others list names of the artists and the selections they were to sing; some even mentioned magic acts and novelty dance numbers. The great David Belasco was well known for some of his recitations, among them, "The Curfew Must Not Ring To-night." As originally performed, it was a very serious dramatic reading. That version has been included here (see page 362). Later versions (like the one illustrated on page 365) turned it into an hilarious spoof of itself.

As olio has evolved at the Imperial and at other melodrama theatres, it is now presented as a 20- to 30-minute segment of variety acts following an intermission after the third act. The traditional announcement, following the final curtain, has become: "And now, ladies and gentlemen, after the actors and actresses have had time to change costumes and makeup, we will present our olio of vaudeville acts!"

It is in this portion of melodrama presentation that satire, spoof and rollicking fun are given free rein. Director, cast, choreographer and musicians all combine to provide variety and spice in the olio program. You can perform a great variety of material from the turn of the century and blend it with numbers from the era of the play. Even many modern numbers lend themselves well to the nostalgic flavor of melo-drama olio.

Song books of the 1890's, as well as earlier collections, are a rich source of material. Songs such as the tear-jerkers, "In the Baggage Coach Ahead" and "Break the News to Mother" are good choices. "The Curse of a Dreamer" and "The Bird on Nellie's Hat" also come from this era. We found "Saloon" (see page 369), a tribute to that bastion of male conviviality, in a private collection compiled by an early vaudeville performer. Some of Robert Service's poetry furnishes excellent elocu-tionary material to add to olio variety.

The original "Curfew Must Not Ring To-night" goes like this:

## CURFEW MUST NOT RING TO-NIGHT
by Rosa Hartwick Thorpe

England's sun was slowly setting o'er the hills so far away,
Filling all the land with beauty at the close of one sad day,
And the last rays kissed the forehead of a man and maiden fair—
He with footsteps slow and weary, she with sunny floating hair;
He with bowed head, sad and thoughtful, she with lips all cold
            and white,
Struggling to keep back the murmur—
"Curfew must not ring to-night."

"Sexton," Bessie's white lips faltered, pointing to the prison old,
With its turrets tall and gloomy, with its walls dark, damp, and cold,
"I've a lover in that prison, doomed this very night to die,
At the ringing of the Curfew, and no earthly help is nigh;
Cromwell will not come till sunset," and her lips grew
            strangely white
As she breathed the husky whisper:
"Curfew must not ring to-night."

"Bessie," calmly spoke the sexton—every word pierced her
            young heart
Like the piercing of an arrow, like a deadly poisoned dart,—
"Long, long years I've rung the Curfew from that gloomy,
            shadowed tower;
Every evening, just at sunset, it has tolled the twilight hour;
I have done my duty ever, tried to do it just and right,
Now I'm old, I will not falter,—
Curfew it must ring to-night."

Wild her eyes and pale her features, stern and white her
            thoughtful brow,

As within her secret bosom Bessie made a solemn vow.
She had listened while the judges read, without a tear or sigh:
"At the ringing of the Curfew, Basil Underwood must die."
And her breath came fast and faster and her eyes grew large
               and bright;
In an undertone she murmured:—
"Curfew *must not* ring to-night."

With quick step she bounded forward, sprang within the old
               church door,
Left the old man threading slowly paths he'd trod so oft before;
Not one moment paused the maiden, but with eye and cheek aglow
Mounted up the gloomy tower, where the bell swung to and fro:
As she climbed the dusty ladder, on which fell no ray of light,
Up and up,—her white lips saying:
"Curfew must not ring to-night."

She has reached the topmost ladder; o'er her hangs the great,
               dark bell;
Awful is the gloom beneath her, like the pathway down to hell.
Lo, the ponderous tongue is swinging,—'tis the hour of Curfew now,
And the sight has chilled her bosom, stopped her breath, and paled
               her brow.
Shall she let it ring? No, never! flash her eyes with sudden light,
As she springs, and grasps it firmly,—
"Curfew shall not ring to-night!"

Out she swung—far out; the city seemed a speck of light below,
There 'twixt heaven and earth suspended as the bell swung
               to and fro,
And the half-deaf sexton ringing (years he had not heard the bell),
Sadly thought the twilight Curfew rang young Basil's funeral knell.
Still the maiden clung more firmly, and with trembling lips
               so white,
Said to hush her heart's wild throbbing:—
"Curfew shall not ring to-night!"

It was o'er, the bell ceased swaying, and the maiden stepped
               once more
Firmly on the dark old ladder, where for hundred years before
Human foot had not been planted. The brave deed that she had done
Should be told long ages after: as the rays of setting sun
Crimson all the sky with beauty, aged sires, with heads of white,
Tell the eager, listening children, "Curfew did not ring that night."

O'er the distant hills came Cromwell; Bessie sees him, and her brow,
Lately white with fear and anguish, has no anxious traces now.
At his feet she tells her story, shows her hands all bruised and torn,

And her face so sweet and pleading, yet with sorrow pale and worn,
Touched his heart with sudden pity, lit his eyes with misty light:
"Go, your lover lives," said Cromwell,
"Curfew shall not ring to-night!"

Wide they flung the massive portal; led the prisoner forth to die,—
All his bright young life before him. 'Neath the darkening
              English sky
Bessie comes with flying footsteps, eyes aglow with lovelight sweet;
Kneeling on the turf beside him, lays his pardon at his feet.
In his brave, strong arms he clasped her, kissed the face upturned
              and white,
Whispered, "Darling, you have saved me,—
Curfew will not ring to-night!"

*One of the men in the background carries the narration in this spoof of "Curfew
Must Not Ring To-night." The other men join in the choruses. Nell (Ellen Mat-
thews), dressed as a country girl, mimes the actions. A swing is suspended from
overhead. On the first chorus, Nell stands on it and gently swings back and forth
toward the footlights. On the second chorus, she swings slightly over the footlights, and on the third, she joins the men in singing the chorus, straddling the
swing, and swings out over the audience.*

And the spoof goes like this:

There is a mournful story of our plucky little Nell—
How she hung her tender torso on the clapper of the bell—
And how she saved her dad that night the curfew did not ring—
This is the touching story that the convicts often sing:

> *Chorus*
> O hang on the bell, Nellie, hang on the bell
> Your poor dad is locked in a cold prison cell.
> As you swing to the left and you swing to the right,
> Remember the curfew must never ring tonight.

It all began when Nellie said, "No, no," to handsome Jack,
And struggled when he tried to kiss her by the railroad track.
Her dad came up to save her as the train came down the line.
The chap fell back across the track and paid the price of crime.

Her daddy was arrested and brought up before the law.
The policeman said, "I'll handle Dad for breaking any law."
Then Nellie came up clean and thought the jury wouldn't care.
They didn't have a sofa, so they offered him the chair.

> *Repeat Chorus*

They pulled upon the bellrope but there was no ting-a-ling;
They couldn't get to business when the curfew did not ring.
Upstairs poor Nell was swinging while below they turned the key.
Then suddenly a voice said, "Stop, your father's been reprieved."

That's the bedtime story that wardens love to tell,
The convicts listen to the tale of plucky little Nell,
And how she saved her dad that night, the curfew did not ring,
And tears run down their faces as in harmony they sing:

> *On the third chorus, the words change to:*
> Oh, hang on the bell, Nellie, hang on the bell!
> Your dear daddy's sprung from his cold prison cell!
> As you swing to the left Nellie, swing to the right—
> No matter when that curfew rings, we're going to swing tonight!

Of course, your choice of material depends upon the special
strengths and talents of the company. A fine tenor voice carries "In the Baggage Coach Ahead" in a strong, serious vein,
while a number such as "Don't Go in the Lions' Cage" can be

*In "Don't Go in the Lions' Cage Tonight," the actress (Valda Claire) wears a circus lion tamer's outfit, with boots. She carries a whip, and a prop chair, if desired. She sings the verses in the voice of the mother, who is confident and a performer, and switches to a child's falsetto for the chorus.*

done by an actress who possesses good comic sense, even though her voice may be far from concert quality.

Ideally, "Saloon" is performed by three men with good singing voices who are able to blend them in three-part harmony. In the Imperial production, the number was done in low light, with the men dressed in rough workmen's clothing. The beer mugs and pail can be actual or mimed, as the men move around a table and chairs down center stage.

A sparkling, lively olio provides that "frosting on the cake," that extra bit of fun and frolic that leaves an audience wishing it all might last just a little bit longer.

# DON'T GO IN THE LIONS' CAGE TONIGHT

Words by John Gilroy

Music by E. Ray Goetz

## "Don't Go in the Lions' Cage" (*continued*)

li - ons look fe - ro - cious and may bite, _____ And when they
get their an - gry fits, They may tear you all to bits, So
don't go in the li - ons' cage to - night. _____
(no, not tonight)

## CURFEW MUST NOT RING TONIGHT

There is a mourn - ful sto - ry of our pluck - y lit - tle Nell, How she
hung her ten - der tor - so on the clap - per of the bell, And
how she saved her dad that night, the cur - few did not ring— This
CHORUS:
is the touch - ing sto - ry that the con - victs of - ten sing: O
hang on the bell, Nel - lie, hang on the bell, Your poor dad is locked in a
cold pris - on cell. As you swing to the left and you
swing to the right, Re - mem - ber__ that cur - few__ must nev - er ring to-night.

# SALOON

Earnest R Llab

I've been look-ing through the dic-tion-ar-y _____ For a word that is run-ning through my mind. _____ Though I love the name of moth-er, I am search-ing for an-oth-er but I must ad-mit that word I can-not find. _____ Can it be that all its glo-ries are for-got-ten _____ And van-ished with the lan-guage of the Greek? _____ If it is it will ev-er lin-ger in my mem-ory _____ As the first word that I heard my Dad-dy speak: _____ Sa-loon, _____ Sa-loon, _____ Sa-loon, _____ It runs through my brain like a tune. _____ I don't like ca-fes and I hate ca-bar-ets, But men-tion sa-loon and my cares fade a-way! It

## "Saloon" (*continued*)

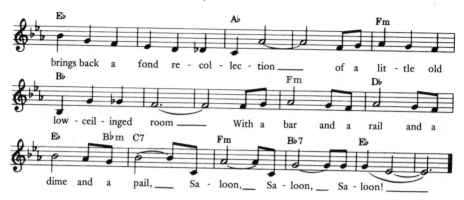

brings back a fond re - col - lec - tion ___ of a lit - tle old low - ceil - inged room ___ With a bar and a rail and a dime and a pail, ___ Sa - loon, ___ Sa - loon, ___ Sa - loon! ___

NOTE: *The composer of "Saloon" is Earnest R. Ball. He spelled his last name backwards here, because he felt this song was so different from the others he had written, such as "When the Sands of the Desert Grow Cold" and "Will You Love Me in December?".*

# KEEP ON THE SUNNY SIDE

Words: Jack Drislane

Music: Theodore Morse

Keep on the sun - ny side And let dull care pass you by. ___ Just fi - gure out you're a long time dead, Don't start to wor - ry or sigh. ___ Weep, and you weep a - lone, Don't give up hope till you've tried, ___ Don't join the crowds that walk un - der dark clouds, But keep on the sun - ny side. ___

# THE CRIMSON STAIN

You have held my heart so close-ly in your keep-ing, It was
pris-oned there for-ev-er at your call: I
can-not take it from you e-ven sleep-ing So I
choose this way to go and end it all. I had
dreamed we two would live in love for-ev-er, Then you
gave the blow that caused the dead-ly pain; So the end of life a-lone the tie can
sev-er, And be-tween our lives there lies a crim-son stain.

# CIGARETTE'S DANCE

**Dance**

# UNDERNEATH THE ARCHES

## LILY OF LAGUNA

She's my la - dy love, she is my girl, my
ba - by love, She's the girl for sit - ting down to dream,
She's the on - ly girl La - gu - na knows. I know she
likes me, I know she likes me, be - cause she said so. She is my
Li - ly of La - gu - na, She is my Li - ly and my own.

## GOODBYE

Good - bye, the gold - en links are bro - ken, ___
___ Good - bye, the part - ing words are spo - ken, ___
___ Good - bye, you have back ev - ery to - ken, ___
___ Good-bye, good - bye, I leave you now, sweet-heart, good - bye! ___

# THE LOUSY MINER

It's __ four long years __ since I reached this land __ In __ search of gold __ a - mong the rocks and sand, __ And yet I'm poor __ when the truth is told, __ I'm a lous - y min - er, I'm a lous - y min - er in search of shin - ing gold.

# GENTLEMAN'S GENTLEMAN

I'd rath - er be a gen - tle-man's gen-tle-man than a gen-tle-man on my own, I would-n't want a ti - tle or a throne __ An - y time I'm feel - ing fri - vo-lous and a - mor-ous, too, I know lots of court - ly la-dies who like my par-lez - vous. I could - n't count the no - ac-count counts whose count-ess - es count on me in-stead, I'm ver-y care-ful not to lose my head __ And though they

# IF I HAD A WISH

# HOORAY FOR GAMBLING

Lively

Hoo - ray for gam-bling and bra - vo for vice! We're thank-ful for po - ker and thank-ful for dice. It may be a sin, but we'll pay the price, Hoo - ray for gam - bling and bra - vo for vice.
*rit.*

# AFTER THE DARKNESS

Slowly

Af - ter the dark - ness, the light will come— Af - ter the clouds, the sun _____ Af - ter the years, with their sor - rows and tears, Glad - ness is sure to come. _____ Though I have trav - elled the road of re - gret, Al - ways the end is in sight. _____ Af - ter the night - time, the dawn will break through— Af - ter the dark - ness, light! _____

Repeat in B♭

# THERE'S NOTHING WE CAN SAY
# BUT JUST GOODBYE

Slowly

There's noth-ing we can say but just good-bye. My
break-ing heart for-gives him, but can I? Don't
shame me with a bribe I can-not take. Our
sa-cred bond your words can nev-er break. Come,
take of me your life of wealth and fame. You
may re-gret me walk-ing in my shame. Don't
tell me that you love me, or prom-ise to think of me— There's
noth-ing we can say but just good-bye.

# I PROMISED TO PROTECT HER

### The Ticket-of-Leave Man

|  | 1964 | 1976 |
|---|---|---|
| Robert Brierly | Manzy Mooney | Steven Leuthauser |
| James Dalton | Dennis MacRae | G. William Skinner |
| Melter Moss | David Shelton | William Bear Henderson |
| Hawkshaw | Michael Brody | John Brownlee |
| Green Jones | Hal Landon, Jr. | Tom Benson |
| Mr. Gibson | Rory Donohue | Steven Hornibrook |
| Sam Willoughby | John Sucke III | James "Rusty" Meyers |
| Maltby | Rory Donohue | Ron Telles |
| May Edwards | Kathleen McCreery | Ellen Schwartz, alternating |
|  |  | with Nancy Pichot |
| Emily St. Evremond | Valda Claire | Linda Woerner |
| Mrs. Willoughby | Jane Ellen Drake | Robin Taylor |
| Detective | — | John Skinner |
| Pianist | Bob Goodnow | Danny Griffith |

### Under Two Flags

|  | 1961 | 1971 |
|---|---|---|
| Lady Venetia | Jeanne Rustemeyer | Kathleen Murphy |
| Countess of Warminster | Sandra Lain | Cynthia Smith |
| Renee Baroni | Nancy Duff | Rena Cook |
| Cigarette | Kendall Clingerman | Georgia Loveless |
| Paulette | Sandra Lain | Cynthia Smith |
| Bouamana | Nancy Duff | Rena Cook |
| Bert Cecil | Ronald O'Hara | Richard Rorke |
| Lord Rockingham | Ben Shelton | David Rieth |
| Rake | Howard Malpas | Jerry Hayes |
| Marquis de Chateauroy | Eldon Hallum | John Clayton |
| Baroni | John Storace | Randall Alderson |
| Entamaboull | John Storace | Randall Alderson |
| Beau Bruno | Dave Kelso | John Skinner |
| Yussef | Bob Cosgrove | Marvin Asher |
| Tiger Claw | David Hardaway | Keith Burkhart |
| Si Hassan | Kasheed Mohammed | Terry Carlson |
| Pianist | Bob Goodnow | Danny Griffith |
| Accordionist | Henry Kenski, Jr. | — |

### The Two Orphans

|  | 1957 | 1968 |
|---|---|---|
| Antoine | Bob Cosgrove | Loring Miller |
| Picard | Frank Talley | Jerry Hayes |
| La Frochard | Shirley Mann | Lynn Bradley |
| Pierre Frochard | Joe Barnaba | Allen Fearon |
| Jacques Frochard | Arlen Dean Snyder | Joe Maltsberger |
| Henriette | Jeanne Miclot | Martha Acker |
| Louise | Nancy Holt | Mary Stephens |
| Jeanette | Sheila Stanker | VanAnn Moore |
| Policeman | Herbert Prizeman | Jerry Yates |
| Baron Maurice | Ron Thompson | Ralph Day |
| De Vaudrey |  |  |
| Count Edmund Levant | Chuck Johnson | John Masterman |
| Clerk | Harold Hahn | Loring Miller |
| Countess Diane Levant | Sheila Stanker | VanAnn Moore |
| Doctor | Harold Hahn | Loring Miller |
| Sister Genevieve | Nancy Holt | Nancy Young |
| Pianist | Max Morath | Danny Griffith |

| After Dark | 1956 | 1972 |
|---|---|---|
| Chandos Bellingham | David Rosario | John Clayton |
| Old Tom | Charles M. Johnson | Jerry Hayes |
| George Medhurst | Richard Morrow | Gerald Lessard |
| Sir Gordon Chumley | Robert B. Pinney | Jimmy Harris |
| Pointer | Bert Hood | Peter Gelblum |
| Eliza | Karen Duke | Rena Cook |
| Rose Edgerton | Mary Platis | Janette Gould |
| Dicey Morris | Patricia Gamble | Ruth Nordgren |
| Jack Crumpets/ | Marvin Hall | John Skinner |
|   Dealer/Butler | | |
| Sally Crumpets/ | — | Shannon Woolley |
|   Barmaid | | |
| Pianist | Max Morath | Danny Griffith |

| Hazel Kirke | 1954 | 1967 |
|---|---|---|
| Dunstan Kirke | David Hardaway | Joe Orton |
| Mercy Kirke | Elizabeth White | Mary Ellen Mathews |
| Hazel Kirke | Shirley Strain | Cynthia Montilla |
| Dolly Dutton | Norma Loy | Gail Allen |
| Met Miggins | Isabelle McClung | Anna Jane Allen |
| Aaron Rodney | Dieter Kiebel | John Masterman |
| Pittacus Green | Tom P. Rea | Robert Montilla |
| Arthur Carringford | Bill McCarthy | William Halliday |
| Emily Carringford | Isabelle McClung | Anna Jane Allen |
| Barney O'Flynn | Kenneth French | Bill Smith |
| Joe and Inspector | — | Richard Ooms |
| Pianist | Max Morath | Danny Griffith |
| Banjoist | — | Jim Tracy |

| The Spoilers | 1959 | 1970 |
|---|---|---|
| Captain Stephens | Arlen Dean Snyder | Phil Ashby |
| First Officer | Steve Callahan | Stephen Boggess |
| Ship's Doctor | Frank Talley | Eddie Fields |
| Roy Glenister | Tom Paxton | Herbert Paul Kouba |
| Joe Dextry | Phil Webber | Jerry Hayes |
| Helen Chester | Sara Sauer | Kate Kelly |
| Arthur Stillman | Arlen Dean Snyder | Phil Ashby |
| Alexander McNamara | Johnny Horton | John Masterman |
| Wilton Struve | Frank Talley | Steve Boggess |
| Cherry Malotte | Marilyn Sue Garrett | Carolyn Chriss |
| Drury Chester | Steve Callahan | Eddie Fields |
| Duchess | Mina Zenor | Debbie Rice |
| Flapjack Simms | John Hazleton | Steve Hornibrook |
| Mrs. Champain | Mina Zenor | Debbie Rice |
| Police Officer | Roy Frankenhoff | Ed Henderson |
| Second Man | Bob Morberly | Ed Henderson |
| Gambler | George Bradley | Tom Cathcart |
| Pianist | Max Morath | Danny Griffith |

# Glossary of Victorian Slang in *The Ticket-of-Leave Man*

**brag**—a card game, similar to poker

**brass**—money

**butts**—a large cask

**cadging**—to get by begging (From Middle English, *cadgear*, to carry wares)

**charity leathers**—clothing, especially shoes, given to the poor by church organizations

**copper**—to bet against

**crushers**—the police (indicating constant pressure of the law upon the lives of criminals)

**darbies**—handcuffs

**dodges**—a clever or evasive plan or device, a stratagem

**dose**—give ample amounts of liquor

**duck**—(as in "duck of a bonnet") dear thing, sweetheart

**flannelback**—common workman. This relates to the Middle English word meaning sackcloth *(flannen)*, probably referring to rough work clothes.

**flimping**—stealing

**flimsies**—counterfeits

**grey dittos**—the drab work clothing supplied by London workhouses to indigent persons who were supplied with the bare necessities of life in return for hard labor

**hair à la Francaise**—hair worn smooth and parted, partially covering forehead, with a knot low on the neck at the back, and a few curls at side over the ears and down on the shoulder. (For evening, tall Spanish combs were worn, made fashionable by the Empress Eugenie, of Spanish birth.)

**Jemmy**—a short crowbar with curved ends, a burglar's tool

**jumping the safe**—picking the locks

**jump the crib**—break into the safe

**mizzle**—disappear like a fog, disperse

**score it down**—refers to the old system of charging against a customer's account

**shiners**—coins

**squeeze**—to force a lock

**swizzle**—tall mixed drink, usually made with rum

**ticket-of-leave**—the official document issued a prisoner who is paroled before his sentence is completed because of good behavior. He must carry the "ticket" with him at all times, but in case of any violation of the imposed restrictions, he is immediately liable to return to prison to complete his term. Thus the name "Ticket-of-Leave Man" was given to any paroled criminal.

**tipple**—alcoholic liquor

**trimmle**—a state of agitation

**trotter**—a foot, especially the foot of a sheep, prepared as food

# Index